Third Edition

PHOTOCOMMUNICATION

A Guide to Creative Photography

David H. Curl

Kalamazoo College
Kalamazoo Institute of Arts
Western Michigan University

A text designed for
first-semester college courses
in art, communication
and photojournalism
and for adult self-study

*The real function of a formal education
is to teach you how to educate yourself
when you're done with your
formal education.*

(Edward Albee, playwright)

Oak Woods Media, Inc.

Library of Congress Cataloging-in-Publication Data

Curl, David.
    Photocommunication : a guide to creative photography / David H. Curl, — 3rd ed.
        p.   cm.
    Includes bibliographical references and index
    ISBN 0-88196-004-7 (pbk.) : $24.95
    1. Photography.   I. Title
TR145.C977 1991
770—dc20   91-22181
                                                       CIP

Printed in the United States of America
with soy-based ink on recycled paper

Published by Oak Woods Media, Inc.
PO Box 19127
Kalamazoo, MI 49019
(616) 375-5621

ISBN 0-88196-004-7

Note: Whenever specific products are
mentioned in the text it should be assumed
that the name is a registered trademark
owned by the manufacturer.

On Vision

So
you've come
to ask me
to teach you photography.

By means of the tools
I shall oblige;
for son,
the mechanics
may be easy.

But
once you have
mastered these,
         please,
do not return
to ask me
         for vision.

For
you must first
learn of yourself
and life in others,
before
you learn
to see.

Judith Baker Martin

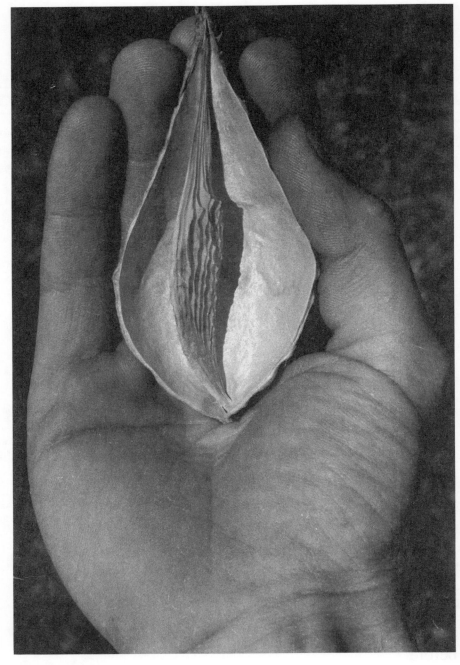

Kenneth Zelnis *Milkweed Pod*

When simple forms are repeated they bring to the eye the kind of pleasure that music brings to the ear.

(Victor B. Scheffer, educator)

Acknowledgements

*As you grow older, art and life become
the same thing.*   (Georges Braque, artist)

Many people must share the credit for any success this book may have as a teaching tool. I am proud that my teachers have included such giants of photography as Ansel Adams, Eliot Porter, Henry Holmes Smith, Jerry N. Uelsmann, and Clarence White, Jr. Many others have shared with me both insight and information.

*Learn from the mistakes of others—you
can never live long enough to make them
all yourself.*   (Fred Tonne, photojournalist)

Those who have taught me the most over the years, however, have been my own students who have shown me that the best way to learn something is to attempt to teach it to others.

*'What is the use of a book,' thought
Alice, 'without pictures...?'*
    (Lewis Carroll, author)

Most of the photographs in this book are typical of the excellent work that can be expected from college students. These fine images were created in response to class assignments and I have given credit to each photographer in the appropriate caption. The spot-news photo by Brian Lanker on page 25 is reproduced by courtesy of the Topeka *Capital-Journal*. Steve Curl and Rich Zesiger created many of the line drawings throughout the book, while those in Chapter Seven were originated by James A. Nemsik. David Knight and Mark Owen provided valuable technical assistance.

Attentive on-call software support from Bill Hanson and Paul Harmelink of SSG LaserWorks made it possible to desktop publish this edition.

*The eternal struggle of art is to leave out
all but the essential.*
    (Oliver Wendell Holmes, poet)

The numerous quotations punctuating and illuminating the text came from various sources—many of which, unfortunately, must remain undocumented. To Scholastic Magazines, Inc. and to the International Fund for Concerned Photography, I am most deeply indebted for permission to quote frequently the words of great photographers as spoken in the remarkable *Images of Man* audiovisual series. *The Daybooks of Edward Weston,* published by Horizon Press and George Eastman House, provided many significant short quotations, as did Ansel Adams' *Basic Photo Series,* published by Morgan & Morgan.

Lloyd Chilton and Dave Novack of Macmillan Publishing Co. made possible the 1978 first edition of this book. Completion of the latest revision was encouraged and expedited by Ardyce Czuchna-Curl and Laura Armstrong. To them, to my students at Kalamazoo College, and to all the other people who helped in so many ways, I offer a humble and sincere thank you!

---

*Let us learn to love
certain forms of madness.
Let us recognize that to alter
the essence of an artist
is to quell that seething genius
so necessary to the beauty
of this planet.*
    (Author unknown)

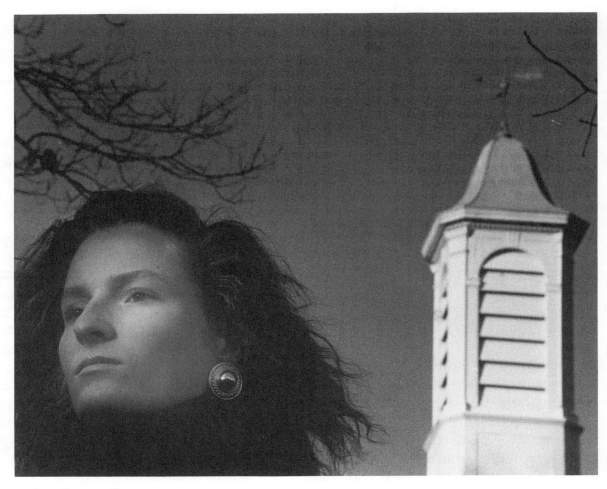

Jorg Jasper *Gwen*

The seasons have changed
And the light
And the weather
And the hour.
But it is the same land.
And I begin to know the map
And to get my bearings.

(Dag Hammarskjold, statesman
—from "Markings")

Table of Contents

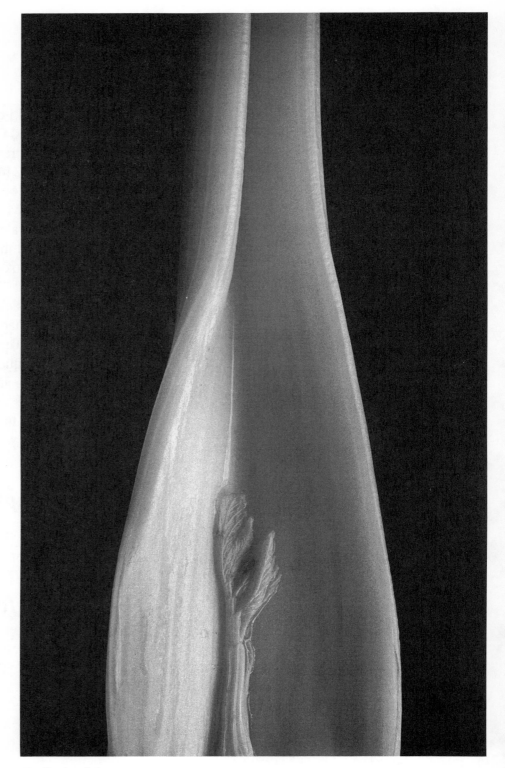

D. Curl *Celery*

...That split second when the familiar suddenly is transformed into the profoundly new... (Larry West, photographer)

Introduction

The "Aha!" Phenomenon

It happened again this morning. The aha! phenomenon when ideas begin to click into place in students' minds. Their eyes light up; sometimes grins flash across their faces. It's the kind of moment a teacher lives for.

I began the discussion by showing the class a large black-and-white photograph of a stalk of celery with a new sprout growing inside it. This image always stimulates perception and comment. After asking, "What is it?" I received the following response:

"A stalk of celery," Mark responded immediately. Then Marlene added, "With a sprout inside."

"OK, that's what it *is*. Now, *what else* is it?" I asked. "Let's try word association. Give me single words...short phrases."

"Growth," Jerrie exclaimed. Other students came up with words such as fresh, crisp, moist, green, growth, rejuvenation, protection and spring.

I turned the photo upside down.

"Birth," said Mary. "A stream of milk being poured from a pitcher," Kevin observed.

Upside down, the growing sprout became also the dangling tail of a horse or a donkey. Held sideways, the image became a landscape of snow-covered hills; then a canoe.

Then I asked, "Where did these ideas come from? Why did we get reactions like these from looking at a picture of a vegetable?"

Most of these students are freshmen and they are quick learners.

Kate, an English major, explained, "It's like *simile* in language. Visual simile is when something *looks like* something else..." Deanna interrupted, "You mean like when we saw that the celery looked like a landscape when we looked at it one way and, upside down, it reminded someone of the rear end of a horse?"

"Yes," Kate continued. "And visual *metaphor* is when an object in a picture represents something abstract or completely different. As when people mentioned spring and birth and growth. A metaphor is a symbol that only has meaning that people bring to it from their personal experience."

How could I have said it better myself?

The best part is that I didn't have to explain anything. The students discovered—spontaneously—a connection between verbal and visual language—between literature and art. Because they observed it themselves, they'll retain the concept and use it. Many of the photographs made by these young women and men in future weeks will reveal tentative new vision. They will perceive before their eyes and lenses familiar subject matter enriched by what Ansel Adams described as *endless horizons of meaning*.

Art *and* Science

Far from enjoying photography as art, many people are more intrigued with the technical aspects of the medium. Some enjoy testing the latest cameras and lenses and comparing films and developers. In science departments, photography courses often are organized around physics and chemistry. Journalism programs emphasize communication. Technical schools teach technique and processes. Many courses are based on the history of the medium. Frequently, instructors teach *about* photography in the hope that students somehow will be able to apply this basic knowledge creatively within their vocational goals.

> *Photography is at once a science and an art...inseparably linked throughout its astonishing rise from a substitute for skill of hand to an independent art form.*
>
> *(Beaumont Newhall, historian)*

At first I taught photography as if it were not an art form but a scientific, academic subject. To my surprise, I discovered that some students were becoming effective photo-communicators not so much because of the facts I had been teaching them, but because of their own terrific internal urge to create—to express their observations and feelings. My students taught me that no one can be taught photography—that one must learn by doing.

To help persons learn...don't give them a lecture full of directions...Get them started doing the very thing they want to learn. (Kenneth Macrorie, educator)

Another mistake I made was to assume that one had to master the fundamentals of technique before he or she would be able to communicate. But now I realize that was a very old-fashioned idea. It's like saying that before a young child can write an excit-

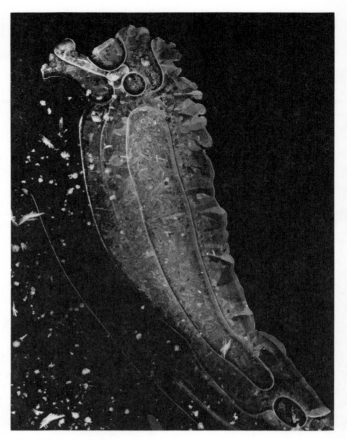

Raimonds Ziemelis *Ambiguity*
What is it—a seahorse? Or is it a photomicrograph of an amoeba or an aerial view of a glacier? Actually, it's a few inches of ice along the edge of a small puddle, but ambiguity of scale creates a provocative puzzle.

ing story about something that interests him or her, s/he must first memorize all the rules of perfect punctuation, spelling, and grammar.

It is more important to generate enthusiasm than to convey knowledge. Knowledge is easily forgotten, while enthusiasm makes anything possible.
(Harold Allen, educator)

Now I think I've learned the secret: first you should become excited about photography—or about writing—by photographing or by writing. Once you get to doing a thing, you'll discover "how to" soon enough. This book will be a handy resource to look up stuff when you're ready for it.

I am excited by the need to render what I personally experience. (Claude Monet, artist)

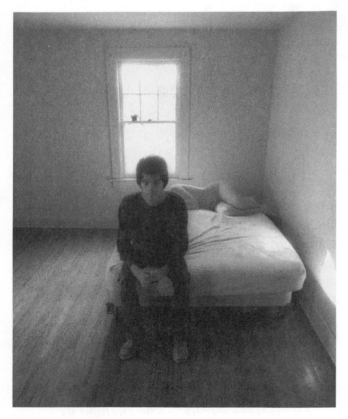

Mickey Howell *Bedroom*
Are you puzzled and intrigued by the bizarre lack of information in this photograph? Why is the room empty except for the bed and the tiny plant in the window? Why are the man and woman juxtaposed in this manner?

Communication Comes First

Art is the affirmation of life.
(*Alfred Stieglitz, photographer*)

Life, or its eternal evidence, is every-where. (*Ansel Adams, photographer*)

Technique is simply the means of convey-ing to the printing paper what the photog-rapher has seen so that someone else might see it too.
(*Margery Mann, educator*)

Technical processes merely are means to an end—means to creating an image that communicates something to someone else or expresses the photographer's feelings or impressions of a situation or subject. Although technique—the essential craft of photography—is important enough to be stressed in this book and in my course, I believe it is a mistake to treat technique as if it were an end in itself.

You can have craft without art; but not art without craft. (*Ansel Adams, photographer*)

For most people, the technical side is the easiest to learn—the hardest part is learning to see and to visualize.

Seeing means perceiving the visual relationships that exist in the world. Visualizing means perceiving visual relationships...as they will exist as trans-lated into a photographic print.
(*Phil Davis, educator*)

Let's take technical details in small doses and invest most of our time in opening up your eyes and stimulating your imagination. Would it surprise you to learn that many top professional photographers don't do any of their own darkroom work? (But at some point most of them learned how). Paradoxi-cally, there are thousands of competent technicians who rarely produce any photographs that, from an artistic point of view, are worth looking at.

I believe in making the best pictures you can, even if nobody likes them.
(*David Vestal, photographer*)

You should start out making photographs that mean something to you, despite technical flaws, and then see how other people react. To my surprise I have found that this simple system works especially well with beginning photographers—those who are not yet aware of what they cannot do because of "limitations" of the medium. Students blossom rapidly within a nonthreatening, nontechnical en-vironment in which they are competing only with themselves. They see more, they see it much sooner, and they are more able to talk with conviction about what they have seen and why they felt it was worth photographing.

Knowledge is power.
(*Francis Bacon, philosopher*)

Imagination is more important than knowledge. (*Albert Einstein, scientist*)

Technique is important in photography—but motivation and self-confidence come first. I have found that nearly all of the technical problems that I would have "covered" in lectures will come out in print critiques. These problems usually appear in the form of questions that are asked when the learner is ready and eager for the answers.

The greatest gift we can give is to help those who want to learn, find out what they love to do. (*Richard Bach, writer*)

An artist is not a special kind of person; every person is a special kind of artist.

(*Eric Gill, sculptor, typographer*)

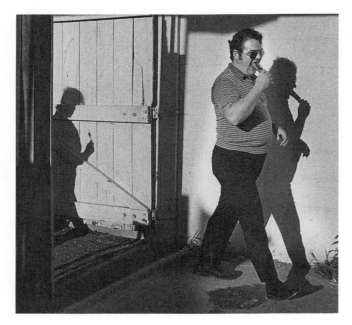

Jim Nixon *Man with Popsicle*
Was your first impulse to laugh when you saw this photograph? But upon second examination, are there sinister elements? Notice the graphic impact of repetition with variation and contrast of both form and value.

Criticism is Important

Criticism...is the analysis of a product or performance for the purpose of identifying and correcting its faults or reinforcing its excellences...Criticism lies at the very heart of education. To learn is to submit oneself to the discipline of a standard, <u>even if the standard is self-created and self-imposed.</u>
(Robert Paul Wolff, educator)

Most people crave response to their work, and most artists will readily admit their dependence on constructive criticism.

One should challenge accepted thinking, particularly one's own.
(Edward Weston, photographer)

Not only is it intriguing to discover what other people see in your pictures, but it's important to find out whether what you're trying to say with your images is getting across. Praise is pleasurable and ego-satisfying, but it's vital that you realize when your own memories of a scene, event or personality remain so vividly in your own mind that you can't be objective about the picture. It's important also to become aware of unforeseen communication barriers that may be present in your work, such as extraneous elements, distracting backgrounds, and careless lab work.

There is a certain exchange going on between a good photograph and the person looking at it.
(William Albert Allard, photojournalist)

It's fun sometimes, to find out what friends and family members see in your photographs. Also, when your work is on display it can be instructive to

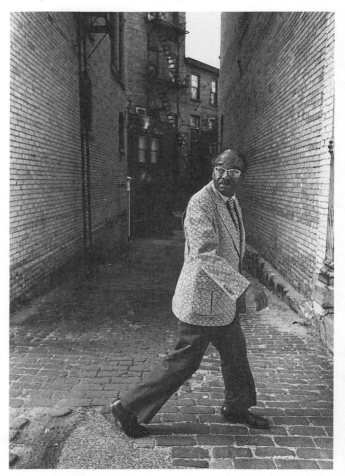

Gary Cialdella *Man in Alley*
Do you wonder why this man is looking back over his shoulder? What is the effect of the converging walls on your interpretation of this photograph?

overhear comments from strangers. But the most constructive critique will come from colleagues and classmates—knowledgeable and sensitive people with an interest as keen as your own in communicating through photographic images. Usually it's helpful to have your instructor or another empathetic "expert" on hand at critique sessions as catalyst and moderator—to keep the comments flowing and to help unravel technical mysteries as they appear.

The truest test of independent judgment is being able to dislike a photograph made by someone you admire—and to admire qualities about a photograph you dislike. (Author unknown)

Why Emphasize Black-and-White?

Color photography is everywhere—in movies, TV, catalogs, books, magazines, newspapers, on billboards and packaging. If color illustrations can have such stunning impact, why bother with black-and-white? I'll tell you why. Because viewing the world in monochrome will teach you to see. Have you wondered why some of the greatest classic motion pictures were shot in black-and-white, decades after color film was available? Have you noticed that black-and-white photos often are used effectively in advertising and in photojournalistic essays?

The successful transformation of color tones into black-and-white values is as essential as image definition and the selection of...composition.
(Thomas W. Leavitt, photographer)

Photographers doing good work in black-and-white must perceive and reproduce the essential graphic elements of the subject: form, texture and contrast—whereas color alone may capture the eye in an otherwise uninteresting image. If you study *National Geographic* magazine, for example, you'll discover that some of the strongest color photographs consist of a limited palette of color. They are composed and lighted so that color often is incidental, rather than the dominant feature of each photograph.

I do not believe any tuition is a better bargain than $100 worth of film put to work in an attempt to make each picture, each roll, better than the last.
(Wallace Hanson, editor)

If first you master black-and-white photography—learn to visualize the essentials of the image—then you can apply what you've learned to create much better color photographs.

One always has to begin with something. One can then remove all appearance of reality: one can run no risk, for the idea of the abstract has left an ineffaceable imprint. It is the thing that aroused the artist, stimulated his or her ideas, stirred his or her emotions. (Pablo Picasso, artist)

Picasso, of course, was a master of abstraction. Simplicity of line and form was the essence of his mature work, and among the strongest are his black-and-white line drawings.

When you go out to paint, try to forget what objects you have before you—a tree, a house, a field, or whatever. Merely think, here is a little square of blue, here an oblong of pink, here a streak of yellow, and paint it just as it looks to you, the exact color and shape, until it gives your own naive impression of the scene before you. (Claude Monet, painter)

Monet painted with a palette of selected hues—pigments of limited color value and muted intensity. Black-and-white reproductions of his paintings reveal Monet's strong sense of framed positive and negative space related by atmospheric perspective—very much like fine photographs of the natural landscape. Viewing the originals, especially the series paintings, one sees how the painter applied color as a subtle transition for the viewer back from abstract form to the reality of subdued color.

You might not be a painter, nor will you necessarily become a professional photographer. But as an "appreciator" of the arts, I hope you will use this book as a stimulus to heighten your own awareness and sensitivity to the shapes, textures and colors of the visual world. Use it as a guide—as you have need of it—to some of the inescapably basic fundamental information; and as a source of comparison, so that you can criticize intelligently and constructively your own work and the work of other photographers.

> *Photography can be an extra sense, or a reservoir for the senses...Photography can teach people to look, to feel, to remember in a way that they didn't know they could.*   *(Edwin H. Land, inventor)*

Looking Ahead

Throughout more than a century-and-a-half of photography, history has preserved images that show us what people looked like, the way they lived, and the things and places that were important to them. Some of those historic images tell us more than they show. Over the years the best of those old photos communicate thoughts and feelings of the artists who made them long ago. This was photography as art.

Will computers and videography make photography obsolete? I don't think so. Here's why.

Computers are dumb until interfaced with human intelligence and imagination. They can only process images that are fed into them. Digital enhancement and manipulation are merely convenient and versatile ways of producing what we have already learned to do with light and chemistry, but in an electronic darkroom we can do things faster, cleaner, and with infinitely greater variation. Soon digital images may rival the quality of pictures produced optically.

There is no substitute for still imaging. Video is a motion picture medium. Although the rules of conceptualizing and framing are similar to still imaging, film and video exist in the dimension of time; still photography abstracts time in a way that even a still video or film frame cannot. Effective still pictures must suggest for the viewer what came before and what might come after the "decisive moment" of exposure, or must tantalyze by withholding this information.

To prepare for the 21st century, think of yourself not only as a photographer, but as an *imagemaker*. Master the skills of visual communication now. Human imagination and creativity never will become outdated. Brains always will be needed to select and conceive images, and some kinds of cameras will be required to capture them.

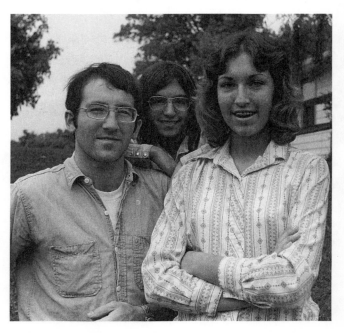

Carmen Anderson *My Family*
Snapshot or portrait? How does one decide? Can one photograph be both a personal recall picture and an image of broader significance?

> ***Note:*** *Whenever masculine pronouns occur within quotations or elsewhere in the text they should be assumed to be gender neutral.*

Photography is a Language *1*

Communicating with a Camera

Photography is a language with which a knowledgeable photographer can produce records, reports, essays, diary-entries—even poetry!

(Ansel Adams, photographer)

Photography is the closest thing we have to a universal medium of communication. Although there are some cultural variations in the way people respond to them, photographs transcend most traditional social and literary boundaries.

I believe that photography can be one of the most powerful means of sharpening human awareness—one of today's most faithful, permanent, and universal means of communication. Through it we can provide an accurate and believable mirror of the human condition—a mirror that mankind must finally face.

(Cornell Capa, photographer)

Photography reaches people on many levels—most of which cannot be classified as art. Photography informs and educates. Much of what we know about the world we have observed in the photographic images presented to us on television and movie screens and on the pages of magazines and books. Photography tempts us and persuades us. It sells us food, furniture, clothes, cars, cosmetics and candidates. It entertains us through motion pictures and television. Photography works for us behind the scenes in countless unapparent ways as an extension of the human eye and the human mind in scientific research, engineering and medicine. Photography for millions of people is a diary for preserving fleeting moments of time. And photography for many of us is becoming, in the words used by Alfred

Stieglitz to define art, "an outer expression of inner growth."

The mission of photography is to explain man to man and each man to himself.

(Edward Steichen, photographer)

Photography is rooted in reality. Nothing is more important to humankind than the transfer of ideas from one person to another. In this process, which we call communication, lies the potential for governments and for individuals to overcome ignorance and misunderstanding. Because it is realistic and therefore believable, photography can be one of the most potent means of communication.

There were two things I wanted to do. I wanted to show the things that had to be corrected. I wanted to show the things that had to be appreciated.

(Lewis W. Hine, photojournalist)

Photographs preserve the present and immortalize the past. They take us to distant places or to places that have never existed. Photographs provide information and add life and excitement to the words of the teacher and the journalist. Photographs answer questions and stimulate curiosity. They often arouse deep feelings and intense emotions.

A good photograph says something so well that it cannot be said better in any other way. It may be factual or poetic; but always it will be so true that from it we can learn of life.

(Beaumont Newhall, historian)

Photographs often help to correct mistaken ideas people have. But because photography is so believable, a careless or unscrupulous photographer or editor can misrepresent events or situations, or may even use photography to tell deliberate lies. This possibility is made more acute because the very presence of press and TV cameras can make an event appear a thousand times more important than other events not covered by the visual media.

Television cannot present the trivial. By being presented even trivia becomes of enormous importance.

(Jay Chidsey, philosopher)

The camera doesn't lie, but photographers often do!

(Fred Tonne, photojournalist)

Because photographs are so believable, we must learn to react to the language of visual stimuli as we should react to written and spoken words. We must learn to ascertain the photographer's or editor's intentions and to recognize the impact of each medium. We must be able to tell when someone is presenting us with facts, appealing to our need to "belong," or addressing us with visual simile or metaphor.

I always wanted to take the best picture I could, one that would satisfy me. But at the same time I wanted to take pictures that would influence people. I wanted to show people that the natural world was valuable for them. This was in a sense propaganda. But I don't think there is anything wrong with certain kinds of propaganda.

(Eliot Porter, photographer)

Visual Literacy

The knowledge of photography is just as important as that of the alphabet. The illiterate of the future will be a person ignorant of the use of the camera as well as the pen. (László Moholy-Nagy, artist)

The grammar of photography is very closely related to that of verbal language, and visual literacy

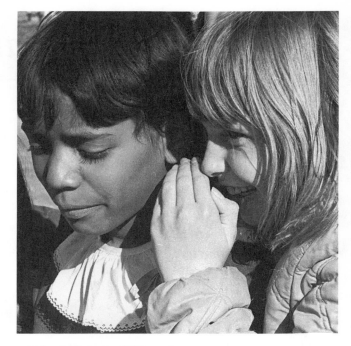

Abigail Pickett   *Whispering*
Can you identify in any way with this picture?

has become as important as the ability to use and understand words. Today's educated person comprehends visual messages and composes clear, even eloquent, visual statements. The most visually literate understand the grammatical parallels of visual and verbal language and have some experience with the tools of visual communication. Perhaps most important, familiarity with visual communication leads to appreciation, as well as healthy, critical skepticism, of the visual arts and mass media.

If these "mass media" should serve only to weaken or corrupt previously achieved levels of verbal and pictorial culture, it won't be because there's anything inherently wrong with them. It will be because we've failed to master them as new languages in time to assimilate them to our total cultural heritage.

(Marshall McLuhan, philosopher)

Commercial TV and film, have, as Marshall McLuhan has suggested, pushed written language toward the spontaneity and freedom of the spoken idiom. At the same time, the media have made us intensely aware that words often cannot communicate true feelings as effectively as facial expression, tone of voice and body gesture. Also there has been widespread fear that literate culture will somehow be "cheapened" by the visual media.

One picture is not necessarily worth a thousand words. But pictures, plus related facts, plus visual presentation, do constitute the language of photography.
(John R. Whiting, editor)

Don't merely record what you saw, but tell others how you felt about what you saw. (Susan Wood, photographer)

The Meaning of Photographs

The purpose of photography may be to portray objects and events realistically or to elicit an emotional response. But the ultimate meaning of a photograph may be altered by differences in the way the picture is made.

Facts are not interesting. It's a point of view on facts which is important.
(Henri Cartier-Bresson, photojournalist)

The weather, for instance, or the time of day can affect the subject being photographed. The point of view or type of lens chosen by the photographer can

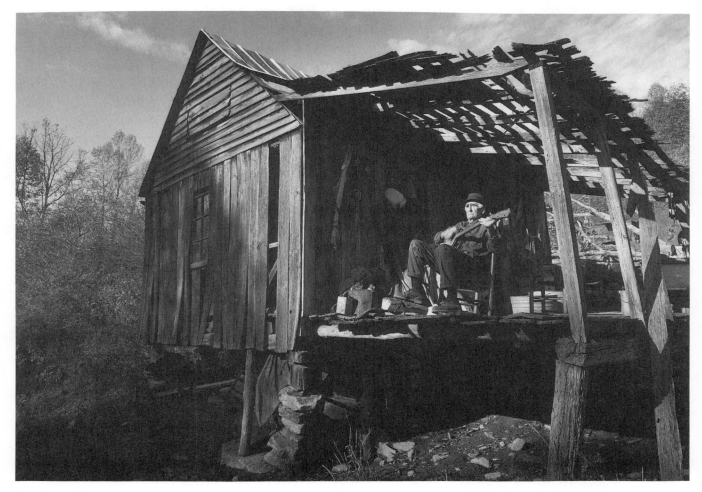

Robert Rowan *Will*
What can we *know* from looking at this picture.
How much must we infer?

make one object seem larger or smaller in relation to the size of other objects. The photographer directs or diverts the viewer's attention by choosing what is to be included or excluded from within the camera's field of view.

Writing about a visual medium tends to make the simple complex. If you want to make photographs, all you do is point the camera at whatever you wish; click the shutter whenever you want. If you want to judge a good photograph, ask yourself: Is life like that? The answer must be yes and no, but mostly yes.

(Charles Harbutt, photojournalist)

The photographer's use of light may mean the difference between a natural-looking picture or one that appears contrived. Light can make the scene appear bright and happy; its absence can make it appear dark and sad or mysterious. When more light is allowed to fall on one part of a subject, people tend to pay more attention to that part of the photograph.

Our responsibility as photographers is to use our technical knowledge and creativity to make images that will be of greatest interest and significance to the people who see them. In doing so we can satisfy ourselves because making photographs that communicate to others can be an active, satisfying experience.

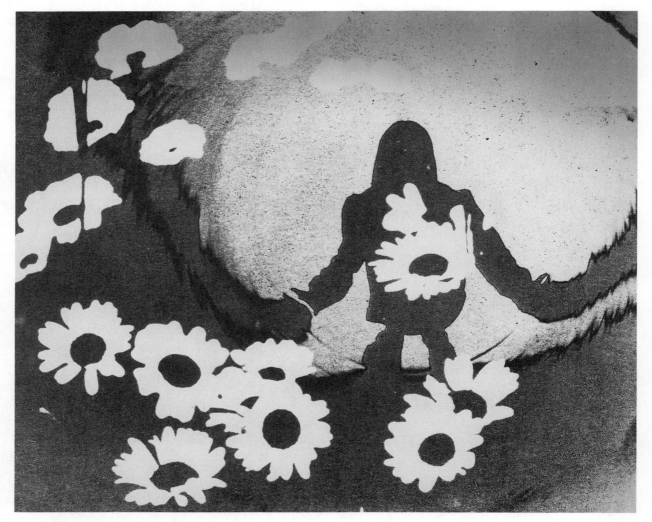

Lowell McCoy *Daisy Pool*
Which is object and which is reflection? What effect is created by the high-contrast treatment of this image?

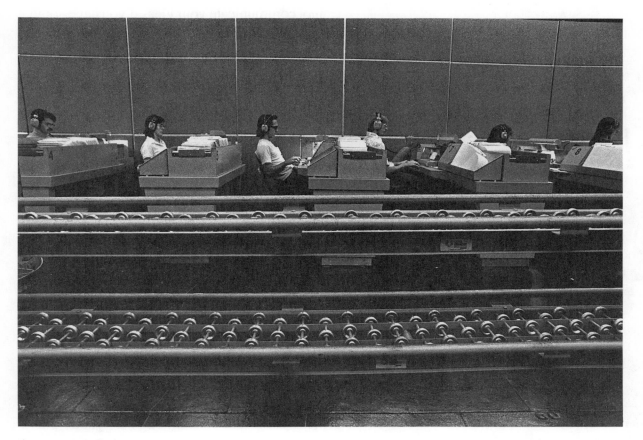

Gary Cialdella *Conveyor*
Does this photograph seem humorous to you or is it frightening? Are these postal workers *on* the conveyor or have they become part of the machines they operate?

The best pictures are made by those photographers who feel some excitement about life and use the camera to share their enthusiasm with others. The camera in such hands is a medium for communicating vital experience.

(Roy Stryker, editor)

Looking at Photographs

Photography, to me, is simply a way of showing to someone else someone or something that has excited me.
(William Albert Allard, photojournalist)

By revealing my own fantasies, I'm also exposing yours! *(Kurt Oldenbrook, artist)*

Looking at pictures can be an active and satisfying experience. When a photograph appeals most strongly to you, it may reveal not only an accurate visual record, but it may also excite your imagination. Perhaps it will stimulate your thinking by reminding you of personal experiences or desires or by challenging you to think new thoughts.

There is no greater esthetic power than the conversion of the familiar into the unbelievably new. *(Edwin H. Land, inventor)*

Many strong photographs stand by themselves as visual experiences without benefit of caption, context, or title; at other times words and pictures work together most effectively to communicate ideas. Photographs can provide information or stimulate interest when words alone might fail; written captions, however, often are required to clarify facts, to

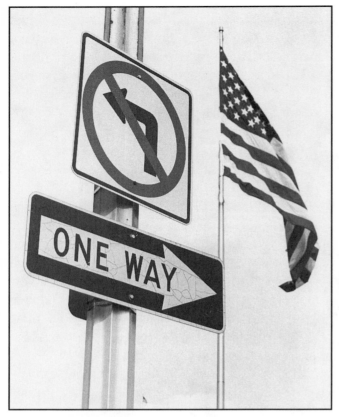

Jorg Jasper *One Way*
Seen together, what message do these three common symbols convey to you? How would you describe the composition?

place a photograph or series of photographs into context, and to call attention to details that the casual viewer might overlook. Some successful photographs need no words at all. Such images appeal to nearly everyone.

You're always looking for the picture that sums it up, the picture that makes a point.
(Brian Lanker, photojournalist)

Think Before You Shoot!

Discovery consists of seeing what everybody has seen and thinking what nobody has thought.
(Albert Szent-Györgyi, philosopher)

A photograph is only as good as the thinking that goes into it. As an artist working independently you cannot communicate your ideas if you have nothing to say; nor, as a professional, can you report an event or communicate a client's ideas if you have no feelings about the subject or about the audience.

By seeing things I could be seen. And by feeling things and capturing those feelings on film I could be felt.
(Bruce Davidson, photojournalist)

Even aloof individuals who claim not to be attempting to communicate any message at all actually say quite a bit about themselves to anyone with whom they share their work. Those of us who consciously attempt to communicate with others need to take a hard look at what we are doing and think about ways to be more articulate. I urge you to consider the following advice:

1. Decide first what you are trying to say or convey to others. Do you want to present information or facts, create emotional impact, or provide esthetic satisfaction? Although a "good" photograph can fulfill any one of these functions, most truly great photographs operate on all three, or at least two of the three levels simultaneously. See what purposes you perceive in "great" photographs that you see.

A photograph that fails to move the viewer and to leave him different than he was before has failed as art because it has failed as communication.
(Harold Allen, educator)

2. Previsualize the essentials of the image. A photograph communicates with subject matter, lighting, perspective, composition and technical quality. All of these elements make up your photographic vocabulary; how well you communicate depends on how well you use your vocabulary. Practice frequently. Seldom do these factors combine themselves by accident into an effective photograph.

I think once you get interested in photographing it makes you very alert to the environment around you. You see much more. (Eliot Porter, photographer)

3. Study every image you see. Look at photographs, paintings, films, and more photographs. When you react strongly to a picture or a movie or TV shot that has real impact, try to analyze the treatment of subject matter in terms of lighting, perspective, composition and technique to see just why it succeeded. Study your own pictures to determine just how each one could be improved. Seek advice from others who are knowledgeable, but most of all be your own severest critic. Look at all the newspapers, magazines and photographic books you can get your hands on. Study their pictures and their page layout. See how the photographs hold your attention (or fail to). Don't copy others' work exactly, but never hesitate to adopt good technique or to adapt good ideas that have meaning for you. Improve on other photographers' successful pictures, but don't repeat their mistakes.

I am the adventurer on a voyage of discovery, ready to receive fresh impressions, eager for fresh horizons... (Edward Weston, photographer)

4. Discover the world around you. Try to see things the way a camera does. Jacques Henri Lartigue wrote that, as a child learning to take pictures, when he ran out of film he would aim his head at a subject he wanted to preserve, close his eyes for a few moments, and then blink his eyelids open and then quickly close them again. Then he would go home and draw with pencil and crayon the "photographic" image he had retained in his mind.

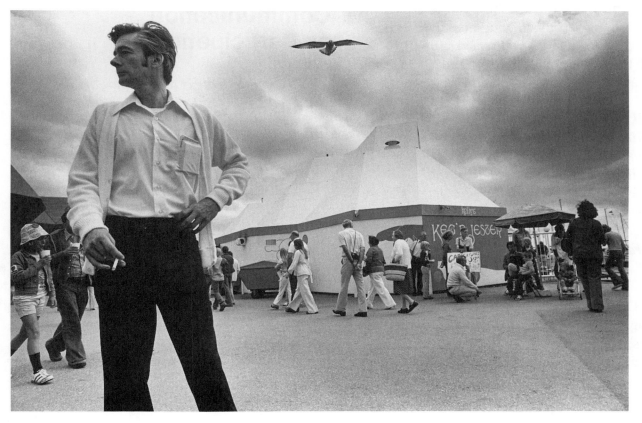

Gary Cialdella *Portent*
Does this photograph suggest that something terrible is about to happen? If so, is it the subject matter or because of experience that you bring to the photograph? Have you seen the Alfred Hitchcock movie *The Birds* or read the original short story by Daphne Du Maurier?

I don't take pictures, pictures take me. I can do nothing except have film in the camera and be alert.

(Charles Harbutt, photojournalist)

The first impression is essential. The first glance, the shock, the surprise.

(Henri Cartier-Bresson, photojournalist)

Like Lartigue, you can teach yourself to "see" by pretending to be a camera. The lens records things in a circumscribed way, and the shutter determines the impression of movement that is to be retained. When you try to see like a camera, notice how every familiar thing changes its appearance under varied lighting conditions and when seen from different points of view. Challenge yourself to notice new things in your everyday environment and to examine familiar things in new ways. Enjoy the different textures, forms and relationships you discover, but don't limit yourself to studying inanimate objects. Most of all, even if you are attracted strongly by the natural landscape, don't be shy about observing people and interacting with them.

Talk to people, but listen to them more. Cultivate a genuine interest in everyone's problems, troubles, successes and achievements, no matter how small. Learn to take everyone for what he or she is worth. Learn to meet every type of person on their own level. In other words, learn to like people!

(Ed Farber, photojournalist)

5. Develop your interest in people. Go to shopping malls and supermarkets, parks and playgrounds; attend concerts, plays, picnics, meetings and social and sporting events. Watch people at these places and activities and observe them at their work or in school. Watch how they sit, lean, laugh, or cry. Watch how they argue, walk, or run. Most of us are interested in pictures of other people, especially when others are shown to be somewhat like ourselves. But it's not easy to photograph people in meaningful and insightful ways. It takes a lot of insight, empathy, patience and persistence.

I try to reveal but not to interpret. I observe but do not intrude.

(Henri Cartier-Bresson, photojournalist)

The photographer establishes an intimate relationship between himself and whatever he is photographing.

(Edward Steichen, photographer)

The camera simply becomes a tool to introduce a person to you...To record the kinds of things that surround him. The kind of country he lives in. The way he lives. The way he works. Hopefully, if the photograph is good, it might even tell you a little bit about the way he thinks. And what he likes to do.

(William Albert Allard, photojournalist)

Communication as Participation

To communicate is to take part...to partake in a joint effort which transforms those so engaged, reconstructs their lives a little and sometimes a lot.

(Edgar Dale, educator)

Communication is often described as a one-way process originating with a sender (speaker, writer, or visualizer) through a medium (speech, written word, photograph, or painting) to a receiver (listener, reader, or viewer). Communication is thus sometimes seen as a linear process rather than a circular or continuous one. Edgar Dale explained that "in one-way communication, the sender assumes that the receiver is a target to be aimed at but with little or no provision for the 'target' to shoot back." In one-way communication there is, as Dale put it, no creative interaction between sender and receiver.

Irresistibly, you share a photograph with someone...and he or she gets a deeper insight into you as well as what you discerned. *(Edwin H. Land, inventor)*

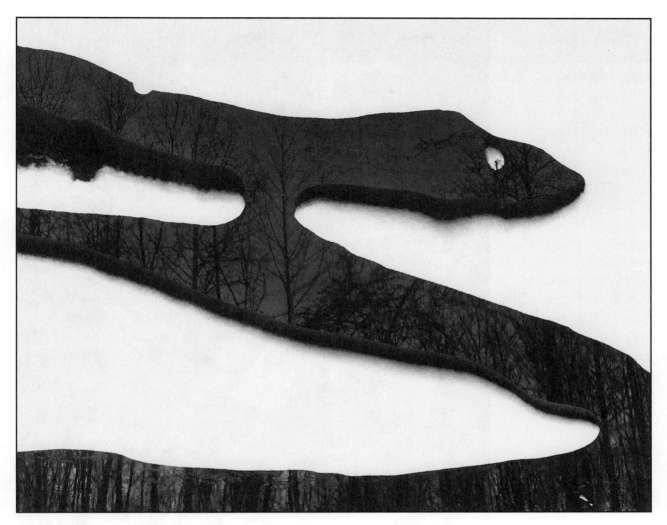

Roger Hansen *Snow and Water*
When viewed from a distance, this winter landscape
becomes an interaction between abstract forms of white
on black—or is it black on white? Which form is
foreground and which is background?

Communication can be defined in a broader sense to mean "to share in common, to participate in." An effective photograph can be a bridge by which people share common experiences. A photograph makes a literal statement: "This is what this object looked like at a certain moment in time," or "these were the participants and this is the setting for an event that once took place." Or the photograph can say, "Share the excitement (or pain or joy or togetherness or aloneness) of these human beings." Or the photograph may speak eloquently of texture, line, mass, balance, light and shade or color. "I was moved by this beauty," the photographer might confide to you through an image, "and I wanted you to share my pleasure." Or the photographer might be saying, "I was horrified and repulsed by what I saw—maybe if you, too, are horrified, together we can begin to change things." Or the photographer could say, "I felt strangely elated (or terrified) when I realized what this image seems to contain—can you help me sort out its meaning?"

To communicate effectively with others, first we must understand ourselves. We must recognize our own strengths and frailties; our hopes and fears; our envies and prejudices. I know of no better means than photography to aid us in the better understanding of our world—and of ourselves.

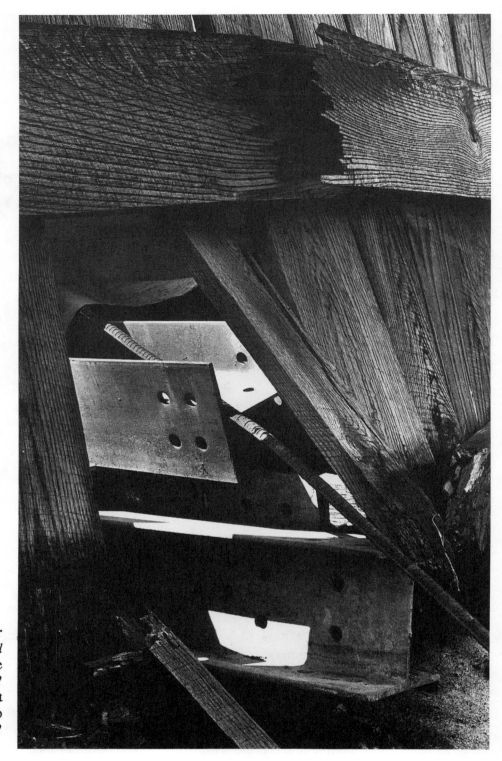

David M. Posther
Splinters and Steel
What kinds of *contrasts* are
evident in this photograph?
Can you imagine an *audible* effect
from this image, in addition to
its visual impact?

*Much is missed if we have eyes
only for the bright colors.*
(Eliot Porter, photographer)

Selecting Subject Matter 2

Two may do the same thing, and it is not the same thing. (Publius Syrus, philosopher)

I've been in places where the photographers were literally elbow to elbow. And yet everyone comes up with a different picture. (William Albert Allard, photojournalist)

What Are You Saying?

A thought is not a thought unless it is one's own. There is all the difference between having something to say and having to say something.

(John Dewey, educator)

Deciding what to photograph isn't so much of a problem if you've developed the habit of seeing. Finding subject matter may not be so hard if you already have a lot to say in the way of social comment, or if there is specific information you have good reason to want to communicate to others. As we summarized earlier, you have to decide what you are trying to say—present information or facts, create emotional impact, share esthetic pleasure, or stimulate the viewer's imagination. When you've decided what you want to do with photography and why, then you can begin to study the how.

I can read in any photo book what the temperature of my developer is supposed to be. However, I want to know what makes a good photograph and the books fail me in that respect. What good is a perfect print of a rotten picture?

(A student)

The anonymous student asks a very good question. Later on in this book I'll discuss plenty of routine details, such as the temperature of your developer and the way you can control image contrast. But before we get into technique, I want you to be making photographs in your mind as well as with your camera. I want you to become so excited about what you're seeing around you that you can't wait to get it down on film and paper.

Let us first say what photography is not. A photograph is not a painting, a poem, a symphony, a dance. It is not just a pretty picture, not an exercise in...technique and sheer print quality. It is, or should be, a significant document, a penetrating statement, which can be described in a very simple term—selectivity.

(Berenice Abbott, photographer)

Selectivity means choosing what to include in your pictures and what to leave out. The choice, ultimately intuitive, is at first conscious and deliberate and you can learn a lot about selectivity by studying other people's photographs. In doing so you'll find yourself going through three stages of photographic awareness: first, noticing; then analyzing; and finally, reacting. When you become interested in photography, you begin to notice pictures that you might not have paid any attention to before.

Learn from the mistakes of others—you can never live long enough to make them all yourself! (Fred Tonne, photojournalist)

And we can learn as well from other people's successes as from their failures—consciously observing and adapting to our own work effective compositional arrangements, lighting techniques and camera angles. As you learn more about visual language you can't help but analyze every aspect of each image, from concept to quality, in the objective way that a competition juror should. Before long you begin to allow yourself to experience real gut reactions, and you start trying to figure out why you (and others) feel the way you do about certain images and why you react differently to others.

There are no new ideas in the world. There is only new arrangement of things.

(Henri Cartier-Bresson, photographer)

If there is something to see and everybody sees it, that is observation. If there is nothing to see, yet you see it, that is poetry. But if you can make something out of nothing and make everybody see it—that is poetry in photography.

(Ernst Haas, photographer)

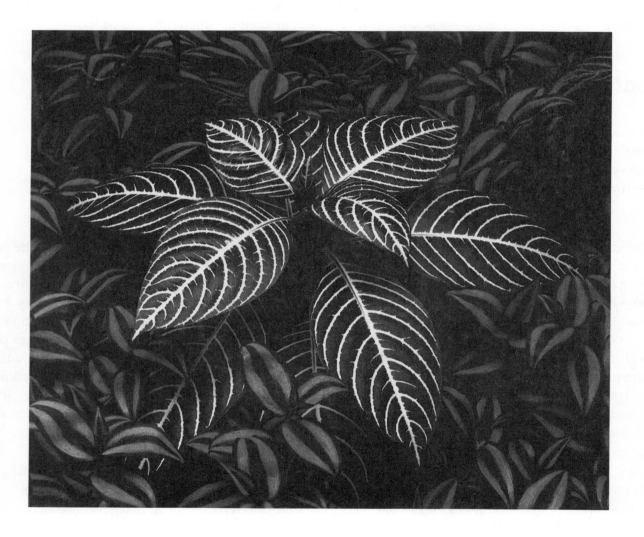

Robert D. Havira *Plant Patterns*
Images of beauty attract attention whether the subject matter is majestic mountains, pretty plants, or attractive people. Repetition is the keynote in this delicately balanced composition. Notice the subtle variations as lines, forms and values are repeated.

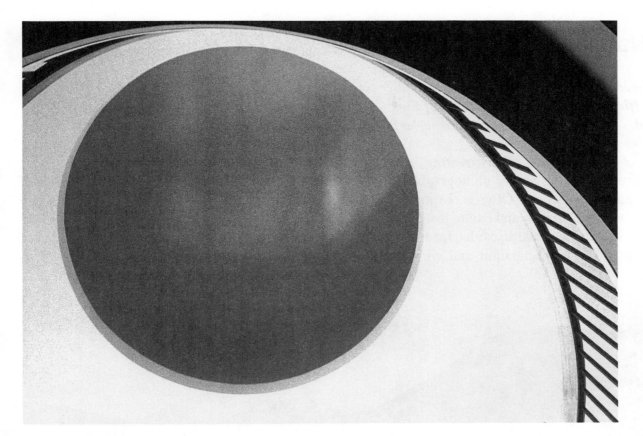

James M. Rhoads *Railing*
A simple, dynamic visual statement can attract a viewer's attention from across a room. Whether the photograph is great or not may depend on whether attention, once captured, can be held and rewarded by rhythms and detailed elements within the image.

If you study the work of great photographers, you can ask yourself, "How would so-and-so have looked at this subject? What portions would probably have been included? At what time of day would the photograph have been made? Or where would he or she have placed the lights? Don't hesitate to "borrow" ideas and styles until you evolve a style of your own. Emulation need not be the same as imitation.

Let other people see the world through your eyes.

(Richard Shirk, photographer)

The seeing process is primarily a purposive searching of the visual environment for instances of order.

(Norman F. Carver, Jr., photographer)

A Visual Vocabulary

The photographic image is different in form and meaning from any other image. It has its own grammar, vocabulary, and interpretation. When and if the student learns this language, he will be able to photographically translate his own thoughts. *(Walter Civardi, educator)*

At your disposal are all of the fundamental elements: subject matter, tonality, contrast, perspective, composition and technique. We'll deal in later chapters with technique, but for now let's examine the other tools of visual vocabulary.

The Natural Landscape

I believe in photography as one means of...affirming the enormous beauty of the world. (Ansel Adams, photographer)

Some of us never tire of discovering, photographing, rediscovering and re-photographing the endless beauty of the world. Often we expose more film when we travel to new and exotic places, but I think that is because we have discarded for a time the blindfold of daily preoccupation and we simply notice more. Often there is at least as much visual excitement at home, but seeing requires looking.

I'm discovering to my delight that there's as much to see and photograph in my own back yard as I have found in any exotic place. (George Herben, photographer)

Our attention is captured by dramatic vistas of grand scale, but don't overlook microcosms of beauty and natural order found on the forest floor or in the streets of your city. Respond to the shouts, of course, but listen for the whispers.

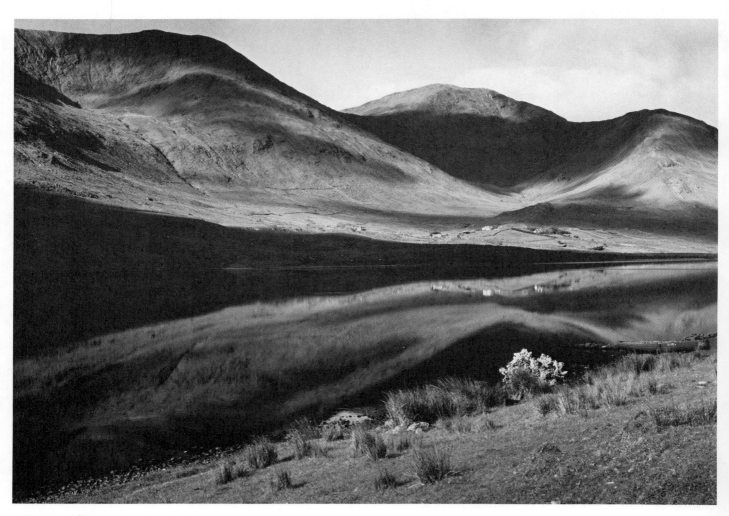

Norman Carver, Jr. *Ireland*
Notice the contrast here between repose and motion as these sensuous lines and forms are repeated and reflected. What compositional role is played by the white flowering bush in the right foreground?

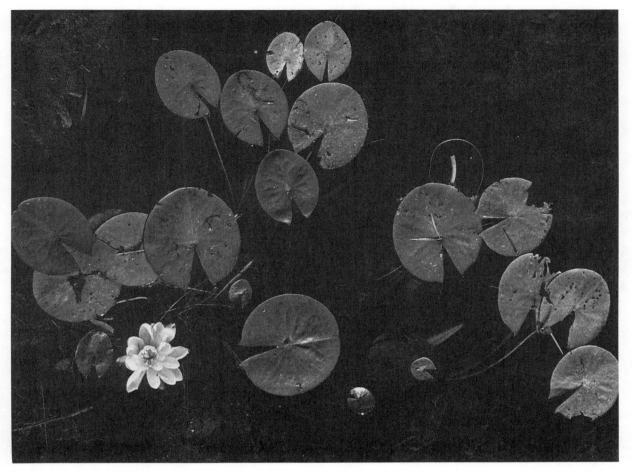

Michael Sarnacki *Water Lilies*
Although the scale is very different from *Ireland* on the
facing page, how are these two images similar in design?

*I photograph nature...because I believe
nature is terribly important.*

(Ansel Adams, photographer)

Traditional views of dramatic and colorful landscapes are popular for calendars and posters because they remind people of idyllic experiences. However, many people who claim not to like any kind of abstract art will be attracted subconsciously to a fine image of recognizable subject matter that is built upon strong elements of graphic design. Some people will be attracted to such an image without really knowing why. Those who do understand visual vocabulary well enough to recognize the underlying order and balance may receive distinct esthetic pleasure from the simple act of viewing such a work.

*I try now to pay more attention to the
earth, to always note such easily taken-
for-granted miracles as sunrises and
moonsets.*   (Stephen Trimble, photographer)

*Only in fragments of the whole is
nature's order apparent.*

(Eliot Porter, photographer)

Less is more.

(Ludwig Mies van der Rohe, architect)

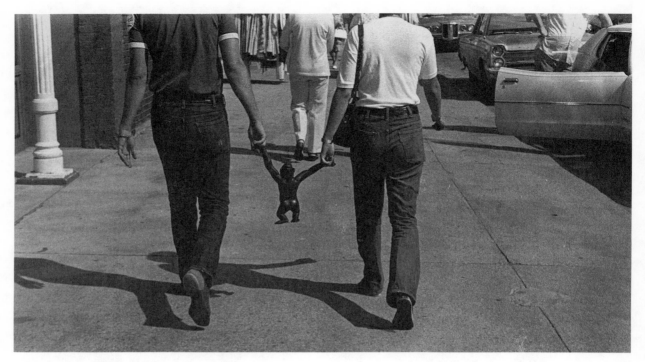

Gary Cialdella *Downtown Pentwater*
(The Humorous) Does the sheer incongruity of this
photograph make you chuckle? It is an instant in
time—an image that could only be photographic—that
succeeds, despite fracturing all the traditional rules of
composition and previsualization.

Michael Sarnacki *Music Festival*
(The Unexpected) Would you quickly dismiss this
photograph because of "sloppy" composition? Or would
you be intrigued enough to study the image long enough
to discover the unexpected surprise within?

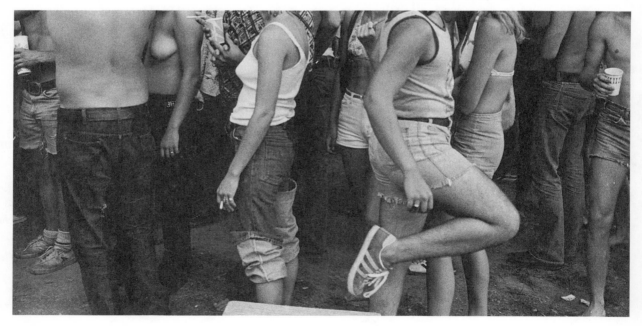

The Social Landscape

I like to take people in their environment...the animal in its habitat.
(*Henri Cartier-Bresson, photojournalist*)

Many contemporary photographers have been turning away from pictorial subjects and toward recording moments of everyday reality—catching people unaware as they interact with one another and with the environment mankind has created on Earth. Bearing a superficial resemblance to the uninspired snapshot, such a photographically immortalized instant sometimes makes a significant comment.

I work with a hand camera, invisibly and quickly...Interacting with the subject changes the nature of the image and its meaning. (*Gary Monroe, photographer*)

Another kind of selective "snapshot" is documentation of mankind. Humorous, tragic, or merely "the way it was," history demands honest recording in every decade of the way people live, look, dress and act.

There is nothing more artistic than to love people. (*Vincent van Gogh, painter*)

Why, in the world of popular culture, are pictures of babies, attractive young men and women, and animals so popular? Perhaps because the subjects and their cute poses are familiar to everyone and

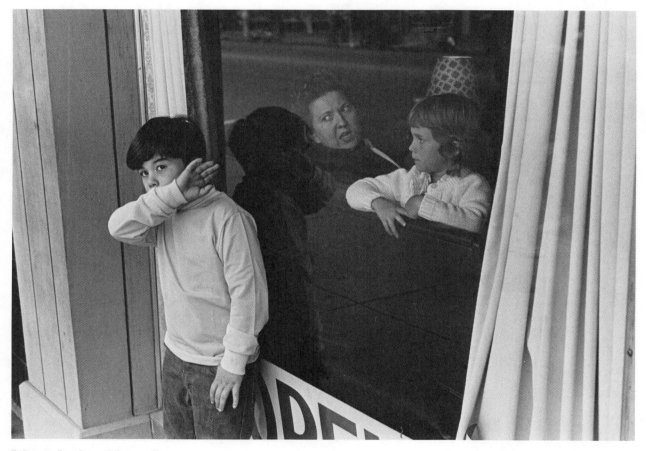

John A. Lacko *Plainwell*
Has this boy been sent from the restaurant for some obscene infraction of table manners? What has he done (if anything at all)? We'll never know, but the photograph poses a provocative puzzle for us as it records a moment of human drama.

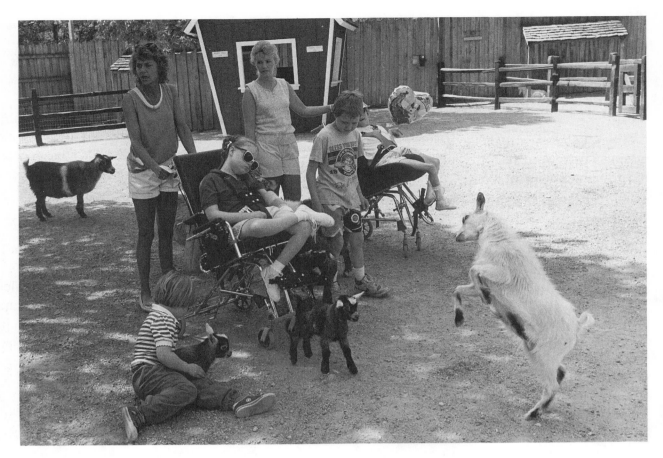

John A. Lacko   *Binder Park Zoo*
Who's paying attention to what? Can you describe the
interactions between people and animals? Besides social
interest, what is the significance here of graphic design?

Jim Nixon   *Mom at Home*
Is this a *snapshot* or a *photograph?* Can it be both? Does it
make a statement about suburban life in America while
presenting some interesting elements of design?

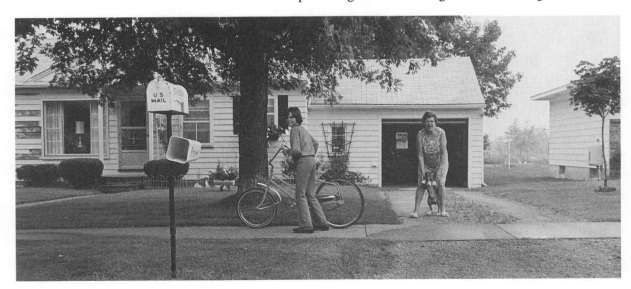

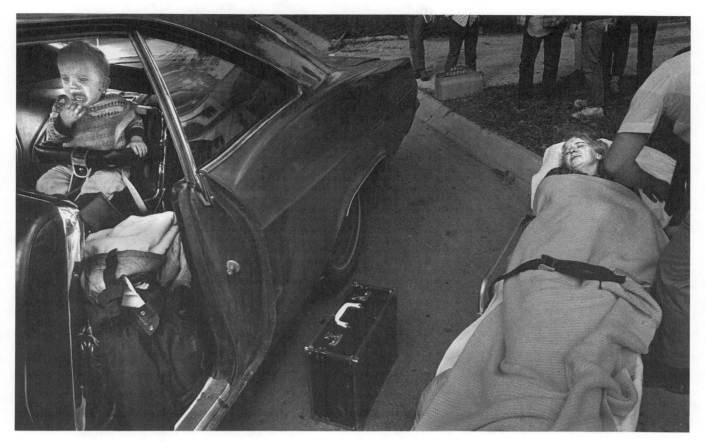

Brian Lanker *Automobile Accident*
What is there about injury and death that appeals to the morbid curiosity of the human mind? Why are people fascinated by the misfortunes of others—could it be that we are secretly relieved that it didn't happen to us? Brian Lanker says, "People seem to have something for tragedies. When they go on in my town, I've got to photograph them." (Photo courtesy of *Topeka Capitol-Journal*).

evoke sentimental ideals of life. Although personal snapshots fulfill this purpose for millions of people, many thousands will happily purchase "professional snapshots" to display on their walls and coffee tables. The fine artist probably won't be concerned much with cuteness and salability, but the skillful professional might even educate a client a bit by sneaking some quality and design into an otherwise ordinary image.

> *I feel you have to strongly like or dislike a subject. You have to care one way or the other. You can't be indifferent.*
> (William Albert Allard, photojournalist)

If you have a natural sense of humor, let it show in your photographs. People respond to a touch of whimsy in an otherwise somber scene, and a natu-

rally comic situation always gets a spontaneous reaction. On the other hand, strong images of tragedy can stir up emotions of sympathy, empathy, indignation, and anger. They can stimulate reactions of commitment or they can result in distrust and disgust. War photographs, for example, and photographs of starving children or accident victims often shake us to our emotional roots as we identify with the plight of the people in the pictures.

> *If...my photographs could cause compassionate horror within the viewer, they might also prod the conscience of that viewer into taking action.*
> (W. Eugene Smith, photojournalist)

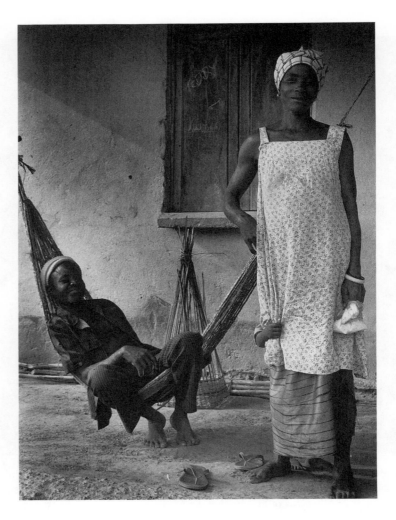

Diane Osborne *Sierra Leone*
What can we learn about our own culture by visiting and photographing people whose lives are different from ours?

John A. Lacko
Auto Swap Meet
What has the photographer documented about the culture of America in the last decade of the 20th century? Of what future interest is such an image?

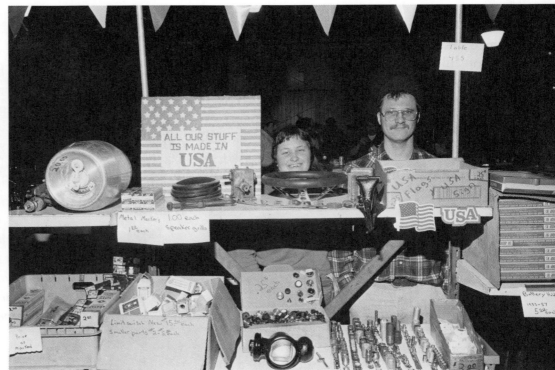

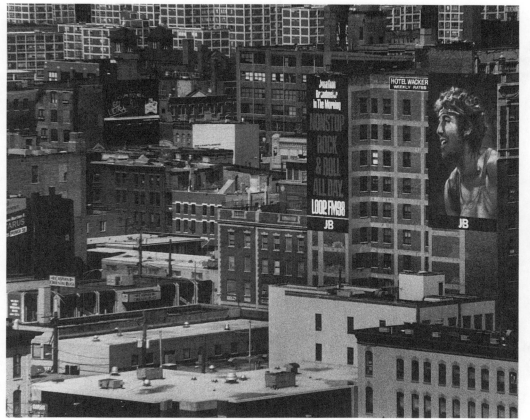

Todd Wickersham
Chicago
In viewing this urban/cultural landscape, what feelings do you have about city life? In addition to the subject matter and the mental images it stimulates, are you aware of geometric relationships?

The Cultural Landscape

The visual soul of America is the highway, a hamburger joint, and a dime store. I love the loneliness and power and craziness of America. It is me.

(Burk Uzzle, photojournalist)

Architectural landmarks were among the first subjects toward which early photographers pointed their primitive cameras. And photographic documentation of today's evidence of mankind's presence—beautiful, ugly, dramatic or mundane—will continue to be valuable to historians of the future.

This mysterious quality of believability or implied truthfulness...raises to the level of art the simplest, most direct snapshot, when the process of selection is in the hands of a creative person.

(J. H. Troup, Jr., educator)

How is *cultural* different from *social?* As I define it, *social* landscape emphasizes interaction between people while *cultural* landscape emphasizes people interacting with the artifacts of human civilization. And then *urban* landscape deals with city life, etc. Of course the categories overlap broadly, but the idea simply is to help us recognize what we are doing. Whatever the subject matter, the important thing is to take an interest in what is going on around us.

Any photographer who takes the time to react to what he is photographing, as well as to aim the lens and push the button...will never feel the same about his subject. (Margery Mann, photographer)

Photography is the simultaneous recognition, in a fraction of a second, of the significance of an event, as well as the precise organization of forms which gives that event its proper expression.

(Henri Cartier-Bresson, photojournalist)

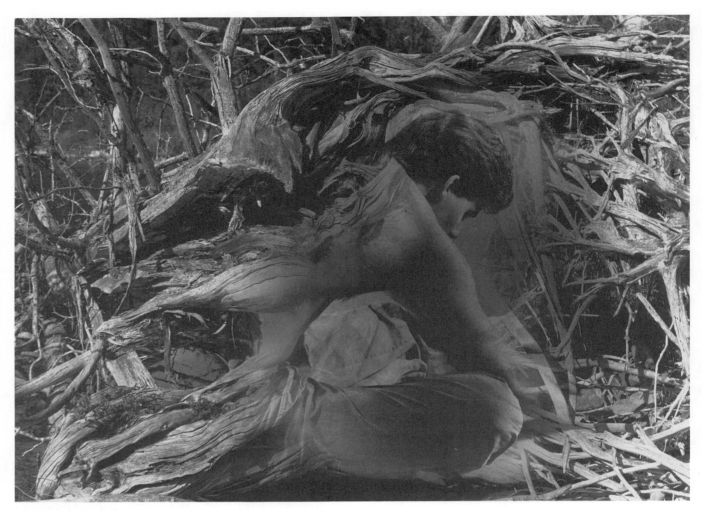

Jeff Keyes *Captive*
In this darkroom-blended image, what meaning is there for you? What might the photographer have had in mind?

The Personal (Inner) Landscape

I like to present a problematic situation and let the viewer in his inventive way come to grips with it on personal terms.
(*Jerry N. Uelsmann, photographer*)

A "stopper" photograph may not always be easy to understand. The secret of its success is in trapping the viewer into studying it long enough to become committed to decoding the visual puzzle or metaphor that the photographer so cleverly hid within it. To establish rapport, you have to offer viewers an intellectual and emotional challenge so personal and so tempting that they are compelled to accept it.

Nothing is ever the same as they said it was. It's what I've never seen before that I recognize. (*Diane Arbus, photographer*)

People love to be surprised and amused by the bizarre. As a movement in art, surrealism involves deliberate distortion of the ordinary, or incongruous juxtaposition of things. If you can shock viewers into spending enough time with your photograph, you can reward them with serendipitous discoveries within the image. The meaning of a photograph does not have to be limited to identification of its subject matter. Try photographing things, as photographer-teacher Minor White suggested, not so much for what they are, but for *what else* they are.

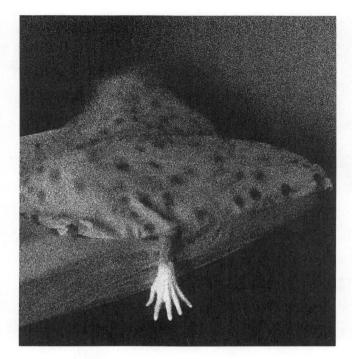

Mickey Howell *White Hand*
This photograph makes my flesh crawl and sends a chill up my spine. Does it have a similar effect on you? Does the murky, grainy tonality of the image affect its psychological impact?

> *To the man who knows nothing, mountains are mountains, waters are waters, and trees are trees. But when he has studied, and knows a little, mountains are no longer mountains, water is no longer water, and trees are no longer trees. Finally, when he has thoroughly understood, mountains are once again mountains, waters are waters, and trees are trees.*
>
> *(Zen philosophy quoted by Edward Weston, photographer)*

Of course some photographs succeed on strength of subject matter alone. Pulitzer prizes have been awarded to photojournalists whose instincts and luck brought them to exactly the right place at the right time and who had the nerve and the presence of mind to release the shutter at the climactic instant of a newsworthy event. But you can carry a camera around your neck for a lifetime—everywhere you go—and never get a single notable news picture.

(But having a camera with you might encourage you to look for strong images of other kinds).

> *Without the influence of the subject matter, there is little reason to find form.*
>
> *(Gary Monroe, photographer)*

> *A photograph should sometimes be more of an intriguing suggestion than an obvious statement.*
>
> *(John A. Lacko, photographer)*

Most good pictures require conscious awareness of the potential of a situation and the skill and patience to make the photograph happen. Good photographs also depend generally on the skillful and fortuitous combination of interesting subject matter with some of the elements of lighting, perspective, composition, and technique.

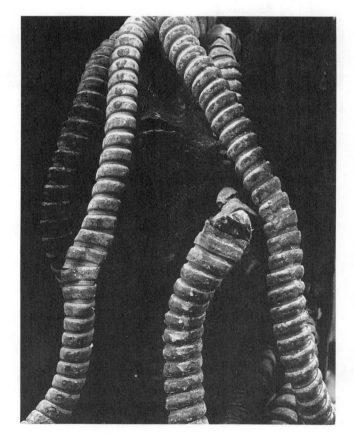

William Beverly *Junkyard*
Besides being what it is...what *else* is it?

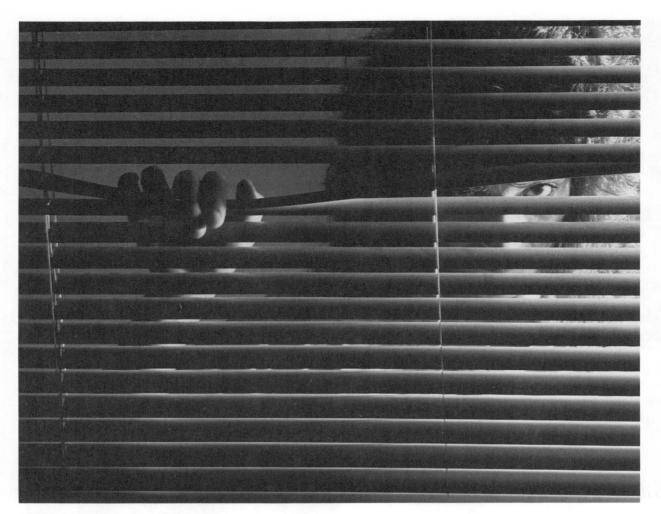

Darren Hathaway *Venetian Blinds*
How do the elements of tonality and contrast affect your reaction to this image?

> *Photography combines those elements of spontaneity and immediacy that say, 'this is happening, this is real,' and creates an image through a curious alchemy that will live and grow and become more meaningful in a historical perspective.*
>
> *(Dan Weiner, photographer)*

Although some photographs can be successful because of their subject matter, there has never been such a photograph that couldn't have had additional impact. Great photographs demand a blending of all the elements of the photographer's visual vocabulary, most prominent of which is light.

> *Wherever there is light, one can photograph.*   *(Ansel Adams, photographer)*

Consider light in terms of tonality and contrast— in other words, what light does to and for the subject matter of the photograph.

Tonality

We live among cultural cliches about color meanings, and stereotypes about tonality. In the North American/European tradition, for example, lightness and brightness imply cleanliness, goodness, hope and inspiration; darkness is often taken to mean the opposite: *blacklist, blackmail, black market, black sheep, "in the dark."*

The ancient oriental symbol of the eternal struggle between good and evil depicts good as white and evil as black or red. In Western movies, we all know who wears the white hats and who wears the black hats. Black, in the culture of the Western world, is the traditional symbol of death and mourning. Perhaps some of the roots of racial prejudice are traceable to ancient myths and taboos about darkness and blackness. Most people instinctively associate dark photographs with sadness, mystery, or ominousness. Lightness usually implies happiness, openness, innocence and hope.

Colors are stereotyped, too—reds, oranges, and yellows are traditionally warm, active, and advancing; whereas greens and blues are considered to be cool, passive, and retreating. Although these conventions are generally accepted, some interesting photographic paradoxes have been created by photographers who were bold enough to violate them.

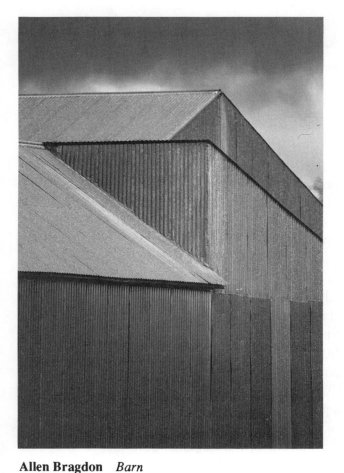

Allen Bragdon *Barn*
What design element dominates this image? Has the composition been strengthened by eliminating much of the building and most of the background?

[When looking at a photograph] we experience a swift, intuitive response to the photograph as a whole—an emotional reaction that cannot be precisely verbalized—resulting from the interplay of shapes, forms, textures, lights, and darks. More or less simultaneously we try to find a rational meaning to the event or situation portrayed. Why is the photographer showing us this particular fragment of time and space? What meaning, if any, did it have for him and may it have for us?

(Arthur Goldsmith, educator)

Contrast

It is two elements which are suddenly in conflict. There is a spark between two elements. There are always two pulls and one cannot exist without the other one. It's these tensions I'm always moved by.
(Henri Cartier-Bresson, photojournalist)

Cartier-Bresson, one of the world's most respected photojournalists, was referring to conflict and contrast between forms and objects, as well as between elements of light and dark and conflicting colors. Contrast (conflict) is a basic element of visual composition.

Photography is possible because some objects and portions of objects reflect more light than others. Shadows, to put it most simply, are crucial. The term contrast refers to the relative brightness, or reflectivity, of various portions of the subject or of the photograph as a whole.

We are...utterly captivated by the problems of light; the gentle, dangerous, dreamlike, living, dead, clear, misty, hot, violent, bare, sudden, dark, springlike, falling, straight, slanting, sensual, subdued, limited, poisonous, calming, pale light. Light. (Ingmar Bergman, film director)

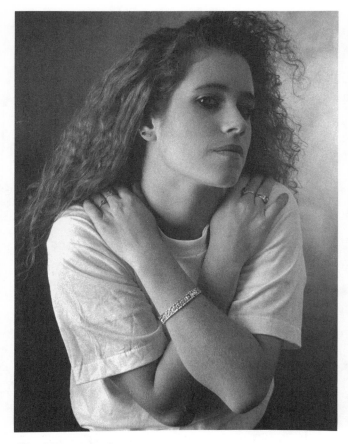

Chad Bennett *Stacy*
Comparing this portrait with *Regan,* on the right, what differences in mood and effect have been created by differences in lighting, posing and composition?

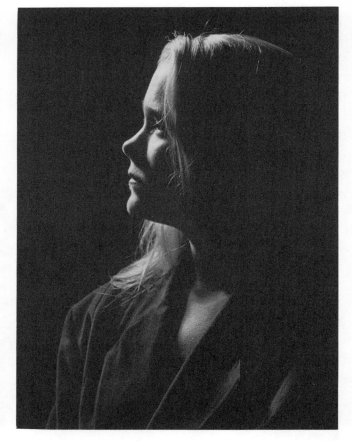

Jorg Jasper *Regan*
Analyze the pose and lighting of this portrait. Where has the key light been placed? What do you think this picture may imply about the personality of the subject?

Soft, low-contrast lighting, in which shadows are diffuse and luminous, often creates a mood of delicacy and softness, even femininity, especially when the image is predominantly light in tone, or *high key*. Contrasts in lighting, on the other hand, tend to form harsh, dark shadows on and around the subject, emphasizing texture and roughness. And remember what darkness may imply! If the predominant mood is extremely dark, there may be mystery (what evil lurks in those sinister shadows?) A photograph that consists mostly of dark areas is said to be *low key*.

> *One of the most beautiful things to do is to paint darkness which, nevertheless, has light within it. (Vincent van Gogh, painter)*

Extreme lighting contrast is often thought to be appropriate for enhancing the rugged appearance of masculine character subjects and for simulating the dramatic effect of stage lighting. As a spotlight singles out the principle performer on a stage, so the *main* or *key* light source draws the viewer's attention to the lightest portion of a photograph.

As you study photographs, notice whether your eye is drawn to the lightest area, and then whether this area is the most significant point, or the center of interest. It's often distracting, for example, to allow a print to have very large white areas in the corners or bright areas in the background that compete for attention. Irresistibly, the eye is drawn away from the primary center of interest. The skilled photographer tries to control the direction and relative contrast of light and to choose which portions of a picture to illuminate.

Chiaroscuro is a term used by artists to describe the placing of light against dark and dark against light. Extraneous detail sometimes is suppressed by placing it in the shadows. Balance is as important between light and dark tones as it is between various hues and intensities of color. Look for the chiaroscuro effect in nature and in works of art. Try to employ it in your photographs.

Perspective

The snapshot is a picture made with the eye only. The creative photograph, on the other hand, is made with the mind.
(Wilson Hicks, editor)

In the broadest photographic sense, perspective means point of view. The term refers to the rendering of lines and surfaces and three-dimensional forms on the flat film plane inside the camera. It refers also to the effect of size relationships and

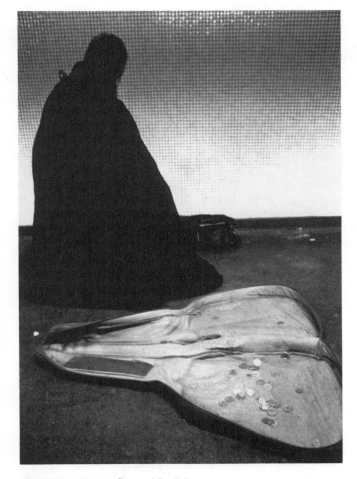

Allen Bragdon *Street Musician*
Notice the chiaroscuro effect here that reinforces this simple composition of strong repeated graphic forms.

camera angle to the viewer's interpretation of the photograph.

Should you correct a distorted rendering of perspective? Although our eyes see parallel lines as converging and straight lines as curved, an accepted convention in architectural and many other forms of photography is that parallels should be rendered parallel and that straight and perpendicular lines should be shown as being straight and perpendicular. With the right kind of equipment, we can either "correct" or deliberately distort perspective, depending on the effect we have in mind.

In size relationships, Biggest=Most Important. That's the general rule, exceptions being made by skillful use of lighting and compositional balance to emphasize areas or objects that are smaller in size.

Nothing exists in itself—it is the relationships between things which are important. (Henri Cartier-Bresson, photojournalist)

When we look up at someone or something, that subject seems to increase in stature and significance, as a child's-eye view of an adult. Conversely, looking down tends by association to diminish or to de-emphasize. Notice the altered feeling of identification when you confront a child or a pet eye-to-eye. Sometimes a change in camera angle adds interest or drama to an ordinary scene.

Composition

The contemplation of things as they are, without error or confusion, without substitution or imposture, is in itself a nobler thing than a whole harvest of invention. (Francis Bacon, philosopher)

J. H. Troup, Jr. observed that, "The camera allows the photographer to select and save rectangular bits and pieces of the all-encompassing, everchanging reality in which we exist...The photographer...applies the camera's frame to nature to include, to exclude, to associate, to disassociate, to isolate designs, and to show significance." In this quotation Troup distills the essence of the difference

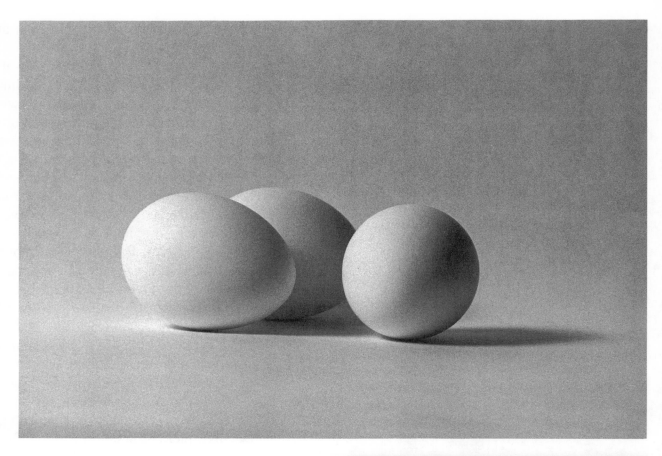

Sally Putney *High Key*
Notice that roundness and texture are retained in the eggs, although only relatively small shadow areas have a value below Zone VI.

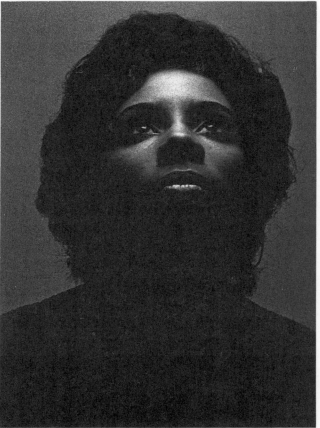

Wallace Kirk *Low Key*
This portrait retains a sparkle and feeling of quality although composed almost entirely of values below Zone V. Loss of separation between the darker zones seems relatively unimportant because attention is diverted to highlights in the eyes and onto the major planes of the face.

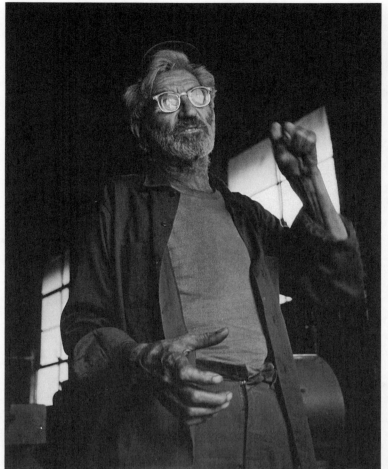

Jim Nixon *Old Man Standing*
Does looking up at a subject increase its apparent stature? Do the hand and arm gestures in this example and the one below contribute to the effects of enhancement and diminution?

Jim Nixon *Old Man Sitting*
What is the effect of viewpoint on psychological interpretation? Are feelings of diminution and vulnerability the result of looking down on a subject, as we are accustomed to looking down on a child?

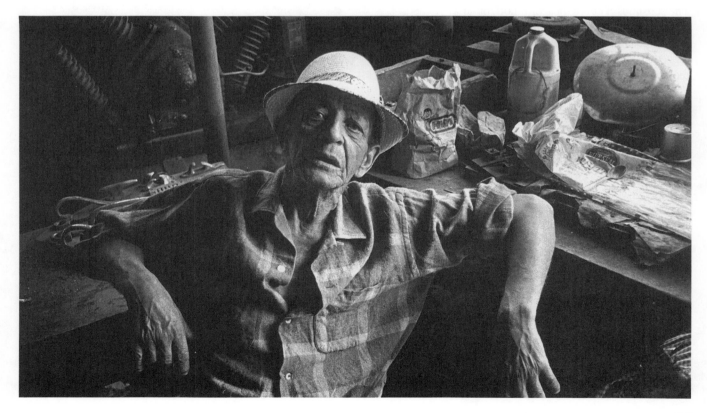

James M. Rhoads *Drainpipe*
Does this combination of vertical format and jagged diagonals strongly imply both height and action? Besides strong graphic elements, this print contains fine textures and unusual spatial relationships.

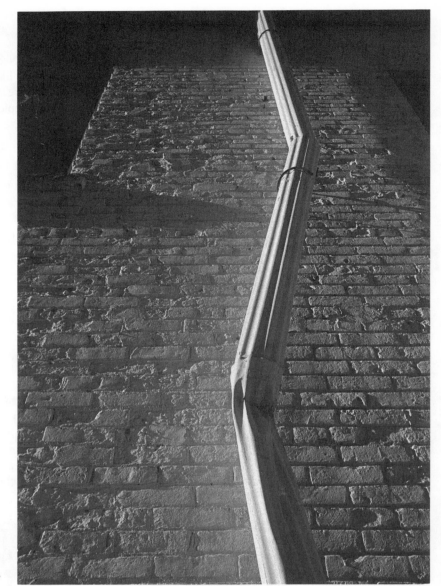

Jim Nixon *Snowscape*
The sensuous S curve, peaceful horizontal format, and restful tonal values of this quiet landscape contrast strongly with the violent jaggedness of *Drainpipe,* above. Do both of these compositions apply the *Rule of Thirds?*

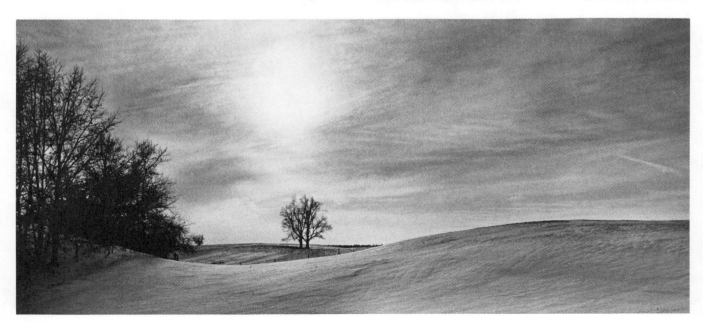

between the work of the painter and that of the photographer.

While the painter starts with simple space (a blank canvas), and then adds basic lines and forms, concluding finally with the complex elements of texture and color, the photographer must do exactly the reverse: the photographer must work from the complex to the simple. From the bewildering array of visual stimuli confronting her or him, the photographer must isolate and select, including the significant elements within the space bounded by the edges of the ground glass or viewfinder, and excluding the extraneous.

> *It's just as important to decide what **not** to include in the frame as it is to decide what to include.* (Gary Monroe, photographer)

> *The camera is dumb!*
> (Garry Winogrand, photographer)

A camera, correctly adjusted, will record an image of everything within its field of view. The camera's eye merely records facts. It is the eye and brain of the photographer that must determine which facts are worth recording and in what way.

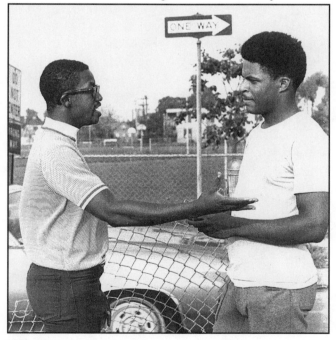

Mel Teague *Conversation*
Do the signs, poles, wheels, fence texture, and other details provide essential supporting information in this photograph or are they distractions?

> *Abstraction releases everyday forms from their everyday associations—allows them to take on new and symbolic meanings.*
> (Norman F. Carver, Jr., photographer)

One self-assignment often recommended to student photographers is to get permission from the owner of a junkyard to come in with camera and tripod on a weekend or holiday when dangerous heavy equipment is not working. Obviously, the biggest challenge in taking pictures in a junkyard is the discipline of searching for pleasing designs and patterns among unrecognizable subject matter. Unburdened by considerations of "What is it?," viewers of the resulting images can share the photographer's joy of discovery.

> *The junkyard proved to me that there are things to photograph everywhere. Until I shot that assignment I didn't believe it.*
> (A student)

Some painters try to produce abstract images by leaving out all identifiable objects. Interestingly, these are the kinds of expressionist images that a perceptive photographer can discover anywhere!

> *More has been written about composition than should have been.*
> (John R. Whiting, editor)

What Whiting means is that iron-clad rules have been set down pontifically through the years by art critics, professors, and jurors. They have used these rules as inflexible criteria for measuring the value of photographs as art. Many of these so-called rules have become so a part of traditional criticism that perhaps the majority of people tend to accept them as gospel and to reject images summarily that fail to follow the formulas. But in the same way that photographs should not be rejected or ridiculed solely because they don't meet certain accepted compositional criteria, neither should empty and meaningless pictures be accepted and praised solely because they do.

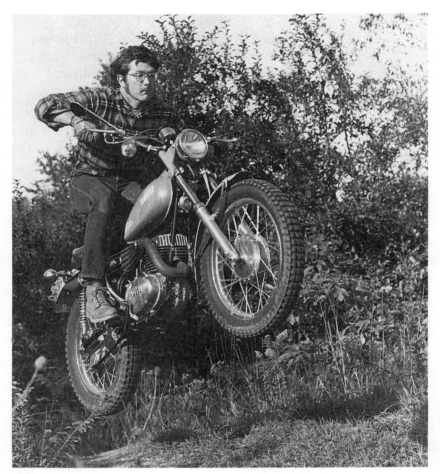

David Knoblauch *Cyclist*

Does it make any difference to you whether the cyclist appears to be moving *into* the frame or *out of it?* In the photograph below, does he seem to be coming to a screeching halt? (If you try photos like this, remind the biker to wear a helmet!)

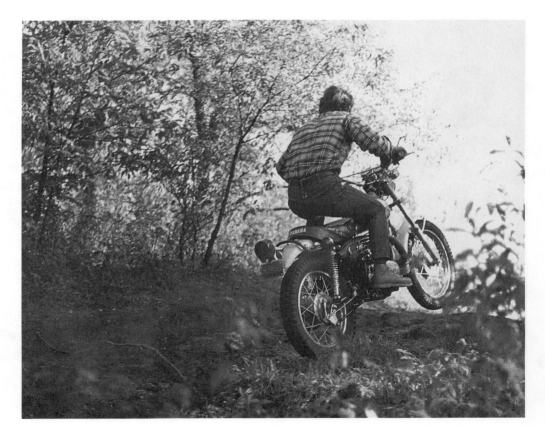

Compositional rules are nothing more than the experience of others that has become accepted. To accept and follow the rules uncritically means to accept other peoples' experience and not to allow yourself to experiment.

(Gerhard Bakker, educator)

The "rules" are worth studying, however, because more often than not they will help you to produce stronger and more successful images. Once you've become familiar with the rules, you can feel free to break them any time you want—but not because of ignorance. Break a rule only when breaking it makes your statement stronger.

Photography is about responding to things.
(Sam Abel, photojournalist)

Photojournalist William Albert Allard has explained that, "When I make what I think is going to be a fine photograph, I feel it. I can feel it in my stomach. And I'd like someone else to feel that also." Part of what Allard means is that he has an innate feeling for design, order and balance—intuition deep inside that says, "Move the camera a few inches to the left..." And, "This is it...shoot!"

By studying other people's photographs, as well as your own, you'll see when the following "rules" have strengthened a picture and when the photographer was right in daring to break them.

The "world" out "there" is as much a <u>projection</u> from inside our heads as it is a <u>perception</u>...[because of this] it is a miracle that we communicate at all.

(Robert Fulghum, philosopher)

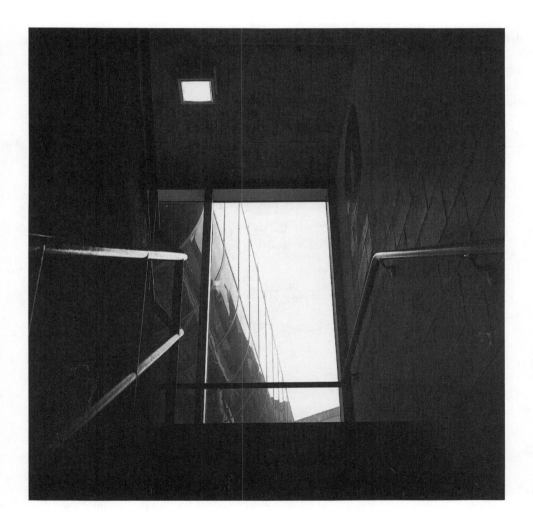

James M. Rhoads
Passageway
Dark on light, or light on dark? Which is foreground and which is background? If the large white rectangle is a window or a doorway, where does it lead—into someplace, or out? The mystery and drama seem heightened by visual contrast and by delicate graphic balance.

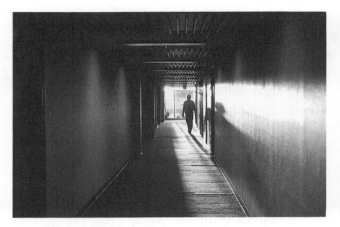
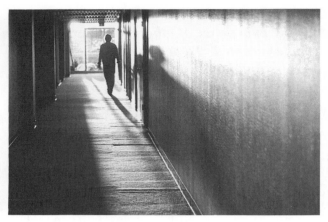

Pat Green *Corridor*

Which cropping do you prefer? The version on the right conforms to the widely stated rule that the center of interest should be placed approximately one third of the distance from either top or bottom of the frame and also about one third the distance from either left or right. This "rule of thirds" provides for a more dynamic composition, but sometimes centering the subject is appropriate. You decide!

The **"Rule of Thirds"** (right) suggests that dominant horizontal or vertical lines and principal subjects be spaced at a ratio of about one-third to two-thirds within the space outlined by the image frame.

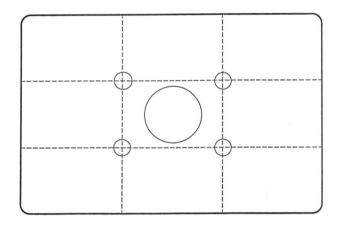

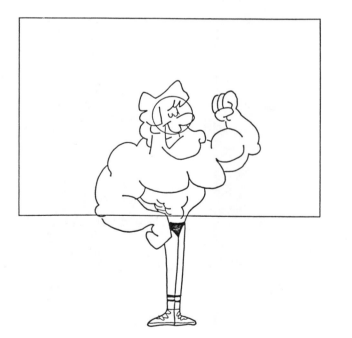
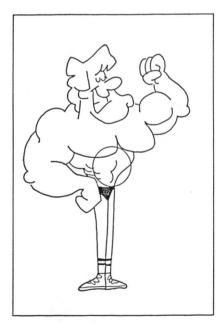

The **"Center Circle Syndrome"** describes the tendency of beginners to place the center of the picture (often a person's head) in the center of the camera viewfinder. Experience teaches us to fill the entire frame, balancing the essential parts of the scene and eliminating everything else. At this point, decide whether to compose horizontally or vertically.

Some "Rules" of Composition:

1. Select a single, dominant center of interest.

2. Place the center of interest away from the center of the picture. Follow the "rule of thirds." (See diagram on page 40).

3. Keep the horizon level, placing it according to the rule of thirds. Don't cut a picture into two equal parts either horizontally or vertically. Keep vertical lines such as buildings and trees parallel with the edges of the frame.

4. Don't allow important tones and textures in your main subject to merge with the background.

5. Fill the frame. Do most of your cropping in the camera viewfinder before you take the picture instead of afterward in the darkroom.

6. Keep extraneous details out of the picture.

7. Don't amputate parts of your main subject at awkward places.

8. Avoid distracting shapes at the very edges of the photograph. Light and bright areas in corners, especially, tend to draw the eye out of the frame and away from the center of interest.

9. Have the main subject facing or moving into the frame, instead of out of the frame.

10. Frame the principal subject with a complementary foreground object. (Especially in scenic natural landscapes).

11. Concentrate attention with leading lines, such as converging diagonals or an S curve that direct the eye into the composition.

12. Employ strong diagonal lines to imply action or conflict.

13. Compose in vertical format to emphasize height and dignity, or to imply potential motion. Horizontal formats may suggest peace and stability.

14. Remember these "rules," but violate them freely when doing so will create a stronger or more meaningful image.

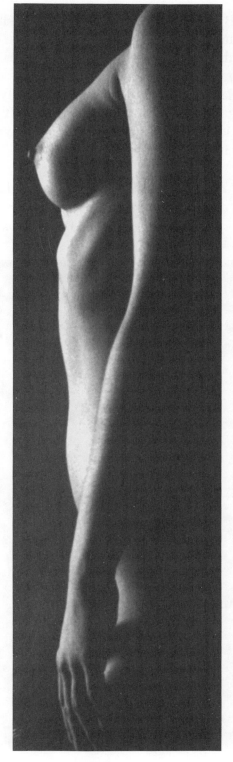

Omar Mangrum *Torso*
Some points from the "Rule of Thirds" apply to this photograph. Sensuous, undulating lines create the image, together with subtle variations in tone. Notice that the black background (negative space) forms an interesting shape of its own.

By observing these rules you'll be able to make pictures that will sell and that will achieve other kinds of recognition. By totally ignoring the rules you risk failure; but sometimes, by deliberately violating them, you may audaciously achieve a fantastically successful photograph. It depends on what else besides composition you've managed to put into your photograph.

To photograph a rock, to have it look like a rock, yet more than a rock..
(Edward Weston, photographer)

Photography is not about composition...Photography is about perceiving the familiar with fresh eyes.
(Gary Monroe, photographer)

Elements of Composition

Fundamental to effective composition are the artist's elements of *form, line, tone, space, texture* and *rhythm*.

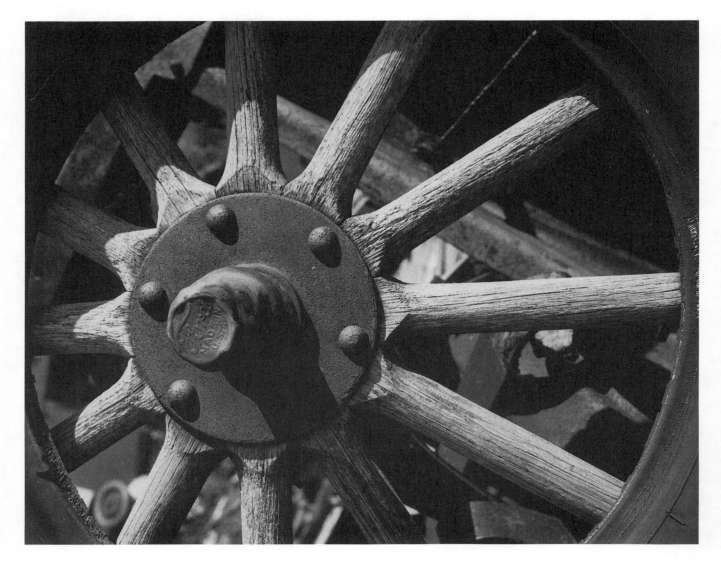

F. L. Feick *Wheel*
Although other elements are important in this photograph, we expect to be able to "feel" the textures of rusty iron and weathered wood. Oblique sunlight and good photographic technique yield an image that does not disappoint us.

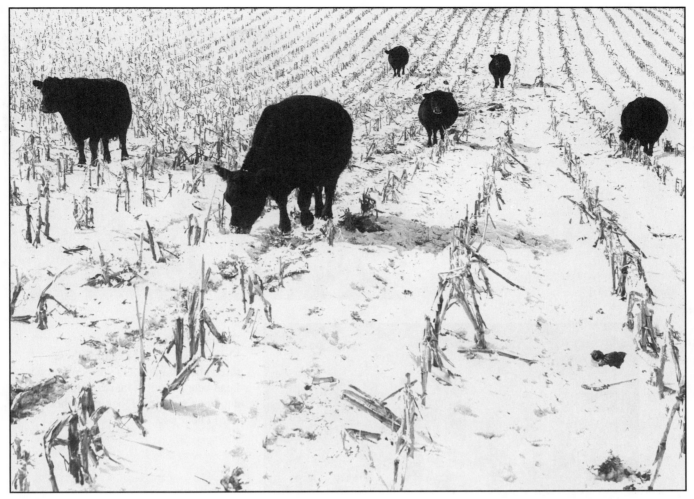

Beth Shirk *Black Angus*
Squint at this photograph. Do the cattle appear to be floating in space? Do their diminishing sizes give an illusion of depth and distance? Notice that the three-dimensional effect is enhanced by the converging perspective of the rows of corn stubble.

Form is the basic underlying shape within a composition. When evident to the viewer, and especially when repeated with variation in size, brightness, or texture, form can become highly significant.

> *When simple forms are repeated they bring to the eye the kind of pleasure that music brings to the ear.*
>
> *(Victor B. Scheffer, educator)*

Line outlines, delineates, and defines form and space within the frame. Strong single or repeated lines may themselves be important elements. The eye and brain tend to group perceived objects into shapes such as triangles, rectangles, etc. Lines that are implied, although they are not actually present, may tend to connect forms and serve as vectors directing eye movement within the composition.

> *The greatest joy for me is geometry. That means a structure...It is a sensuous pleasure, an intellectual pleasure at the same time, to have everything in the right place.* *(Henri Cartier-Bresson, photojournalist)*

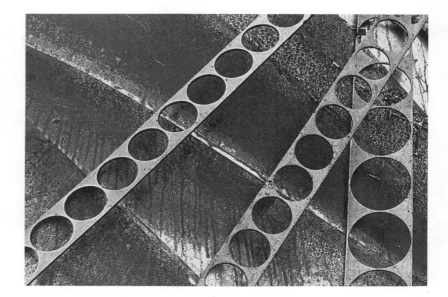

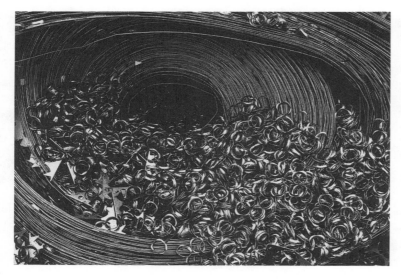

William Beverly *Rhythms*
I hear music when I examine these
three photographs. Do you? With one
I can hear a strident march, with
another a waltz, and looking at the
third I hear jazz.

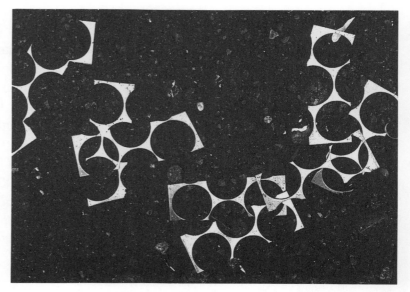

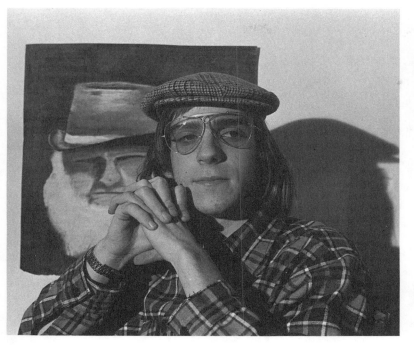

Elaine Logie *A Friend*
Notice in this portrait that the subject's face and cap are *repeated, with variation,* both in the painting and in the shadow on the wall.

Jack Urban *Precast*
The photograph below contains all the compositional elements of *form, line, tone, space, texture, rhythm, and contrast.* Do you find it interesting from a graphic point of view? Is it also a bit mysterious, as a visual puzzle of unknown scale? Does it surprise you to learn that these are edges of precast concrete steps lying on their sides?

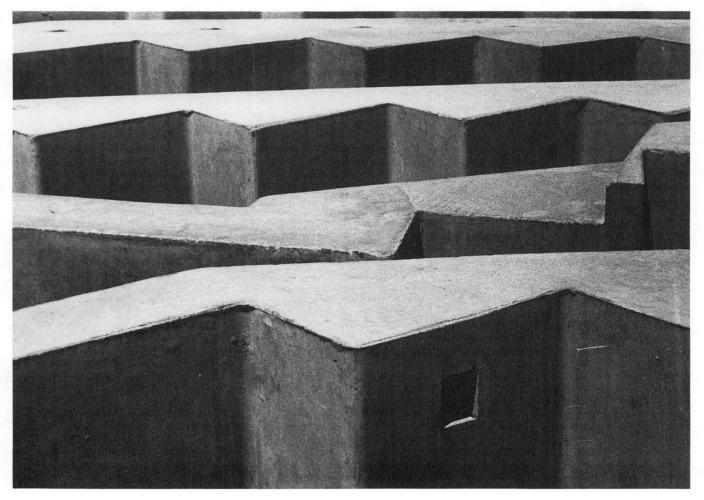

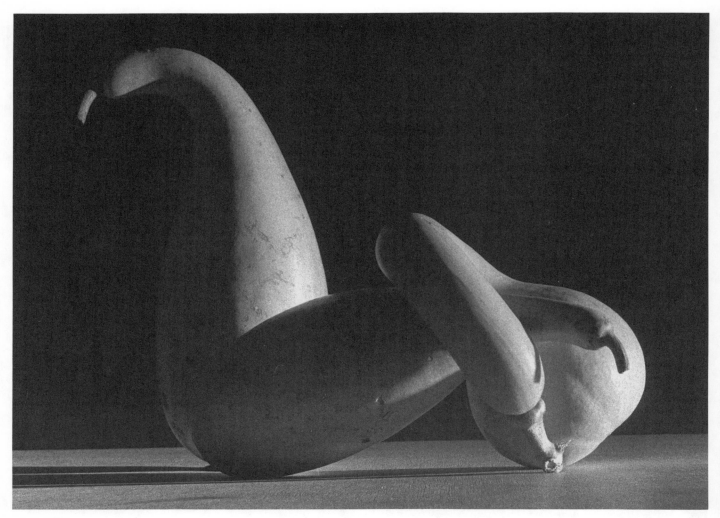

Jack Sizer *Gourds*
(Visual analogy) Although the forms
in these two photographs are far from
identical in form, texture and size, are
they not visually very closely synony-
mous?

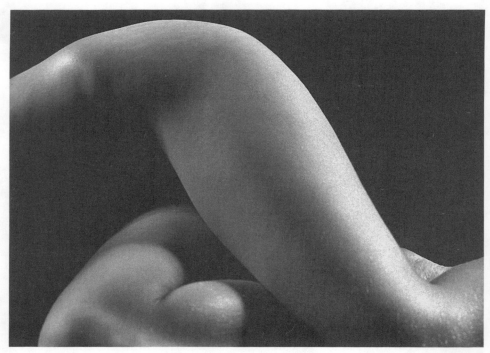

John Stites *Figure*

Tone is the relative value or reflectiveness of a given area within the image. The term also can describe the overall lightness or darkness of the entire photograph. Whether in shades of gray or color values, tones can be contrasted, harmonized, or merged, depending on the effect you want to achieve.

Creativity is the ability to relate previously unrelated things. *(Paul Smith, educator)*

Space is the field or background surrounding objects within the frame. Whether the background remains in the background, in what is sometimes referred to as negative space, depends in part on the relative tonal values present in the image. If the main subject merges with the background, both form and space may be poorly defined. On the other hand, contrast of either line or tone can be used deliberately to separate the subject from the background (form from space or, in psychological terms, figure from ground).

You can think of [texture] as form on a smaller scale. It describes the finer parts of a pattern. When you see a spider web at a distance you think of its texture, but when you look closely at one you think of its form...As you bring your eye closer to the bark of a tree you gradually lose the feeling of texture and begin to see bold lines and curves. Now you see how form and texture are related by scale.
(Victor B. Scheffer, educator)

Texture is another element of beauty and interest. Texture in a photograph is roughness or smoothness that you can "feel" with your eyes: tree bark, sand, or skin that your mind vicariously can caress and explore.

Architecture is frozen music.
(J. W. von Goethe, poet)

Rhythm and *repetition* are everywhere—in music, in architecture, in the human body, in nature. Form is the basic thematic statement of the composition. Form is the basic plan. Everything else is either support, repetition, or embellishment. In music, syncopation is the term used to describe unexpected interruptions in rhythm. The principle of syncopation applies also to the visual arts as a form of repetition with variation.

Whenever I can feel a Bach fugue in my work I know I have arrived.
(Edward Weston, photographer)

Rhythmic, repeated patterns of line and form can be interesting in themselves. But even more exciting images can be created if the pattern is varied by one single item being different from the rest—contrasting in size, shape, value, texture or direction. As in musical composition, repetition with variation usually is a strong basis for an interesting visual composition. When you repeat form and line with variation, the variation can be slight irregularity or it can be gross distortion, depending on how subtle you want it to be.

Conflict and Contradiction

Social landscape is like jazz—improvisation and spontaneity. There is tension between form and content.
(John A. Lacko, photographer)

Contrast means the visual difference between light and dark tonal values. The term *contrast* also can be used to mean conflict or contradiction between opposites.

Opposites will always be present in any photo, but in the bad photo they will be at war with each other and not working as a team. For example, background objects will interfere with the foreground, highlights will blast while shadows are impenetrable. *(Nat Herz, photographer)*

Dynamic balance is a compositional way of placing unlike elements into equilibrium. Strong photographs often are filled with opposites—not only light versus dark, large versus small, rough versus smooth, but opposing and contradictory ele-

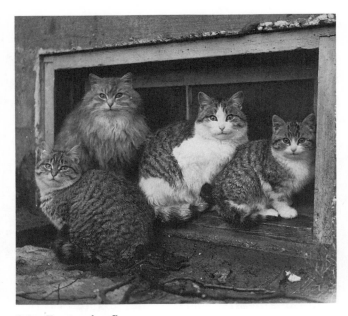

John Bartocci *Cats*
In this simple photograph the fundamental compositional device is repetition with variation. Analyze the elements of form, line, tone, space, texture, rhythm, and contrast.

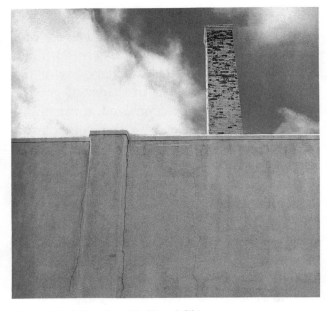

James M. Rhoads *Wall and Chimney*
Much of the interest in this strong, yet simple design derives from subtle variations in value and tone.

ments: flesh and steel, high and low, youth and age, birth and death, growth and decay, joy versus sadness, moving versus still, sun versus ice, rectangle versus circle, straight versus curved. Visualize in terms of contrasts and contradictions. Deliberately build your images around them.

> *I don't know any formal rules of composition...Composition is simply the strongest way of seeing.*
> (Edward Weston, photographer)

Think in terms of contrasts in size, shape, tone, texture, direction, mood, color and content. Composition is the sum total of all the elements we've described, put together not mechanically or ritualistically, but assembled with a real feeling for the effect you want to achieve.

> *I get a greater joy from finding things in nature, already composed, than I do from my finest personal arrangements.*
> (Edward Weston, photographer)

Many photographers look consciously for compositional elements, and many abstract photographs depend solely on these elements as their reason for existing. Photojournalist Henri Cartier-Bresson said,

however, that although he was always intuitively aware of geometric structure, "you can't go shooting for shapes, for patterns..." But in order to make successful images of the kind Cartier-Bresson made of people and events, you must always be subconsciously aware of compositional elements and ready to release the shutter at "the decisive moment" when subject matter and compositional elements are in appropriate harmony or conflict.

> *Photographs come from the moment in the process of cognition before the mind has analyzed meaning or the eyes design...Photographic design is...spontaneous, instinctive, even subconscious.*
> (Charles Harbutt, photojournalist)

Therein lies the greatest element of skill in photography and the one aspect that it is most difficult to teach. Only by studying thousands of images and by making countless photographs yourself, both on film and in your mind's eye, can you teach yourself to be a really superb photographic communicator.

> *I photograph something to see what it will look like photographed.*
> (Garry Winogrand, photographer)

Cameras and Lenses 3

The camera is an instrument that teaches people how to see without a camera.

(Dorothea Lange, photojournalist)

The camera is at once an expedient to communication and a barrier to expression. This paradox is explained by the fact that while many people recognize the camera as an indispensable tool for recording and preserving impressions of the world, others have considered it to be an intruder—an obstacle—a contraption that mechanizes and dehumanizes the act of "creating" a picture. This contradiction illustrates one of the most charming characteristics of humanity, however: that people are pleased and satisfied by different things, methods, approaches, and results. Because cameras have certain characteristics that make photography unique among media, I can assume that you have more than a casual interest in what cameras can do for you, or you wouldn't have read this far.

The camera need not be a cold mechanical device. Like the pen, it is as good as the [person] who uses it. It can be the extension of mind and heart.

(John Steinbeck, writer)

The Basic Camera

All types of cameras have the same basic parts:

1. Light-tight box.
2. Holder and transport system for light-sensitive film.
3. Lens to form an image on the film.
4. Diaphragm, or aperture, to control the amount of light passing through the lens.
5. Shutter to control how long the film is exposed to light.
6. Viewfinder for aiming the camera and composing the image.

All cameras except the very least expensive have a means for moving the lens forward or backward to adjust for sharpest focus, variable shutter speeds, and a diaphragm with an adjustable aperture to allow more or less light through the lens.

The question, "Which is the best camera for me?" can only be answered by asking further: "What kinds of pictures are you going to take?" and "How will your pictures be used?"

No one camera can do all photographic jobs equally well. Although one of the popular pocket-sized automatic cameras may suffice for family snapshots, to do "serious" photography you'll need to know about the various styles and formats of advanced or "professional" cameras and the kinds of work each does best. Let's examine the advantages and disadvantages of the five major types of professional quality cameras.

Technology doesn't mean. It is means.

(Robert Rauschenberg, artist)

Parts of a basic camera

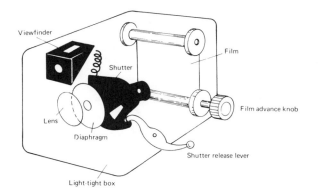

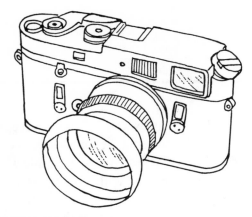

35mm rangefinder camera

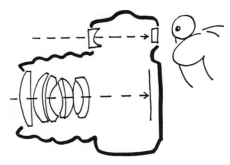

Popular Camera Formats

Rangefinder, 35mm

Advantages: Very light and portable, cameras such as the famous Leicas and their compact, lower-priced descendants are easy to handle rapidly and easy to focus in dim light. 35mm film magazines contain up to 36 exposures, reducing the cost per frame to a minimum. Interchangeable "fast" lenses of excellent quality allow shooting by existing light in many situations. A relatively quiet shutter simplifies unobtrusive "candid" shooting and many recent models feature automatic control of shutter speed, aperture, focusing and flash for quick, "no-think" shooting.

Disadvantages: As with all 35mm cameras, the tiny negatives or transparencies scratch easily, so they must be handled with special care. Extreme enlargement tends to make the grain of the film visible and to increase trouble from dust, scratches, and fingerprints and to make more objectionable the blur resulting from camera movement. Different viewpoints of lens and viewfinder (parallax) make it difficult to frame and focus accurately when working closer than two or three feet from the subject, unless special attachments are used. Forgetful photographers have been known to leave the lens cap on while shooting. Lenses are not interchangeable on many compact cameras and the automatic features actually can be limiting to "serious" photographers.

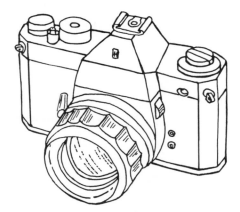

35mm single-lens reflex

Single-Lens Reflex (SLR), 35mm

Advantages: A very popular, convenient and versatile camera, especially when equipped with prism viewfinder and automatic diaphragm (both features are standard on most models). SLRs such as Canon, Minolta, Nikon, Olympus, and Pentax are similar in operation to rangefinder cameras, but the large, bright prism viewing screen simplifies focusing and accurate framing especially when shooting extreme close-ups and when using telephoto and zoom lenses. The ability to view the subject and focus the image through the lens is the most important advantage of the SLR. This feature allows predetermination of depth of field and selective focus effects and makes possible the use of extensive systems of lenses of various focal lengths and many special-purpose accessories. Latest models offer programmed electronic automation of exposure and focus. Still-video cameras basically are single-lens reflexes that record the image on a miniature computer "floppy" disk instead of on film. Somewhat bulkier than conventional cameras, their operation is very similar.

Disadvantages: As with all 35mm films, negatives must be handled very carefully because scratches, fingerprints and dust can cause problems. Most SLRs are somewhat heavier and bulkier than most rangefinder cameras. Certain models are hard to focus with some lenses in dim light and when following action, although many SLRs provide a bright prism or split-image focusing system in the center of the ground-glass focusing screen. A relatively noisy mirror and shutter tend to call attention to the photographer at quiet events such as concerts and weddings, and movement of the mirror may shake the camera during long exposures. Momentary image blackout is a problem when shooting rapid action and with flash, because you can't see through the viewfinder at the very instant of exposure. Older-type lenses without an automatic diaphragm are troublesome because it's easy to forget to set the lens opening each time before shooting. Electronic automation can be a liability in case something goes wrong with the mechanism or if the battery fails. *Autofocus* lenses used carelessly can yield *out-of-focus* pictures.

Single-Lens Reflex, Medium Format (6x7, 6x6, or 6x4.5 cm)

Advantages: 120-size roll film yields images two to four times larger than 35mm, lessening the problems of grain, dust, scratches, and camera movement. The larger ground-glass viewing area of

6 x 4.5cm single-lens reflex

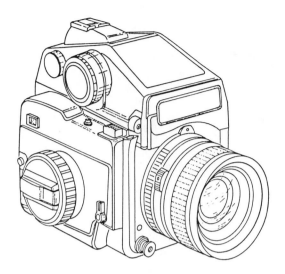

medium format cameras such as Bronica, Hasselblad, Mamiya, Pentax and Rollei simplifies composition and focusing and allows predetermination of depth of field and selective focus effects. Extensive accessory systems are available, including replaceable backs that permit changing film type in mid-roll and use of Polaroid instant film.

Disadvantages: Noisier and much heavier and bulkier than 35mm SLRs. 120 film is economical, although more expensive per frame than 35mm. Cameras and accessories are very expensive.

Twin-Lens Reflex, Medium Format (6x6 cm)

Advantages: Convenient and rapid in operation, with the advantage of 120-size roll film negatives. This so-called 2 1/4-square format was once very popular. Today larger camera stores may have several models of used Mamiya, Rollei and Yashica cameras available at a relatively moderate cost.

Disadvantages: Somewhat bulky. Most models do not accept interchangeable lenses, and few acces-

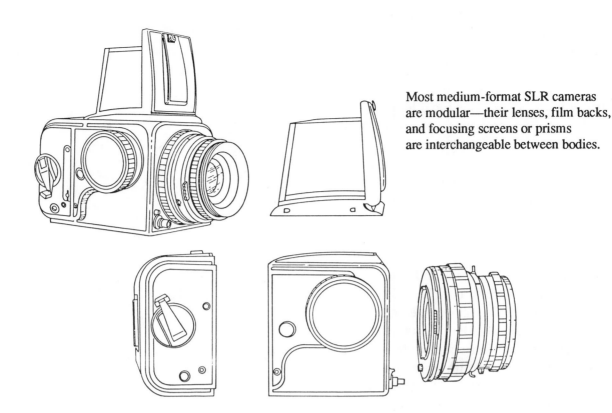

Most medium-format SLR cameras are modular—their lenses, film backs, and focusing screens or prisms are interchangeable between bodies.

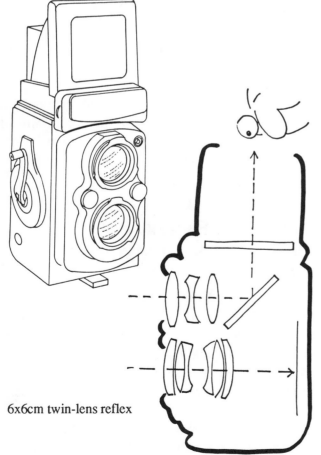

6x6cm twin-lens reflex

sories are available. Unless an auxiliary prism is attached, focusing below eye level is required and this point of view may be inconvenient. The image is also reversed left-to-right. Parallax between the two lenses prevents accurate framing for copying and extreme close-ups.

View Camera, Large Format (4"x 5"and larger)

Advantages: Enormous negatives and transparencies reproduce with such high quality that large format cameras often are first choice in the commercial studio and by many photographers who concentrate on the natural landscape. A favorite for photographing building exteriors and interiors, furniture, food, packaged products, etc. because swing, tilt, rise, and shift adjustments of both front and back can correct perspective distortion and maximize depth of field. View cameras are good for copying and graphic arts work because of the large negative

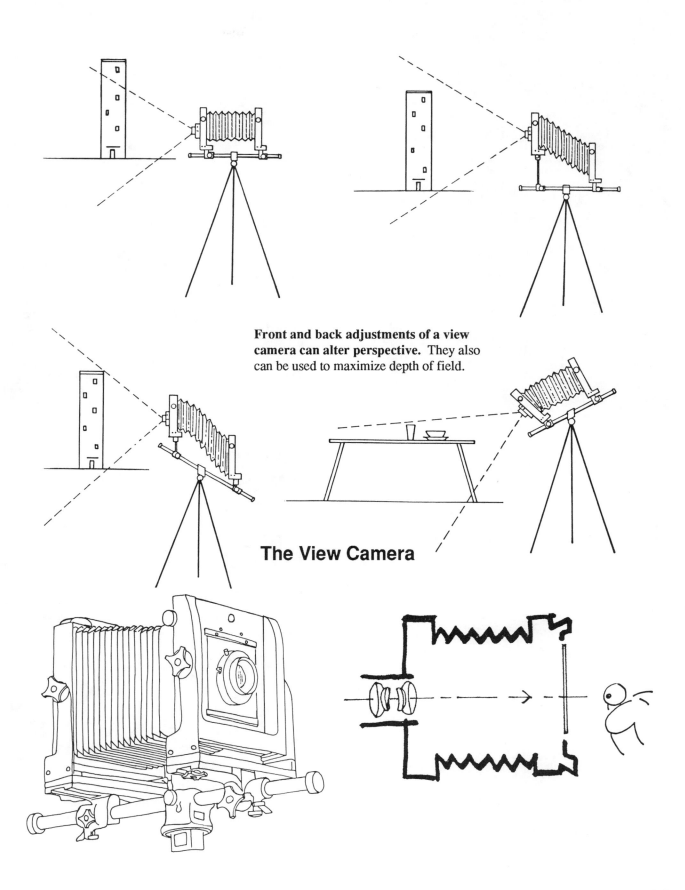

Front and back adjustments of a view camera can alter perspective. They also can be used to maximize depth of field.

The View Camera

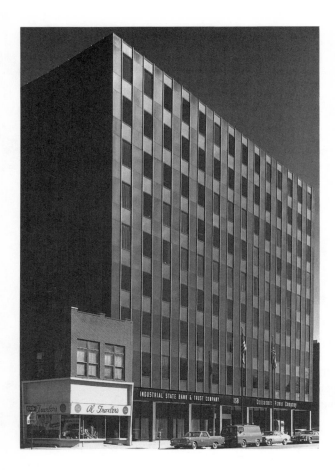

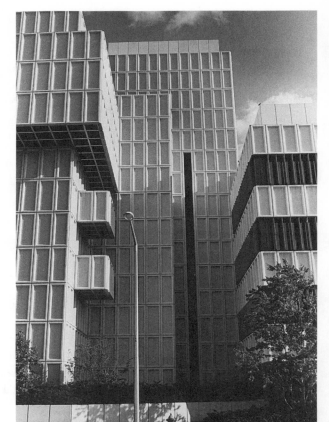

Jim Nixon

The building at left, above, has been corrected so that all vertical lines are parallel. This was achieved by placing the planes of both the back and the front of the view camera exactly vertical. An orange filter darkened the sky, allowing the large dark building to project forward. **The building on the right was photographed with a 35mm camera.** Should the vertical lines be parallel, or does the convergence give a feeling of soaring height?

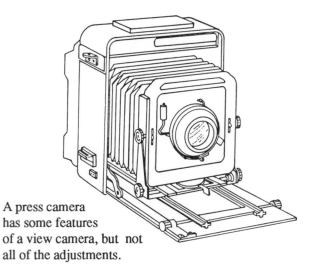

A press camera has some features of a view camera, but not all of the adjustments.

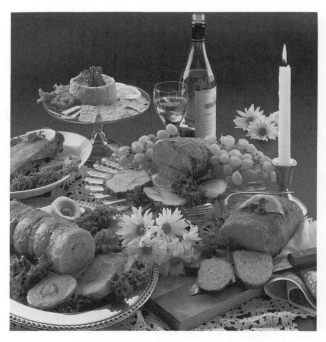

For this food illustration, the view camera back was adjusted vertically to keep the candle and wine bottle parallel. To maximize depth of field, the front of the camera was tilted downward until objects were in focus at both front and rear of the table setting.

size (up to 8"x10" and even much larger!) and the wide variety of specialized types of film available. Large sheet film negatives allow retouching, if desired, and permit great enlargement or fine quality contact prints. The large ground-glass screen in the camera back simplifies careful composition and focusing.

Disadvantages: View cameras are not very portable; they must always be set up on a tripod or heavy studio stand. View camera lenses are slower and have less depth of field than comparable lenses for smaller cameras and the image on the ground glass is upside down. Rapid shooting is difficult because several things must be done by hand before and after making each exposure. Sheet film is expensive, and film holders awkward to handle. The holders usually must be loaded individually in a darkroom or light-tight changing bag and kept protected from bright light. Although many of the world's most respected photographers have used view cameras extensively, this bulky instrument is not suitable when the photographer is in a hurry or has to travel light. A press camera such as the classic Speed Graphic is an obsolescent variety of the view camera, but with some features that allow hand use, such as rangefinder focusing and synchronized flash.

There was a time when I lived behind the camera, hiding behind it. There was only this huge camera walking around. My legs were wrapped around the base. My arms were sort of up on top and would reach to click the shutter. It was that big a thing. Now the camera is so small, it's like it's not even there.

Brian Lanker *(photojournalist)*

Specialized Cameras

You might want to own one or more special-purpose cameras in addition to your regular equipment. A Polaroid "instant" camera, for example, or an accessory Polaroid back can be very useful for checking lighting arrangements or composition before exposing conventional color or black-and-white film.

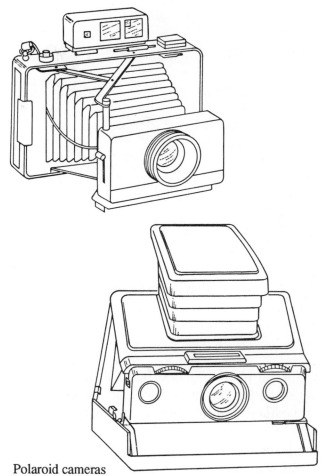

Polaroid cameras

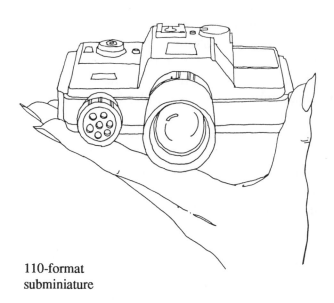

110-format
subminiature

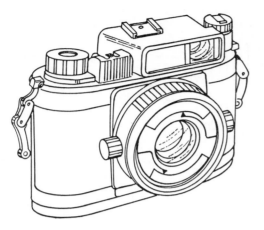
Underwater camera

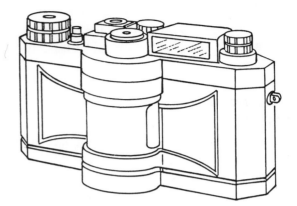
Panoramic camera

Instant photography offers unusual spontaneity in portraiture because photographer and sitter can immediately critique the expression, pose, and lighting. Some instant films yield negatives that later can be enlarged conventionally.

Subminiature and half-frame 35mm cameras were introduced mainly for reasons of film economy, but like the negatives from 110-size cameras and 16mm, disc, and other subminiatures, enlargements from the tiny negatives are limited severely by problems of sharpness, grain, dust, and scratches.

Large format panoramic cameras were popular in the nineteenth century, and a few types are available today that use 120 roll film. Producing an extremely long narrow image, the novelty of the format appeals to imaginative landscape and experiment-minded photographers.

Although waterproof underwater housings can be bought or built for many cameras, the popularity of scuba diving and other water-related sports such as rafting, canoeing and water skiing has created a market for watertight 35mm cameras such as the Motormarine and Nikonos that simplify taking pictures in wet places and reduce the risk of dunking a conventional camera.

Some people enjoy owning and using unusual cameras or actively collecting antique, classic, or unique equipment. Organizations catering to camera collectors publish newsletters and sponsor exhibits and sales.

There are times that I would like my cameras to be a complete and true extension of myself.
(William Albert Allard, photojournalist)

Choosing a Camera

After becoming familiar with the various types of cameras and deciding on the format you prefer, you have to face the dilemma of choosing a particular make and model from the many quality cameras available. That's not so easy, because investing in a camera is a lot like buying a car—the conscientiousness of the dealer may be more important in the long run than the brand you purchase or the price you pay. As almost any kind of car will get you where you want to go, so there are literally dozens of cameras, each of which will make excellent photographs if intelligently used.

Personal preference is very important in choosing a camera, so it's important that you work with a knowledgeable salesperson who will help you select the best equipment for your needs, preferences,

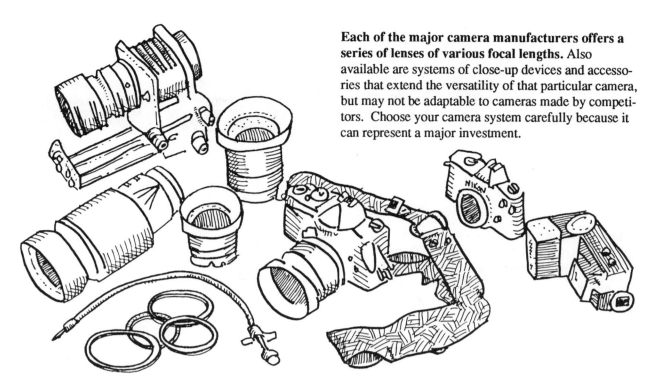

Each of the major camera manufacturers offers a series of lenses of various focal lengths. Also available are systems of close-up devices and accessories that extend the versatility of that particular camera, but may not be adaptable to cameras made by competitors. Choose your camera system carefully because it can represent a major investment.

and budget. If you encounter impatience or ignorance I suggest you take your business elsewhere.

You'll want to try the "feel" of various cameras, because different models employ different focusing systems and the viewfinder images vary significantly in brightness, relative size of the image, and ease of focusing. Placement of the controls may seem more convenient for you on one camera than on another. If you handle several, you'll probably find that you prefer the feel of one model over another.

If you're thinking of going into photography seriously, your dealer can advise you on which camera manufacturers offer systems of quality lenses and accessories that are likely to be available as your interests, needs, and financial resources grow. And your dealer should be the kind who will see to it that you receive prompt and proper service when you need it and perhaps even loan you a camera in an emergency.

Although price isn't everything, many local camera stores will meet the advertised prices of mail-order and discount competitors. They know that if you're satisfied you'll come back to buy accessories, supplies, and services. If you're considering the purchase of a used camera, be sure to study "How to Test Your Equipment" in Chapter Four.

Exposure Controls

A photographer needs a short-circuit between his brain and his fingertips.
(Alfred Eisenstaedt, photojournalist)

In photography you've got to be quick, quick, quick, quick. Like an animal and a prey. (Henri Cartier-Bresson, photojournalist)

People who earn a living with their cameras or who use photography as a creative or scientific tool know that there isn't time to make calculations every time they want to take a picture. Like driving a car, playing a musical instrument or riding a bicycle, the technical processes have to become second nature so you can concentrate all your psychic and emotional energy on perceiving and selecting the perfect arrangement and the decisive moment. For many beginners, the most difficult and confusing aspect of photography is exposure. Fortunately, there are only a few simple principles to learn.

The camera should become an extension of your eye, nothing else.
(Ernst Haas, photographer)

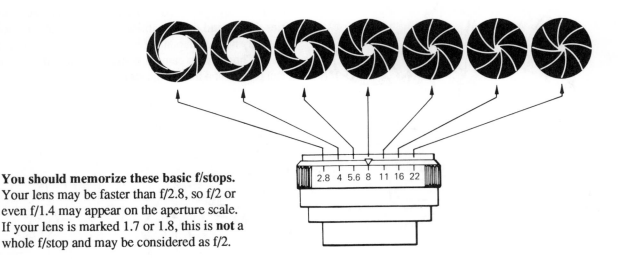

You should memorize these basic f/stops. Your lens may be faster than f/2.8, so f/2 or even f/1.4 may appear on the aperture scale. If your lens is marked 1.7 or 1.8, this is **not** a whole f/stop and may be considered as f/2.

E = I x T

Yes, it looks like algebra, but don't panic! This little equation tells it all: Exposure = Intensity of light x Time. That's it. Exposure means the total amount of light reaching the film and that quantity is very important because it has a lot to do with the quality of your negatives and color transparencies. Underexposure is the result of not enough light affecting the emulsion of the film; overexposure is from too much light.

The amount of light reaching the film is controlled both by the size of the lens aperture (f/stop) and the length of time the shutter is allowed to remain open (shutter speed). You should be in control of both factors.

Lens openings (f/stops)

The larger the lens opening, the more light that gets through at any given shutter speed. The numbered apertures (f/stops) on most lenses are spaced so that moving from one full f/stop to the next will result in either doubling or halving the amount of light passing through. "Opening up" the lens (larger aperture opening) increases the light, while "stopping down" the lens (smaller aperture opening)

reduces the light. So far, so good? The confusing part is that the f/stop numbers on lenses are the opposite of logic: *the larger the f/number, the smaller the aperture.* Remember that!

Although the entire range of numbers from f/1 to f/64 will never appear on any one lens, you should memorize at least the basic scale of f/stop numbers shown in the illustration above. Don't be misled by half-stop "click" indentations on your lens—these are to make it easier for you to make in-between settings. The half-stops are not part of the regular scale for calculating exposure.

An easy way to remember the stops is that the numbers are cut in half (or doubled) every other number. But don't try to use the same arithmetic in calculating exposure. The amount of exposure increases or decreases by a factor of 2x between every adjacent pair of full f/stops on the scale. Very

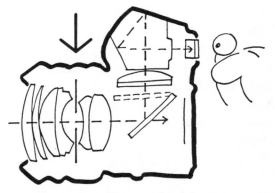

The aperture is located between lens elements

The *speed* of a lens (maximum f/number) is determined by dividing the focal length of the lens by the diameter of the maximum aperture. *Focal length* is the distance from the optical center of the lens to the focal plane (film surface) when the lens is focused on infinity.

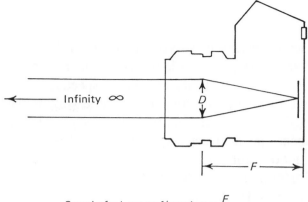

Speed of a Lens or f/number $= \dfrac{F}{D}$

few lenses stop down to f/45 or f/64, although many go as far as f/22 or f/32. Many lenses for small cameras do not stop down smaller than f/16.

> **The _larger_ the f/number, the _smaller_ the lens opening. Smaller f/numbers stand for larger apertures.**

If the maximum aperture on your lens shows an odd number such as f/1.8, f/3.5, or f/4.5, this number will not be a full stop larger than the next smaller f/stop. Because the speed of a lens is expressed in terms of its largest f/stop (largest opening=smallest number), manufacturers like to impress people with a slightly lower f/number (larger aperture). These irregular apertures, however, are only slightly larger than the next whole f/stop, and for practical purposes you can ignore the difference. An f/1.8 lens, for example, is only negligibly faster than f/2. An

f/2 lens is considered *fast*, whereas a lens with a maximum aperture of only f/4.5 would be comparatively *slow*. Don't be misled into thinking that an f/1.2 or f/1.4 lens is significantly *better* than an f/2 lens. Although the f/1.4 will be a full stop faster than the f/2 (and may be a little easier to focus in dim light), you will be paying for extra glass that you may seldom use and also will be sacrificing some sharpness at the wider aperture.

Shutter speeds

The other important variable in controlling exposure is the shutter speed. The speeds in the table below are the standard markings found on most modern cameras. Each speed is expressed in terms of a fraction of a second, down to one full second. Some electronic cameras include shutter speeds of 2, 4 and 8 full seconds. Nearly all cameras have a setting marked "B" which allows the shutter to be held open as long as the release button is depressed. Some cameras also have a "T" setting that opens the

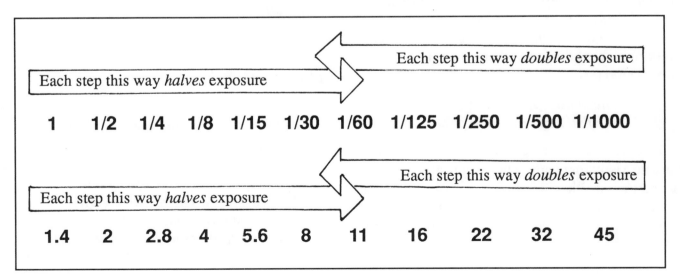

shutter when the release is depressed, then closes the shutter or drops the mirror when the release is depressed a second time. The shutter speeds (except B and T) affect exposure in the same way as the f/stops—that is, each change from any speed to the adjacent speed effectively *doubles* or *halves* the amount of light reaching the film at a given f/stop.

Sometimes a symbol will appear next to one shutter speed, usually 1/60 or 1/125 second, or one of those speeds will be marked in red. That should be the setting to be used for flash. (Learn more about flash in Chapter 9).

Shutter speed and lens opening work together

Many combinations of f/stop and shutter speed will admit the same amount of light, resulting in identical total exposure. Using the next slower speed, such as 1/60 of a second instead of 1/125, admits light for twice as long. This gives the same effect on exposure as opening up the lens aperture one full f/stop, such as f/8 instead of f/11, which doubles the amount of light passing through. Thus an exposure of 1/30 at f/16 will produce the same exposure on the film as 1/60 at f/11, 1/125 at f/8, 1/250 at f/5.6, 1/500 at f/4, or 1/1,000 at f/2.8.

Do you see how the lens opening and shutter speed are interconnected? Once you have determined the correct total amount of light your film needs for a particular photograph, then you have a choice of camera settings. You could choose a small aperture (f/16) to keep objects in focus both near and far (depth of field) or select a fast shutter speed (1/1,000) to "freeze" a moving subject. In either case you would then adjust the other control to admit the correct amount of light to expose the film properly.

> *One shutter speed change =*
> *one f/stop change in exposure.*

Practice setting your camera until you can compensate easily for changes of several stops of speed or aperture in either direction. You can set the lens between f/stops to make minor exposure adjustment (for example, halfway between f/5.6 and f/8). But don't set the shutter between marked speeds.

Before trying to use any automatic camera, please read the instruction book!

Setting Automatic Cameras

When locked into either *aperture priority* or *shutter priority* mode, cameras with automatic exposure control do all the calculating and compensating for you. But because cameras differ in how they should be set, be sure to study your owner's manual.

In *shutter* priority, whenever you set the shutter speed, the camera will choose the appropriate lens opening. In *aperture* priority mode, when you select an f/stop to control depth of field, the camera will adjust the shutter speed. Usually these settings can be read either in the viewfinder window or from a liquid crystal display on top of the camera. Many newer cameras have one or more *program* settings that will select *both* aperture and shutter speed. If you buy one of these cameras, be sure it also can be set manually. The owner's manual will explain your choices of programmed modes and tell you how to override the automatic features. Chapter 5 in this book describes how to determine correct exposure and how to suspect when the exposure meter in your camera may be giving you wrong settings. Please read that chapter now if you're going out right away to take pictures before reading more about cameras and accessories.

> *Automatic simply means that you can't*
> *repair it yourself.*
> *(Mary H. Waldrip, photographer)*

The Lens

> *A camera has but one eye—the lens. It*
> *can record only a fragment of the visual*
> *world. The photographer provides a*
> *second eye. This is the eye of selection.*
> *The artist has a Third Eye, the eye of*
> *creative imagination. It is this Third Eye*
> *that can penetrate into our inner world.*
> *(Author unknown)*

Most camera lenses consist of three or more separate glass elements instead of a single piece. The sharpest and fastest lenses have many elements. Remember that lenses should never be taken apart except by an experienced camera repair technician!

The lens projects a sharp image onto light-sensitive film in the back of the camera. The size of this image is determined by the focal length of the lens.

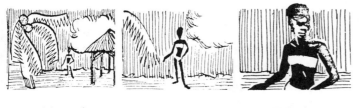

Wide angle   Normal   Telephoto

Focal length

The focal length of the lens affects how large the image will be on the film and how wide or narrow the angle of view. Because different cameras are designed to use different sizes of film, different types of lenses are needed. The size of the image projected on the film by a lens and the distance the lens must be from the film to form a sharp image are directly related to its focal length. This number usually is engraved on the lens mount in millimeters and is a measure of the distance between the optical center of the lens and the film when the lens is focused on a distant object (infinity). 25mm equals approximately one inch.

A so-called "normal" lens has a focal length about equal to, or slightly longer than, the diagonal of the image produced on the size film to be used in that camera. For example, a square negative made on 120-size roll film measures about 80mm diagonally from corner to corner. Therefore, the normal lens for a 6x6cm reflex camera has a focal length of approximately 80mm. 35mm cameras are normally supplied with a lens of 50mm to 58mm focal length, slightly longer than the diagonal of the image. As you know, *35mm* refers to the *width of the film* in a 35mm camera. A *35mm lens* on a 35mm camera would be a moderately wide-angle lens (shorter than "normal" focal length).

An 80mm lens will always project the same sized image of a given object whether the lens is designed for use on a 35mm camera or on a 4x5. An 80mm lens will be a moderate "telephoto" if mounted on a 35mm camera, normal on a 6x6cm camera, and wide-angle if its field of coverage is broad enough to cover 4x5. When the focal length is much shorter than the film diagonal, the lens is said to be wide-angle, projecting a smaller image of each object in its field but including a wider angle of view. When the focal length is longer than normal the lens is said to be a long-focus or telephoto lens, and it will form a larger image covering a narrower angle of view. Image size is always directly proportional to focal length. That is, the image formed of a given object by a 200mm lens will be exactly twice the height of the image of the same object at the same distance formed by a 100mm lens, regardless of the size and format of the film and camera. This rule applies also to variable focal length zoom lenses.

Focusing

No lens is capable of recording all objects sharply at various distances within its view. Because of this, the lens must be adjusted (focused) within a certain range of distances so that all desired objects are sharp. Some adjustment of focus is possible on all but the simplest snapshot cameras. These are permanently focused at about 15 feet, which gives acceptable, although not sharp, focus on everything from about five or six feet from the camera out to infinity (as far as the eye can see).

Focusing is nothing more than moving the lens nearer or farther from the film plane with a threaded or geared mechanism. One of the latest trends in camera design is automatic focusing.

Autofocus lenses make it easy to "grab" unexpected subject matter, but many pros find them inconvenient. Experienced photographers learn to prefocus according to estimated distance and then to shoot when action is at its peak. The problem is that autofocus lenses can be slow to react and they will focus on the background or foreground unless the main subject is in the center of the frame. If your camera focuses automatically you should study the owner's manual to find out how to "lock-in" the focus manually or turn off the autofocus feature.

Close-ups

If your pictures aren't good enough, you aren't close enough.

(Robert Capa, photojournalist)

Simple cameras do not permit the lens to be moved out far enough from the film plane to focus correctly on close-ups. View cameras and some reflexes have a flexible bellows connecting the lens mount with the body of the camera that can be extended for focusing on very near objects. Most 35mm cameras focus normally to as close as one and one-half to three feet, depending on the construction of the lens mount, but require extension tubes, bellows attachments, or supplementary close-up lenses that fit in front of the normal lens for photographing subjects that are closer than that. Although supplementary close-up lenses often are referred to as "portrait attachments," this term may be misleading, for most portraits do not require the use of such lenses. The close range the lenses allow tends to distort the shape of the subject's features (see Chapter 9). Extreme close-up attachments are best suited to copy work and to nature and scientific subjects.

The Viewfinder and Parallax

With cameras other than single-lens reflex and view cameras, the lens that actually takes the picture doesn't "see" exactly the same area that the viewfinder sees.

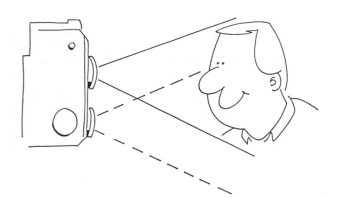

Parallax

This difference isn't very important on medium or distant shots, but when focusing up close the difference becomes significant. You may find, for example, that although your subject was perfectly framed in the viewfinder, the picture itself is cut off at the top or is off-center. This often happens in copying and in close-up pictures made with a rangefinder camera or a twin-lens reflex.

The difference between what is seen by the taking lens and by the viewfinder is called parallax. Some cameras have minimized the parallax problem by the use of adjustable viewfinder masks or prism lens attachments.

Although single-lens reflex viewing systems are free from the parallax problem, you may find, if you do much critical copy work or close-up photography, that the frame edges of your viewfinder are not precisely accurate. This may be true especially along the edge of the viewfinder corresponding to the bottom edge of the mirror and the problem may become more acute when using extra-long telephoto lenses. The only way to solve this is to run careful tests, measure the error, and compensate as required.

Depth of Field

Depth of field is the distance between the subject distances nearest and farthest from the camera that will be acceptably sharp in the finished photograph. The extent of this area of sharp focus is very important; most of the time you'll probably want the greatest depth of field possible. Except when the background would be distracting and should be kept deliberately out of focus, sharp detail in both foreground and background usually improves the picture. Depth of field increases when a smaller lens opening is used (f/16 instead of f/8) or when the camera is moved farther from the subject.

Lenses of short focal length give proportionately greater depth of field than longer lenses. This is one advantage offered by 35mm cameras. View cameras have means of increasing depth of field by adjusting the angle between the lens mount or film plane of the camera and the principle plane of the subject.

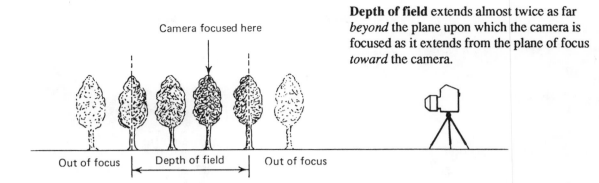

Camera focused here

Out of focus | Depth of field | Out of focus

Depth of field extends almost twice as far *beyond* the plane upon which the camera is focused as it extends from the plane of focus *toward* the camera.

Most lenses for 35mm cameras (except some with automatic focusing) have a depth of field scale engraved on the lens mount. Using this scale makes it easy to predetermine whether certain subjects will be within the area of acceptably sharp focus when the picture is taken. View cameras and most single-lens reflexes have provision for visually determining depth of field by viewing the subject with the lens stopped down.

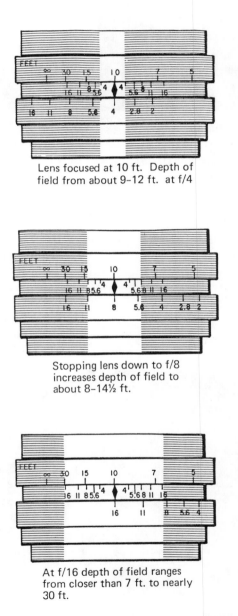

Lens focused at 10 ft. Depth of field from about 9–12 ft. at f/4

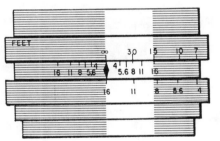

Focusing the lens on infinity (∞) wastes depth of field. Note near limit is 15 ft. when aperture is set at f/16.

Stopping lens down to f/8 increases depth of field to about 8–14½ ft.

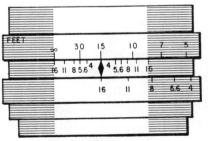

By focusing at nearest limit of depth of field at infinity (hyperfocal distance)—in this example, 15 ft. at f/16—depth of field extends from about 8 ft. to infinity.

At f/16 depth of field ranges from closer than 7 ft. to nearly 30 ft.

Hyperfocal focusing is a way to preset your camera for maximum depth of field, as for sports and travel photography.

Depth of field depends upon both subject distance and lens opening. Some lenses have a "double f/stop" scale that indicates depth of field at any given setting (here shown within the white band).

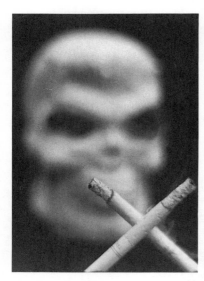

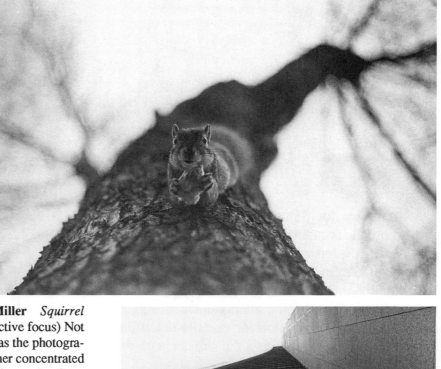

Abdel Alsoliman
No Smoking
A large lens opening (f/2.8) and a close working distance resulted in very shallow depth of field in this allegorical image.

Nancy Miller *Squirrel*
(Selective focus) Not only has the photographer concentrated attention on her furry friend, instead of on what would have been a very "busy" and distracting background of branches and bark texture, but she has shown us the importance of looking elsewhere for pictures than straight ahead at eye level.

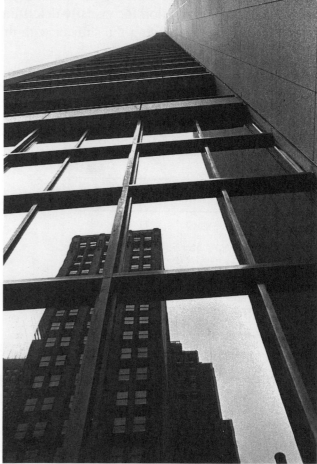

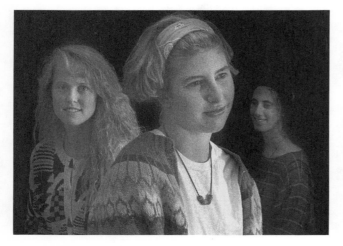

Erich Hammer *Classmates*
(Depth of field) The camera was focused on the middle girl (on left in picture) and stopped down to f/16 to keep everyone in focus.

Jim Nixon *Windows*
Here the lens was stopped down to f/16 and focused between the plane of the windows and the reflection to keep all parts of the image in sharp focus.

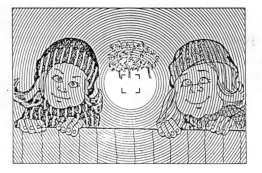

(1) Lens focuses automatically on the background (or meter exposes for the background)

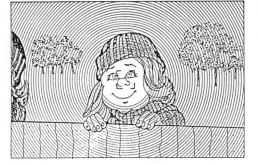

(2) Move camera so lens focuses on subject, and meter reads proper area. Hold down lock.

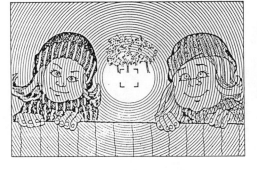

(3) While holding down the lock button, reframe the image and take the picture.

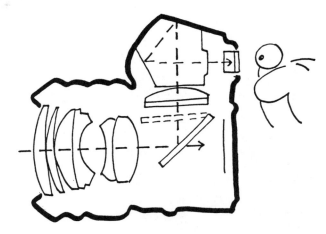

How to keep *autofocus* lenses from giving you *out-of-focus* pictures

(Left) Autofocus lenses tend to focus on the center of the picture. When the main subject is not in the center, you may need to move the camera to center on the subject, focus, then hold down a "focus lock" button or depress the shutter release halfway, reframe the picture, and shoot. Do the same thing for metering exposure when the background is much brighter or darker than the main subject.

Two SLR Focusing Systems

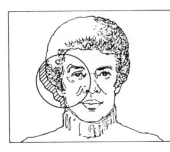

Out of focus

Split Image

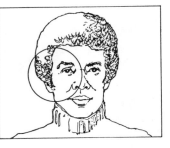

In focus

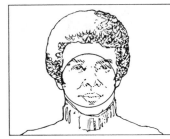

Out of focus

Ground Glass or Microprism

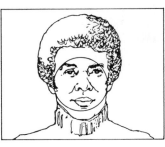

In focus

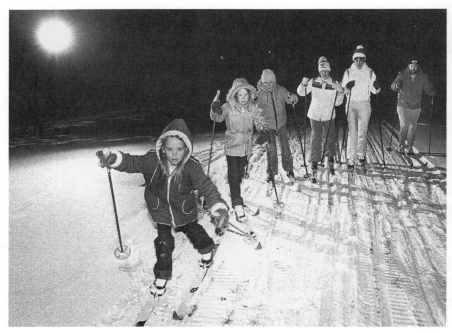

Ardyce Czuchna-Curl
Night Skiers
A wireless slave flash unit (showing in the picture at upper left)
simulated natural light, while a
second flash on camera filled in
foreground shadows.

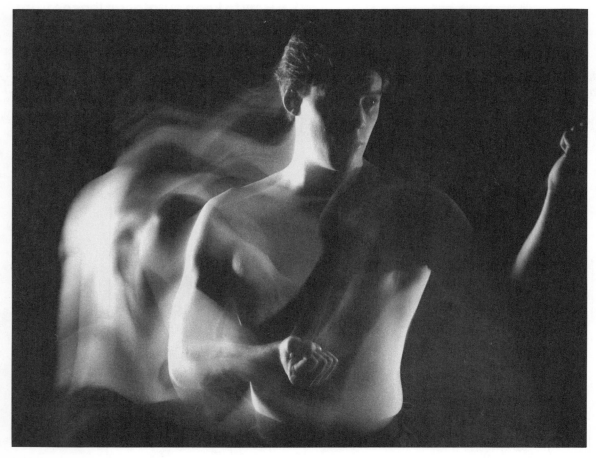

Jeff Keyes   *Flow*
Notice how in this 1-second exposure the illusion of
motion is strengthened by combining sharpness and
blur. Edge lighting enhances the effect.

The Shutter

Photography's most unique characteristic is the ability to preserve eternally a moment out of time. It is the camera shutter that makes this possible, together with highly sensitive film. We take these things for granted today, but because of the handicaps of their primitive equipment and materials, early photographers were unable to record anything that moved. A portrait sitter had to hold unnaturally still or have his or her head clamped firmly to prevent movement during an interminable exposure time of from several seconds to several agonizing minutes. Have you wondered why there are so few very early photographs of young children, animals, sporting events, or battle scenes?

Modern equipment and materials give us a choice of whether to "freeze" motion for examination of minute detail or to attempt a more subjective approach by deliberately allowing a moving subject to be blurred, thus preserving a feeling or interpretation of action.

Stopping motion

The choice of shutter speed is yours (unless your camera is set on *program*). A speed of 1/60 of a second will "stop" a person walking toward you at some distance, but it will take a higher speed, say 1/250, if the subject is closer to the camera or is walking directly past. Moving vehicles and fast-action sporting events usually call for 1/1000 to freeze the action. If you're a nature photographer you may find that the wind will move blossoms and leaves so much that you can't get a sharp image at less than 1/250 or 1/500.

Close-up photography often requires a very small lens opening to gain depth of field, but the resulting slow shutter speed can cause motion-stopping problems. This is when you need a tripod.

Camera movement can be as serious a trouble-maker as subject movement. Most people are unable to hand hold a camera steadily at shutter speeds slower than 1/60 of a second. The negative may look all right, but enlargement will show the telltale directional blur that proves the camera wasn't steady enough at the moment of exposure. Long focal length lenses are especially hard to hold steady because they magnify movement in the same proportion that they magnify the size of the image.

The goal of every artist is to stop movement, which is life...and to maintain it fixed so that one hundred years later, when a stranger may gaze at it, it will once again move, because it is life.

(William Faulkner, writer)

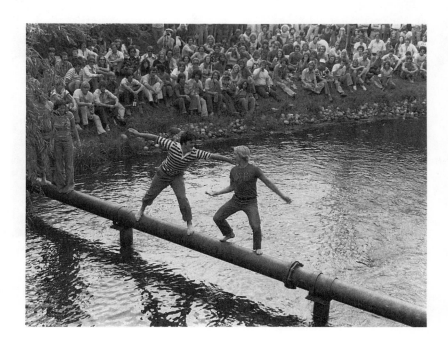

Scott LaVacque *Contest*
A shutter speed of 1/125 second was fast enough to "stop" the action because the photographer waited for a moment when the combatants' positions implied movement that was not actually happening (note the slight blur of the left hand of the man on your right).

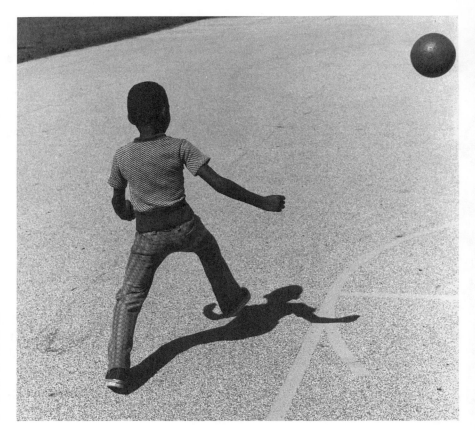

Barbara Bergy *Boy and Ball*
A shutter speed of 1/1,000
second froze the movement of
the boy, his shadow, and the
ball into a dynamic compostion
full of tension and graphic
contrast.

Andrea Rubenstein *Stairway*
Do you react differently to these two images of the same stairway? Do the
vertical format, the tilted angle, and the blur from camera movement intensify
the feeling—the fear—of falling?

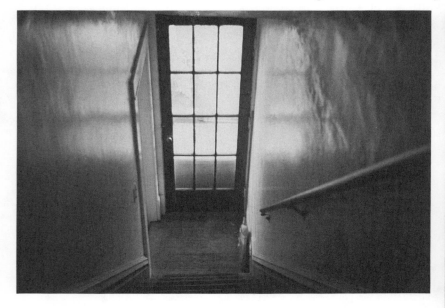

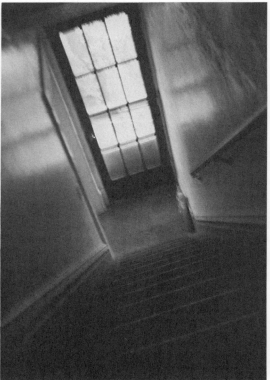

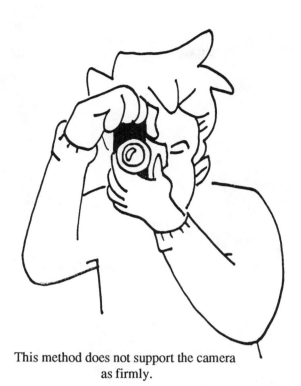

This method does not support the camera
as firmly.

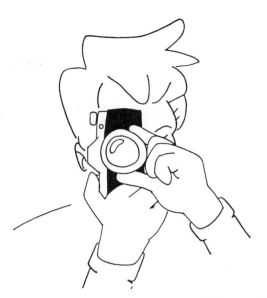

Thumb releases shutter, left hand supports lens
and focuses. Elbows press against body.

Hold the camera steady!

Hand holding a camera requires the same steady nerves and concentration needed for accurate target shooting with a rifle. The camera strap can serve as a steadying sling, as well as a carrying strap. Hold the camera firmly against your face, even if you're wearing glasses, and brace your elbows firmly against your body. Squeeze the shutter release smoothly—don't punch it or jab it!

Usually we want to make sharp images, but can you imagine bad (blurred) pictures that are good?

Creative blurring

There are a couple of different ways to record blurred, subjective action: (1) move the camera along with the subject (panning) and (2) hold the camera still while the subject moves past.

To pan, follow a rapidly moving subject through the viewfinder, using slow film (ISO 25-100) at a very slow shutter speed—perhaps 1/8 of a second. Continue moving the camera while you depress the shutter release. The image will disappear temporarily, but you should continue to try to stay lined up with the moving subject.

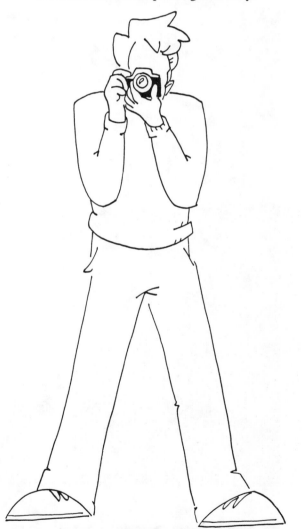

Feet spread wide apart, both elbows braced against
body. Left hand supports lens and focuses.

Jim Nixon *Turnstyle*
Do you get the feeling of a surging crowd? The effect was obtained by hand holding the camera at a shutter speed of one second and panning with the people as they burst through the turnstyle at the opening of a carnival.

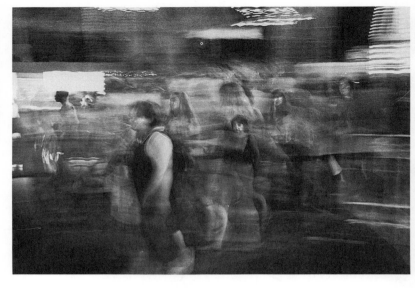

Karen Erickson *Fireworks*
The unsteadiness of a hand-held one-second exposure adds interest to what otherwise would have been a routine burst of fireworks.

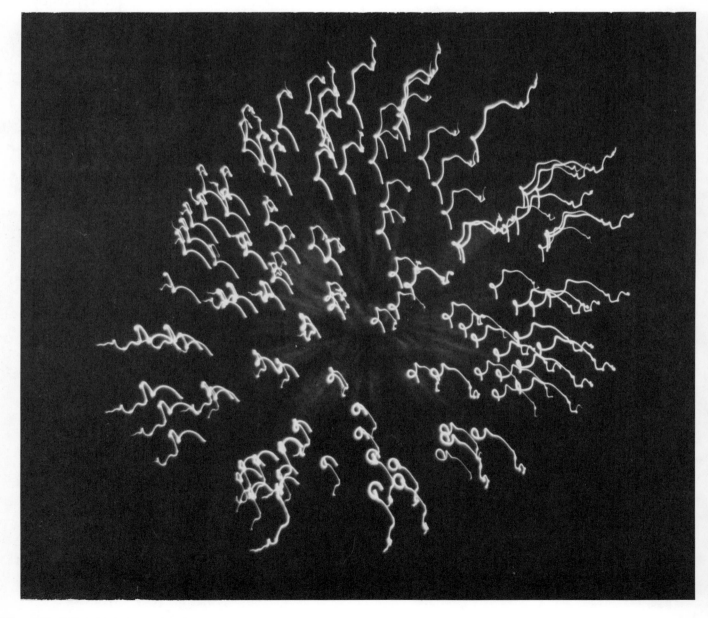

To show subject motion, mount your camera on a tripod and let the subject's movement trace a blur at various slow shutter speeds. You may be surprised at the interesting illusion of motion.

Most modern 35mm single-lens reflex cameras contain focal-plane shutters—so called because the shutter curtain moves across the camera body directly in front of the film. Lenses can be interchanged more conveniently and less expensively on a camera with a focal-plane shutter because each lens need not contain its own shutter. Most larger-format cameras use between-the-lens shutters with maximum speeds of generally 1/500 of a second, allowing flash synchronization at all speeds. Unfortunately, the curtain of most focal-plane shutters is not fully open at speeds faster than 1/60. This is something to think about when buying a new camera. Certain 35mm SLRs will synchronize flash up to 1/250 making it possible to use fill-in flash outdoors in sunlight and to minimize "ghost" images when shooting with flash under bright ambient light such as at sporting events. Some cameras provide an option of "rear curtain sync" which allows the flash to be fired at the end of a long exposure so that a sharp image may be combined with a blurred one in a single exposure.

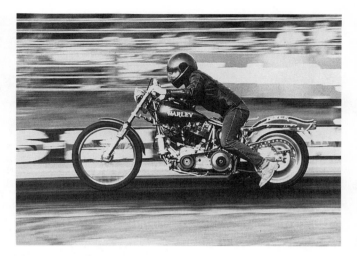

Ricky Don Meek *Harley*
This cycle was moving so fast that panning at 1/60 second with a 200mm lens gave a strong illusion of motion.

David Knight *Dancer*
The dancer moved in front of the camera, which was mounted firmly on a tripod, during a one-second exposure. Notice that her brief pauses left distinct images connected by flowing lines, suggesting the grace of the dance.

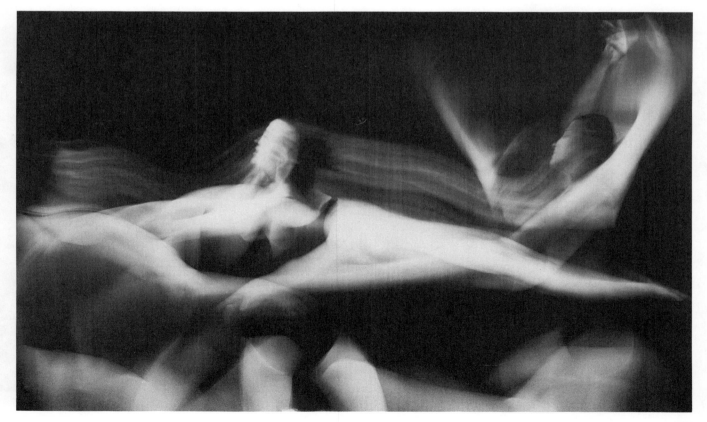

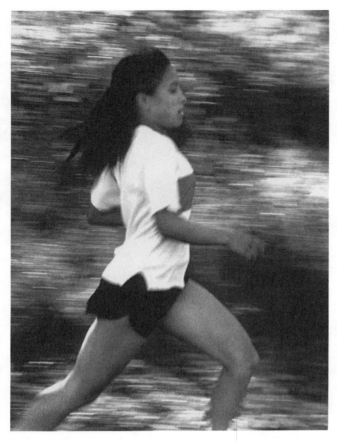

Erich Hammer *Running Girl*
Panning the camera at 1/30 second as the subject ran past gave a feeling of breathless speed.

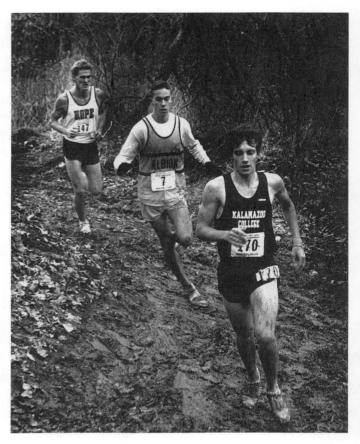

Erich Hammer *Cross Country*
Because these runners were moving directly toward the camera, their motion was nearly frozen at 1/250 second.

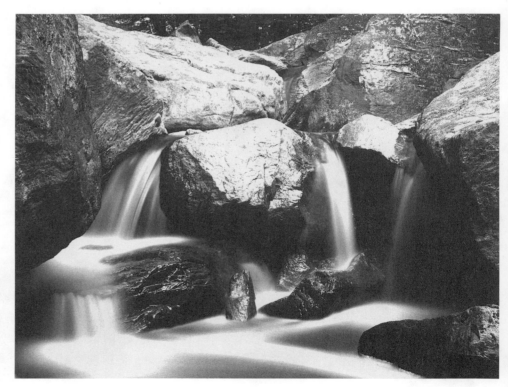

David Knight *Waterfall*
Obviously, both rocks and camera remained motionless during this eight-second exposure, but the moving water has taken on a metallic, flowing quality.

Camera Care

Your camera is a precision instrument that deserves good care. It represents a sizable investment and it will give the best results when protected from dirt, moisture, and physical abuse.

Cleanliness is very important. A common misconception is that dust on the lens will cause spots on prints. This is not true—a layer of dust on the camera or enlarger lens will at most reduce the contrast of the image slightly, and it may degrade the sharpness. But dust may cause permanent scratches if you're careless about how you clean the glass surfaces.

The proper way to clean a lens is first to blow or gently wipe away surface dust with a very soft brush. Sand or rough particles can make deep scratches if rubbed, so be especially careful. Fingerprints or water spots can be removed by wadding a sheet of camera lens tissue into a loose ball and moistening it with a couple of drops of lens cleaning fluid, then wiping the lens surface gently in a circular motion. Don't pour the cleaning solution directly onto the lens because it can seep inside between the glass elements. Dry with another loose wad of lens cleaning tissue. Don't use cleaning products designed for eyeglasses.

Although a little dust on the outer surfaces of the lens may not be very serious, dust, sand, and film fragments inside your camera may cause jamming of some part of the mechanism or the tiny particles may leave images of themselves on your negatives. Blow out loose dirt and dust or wipe it out with a cotton swab, but be very careful not to touch the shutter curtain or the mirror.

The best way to have a clean camera is to keep it from getting dirty. Invest in a durable, padded case for your equipment. Keep caps on both ends of lenses when they're not in use. For the lens that stays on your camera most of the time, a *UV, haze,* or *skylight* filter (practically colorless) kept over the lens at all times provides excellent protection against abrasion, dust, sand, and moisture. Opaque lens caps are a nuisance and, after all, it's a lot cheaper to replace a filter than to buy a new lens.

A few raindrops falling on your camera are not

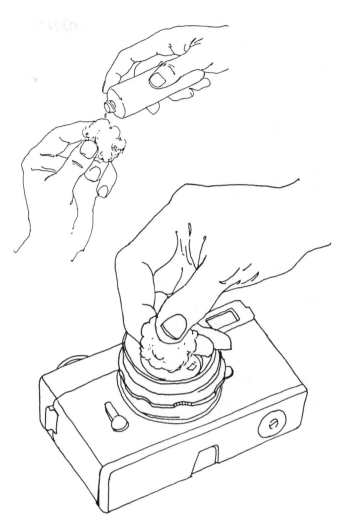

A clean lens is essential for clear pictures. Protect your lenses with lens caps or clear glass filters, cleaning them only when necessary using the recommended procedure.

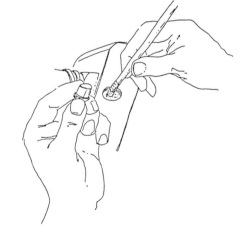

When batteries die, so may your camera. Sometimes wiping the contacts with a pencil eraser will restore operation if the battery still has life in it.

likely to cause permanent harm, although a good soaking probably will. Salt water is an especially voracious enemy of lens coatings and metallic finishes, so a filter over the lens and even a plastic bag over the camera will help if you're going sailing. If your camera should ever become thoroughly immersed, especially in salt water, rinse it out immediately in a container of fresh water; then if you can't get it to a repair shop right away while it's soaking, dry it out as rapidly as possible with warm air from a hair dryer. Operate the mechanism occasionally while it is drying to keep it freed up. Wet film can be saved if it can be processed within a few hours. Seal the film in a jar of fresh water until it can be processed.

Photographers who travel often run into vibration problems. The vibration from a plane, train, motorcycle, or car eventually may shake loose some vital screws, so retighten the visible screws periodically with a jeweler's screwdriver and plan to carry the camera around your neck or over your shoulder instead of having it travel in the baggage compartment. Aside from Customs difficulties and possible theft, another reason for carrying your camera is that you can request a visual security inspection at the airport instead of having your loaded camera pass through a potentially harmful X-ray machine. I have found most airport security people to be cooperative and usually they will hand inspect my camera. I remove film magazines from their opaque containers and place them together in transparent plastic storage bags so they can quickly be handed through security. An alternative is to purchase lead foil containers from a camera store and leave the film in your luggage. One trip through most airport X-ray machines probably won't harm film slower than ISO 1,000, but the effect is cumulative. So take care.

Extreme heat and cold

The trunk or glove compartment and the ledge of the rear window of your car are among the poorest places to put a camera. The intense heat within a closed automobile in the sun not only can fog the film in the camera or cause color shifts, but it may actually cause lens elements to separate, lubricants to liquify, and batteries to deteriorate.

Tropical heat and humidity are especially troublesome, as fungus will grow rapidly on film and it may eat away some lens coatings and even etch itself into the glass. Don't leave film in the camera any longer than necessary. Store your camera in an air-conditioned room, a dehumidified closet, or in a sealed box containing a desiccating agent such as silica gel. An insulated beverage cooler will help protect your film and camera against extreme temperatures for a few hours.

Arctic conditions cause different problems. Although cold is less likely than heat to cause damage, low temperatures can weaken batteries and cause lubricants to congeal. Carry the camera under your coat between shots and your body heat should keep it warm enough to function.

Another winter problem is static electricity. Static can make lightening-like imprints on your negatives. Avoid this problem by manually advancing or rewinding film slowly.

If your equipment has become thoroughly chilled, don't bring it into a warm room where moisture can condense on it (and in it). Let it warm up gradually or seal the cold camera and lenses in plastic bags before bringing them indoors. Avoid putting equipment and film near heaters and radiators.

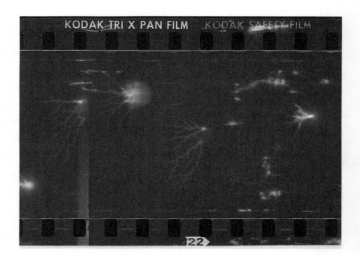

Static in action. This negative is not a photograph of a thunderstorm, a nuclear explosion or a fireworks display. What you see is an actual example of a very bad case of static electricity. Static discharge occurs in very cold weather when the relative humidity is low. It can be avoided in manually operated cameras by advancing and rewinding the film slowly.

Care of batteries

Batteries can fail without warning—functioning one day, dead the next. The tiny energy cells that power exposure meters and electronic features on many modern cameras should last a year or more. They can be tested, so be sure to find out how to do this. Put in fresh batteries before leaving on an extended trip, and carry spares.

Alkaline flash batteries require frequent inspection to remove the white powder that collects on the terminals and causes flash failure. A rough cloth will shine up the ends of the batteries; a pencil eraser is a handy tool to reach down inside the battery compartment to shine up the contact terminals there. Remove the batteries altogether if the camera or flash isn't going to be used for several weeks. Put them in a zip-lock plastic bag and store them in the refrigerator. Freezing will prolong the life of film, but freezing is *not* good for batteries.

Loading Film

Imagine shooting a roll of great pictures, then developing the film and finding it blank. This is a common problem, but it is preventable because film loading errors seem to cause most of the problems encountered with using an unfamiliar camera. Even though the film may not be advancing, most 35mm cameras will act as if everything is OK and even the exposure counter will register.

Here's how to keep this disappointing experience from happening to you: When you load your 35mm camera, be sure the film leader is firmly attached to the take-up spool or, if your camera is automatic-loading, pulled out to exactly the right length and laid against the indicator mark. Check to see that the film sprocket holes are engaged with (or lying directly over) the sprocket teeth on both sides. Be sure the film is flat and lined up correctly before closing and latching the camera back.

If your camera has a motorized rewind and no hand rewind crank, then you should consult the owner's manual to see whether there is a warning signal if something is wrong when you press the film advance to begin the roll.

Manually operated cameras are easy to check, because the rewind crank or knob will turn as the film advances. Here's how to take advantage of this feature:

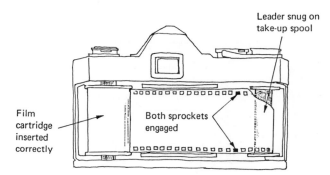

Leader snug on take-up spool

Film cartridge inserted correctly

Both sprockets engaged

Most problems with film loading are caused by being in too much of a hurry. Take your time. Don't short-cut the procedure. Check every step.

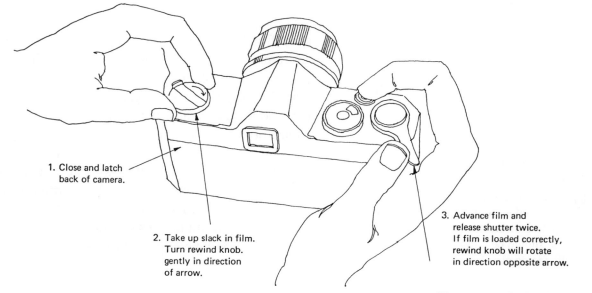

1. Close and latch back of camera.

2. Take up slack in film. Turn rewind knob. gently in direction of arrow.

3. Advance film and release shutter twice. If film is loaded correctly, rewind knob will rotate in direction opposite arrow.

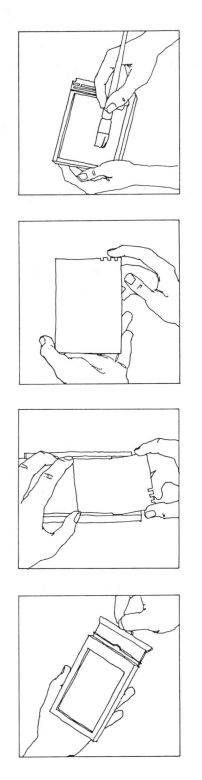

Sheet film holders must be kept free of dust. In the dark, each sheet of film is loaded separately beneath the retaining guides on one side of a holder. The dark slides should be inserted with the silver sides of the handles facing out to indicate unexposed film. After exposure, the slide should be reinserted with the black side of the handle facing out.

After latching the camera back, press the film advance lever until it stops. Then turn the rewind knob or crank in the direction of the arrow (clockwise, as if you were rewinding the film after exposure) until you feel slight tension. Stop. Release the shutter and advance the film one more frame, watching the rewind knob as you turn the advance lever. The rewind knob should rotate counterclockwise, opposite to the arrow, showing that the film is moving. Check this from time to time as you advance the film to avoid the embarrassment of shooting 36 exposures on the same frame.

Most 120-size roll film cameras have an arrow inside the film magazine that must be lined up with an arrow printed near the beginning of the film backing paper. Lining up these arrows sets the exposure counter.

Sheet film handling creates a set of different problems, principally because most films must be handled in total darkness. Sheet film holders should be blown or brushed free of dust before loading, and the dark slides must be positioned correctly. Nearly all sheet films are notched so that you can feel the notches with your right index finger if the film is held correctly for insertion into the holder. Guide the film under the retainers with your left hand, then fold over the hinged end flap and insert the dark slide all the way, with the silver side of the handle facing out. Lock the latches. Don't forget to rewrap the leftover film and put it back into its light-tight box before turning on the lights!

All cameras should be loaded and unloaded in the shade or indoors, never in bright sunlight. Even sheet film holders tend to leak light if the dark slides are removed and inserted in direct sun, so shade the camera if possible when this is done. Never force any of the adjustments or controls on any camera. If film should jam for any reason, unload the camera in a darkroom or inside a lightproof changing bag.

Although these tips and suggestions won't ensure that all of your photographs will be significant and visually exciting, avoiding the common mistakes mentioned above will help to increase the odds that your important images will not be lost because of malfunctioning equipment or a careless error.

Camera Accessories   *4*

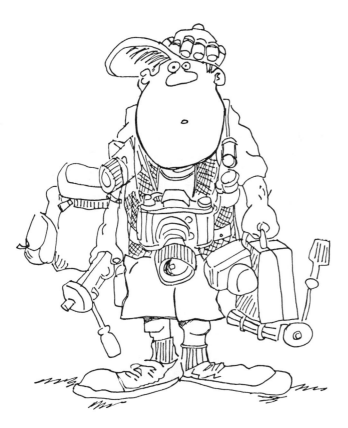

hand and twist it—and get a bigger tripod than you think you need. Although you may curse the weight of a bulky camera support when you're backpacking or photographing in the field, you'll be glad when you finally compare your sharp negatives and prints with the fuzzy ones you used to get.

Nature photographers often choose a tripod with legs that spread wide for low camera angles. Many users prefer flip-type leg locks to the kind that twist. Check out different types of heads and camera mounting devices. Some 35mm users enjoy the simplicity of a swiveling ball head with a single knob to lock it in position; others prefer a pan head or the double tilting kind. Try before you buy!

There are emergency substitutes for a tripod, such as a C-clamp equipped with a swivel tripod head, or a six-foot length of lightweight chain or nylon line fastened to a 1/4 x 20 threaded eye bolt (you step on the end of the chain or line and stretch it tight). But eventually you'll need a substantial tripod, so make this important investment as soon as you can afford it.

What to Look For

Buying a camera is only the beginning. There are a lot of other ways to invest in photographic accessories and gadgets. A few of the items displayed in stores and advertised in magazines are essential. Some are useful for special purposes, while others are merely toys. This chapter will help you decide what you really need and how to get the most for your money.

Tripod

First and most important, you'll need a tripod. A sturdy tripod is essential for absolutely sharp pictures, although most beginning photographers aren't convinced that they need one until they make their first *big* enlargements. Pick a tripod that won't wobble when you press down on the head with your

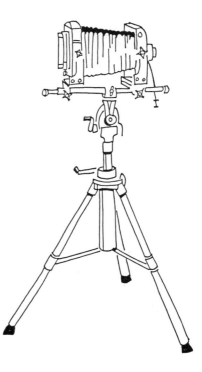

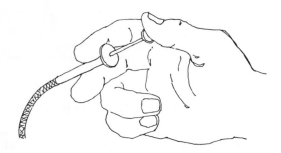

A cable release will give you sharper pictures. Use one whenever the camera is mounted on a tripod or copy stand.

Cable release

Then, when you're using the tripod, you'll need a cable release to trip the shutter without jarring the camera. A metal or cloth-covered cable release about ten inches long will screw into a threaded socket in or near the shutter release button of most cameras and permit you to squeeze the release much more gently than you can with your finger. Some newer electronic cameras, however, don't have a cable release socket. For these you may need a remote electronic release that plugs into the camera body.

Lens shade

A lens shade, or lens hood, is another essential accessory. Screwing directly into the threaded outer rim of your lens, the shade will help prevent stray light from entering from just outside the field of view of the lens. This light causes flare spots or streaks on the negative and may reduce the contrast of the image significantly.

Either the rigid metal or collapsing rubber kind of shade is OK, but be sure that the threads are of exactly the right pitch and diameter to fit your lens (you may need to buy separate shades for different lenses). If you're not using a reflex camera, be sure that the shade doesn't obstruct the viewfinder or rangefinder window. You can't use a lens shade with some wide-angle lenses because it will cut off the corners of the image, so always use a shade of the proper depth for that focal length.

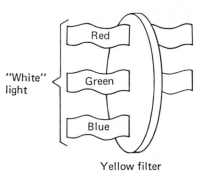

Yellow filter

A *yellow* filter is commonly used to darken skies in black-and-white photography. It absorbs blue light and transmits other colors. What is the visual effect of a yellow filter on a black-and-white *negative*—will the sky appear darker or lighter than if the filter had not been used?

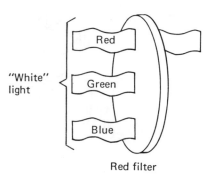

Red filter

A *red* filter transmits red light but does not pass other colors. Red objects therefore will be rendered very light in a black-and-white print, while objects that are predominately green or blue will appear darker.

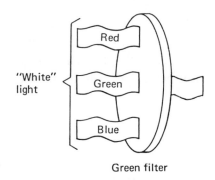

Green filter

A *green* filter transmits green light, absorbing red and blue. In black-and-white photography, what effect would a green filter have on the image of a red apple among green leaves?

Filters

Filters are handy for special effects, but you won't need nearly as many as you'll be tempted to buy. A UV, *haze*, or *skylight* filter will be a good investment as a permanent transparent lens cap. The filter will protect each expensive and delicate lens from moisture and abrasion and minimize the number of times you'll have to clean the lens surface. Cleaning a filter is easier and much less risky than cleaning the lens, and if the filter gets scratched, you can throw it away and buy another.

Colored filters affect contrast

Colored filters are used in black and white photography to darken or lighten a particular color as it will be reproduced in the final print.

To understand how a filter works you should know that visible "white" light is made up of all the colors in the visible spectrum. The primary colors of visible light are red, green, and blue.

When you see a red object you are seeing red light that has been reflected from the object. The object has absorbed all the other colors, reflecting only red. If this red object is photographed through a red filter, red light is passed through to the film, but any green or blue light present is absorbed by the filter. Because the image is formed only by red light, the red object photographed will appear dense on the negative and light on the print. Anything green or blue in the picture will not be recorded with much density on the film, and will print very dark.

Yellow light is made up of red and green light. If you put a yellow filter in front of your camera lens, the filter will pass red and green light easily, but it will hold back the blue. The red and green light combine to form yellow light, which records the image. When a yellow, orange, or red filter is used, blue areas record as lower densities on the negative, thus appearing darker in the final print. A common use for a yellow, orange, or red filter is to darken a blue sky, giving added contrast between white clouds or buildings and the sky. Here's a quiz question: Why won't a filter give this effect when the sky is overcast?

A green filter yields just the opposite result of a red filter, lightening greens and darkening reds and blues.

The effect of filters on black-and-white films is to lighten or darken colors. The rule to remember is: If you want to render a color lighter in the final print, select a filter the same color as the subject to be lightened or one that will transmit that color of light. If you want an object to appear darker in the print, use a filter that will not pass that color. A filter will darken objects that are its complementary or opposite color. For example, if you want to make a red object appear darker, use a blue or a green filter. A red filter would make the red object photograph lighter than it actually appears; so would a yellow filter, although to a lesser degree.

Filters for copying

Other important uses of filters in black-and-white photography include the improvement of contrast between colored lettering or lines and the background on signs, posters, or architectural drawings. Blue printing on a white background, for instance, won't show as much contrast in a photograph as the original appears to the eye. Photographically copying the document with a red filter will darken the blue considerably, thus increasing the contrast and readability of the reproduction.

Filters, close-up lenses and lens shades can be purchased with screw threads to fit most lenses. Unthreaded and gelatin filters can be attached with adapter rings and filter frame holders. When many attachments are combined as in this illustration, the corners of the image may be cut off (vignetted).

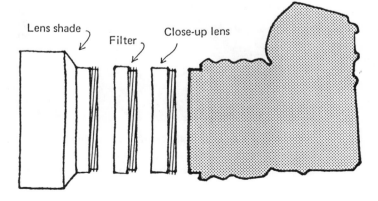

Lens shade   Filter   Close-up lens

Suppose that you want to copy a faded, yellowish-stained old document to make the writing (in black or blue ink) more legible. What filter would you use? A yellow or orange filter would record the yellow as white on the final print, increasing the contrast between the writing and the stained background. Here's another problem: What filter would you use to make a black-and-white copy of an old photograph stained yellow by age and improper storage? Right. Blue. The filter will render the faded, yellowish image darker and so it will be possible to restore much of the original contrast in a print made from the copy negative.

Remember the rule about filters transmitting their own and related colors and blocking opposite or complementary colors and you'll be able to determine whether a filter will create the effect you want.

A polarizer reduces reflections

A filter useful with color film as well as black-and-white is a polarizer. For autofocus lenses and certain metering systems you need a special type of *circular* polarizer. What this dark-gray looking filter does is to remove many detail-obscuring reflections from non-metallic surfaces such as glass, water, and polished wood without affecting the relative intensities of colors. You simply rotate it until you see the effect you want. Because blue sky is polarized, the filter also will darken blue skies to

some extent, depending on the angle between the sun and the camera-to-subject axis. When shooting with color film a polarizing filter will intensify the contrast between blue sky and clouds, snow, or autumn leaves about the same way as a yellow filter affects black-and-white. You'll get the most dramatic effects on a clear day, shooting upward at a right angle to the sun.

Polarizers can be placed over light sources as well as on the camera lens. When you do this you can completely eliminate surface reflections from printing inks and painted surfaces. This technique is especially useful when making slides of artists' original works, and from books.

Filters require exposure change

Although filters are very useful, there is also a drawback. Because all filters except the "transparent lens cap" type absorb some of the light, you'll have to increase the exposure to compensate. Most cameras with through-the-lens exposure metering will compensate automatically for the density of the filter; however for the most accuracy it's best to make the reading before putting the filter over the lens, then increase the exposure as shown in the table. You can either open up the lens aperture or slow the shutter speed by the number of stops indicated. When using a hand-held exposure meter you can divide the exposure index by the filter factor and set that lower ISO number into the meter.

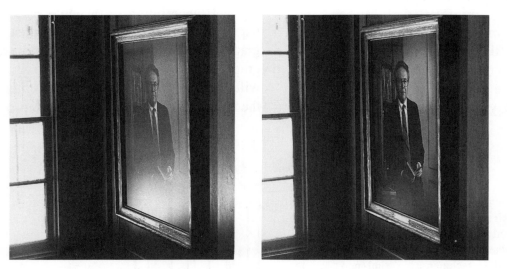

A polarizer can eliminate certain kinds of glare and reflections. In this detail from a building interior, notice the reflections on the surface of the portrait and the wall paneling in the photo on the left. On the right, a polarizer has made the reflections much less noticeable.

Filter Color and Type	Factor	Number of Stops Increase
Yellow (#8 or K2)	1.5x	two-thirds stop
Orange (#15 or G)	2x	one stop
Green (#11 or X1)	3x	one and one-half stops
Red (#25 or A)	8x	three stops
Polarizing	3x	one and one-half stops

The daylight filter factors for most black-and-white films and for the most commonly used filters are shown in the table above. These factors should be verified from the film manufacturer's data sheet for individual types of film, especially when working with incandescent lights.

Neutral density filters reduce exposure

Sometimes there's too much light, especially outdoors with fast film or when working in the studio with high-intensity electronic flash. Neutral density filters reduce the amount of light passing through the lens without affecting anything else. Use an ND filter when you need a slow shutter speed for panning or blurred motion effects or a wide lens opening for selective focus.

Neutral density filters come in various densities and they can be stacked together. Most commonly used are ND .30 (1 stop), ND .60 (2 stops) and ND .90 (3 stops).

"Creative" filters for special effects

Here's where it's easy to spend a lot of money. It's hard to resist buying an entire series of special effects filters and the adapter kit to attach them to your lenses.

Several companies make sets including close-up, diffusing, fog, infrared, split-field, center spot, cross-star, multi-image, multiple-exposure, and many more. Sales people be happy to show these to you at a camera store.

Filters for color control

We suggested using a UV or *skylight* filter as a lens cap. This filter also will absorb excess ultraviolet. It also will improve color pictures taken in shade or on a heavily overcast day by reducing excess bluishness. With both color and black-and-white films the *UV* or *skylight* filter also reduces the effect of haze in distant landscape and aerial photos without requiring an increase in exposure.

Filters intended solely for color photography fall into three categories: compensating, correction, and conversion. *Compensating* filters (CC series) are for making minor changes in the color balance of light used to expose color films and papers. *Correction* filters such as the FLD filter for daylight color film in fluorescent light, and the warming 81 series and cooling 82 series, are intended to improve the accurate reproduction of colors when the illumination present differs slightly from the color temperature for which the film was balanced. *Conversion* filters (such as the bluish 80 series and the orangish 85 series) enable the use of color film balanced either for daylight or incandescent illumination to be exposed with the other kind of light.

Filter factors for color-compensating, color-correction, and color-conversion filters are included in the film or filter manufacturer's exposure recommendations.

Filter formats

Although the most commonly used filters are available in either dyed or laminated glass for durability, each type is available also in a less costly but more delicate gelatin sheet form that is practical for studio use. All filters either screw directly into the front of the lens mount or they slip into an adapter ring or holder. Be sure to get the right diameter and thread size to fit your lens. If you own lenses with different front thread sizes, you can buy filters to fit the largest lens and purchase step-down rings to adapt those filters to the smaller diameter lenses.

Exposure meters

If your camera has a built-in, through-the-lens exposure meter, it isn't essential to acquire a separate meter. On the other hand, if you try to make very precise readings of small subject areas in order to place these areas in the proper exposure zones, you'll appreciate a precision hand-held *spot* meter with a relatively narrow angle of view. Especially for natural landscape and architectural subjects, it's very convenient to be able to read the brightness of a small area from a distance. A meter with this feature is a worthwhile accessory.

For studio and copy work with either incandescent lights or electronic flash, the appropriate type of *incident* light meter is desirable because its spherical light-integrating cell gives precise "Zone V" readings regardless of backlighting or variations in background brightness.

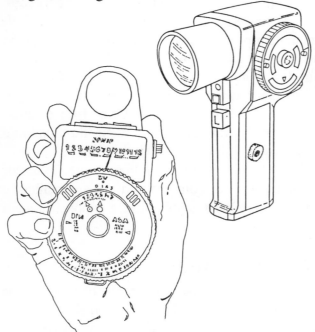

Wide-angle and telephoto lenses

Before buying expensive lenses It's a good idea to wait until you've had a chance to find out what your most comfortable shooting distances are. For street photography with a 35mm camera, for example, many photographers prefer the wide-angle coverage and great depth of field of a 35mm or 28mm focal length lens because it allows them to work freely in the midst of a crowd of people without cutting off heads and feet. A wide-angle lens even allows shooting "from the hip" without putting the camera up to the eye. Other photographers feel more comfortable picking off their prey from a safe distance, hiding behind a 200mm or 300mm telephoto or a long zoom lens.

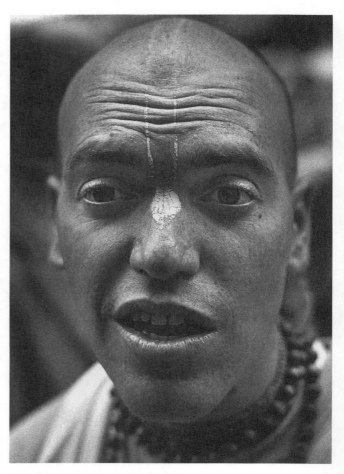

Jim Nixon *Hare Krishna*
A pre-focused wide-angle lens permitted this confrontational close-up. Would you feel more comfortable using a longer focal length?

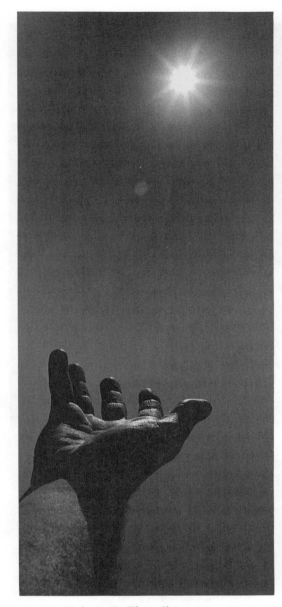

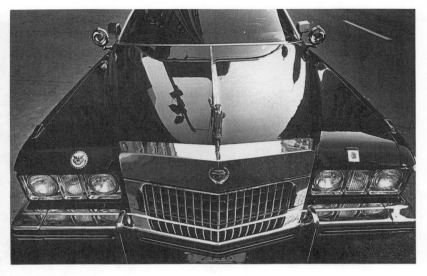

Jim Nixon *Limousine*
Wide-angle lenses tend to increase size differences between near and far objects, or between parts of the same object. In this case a 24mm lens has made the vehicle appear even more massive and sculptural than it actually is.

Jim Nixon *Chicago*
A moderately wide-angle lens makes street photography more convenient in crowded places.

Raimonds Ziemelis
Hand and Sun
An extremely wide-angle lens (21mm) was necessary to allow the photographer to include his own right hand in the picture while holding the 35mm camera in his left hand.

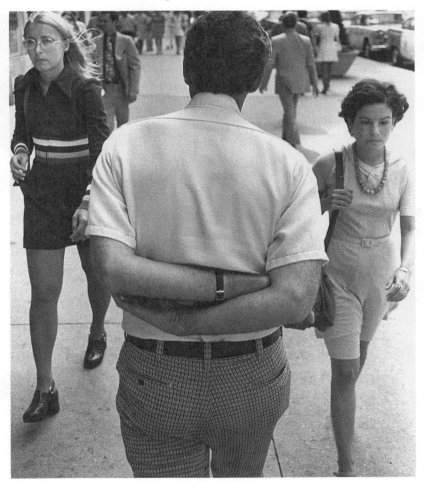

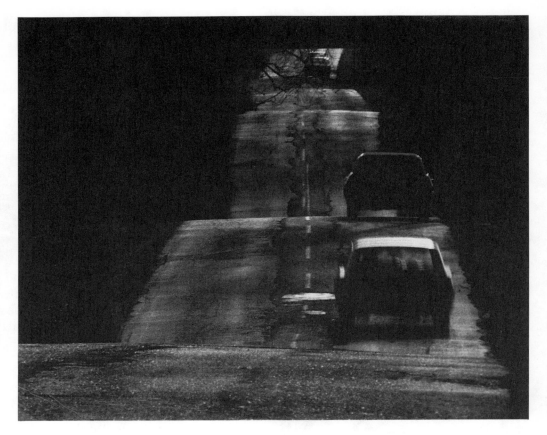

D. Curl
West "H" Avenue
The cumulative compression of depth produced by telephoto lenses is especially apparent with extremely long focal lengths. More than a quarter mile of roadway is visible in this photograph made with a 400mm lens on a 35mm camera.

Jim Nixon *Self-portrait*
A "fish-eye" lens produced this unique image, which the photographer enhanced through the use of maximum printing contrast and the Sabattier effect. The image is reversed because the final print (on the right) was printed by contact from a "solarized" paper positive print.

Jim Nixon *Self-portrait (normal print)*

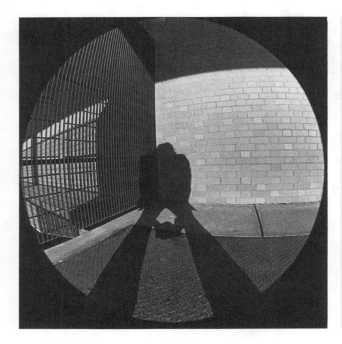

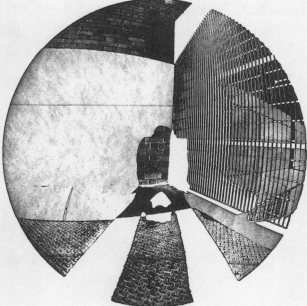

Choose lenses you need

A focal length of about 105mm is very popular with portrait photographers who work with 35mm cameras because the 105mm lens yields a full head and shoulders image without the photographer having to be embarrassingly close to the subject. Wide angle lenses tend to distort facial features on close-ups, whereas very long focal lengths flatten perspective and lose the feeling of roundness. Other than for specialized sports or nature photography, few people ever get their money's worth of use out of extreme telephotos (300mm and longer).

A fish-eye lens (extreme wide-angle) is an expensive toy for most photographers, distorting perspective so seriously that the effect is usable mostly as a novelty or for unusual architectural or recording requirements. Considering the amount you'll probably use it, a fish-eye lens probably should not be a high-priority item in your photographic budget.

Zoom lenses

A zoom lens can be a luxurious convenience for the traveler who wishes to be prepared to record exotic landscapes, snatch unposed portraits, or follow the action of a bullfight without bothering to change lenses.

Because variable focal length zoom lenses contain many elements, users generally sacrifice maximum aperture and some corner-to-corner image sharpness in exchange for the convenience of carrying a single camera with only one lens. An alternative popular with professionals is to maintain separate camera bodies equipped with favorite focal-length lenses, switching rapidly between cameras rather than changing lenses or zooming. Either way involves carrying extra weight and bulk.

Lens extenders

A lens extender is a relatively inexpensive way to make a long telephoto out of a shorter focal length lens. The trouble is that aberrations present in an inexpensive extender will bring down the image quality of an expensive, high-quality lens to that of the lowest denominator—usually the extender. If you can afford it, it's a better investment to buy quality lenses of needed focal lengths (or a good zoom lens) than to try to stretch a normal lens into something that it isn't.

Close-focusing attachments

When you want to take a close-up picture of something really small, you will probably need a special camera attachment. There are several choices, the least expensive being close-up lenses that screw like filters into the front of a regular lens. These supplementary lenses are available in various strengths—+1, +2, +3, and +4 diopters—and they can be used singly or combined to allow you to focus on objects down to a few inches from the camera.

Because the lens isn't physically moved out farther from the film, close-up lenses require no exposure correction. But they do tend to cut down on the sharpness of the image, especially around the edges. Because of this problem, you should stop down the lens as far as possible, not only for sharpness, but because you'll need all the depth of field you can get when you're working that close to the subject. Framing close-ups is no problem with a single-lens reflex, but you'll have to measure the distance very carefully, according to the manufacturer's table, if you're using a rangefinder camera.

Another way to get a normal focal length lens to focus close enough to the subject for *macro photography* (the photographing of very small objects) is to employ *extension tubes*. Tubes of different lengths are available for most single-lens reflex cameras, some of which actuate the automatic diaphragm mechanism (very desirable). Of course the screw threads or bayonet lugs on the tubes have to line up perfectly with your particular camera. Normal lenses sometimes are attached to extension tubes in reverse—that is, screwed onto the tubes with the rear lens element facing toward the subject. In this way the image may be sharper.

A *bellows attachment* is another solution, more flexible than extension tubes, that allows you to focus down to about 1:1 (where the image is the same size as the object). Both bellows and extension tubes require a greater increase in exposure the closer you get to the subject. The table on the next page gives approximate exposure increase factors for 35mm cameras at various field sizes.

Attachments enable you to focus the camera very close to the subject. In addition to a macro lens, most single-lens reflex camera bodies will accept a system of close-up accessories including extension tubes and/or focusing bellows

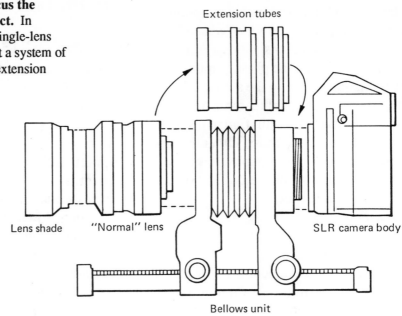

Extension tubes

Lens shade "Normal" lens SLR camera body

Bellows unit

A macro lens may be best

The ideal close-up device for most 35mm SLR cameras is a *macro lens*. Generally of normal focal length or longer, the macro lens is especially corrected to give extremely sharp images at close focusing distances. Most macro lenses are designed to focus continuously from infinity almost to 1:1 (life size) without exposure compensation or other manual adjustment.

The lens reveals more than the eye sees.
(Edward Weston, photographer)

Approximate Exposure Correction for Close-up Photography with 35mm Cameras Using Extension Tubes or Bellows*

Length of area photographed (in.)	12	6	3	2½	2	1½	1¼	1	¾	½
Length of area photographed (cm)	30	15	7.6	6.5	5	3.8	3.2	2.5	2	1.2
Open lens by (f/stops)	⅓	⅔	1	1⅓	1⅔	2	2⅓	2⅔	3	4
Or multiply time by factor of**	1.3	1.6	2	2.5	3.2	4	5	6.5	8	16

*These corrections may not be necessary if your through-the-lens exposure meter and automatic diaphragm mechanism are coupled with the close-up system you use. Certain macro lenses automatically adjust the diaphragm as the lens is focused. Check your instruction manual for verification.

**Note: At exposure times of one second or longer, you will have to make additional correction for reciprocity departure. At one second, your corrected exposure will require opening one additional stop or lengthening the time to two seconds. Open up two additional stops at ten seconds or lengthen the time to 50 seconds. Interpolate or extrapolate as necessary.

Brand names and quality

There's hardly anything in the world that someone cannot make a little worse and sell a little cheaper, and the people who consider price only are this man's lawful prey.   *(John Ruskin, publisher)*

The best lenses generally carry the camera manufacturer's name, but they also are the most expensive. I believe that you should buy the best you can afford, because "cheap" equipment will be outgrown in a hurry. An amateur photographer may never notice that his or her lens isn't sharp in the corners of the image, because their pictures are small, discount store processed snapshots of people standing in the middle of the frame. But if you are doing big enlargements of subjects with important detail, you'll learn very quickly the limitations of your lenses. Some helpful hints about how to test equipment appear later in this chapter.

Self-timer

A self-timer is a delayed-action gadget that lets you take your own picture. If your camera doesn't have a self-timer built in, you can buy one that either screws into the cable release socket or plugs into the camera body and trips the shutter after a preset delay of ten seconds or so—long enough for you to run into the scene and pose. Narcissistic? Maybe, but handy sometimes. Another use for the self-timer is to release the shutter gently at slow shutter speeds when you might not have a cable release with you.

Motor drive

The battery powered motor drive is gaining in popularity even though it adds considerably to the bulk and weight of the camera. Valuable especially for sports and nature sequences, a motor-driven film winder can allow you to expose as many as four frames per second! Rapid film advance and rewind and multiple exposure features are built into the newer fully-automatic cameras.

Flash attachment

A flash is another popular accessory because it allows you to make pictures in very poor light and to fill in excessively dark foreground shadows in bright sunlight. A flash unit mounted on the camera is hardly the ideal light source, as we'll discuss in Chapter 9, but it is a way of getting an image when there is not enough existing light.

The cost of an electronic flash unit varies with the light output of the unit and depends on whether you purchase such desirable features as automatic exposure sensing and provision for bouncing the light off the ceiling to get a shadowless, more flattering quality of light. The easiest flash to use will be the *dedicated* unit that is designed to go with your particular model camera.

Manual flash units generally have a dial mounted on them for calculating the correct f/stop for tests at various distances, for films of the ISO number you set into the dial. Or you can make up your own flash guide number, determined by tests.

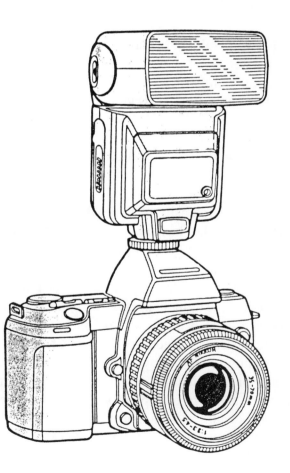

Jim Nixon *Boxer*
Electronic flash is the only practical way to stop very fast action when there isn't enough existing natural light. Although a slower shutter speed, such as 1/60 second, may be required to synchronize the flash (notice that some background illumination has been picked up), the duration of the flash—usually 1/1,000 second or faster—determines the actual exposure time. Because the flash was held a few feet from the camera, a feeling of roundness was retained in the subject and the lighting appears to be from natural sources.

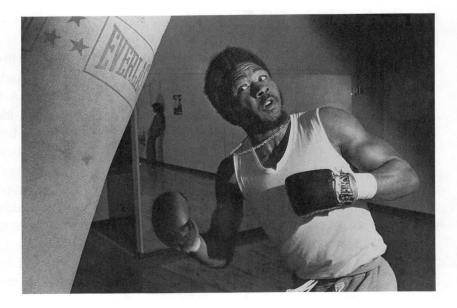

To calculate flash exposure, simply divide the guide number by the distance from flash to subject to determine the f/stop. For example:

$$\frac{\text{Guide Number}}{\text{Flash-to-subject distance}} = \text{f/stop}$$

Guide number = 110
Distance   = 10 feet

$$\frac{110}{10} = 11 \qquad \text{f/stop} = \text{f/11}$$

Because light intensity depends directly on the distance between the flash unit and the subject, you can produce unprintable negatives if the flash unit is mounted on the camera and if there is great depth of field in the picture. Near objects will, of course receive most of the light, being grossly overexposed while objects farther away will be underexposed. Automatic flash units expose for the nearest surface, whether or not that is what you want to emphasize.

Bounce flash yields the most natural effect, but may require about two stops more exposure than direct flash because of the absorption of light by the ceiling and because of the extra distance from flash to ceiling to subject. If your flash unit is not of the "hot shoe" type that makes its own direct connection to the camera, be sure to plug the flash cord into the X contact for electronic flash (older cameras had M and/or FP contacts for flashbulbs) and use the shutter speed recommended in your owner's manual—usually 1/60 or 1/125 second on 35mm single-lens reflexes.

Carrying case

Now that you have all this equipment you need a fitted case to put it in. Only tourists seem to carry the so-called ever-ready (never-ready) case that's fitted to the shape of the camera. Although these cases do provide some protection, most serious photographers find them a nuisance to work with, preferring to wear their camera(s) uncovered while shooting and to keep each camera body, lens, and accessory in its own compartment in a larger case or shoulder bag. Such cases can be purchased in light- and heat-reflecting aluminum, fibreboard, or flexible, padded cordura nylon. They usually are lined with foam inserts that you can arrange to custom fit your equipment. If you worry, however, about being the target of a camera thief, you may decide to use, instead of a regular camera case, a somewhat battered businessman's briefcase or student's bookbag that doesn't shout "photographer" to the world. Speaking of "wearing" equipment—photographers' vests are very popular. They're secure and convenient and have enough pockets for everything.

How to Test Your Equipment

After becoming familiar with a new camera or accessory you shouldn't need to worry much about further testing if you've bought it from a reputable dealer. The store probably will guarantee the equipment to your satisfaction. But after the warranty has expired, or if you're tempted to buy used equipment by mail or from an ad in the newspaper, you ought to know what to look for to avoid expensive repair bills.

Always be wary of equipment that looks badly beat up. That usually means that the previous owner didn't take very good care of it and that there may be some internal problems, as well as the external defects that show. Most manufacturers' service centers charge a minimum fee for handling a camera, whether the problem is simple or not, although you may be able to find a congenial local repair technician who will make minor adjustments for you without charging for a complete overhaul. Major repairs could cost more than a used camera is worth so a "bargain" may turn out not to be such a good deal after all.

Testing a camera

Here are some things to look for if you're thinking about buying a used camera: First check the lens for scratches. Reject it if these are severe, especially if scratches or dust appear to be inside the lens—an indication that the lens has been disassembled. A few tiny air bubbles in the glass will not cause trouble, however, and are a slight manufacturing defect that usually can be ignored. If the lens mount fits loosely and if the diaphragm setting ring or focusing ring either turns hard, grabs, grinds, or turns too loosely, suspect excessive wear or dirt in the mechanism.

Open the back of the camera and trip the shutter several times. Observe the automatic diaphragm at different f/stop settings. The diaphragm should stop down smartly when the shutter release button is pressed, and then open right up again with no delay after each exposure.

Test the exposure meter by reading light and dark subjects indoors and out. Compare the indicated camera settings either with another meter of known accuracy or estimate with the "Sunny 16" rule (pp. 95-96) or with an exposure table. Be sure the meter needle doesn't stick or move erratically—a sure sign of needed repair. If the camera has either a liquid crystal or LED readout, the figures should be legible and should change appropriately as you read areas of different brightness.

Try each of the shutter speeds several times to see whether they are consistent and whether they seem to be proportional to the amount of time the shutter remains open. If in doubt about the shutter, have it checked by someone who has an electronic shutter tester. A shutter that sticks open at any of the speeds may need an expensive overhaul.

Check out the focusing system by focusing sharply through the camera eyepiece at objects at various distances; then compare readings on the lens distance scale with your measured or estimated distances.

You can make an actual test of the coverage and resolving power of a lens simply by mounting the camera on a sturdy tripod and photographing the classified ad page from a newspaper. Tape the newspaper up on a wall in strong, even light. Fill the entire viewfinder with the image of the newspaper page, focus very carefully, and then make an exposure at each f/stop on the lens.

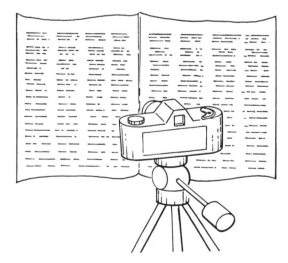

Photographing a newspaper classified ad page is a practical way to test a lens. Study the negatives with a magnifier to check sharpness and covering power at different apertures.

You'll have to compensate by adjusting the shutter speed, of course, to maintain proper exposure. Keep a record so that you can tell which negative was exposed at each f/stop; then when you study the negatives with a hand magnifier you can tell easily whether you can read the printing out to the edges of each frame. You may find that your lens is like most others, in that the edges of the negative tend to be somewhat less sharp than the center until you stop down to about f/4 or f/5.6, at which point the image becomes more uniformly sharp.

Shooting a roll of film in the camera may reveal more than just the quality of the lens. If the frames overlap or show uneven spacing between frames, the film advance mechanism may require repair. If there are any light leaks you'll see dark streaks or spots (light if you're exposing color slide film). A scratch along the length of the film may indicate a rough spot either on the camera body aperture or on the film pressure plate.

Testing flash synchronization

Electronic flash synchronization can be tested by opening up the back of the camera (with no film in it), aiming the lens at a light-colored wall, and flashing a "picture." Don't forget to turn on the flash unit and let it charge up (there usually is a "ready" light that comes on). Set the camera for the proper flash shutter speed (probably 1/60 or 1/125). If there is a cord attached to the flash, be sure that it is plugged into the proper place on the camera and that the lens is set to the widest aperture. You should see a brilliant flash through the lens at the exact instant that the shutter is wide open. If you see only a partial frame, either the wrong shutter speed has been selected or there is a real problem.

If you have any doubt about the condition of equipment you own or intend to buy, be sure to get the advice of a responsible dealer, a repair technician, your photo instructor, or an experienced photographer friend. If your equipment does need repair, be sure that it goes to a reliable service shop and be sure to get a written estimate of the cost.

Contemporary cameras are marvelous precision instruments. Care for yours respectfully and it will serve you well.

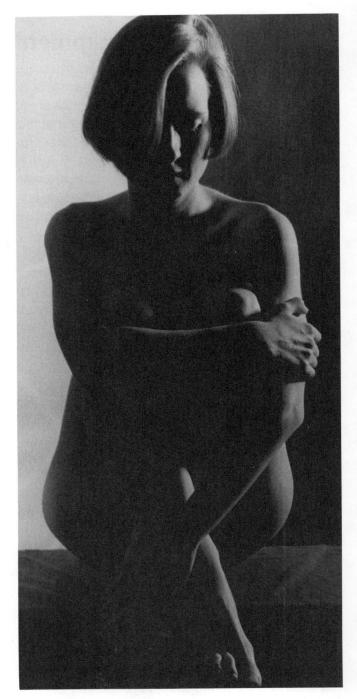

Michelle Campbell *Chiaroscuro*

The mastery of studio light is basic to the transformation of the ordinary into the special.

(Ken Marcus, photographer)

Films and Exposure 5

Getting it on Film

Although you'll discover later how to work some "magic" in the darkroom to improve the quality of your prints, you must remember that if detail isn't present in the negative, you can't print it. Photographic films have certain inherent limitations that have to be learned about and lived with. In this chapter you'll have a chance to experiment enough to find out how far you can err in exposure and development and what kinds of controls are possible.

Characteristics of black-and-white films

There are many types of black-and-white films. Some, such as high-contrast copying and infrared, are intended for specialized use, but there is a wide variety of general purpose films. One type is chosen instead of another for one or more of the following reasons:

Speed

Exposure index (EI or ISO) is a measure of relative sensitivity to light. A film rated 400 by the manufacturer is assumed to be four times as sensitive as a film rated 100. The slower film (100), therefore, would require four times as much exposure, (two f/stops more) than the faster film (400). Under certain conditions, experienced photographers sometimes rate film at a speed different from that recommended by the manufacturer.

Grain

Grain is the extent to which the tiny silver particles forming the image tend to clump together and form a mottled, or spotty effect. Generally, the faster the film (higher EI or ISO rating) the more tendency there is for grain to become visible upon enlargement of the negative. Color transparency films are composed of dye images instead of silver grains, but high speed color films also tend to show a grainy look when slides are projected or enlarged.

Color sensitivity

Black-and-white film is either panchromatic (sensitive to all colors of visible light) or limited in sensitivity to only part of the spectrum. Because nearly all films today are panchromatic they must be kept in total darkness until processing is complete. A few special-purpose process and copying films, however, may be handled and developed under a red or yellow safelight.

Contrast

Contrast refers to the relative differences in density between dark and light tones in the negative image. In both black-and-white and color, slower (lower EI or ISO) films tend to have more inherent contrast than faster films. Generally, low speed, finer grain and higher contrast tend to go together in some films, whereas high speed, more noticeable grain and lower contrast are common characteristics of others.

Latitude

Another important characteristic of film is latitude—that is, the amount the film can be underexposed or overexposed without serious loss of image quality. Although color transparency (slide) films are limited in latitude to within about one f/stop, modern black-and-white and color negative films can compensate for human or mechanical error within as much as two or three f/stops and still produce a printable negative.

With *negative* films it is better to err on the side of *too much* exposure rather than too little. If there is enough exposure to record density in the shadow areas of the negative, it can be printed; if there is not

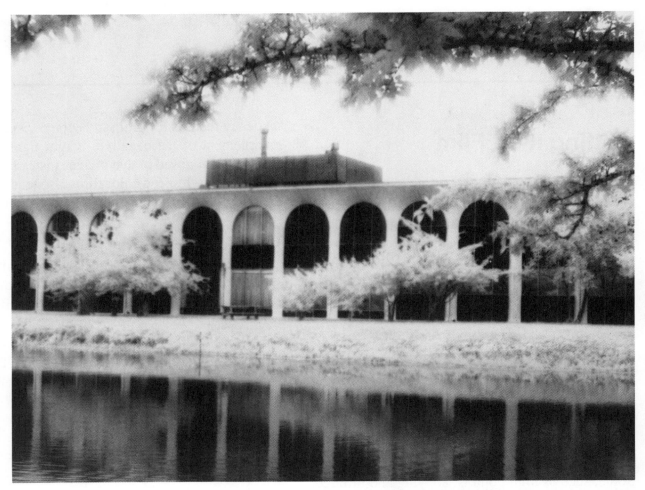

Robert Fleming *The Forum Building*
Infrared film records familiar things with an eerie
difference. This specially sensitized film must be
exposed through a deep red filter to eliminate most
visible light.

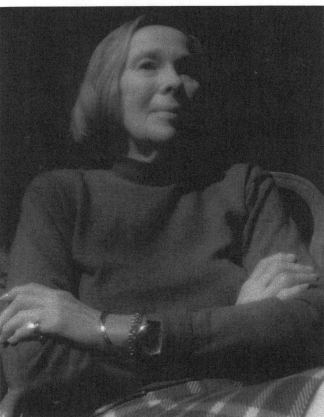

Todd Wickersham *Grandmother*
In another example of infrared, notice the unusual
rendering of skin tones. Also characteristic of
infrared film are accentuated grain and a soft,
diffuse image quality.

enough density, the missing shadow detail cannot be restored in printing. Greatly overexposed negatives produce grainy and unsharp prints. The rule is exactly opposite for reversal films such as color slides. Because of their limited latitude, color transparency films usually should be exposed for the important *high* values, to prevent light skin tones, textured snow or sand, etc. from being too light and "washed out." Slides that are too dark are the result of underexposure.

Reciprocity

This will bother you when making very long time exposures. It also can be a problem with flash duration shorter than 1/1,000 second. Reciprocity is another word for the $E = I \times T$ rule that says lens opening and shutter speed relationships are linear. They are, except for very long and extremely short exposures. Reciprocity *departure* will affect exposures of one second or longer. For example, with Kodak T-Max 400 film and a metered exposure calling for one second, you should open the lens about 1/3 f/stop. Ten seconds should be increased to at least 15 seconds or open 1/2 stop. 100 seconds should be 300 seconds, or open up one and one-half stops. For precise reciprocity corrections, refer to the film manufacturer's published data.

Choosing a film

Because switching between films can be confusing, my advice to beginners is to select one film and stick with it until another type is needed. Many people standardize on a 400-speed film because photos can be made in available light with a hand held camera where a slower film would require a tripod. 35mm negatives from 400-speed film usually can be enlarged to 8"x10" before the grain becomes objectionable. Some photographers expose 400-speed film at a higher or lower exposure index. On pages 122-123 you will find a method for determining an optimum "working" exposure index for your choice of film, exposed with your meter, in your camera, and developed following your own standardized procedure.

When fine print quality is more important to you than convenience or action-stopping, a slower film will be called for. Except in extremely bright light,

slow film will require a slow shutter speed, particularly when you stop the lens down to get depth of field. This will mean using a tripod.

Very slow, fine-grained films are appropriate when enormous display enlargements are to be made, when increased contrast is desirable, as in copying documents, or when you want to reproduce extremely fine detail and texture in the subject.

Characteristics of Color Films

Speed, grain, contrast, latitude and reciprocity

These characteristics apply to color films as they do to black-and white, but there are some differences.

Color films also are available in a wide range of speeds. As with black-and-white, grain is proportional to speed, so select fast film when you have to shoot hand-held under existing light. Use slow film when you can mount your camera on a tripod and stop down the lens, or when using flash. Also, slower color films are the best choice when you want maximum contrast.

Color negative films are almost as tolerant of over- and underexposure as black-and-white; but with color transparency (slide) films, latitude is very limited. When in doubt, the rule with negative films is to be sure to give enough exposure to record detail in the shadow areas. Transparency films require just the opposite: be sure not to overexpose and "wash out" the important highlight values.

Reciprocity departure is even more critical with color not only because of getting adequate exposure, but because the color balance may shift in unwanted ways. Special color films intended for long or short exposures are available in medium and large format to aid the professional.

Color balance

Color transparency (slide) films are manufactured specifically for exposure under predictable lighting conditions, either daylight or incandescent. Except for special effects, the colors of light should not be mixed. Fluorescent light is an example of misleading appearance and it doesn't even appear on

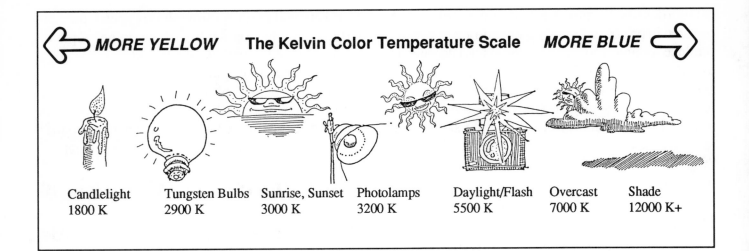

Candlelight	Tungsten Bulbs	Sunrise, Sunset	Photolamps	Daylight/Flash	Overcast	Shade
1800 K	2900 K	3000 K	3200 K	5500 K	7000 K	12000 K+

the Kelvin scale (above). Because of their overall bluish appearance, fluorescent lights would seem to balance with daylight color film. But so-called "daylight" fluorescents usually are extremely weak in red. They give an unpleasant greenish color on film, unless compensated for with a magenta filter.

Electronic flash illumination is very close in color to the light for which "daylight" color films are balanced. Incandescent (tungsten) lamps appear quite a bit warmer, more toward the lower end of the Kelvin color temperature scale (see table). A picture will appear overall yellowish-orange if photographed under incandescent light on color film balanced for daylight or electronic flash. Conversely, moonlight effects can be obtained by slightly underexposing color film that is balanced for incandescent illumination, in daylight, without the appropriate conversion filter.

Although nearly any kind of color film can be filtered for acceptable color balance under standard kinds of illumination, it's best to get the right kind of film in the first place, making any minor adjustments in exposure or filtration according to the manufacturer's instructions.

Most color negative films are balanced for daylight and flash. That's why photofinishers' prints from negatives exposed by incandescent light often look strongly orange. The automatic printer was set for "normal" daylight/flash balance. Good custom prints can be made from these negatives, but the printing filtration must be adjusted. An alternative is to use a bluish filter over the camera lens when taking the pictures.

Storing Films

Whether black-and-white or color, you'll do best to buy fresh film and store it in a cool, dry place. Factory sealed packages of film will keep well for two years or more in a refrigerator or freezer, even well past the expiration date printed on the box. But to prevent moisture condensation, allow at least half an hour for refrigerated film to reach room temperature before unsealing the package. Frozen film should thaw for at least an hour before the seal is broken. Film that has been stored in a hot, humid place may show gray or greenish overall fog or poor color quality. This is why outdated film may not be a bargain unless you can be certain that it has been refrigerated.

Loading Bulk Film

Should you buy bulk film? Some experts recommend it and others don't, although the economy of purchasing 35mm film in 100-foot rolls is very appealing. If you shoot enough pictures to use the nearly 700 exposures you get from a 100-foot roll before it goes out of date, the cost per shot with bulk film will be less than half what it would cost to buy factory loaded film magazines. But on the other hand, you have to invest in a bulk film loader and a supply of reloadable magazines. And bulk loading takes time and care.

The best reason for *not* using bulk film is the danger of scratches, fingerprints, or fog. With so-called daylight film loaders, the film may have to pass between felt light-trap pads four times instead of only twice with commercially loaded film. Furthermore, there is more than twice the risk of an embedded speck of sand or grit gouging the entire length of a roll because the felt lips of the loader and the reused magazines are less likely to be clean. Light fog will occur at both the head and tail ends of each roll (you have to be careful not to shoot right up to the very end—stop one or two exposures short), and there is always the possibility that someone might accidentally unscrew the lid of the loader and fog your entire bulk-film supply.

Some special films, however, are available only in long rolls. And it is convenient to be able to load short lengths of film for testing and for special processing. If you do load bulk film, be careful to handle the film only by the edges or by the very end; be sure to use strong enough tape (3/4-inch masking tape will do) so the film doesn't pull off the spool; inspect all felt light trap lips for dirt; blow out dust from inside the magazines; and beware of light fog. Be sure to insert the spool in the magazine shell so that the long end of the spool will point toward the bottom of the camera when it is loaded. Most cameras will require that you trim the leader to fit the takeup spool.

Bulk loading, like everything else in photography, is subject to Murphy's Law.

Nothing is as easy
as it looks.
It will take longer
than you think.
If anything can go
wrong, it will.

(Murphy's Law)

Determining Exposure

A good exposure meter is a very valuable tool, but personal judgment is still important. If your meter is working correctly and you use it intelligently, you will make more printable negatives and projectable slides. Fine prints can best be made from properly exposed negatives. But since most meters are programmed for "average" conditions, you will need to learn when to manually override the camera's settings.

Both your meter and your judgment will be needed when taking pictures in deep shade, indoors with available light, or whenever the subject is backlit or unusually light or dark. If in doubt, *bracket*—that is, expose at the setting you think is right; then, to make sure, shoot more frames at one-half or one stop more and less, depending on the subject. Even professionals do this. Many cameras have a "backlight" setting that gives one or two stops more exposure. Others have plus or minus adjustments. Bracketing can be done by adjusting the shutter and aperture manually or by resetting the film speed. Read more about bracketing and exposure compensation in the zone system section later in this chapter.

Good judgment comes from experience,
and experience...well, that comes from
bad judgment.   (Anonymous)

The "Sunny 16" rule

What can you do if your meter malfunctions or the battery dies? If you're working outdoors there can be two ways out: First, refer to the film manufacturer's instructions printed on a data sheet or inside the box. The second solution is to use the "Sunny 16" rule. Here how it works:

Exposure for an "average" subject, outdoors on a sunny day between about 10:00 a.m. and 4:00 p.m., equals the EI or ISO of the film *as the shutter speed* at aperture f/16. For example, with 400-speed film the settings under "Sunny 16" conditions would be 1/500 at f/16. 100-speed film would require 1/125 at f/16. (Your shutter probably isn't marked for 1/400 or 1/100, so use the closest setting).

But what if it's not a sunny day? Try this: For hazy sun, open up the lens to f/11. For light overcast, open up to f/8. If the sky is heavily overcast, or if your subject is in open shade on a sunny day, your basic settings for 100-speed film will be about 1/125 at f/5.6. 400-speed film will require 1/500 at the same f/stop range; 64-speed film would require 1/60, etc. Remember, this is the *basic* exposure. For depth of field and for action photos you can compensate between lens openings and shutter speeds all you want, as long as you maintain the basic relationship according to the speed of the film and the amount of light on the subject.

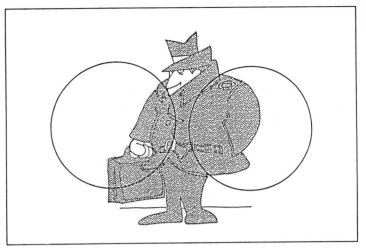

Averaging

How meters work

Most built-in exposure meters average the brightness of the entire field of the lens by reading samples (see diagram). Such meters are designed with the assumption that the average photographer will be shooting subjects of overall average brightness. So-called *center weighted* meters assume that you're going to place the most important area of your subject in the center of the viewfinder and that you want that central portion reproduced as a middle gray. *Spot* meters scan an even smaller central area so you can move the camera around and compare the brightness of subject and background. Finally, *matrix* metering scans many areas of the camera's field of view, and feeds the readings to a microprocessor which attempts to figure out which is subject and which is background and integrate this data into a compensated exposure setting the way it would be done by an experienced photographer.

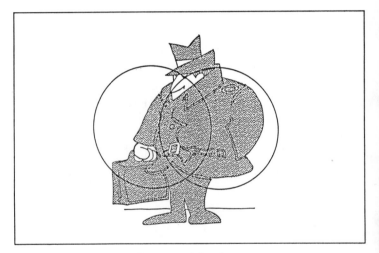

Center weighted

Exposure meters built into cameras are of the *reflected light* type, and they are all subject to the same limitation: they are designed to convert everything they read into an average middle gray. This averaging feature simplifies exposure determination, but it also can be seriously misleading if the subject is not of average brightness. With many types of subject matter, if you want to reproduce black and white with a full range of gray tones in between, you have to learn to use the meter to help you previsualize what the final print is going to look like if properly exposed.

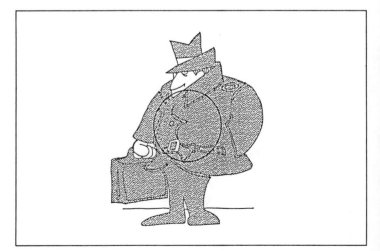

Spot reading

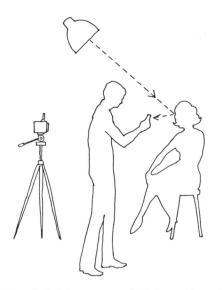

A reflected-light meter reads light reflected from the subject. The meter should be held so that it neither reads its own shadow nor is affected by background brightness.

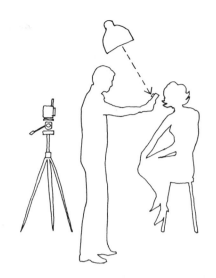

An incident light meter reads light falling on the subject. It is not affected by variations in brightness of the subject or background.

Reflected light meters

A hand-held meter should be brought in quite close to the part of the subject you're reading, but don't get so close that you read the shadow of the meter or your own shadow. Why get so close? Because if the background or adjacent areas are significantly brighter or darker than the area you want to expose for, the meter will include those areas and make the reading inaccurate. Spot meters, of course, are designed to read a very small area from farther away.

Cameras with built-in meters can be handled as if the entire camera were the meter: move in very close for the reading, note the settings called for, and then back off to shoot from the same angle from which you made the reading. If the meter display changes, ignore it. Leave the camera set as indicated when you made the close-up reading. When in automatic mode, lock in the settings while making the reading, then back off to shoot.

> *The ability to anticipate...the final print while viewing the subject makes it possible to apply the...controls of the craft... to achieve the desired result.*
>
> *(Ansel Adams, photographer)*

Incident light meters

Many meters come with incident light adapters and some meters are designed primarily to read the light falling on the subject, rather than the light reflected from it. These are called incident light meters and most flash meters are of this type. Incident readings should be made with the meter pointed *toward the camera* from the subject's position (see diagram). Extreme highlight and shadow values, stray light, and background brightness have little effect on an incident light reading, so this technique is especially recommended for color photography, for copy work, and for situations in which the lighting is uneven or when small objects are being photographed against a contrasting background.

Because of their more limited exposure latitude, color reversal films usually must be exposed close to the standard 18 percent middle gray to which meters are calibrated. Although the incident light method will eliminate false readings from unwanted values, it does not separate the important light and dark areas in the subject. These high and low values are very significant in black-and-white work because you can control the range of values in the brightness scale by manipulating exposure and development. The best way to get really superb black-and-white negatives is to use an accurate reflected light meter, following a procedure known as the zone system.

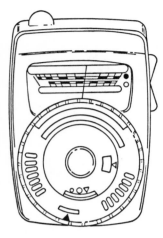

A reflected-light meter with incident-light adapter.

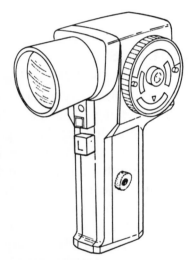

A reflected-light spot meter.

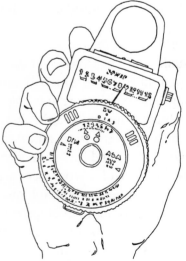

An incident-light meter.

Zones of Subject Brightness

Low values	Zone 0 (five stops less)	Complete lack of density in the negative image, other than film base density plus fog. Total black in print.
	Zone I (four stops less)	Slight tonality, but no texture. Unlighted interiors through open doorways. Practically indistinguishable in print from total black.
	Zone II (three stops less)	First suggestion of texture. Deep tonalities representing the darkest part of the image in which some detail is required.
	Zone III (two stops less)	Dark, textured materials such as dark clothing, hair, and fur. Low values showing adequate texture in the print.
Middle values	Zone IV (one stop less)	Average dark foliage. Dark stone. Landscape shadow. Recommended shadow value for portraits in sunlight.
	Zone V (meter reading)	Clear north sky. Dark skin in sunlight. Gray stone. Average weathered wood. (*Note:* This is the 18 per cent middle gray for which exposure meters are calibrated.)
	Zone VI (one stop more)	Average Caucasion skin value. Light stone. Average sand. Shadows on snow in sunlight.
High values	Zone VII (two stops more)	Very light skin. Light-gray objects such as concrete walls and light-colored hair and fur. Average snow or light sand with acute side lighting.
	Zone VIII (three stops more)	Whites with textures and delicate values (not blank whites). Snow in full shade. White painted surfaces. Highlights on Caucasian skin.
	Zone IX (four stops more)	Glaring white surfaces. Snow in flat sunlight. White without texture. Light sources and reflections. Usually represented in the print by the maximum white of the paper surface.

Adapted from Ansel Adams, *The Negative*, New York Graphic Society, 1981, p. 60.

Most...photographers...forget that they are never photographing an object, but rather light itself. Where there is no light, they will have no picture; where there is remarkable light, they <u>may</u> have a remarkable picture.

(*Galen Rowell, photographer*)

The Zone System

Developed by Ansel Adams for his own use and written about by Adams and many other photographers, the zone system forces you to carefully previsualize your subject matter as you want it to appear in the final print. You must observe and compare the important tonal values in each scene you want to photograph, mentally placing each value at the desired place on a ten-step gray scale. Each step of the gray scale is referred to as a zone (see table).

The zone system is based on the ancient photographers' axiom, *"Expose for the shadows and develop for the highlights."* Photographers relied on this principle long before the invention of exposure meters and panchromatic films. The old-timers judged exposure by examining the brightness of the shadow areas of the image as they appeared on the view camera ground glass, exposed according to experience, and then developed their slow glass plates or films by the light of a dim red bulb or lantern until the highlights appeared to be of the proper density.

The principle of the zone system applies today with black-and-white films and can be very helpful in exposing color, although the development controls cannot be used with color.

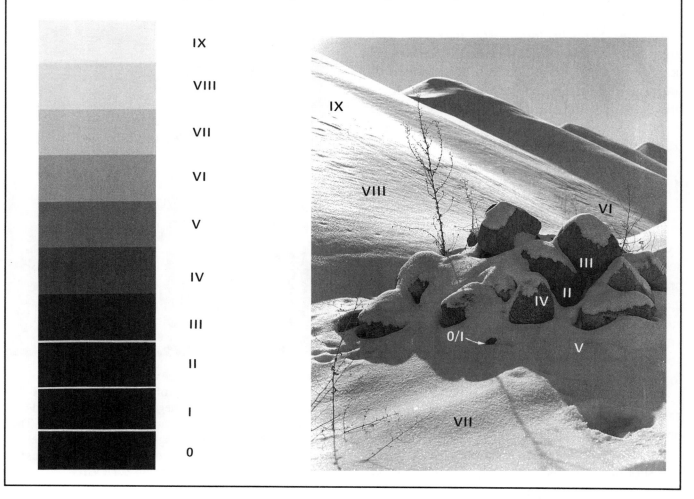

Ron Null *Snow Mountains*
This subject contains a full range of tonal values. So does the original photograph. Although printing inks cannot show separation between the extreme values at both ends of the scale, zone numbers have been placed in the photograph to indicate approximately what the corresponding steps would be on the ten-step gray scale used in the zone system. Each step, or zone, represents the equivalent of one f/stop difference in negative density.

Shadow density in the negative is determined largely by exposure, more or less independent of development time, whereas highlight density increases very rapidly in proportion to length of development. If it weren't true that low and high negative densities responded differently to development, the zone system wouldn't work. Remember, the rule is to expose for the shadows (lower values—Zones I through IV) and develop for the highlights (higher values—Zones VI through IX). Ideally, you would read and place on the gray scale each important zone appearing in the subject. However, if you place even *one* zone correctly on the gray scale, all the other zones will fall into their relative places within the limits of the film used and the development given.

Placing brightness values

There are five different ways of determining exposure with the zone system, the first four of which are timesaving shortcuts: (**1**) the *darkest important shadow* method, (**2**) the *most important highlight* method, (**3**) the *substitute reading* method, (**4**) the *standard reading* method (recommended for color), and (**5**) the *brightness-range* method, which gives you control over black-and-white negative contrast as well as density. When you understand the principle of the zone system and are able to previsualize the zones into which significant subject brightnesses should fall, you'll be able to choose the best method for each situation.

1. Darkest important shadow

This method is simple, yet it keeps you from losing significant shadow detail in a subject such as a dark rock formation, dark animal, or a woodland scene with spotty areas of sunlight and shade. If you previsualize the zone into which the darkest important values should fall (usually Zone III) and expose so that zone is placed correctly on the gray scale, you'll record the textures in those dark areas. Other zones in the scene then will fall into place according to their relative brightness.

If the higher zones don't fit the gray scale, you can develop the film so they do. If the negative is properly exposed and developed you should be able to tell the difference in the final print between areas that should appear as Zones VI, VII, VIII, and IX.

When you make a close-up reading of the darkest important shadow areas the meter will give you a *Zone V* reading (middle gray). Unless you want those shadow areas to *be* Zone V, you'll have to convert the reading to the correct zone. The easiest way to do this is to count zones as you *stop down the lens*. If the chosen shadow area should be Zone III, simply read the meter to determine the f/stop for making that area Zone V; then count "Zone IV" as you close down one stop and "Zone III" as you close down another stop.

For example, a direct, reflected-light meter reading of a dark, textured area indicates an exposure of 1/30 at f/8. You know that this setting would be the correct exposure to render that area as Zone V, but

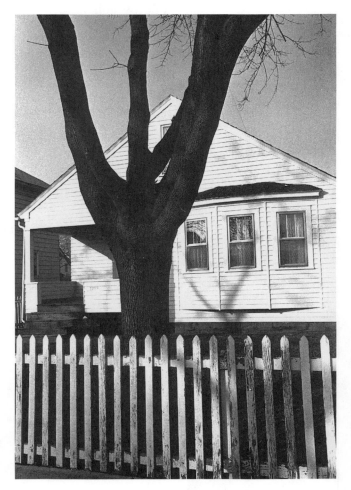

Gary Cialdella *White House with Picket Fence*
The extreme brightness range of this subject calls for N-(minus) development of the negative. Exposure should be based on Zone III to retain detail in the dark tree bark. The difference between reflected-light meter readings of the bark and the brightest portions of the white painted house indicated N-2 development to retain Zone VIII.

you want it to reproduce as Zone III. So as you stop down from f/8 to f/11 you say to yourself, "Zone IV"; as you stop down one more stop to f/16 you say, "Zone III." Of course you can leave the aperture alone and adjust the shutter speed instead. Suppose you choose f/16 because you want maximum depth of field. Your meter indicates 1/8 at f/16. How would you place Zone III? *Increase the shutter speed* two "stops" from 1/8 to 1/30.

The rule is to give *less* exposure than the meter says to place Zones I through IV. If you were basing exposure on higher values instead of lower values, you would give *more* exposure than the meter indicates to place Zones VI through IX. No change is necessary to place Zone V, because the meter reads directly for Zone V. Count zones only on the marked shutter speeds or on the numbered f/stops of the regular scale (that is, f/5.6, f/8, f/11, f/16, etc.).

Don't count the halfway click stops that may be on your lens. They are there simply to help you make slight adjustments in exposure.

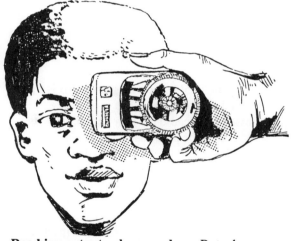

Read important values up close. But when making a close-up reading, be careful not to include your own shadow!

2. Most important highlight

Choose this method when shadows are less important than light skin tones, snow texture, or other values above middle gray. This also is usually the most convenient metering method for color reversal (slide) films.

Instead of reading the shadows, you read the skin tone or other light value directly with your meter and place that Zone V reading on the chosen zone. For example, in an outdoor portrait of a white person in full sunlight the brightest side of the face reads 1/125 at f/16. You want the skin not to record as Zone V, but as Zone VI, so you *open up the lens one stop* from f/16 to f/11, saying to yourself, "Zone VI" as you set the aperture. If instead of a face, you've read side-lighted, textured snow or light sand, you would *open up two stops* from the Zone V reading to place the snow or sand on Zone VII. If you wanted to record flat lighted snow or sand as Zone VIII, you would open up the lens *three stops,* from f/16 to f/5.6 or leave the aperture at f/16 and *slow the shutter* three "stops" from 1/125 to 1/15.

In some cases you may have to lose background detail in order to place the most important values in their proper zones; but be careful not to let your meter include those unwanted background areas in its reading. If you remember to read the single most important value (usually skin tones if people are in the picture) and place that value in the desired zone, you won't be misled by the background. Since your meter can't tell what the most vital part of the subject is, it will average everything you allow it to read into a Zone V middle gray.

3. Substitute reading

A variation of the *Most Important Shadow or Highlight* methods, a substitute reading is useful when it's impossible or inconvenient to approach the subject for a direct, close-up meter reading. You could read nearby snow to substitute for snow in similar light on a distant mountain peak. Or the trunk or foliage of a large nearby tree can substitute for trees on the other side of a river.

The important thing is to be sure that the light conditions are the same, that you hold the meter properly to avoid false readings from contrasting background values, and that you count out the zones correctly as you adjust lens or shutter settings from those indicated by the meter for Zone V.

Before [Ansel Adams], people thought mountains were made out of stone. He demonstrated they were made out of light and were never the same twice.

(John Szarkowski, museum director)

4. Standard reading

Appropriate for exposing color films of limited exposure latitude, the *Standard Reading* method is based on consistent Zone V readings from an 18 percent gray card or incident-light meter or on reflected-light readings from some other standard value. Flash meters usually read incident light and are calibrated for Zone V. Other than a gray card, the most commonly used reflective value is the back (or palm) of the photographer's hand. Since light skin generally reflects at Zone VI in full light and dark skin at Zone V, this is a uniform standard that's always available.

Color films normally should be exposed for Zone V, allowing the higher and lower values to reproduce wherever they fall on each side of middle gray. Note that this is what you're doing when using the *Most Important Highlight* method.

As with a black-and-white portrait, you would open up one stop in color if you've read Zone VI skin instead of a Zone V gray card. You would do this because the meter has read the skin tone not as Zone VI, but as Zone V middle gray. Color reversal films ordinarily do not have enough exposure latitude to place zones more than about one stop away from "normal," although there might be exceptional circumstances.

When your experience doesn't allow you to completely previsualize the result, bracketing is a good practice and pros do it every day. Bracketing means making one exposure at exactly what your meter reading and calculations indicate, and then making another exposure at one-half stop, one stop, or more additional exposure and another at the same amount less exposure. When experience tells you that it's a waste of film to bracket both directions, such as long exposures when reciprocity is a problem, then simply extend bracketing as needed.

5. Brightness range

The *Brightness Range* method gives you greatest control over all the zones of subject brightness. At its most complex, this approach calls for reading each subject area separately with a spot meter and plotting these readings on a gray scale so that the brightness of each part of the subject is matched to the optimum zone. If the subject brightness scale doesn't match the scale of zones, then plus or minus development of the film is indicated (only for black-and-white).

At its simplest, the *Brightness Range* method calls for reading only the lowest and highest significant values (frequently Zones III and VII) and averaging the two readings. You might choose, for example, to read both a Zone III tree trunk and Zone

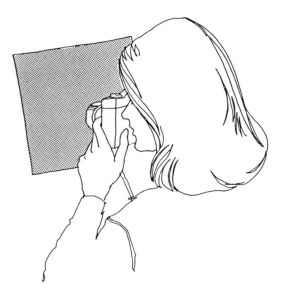

An 18% neutral test card (gray card) is the standard to which exposure meters are calibrated. Because the gray card represents Zone V it can be used as a standard reference in practically any situation. When you determine exposure from reading a gray card, place the card so it receives exactly the same amount of light as the principal subject. Move in close with your meter—or your entire camera if using through-the-lens metering. Be careful not to read the area beyond the gray card or to read your own shadow!

Your hand can serve as a "gray card" if you place the reading on the appropriate zone.

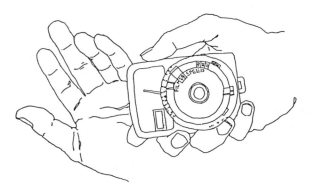

VII side-lighted snow. Reading from the tree trunk, the meter indicates 1/125 at f/5.6, while the snow indicates 1/125 at f/22. Remember that these exposures would render both the high and low values as Zone V middle gray. The difference between the readings is exactly four stops (four zones), which it should be, and an exposure of 1/125 at f/11, halfway between the extremes, would place both the tree trunk and the snow within the limits of the film and reproduce all values in between. This is exactly the same setting you would have obtained had you placed separately either Zone III or Zone VII or based the exposure on a Zone V gray card reading.

Averaging the highest and lowest readings is a timesaving technique when both high and low values are the same number of zones above and below Zone V middle gray. But averaging doesn't work if all or most of the zones are skewed to either side of Zone V. In a very low-key subject, for example, the values may range from Zone II through Zone V, with nothing lighter than Zone V, except perhaps a tiny catchlight or reflection that isn't measured by the meter. In this case, the exposure should be based on the Zone V reading to place all of the low values properly. An average exposure would place the Zone V value between Zones III and IV, adding unnecessary density to the entire negative.

Similarly, a high-key subject with a tonal range extending from Zone VI through Zone IX may not contain any low values, or the low values may be so small as to be insignificant in determining exposure. An average setting halfway between Zones VI and IX would result in an undesirably thin negative, so the exposure should be anchored to Zone VI.

With many subjects, reading the highest and lowest important values and setting the exposure halfway between will result in a Zone V average, the same as a single overall reading of the entire subject or an incident-light reading. With other subjects, however, the averaging method may lead you astray either because the significant zones don't fall equally on both sides of Zone V or because the brightness range from highlight to shadow may be greater than the film can record. This may result in an unsatisfactory compromise of underexposure at the shadow end of the scale and overexposure of the highest values. When this happens, the print will lack shadow detail and high values will be "washed out."

Adjusting contrast by development

Black-and-white film will reproduce at best a range of only eight zones with detail from deepest shadow to brightest high value. This means that Zone VIII can be no more than 128 times as bright as Zone I. If you detect a greater brightness range than eight zones, or 128:1, you won't be able to record the entire gray scale properly unless you reduce the subject contrast. One way to do this (necessary for color) is to increase the amount of light in the shadows with flash or a reflector or decrease the brightness of the highlights by shading them. With black-and-white you can reduce the contrast of the negative by developing it for less than the normal time.

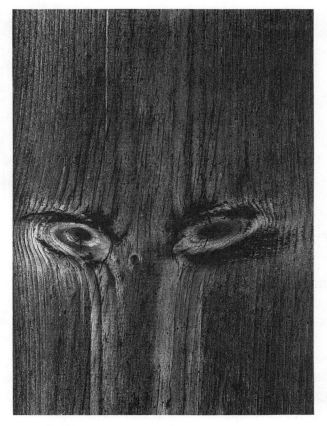

John Griffioen *Pine Board*
Do you see, in this photograph, a board or a baboon? Or is the image, for you, composed solely of textures and convoluted lines? With nearly all the values Zone IV and darker, this is an excellent example of the kind of subject matter that requires N+ development.

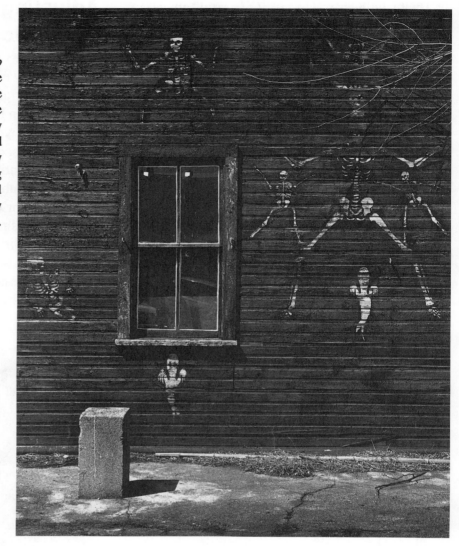

D. Curl *Abbott's Magic Shop*
Nearly all the texture of this bizarre
building was in the weatherbeaten Zone
III black paint. Careful placement of the
wooden siding on Zone III was necessary
to avoid underexposure. Extended
development (N+3) increased the density
of the white painted figures, enabling
them to print as Zones VII and VIII and
the tiny white areas around the window
panes as Zone IX.

Compression

Let's take an example in which the development time should be reduced. Suppose a Zone III tree trunk reads 1/125 at f/5.6, while the Zone VII snow reads 1/125 at f/32. That's a *five*-zone difference instead of the desired *four* zones. In this case, normal *minus one zone* (N-1) development is indicated. If the tree trunk and the snow were *six* zones apart when the difference should be only four zones, correct development would call for normal *minus two zones* (N-2).

> ### *One zone = One f/stop*

Expansion

Suppose you want to expand, instead of compress, the placement of the highest values. For example, you're shooting the scene just described, but on a very dull overcast day. The Zone III tree trunk reads 1/30 at f/4, while the snow reads 1/30 at f/11. The difference between Zone III and Zone VII is only *three* stops instead of the desired four, so normal development *plus one zone* (N+1) would be indicated. If you wanted the snow to be rendered as Zone VIII, you'd want to extend development to normal *plus two zones* (N+2) to bring the high values up where they belong. Otherwise your print would seem gray and flat.

The *brightness range* method is very convenient for determining exposure if you're using sheet film and can develop single sheets according to whether you want to expand the brightness range (N *plus*) or compress it (N *minus*). Advanced photographers who work with roll film and who can afford to own extra camera bodies or extra film backs, often load one camera or one back with film to be developed normally, reserving and marking another body or back for either minus or plus development. You'll learn much more about zone-system development in Chapter 6.

Problems with Exposure

A sensitive and accurate exposure meter is indispensable for making fine quality photographs under varied lighting conditions. But the meter won't solve all of your problems. Your meter may not be entirely accurate; it may read consistently high or low. If the shutter speeds of your camera are slightly inaccurate in the same direction, you may find that the film speed for which you should set your camera is different from the rating indicated by the film manufacturer. Slight differences in processing technique may also affect the way you rate the film. If you have doubts about the accuracy of your equipment or the quality of your results, ask your instructor or someone with a densitometer or an electronic shutter speed tester to examine your negatives and perhaps to test your camera.

A person who works
with their hands
is a laborer;
a person who works
with their hands and head
is a craftsperson;
and a person who works
with their hands, head
and heart
is an artist.

(Author unknown)

[Imagemaking is] like inventing a
language at the same time I am
using it.

(Jerry N. Uelsmann, photographer)

Take notes

Don't be lazy about taking notes and keeping records of your exposure settings, especially in unusual situations. There's nothing wrong with making a mistake the first time, but keeping careful records will save you the embarrassment, frustration and expense of repeating errors. You'll soon learn to estimate the proper exposure in many situations, verifying it with your meter. And you'll learn to compensate for unusual lighting conditions by varying exposure and development.

The only way to become a skilled photographer is to make lots of photographs. Be prepared to use plenty of film, but expose it systematically. follow careful meter readings or printed exposure guides, but keep accurate records of every frame you expose. When the film is developed, compare your negatives with the exposure data. Then you won't repeat your mistakes.

You'll be wise to use a single kind of film most of the time and to standardize on processing. To learn the most about what your camera can do, don't limit your photographic activities to average scenes on sunny days. Look for chances to make pictures indoors, in bad weather, and under pressure. This additional experience will make you a much better photographer.

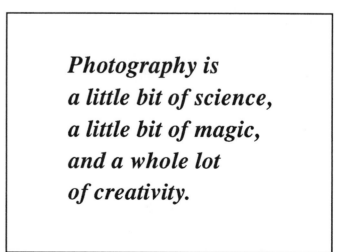

Photography is
a little bit of science,
a little bit of magic,
and a whole lot
of creativity.

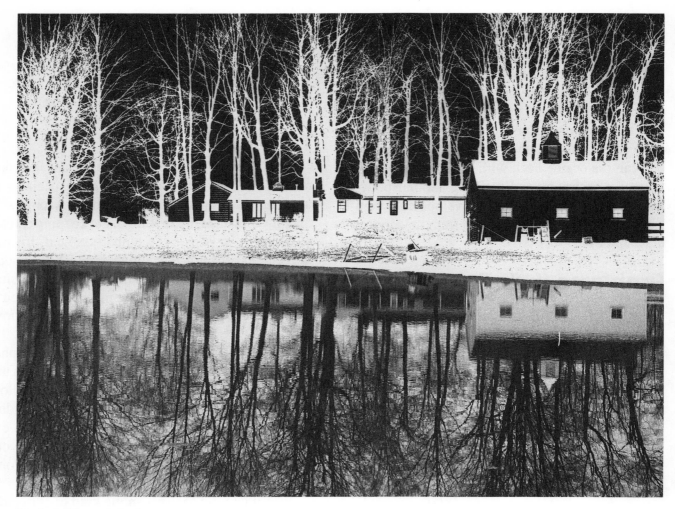

Kevin Miller *Lakeshore*
Both negative and positive images were cleverly juxtaposed
in a single enlargement. The original negative was printed
and then a film positive was printed on the same sheet of
paper. An opaque paper mask was cut carefully to parallel
the shoreline.

*Black-and-white photography has a
potential for luminosity unequaled by any
other medium. Its incomparable range
allows me to contain both the material
weight of reality and the ethereal weight-
lessness of light. I can create monochro-
matic images that appear to glow from
within, radiating a strange and wonderful
inner light.* (Sally Gall, photographer)

Processing Black-and-White Film   *6*

The Negative

Film that has been exposed in the camera contains an invisible latent image made up of tiny silver particles that have been changed by light. These exposed silver particles suspended in the film's emulsion layer turn dark during development and form a visible negative image in which light and dark tones are opposite to what they were in the original scene.

Dark and light tones are reversed

Light parts of the subject reflect more light onto the film, so those areas of the negative appear dark because they are filled with more opaque silver particles than the shadows. The darkest parts of the subject appear nearly transparent on the negative because very little silver has been deposited there.

After film has been developed, the silver grains that were not used to form the negative image are still sensitive to light. An acid-hardening fixing bath dissolves the unexposed silver, making the film safe to examine by ordinary light and more resistant to physical damage. After fixing, the amount of silver remaining in a given area of the negative determines its density or opacity.

Although not absolutely necessary, an acetic acid stop bath or a water rinse often is used between developer and fixer to stop development quickly and evenly and to make the fixer last longer.

Following the fixer, a bath in running water washes away chemicals remaining in the emulsion, so that the negatives do not become stained or faded.

Do it in the dark!

Most films must remain in total darkness until after they have been through the developer and fixer. Processing may be carried out in ordinary room light, but first the film must be loaded into a light-tight developing tank in a completely dark room or changing bag.

Commercial labs process color film with automatic machinery, but you can develop color negatives and most slide films in exactly the same type of tank used for black-and-white. Different chemicals are required for color, and even more care must be taken with temperature, time and agitation.

Be careful; practice the process

Carelessness has no place in the darkroom. The only way to get consistently good negatives is to control accurately the temperature of the chemical solutions and the length of time the film is in each one. It's also very important to keep everything clean, because pictures can be ruined by chemical contamination or stains caused by hands and equipment that have not been washed and dried after being used.

Roll-film developing tanks are available both in stainless steel and in plastic. The metal ones require more practice to learn to load, but they are more durable and require less chemicals per roll. The tanks are light-tight and have a hole in the cover through which solutions are poured in and out. Always follow the film manufacturer's instructions about development time, temperature and agitation unless you're quite sure of your reasons for doing otherwise.

> *There is a painful lapse [of time] between the...making of a photograph and looking at it. The proof of that is that every photographer wants to rush right into the darkroom and see what he has done.*
>
> *(Walker Evans, photographer)*

Ten Tips for Darkroom Safety

1. Be careful with chemicals! Although few photographic chemicals are toxic in the concentrations generally used, the acetic acid in stop bath and fixer, and the bleach used in color processing, might cause serious eye damage. Wear eye and hand protection when mixing solutions from powders and concentrates. Be sure that copies of chemical safety data sheets are available in case of emergency. If someone should drink photo chemicals they should get medical help.

2. Never pour water into a concentrate. When preparing working solutions always start with water and add stock solution to make the amount needed. If any chemical gets splashed into your eye, flood the eye immediately with running water from a hose or eyewash, rinse it for several minutes, then go to a doctor.

3. Ventilate the darkroom. Don't breathe chemical vapors in a closed room with inadequate air circulation.

4. Don't expose your skin unnecessarily to chemicals. Learn to slide prints and sheet films into the tray without getting your hands wet. Some people wear latex gloves or use print tongs to transfer prints and films between trays. Whenever your fingers touch chemicals, rinse in water and dry them immediately, especially if you're susceptible to skin allergies.

5. Keep your hands clean and dry. Don't handle equipment or sensitized materials with wet or damp hands. To avoid constantly having to rinse and dry your hands while making prints, you may prefer to use print tongs or gloves. Some photographers like to keep one hand dry all the time for handling negatives, paper and equipment, using the other hand for carrying prints through the solutions. Rinse your "wet" hand or tongs in water between processing steps.

6. Don't be sloppy. Avoid dripping chemicals onto the darkroom floor or getting any chemicals on counter tops, squeegee boards, or equipment. The evidence of sloppiness with chemicals shows up after spilled solutions dry, leaving stains, corrosion and airborne dust. If you want to take a print out of the fixer to inspect it, rinse the print in water and place it in an empty tray before carrying it around. Because it is most likely to be spilled, fixer is the greatest contaminator in photography. Always wash it off your hands before touching anything, even the towel. Don't let it splash around the darkroom.

7. Mop up spills. Someone could be seriously injured from falling on a wet and slippery darkroom floor. So clean up all spills immediately, whether chemicals or merely water.

8. Dispose of chemicals properly. Noncommercial amounts of photo chemicals are not considered to be serious pollutants in ordinary sewage disposal systems. But be sure that when you dump chemicals down the drain you rinse out the trays, tanks, and sink with plenty of running water. Not only does rinsing keep everything clean for the next user, but the water further dilutes discarded chemicals. Many large labs sell silver recovered from used solutions.

9. Beware of sharp instruments. The safest kind of paper cutter for darkroom use is the rotary type with a covered blade. Never cut a wet print, because it may tear or jam the cutter. Be especially careful when using scissors in the dark.

10. Don't smoke. You already know what this habit does to your own body and to the lungs of other people forced to breathe the same air. Darkrooms are very confined spaces, often without rapid ventilation. Ashes always make a mess. An abandoned butt can burn down a building.

Getting Ready

It's easy to develop roll film, either black-and-white or color. The hardest part is getting the film loaded properly onto the metal or plastic reel that fits into the developing tank; but after a bit of practice, you'll feel confident of your skill. *Try it several times with practice film.* If you're using a stainless steel spiral reel, I recommend practicing *at least 100 times* with your eyes closed! By then your fingers will learn the touch they need to detect problems and you probably won't mess up your real film.

The following outline is presented to help guide you through the first few black-and-white rolls. Because each color process is somewhat different from the others and the time and temperature requirements are more rigorous, it's important to follow the manufacturer's instructions explicitly. You'll have few problems if you're careful and practice each step in the process several times until you feel fully acquainted with the procedure.

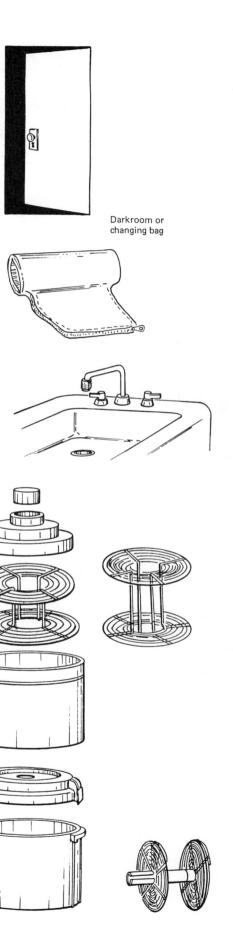

Darkroom or changing bag

Have all chemicals and equipment ready

*Items in **bold type** you'll need; others are optional:*

- **Darkroom** with running water, or dark closet or changing bag and access to a sink.
- **Developing tank with reel and cover** (a cap is required for most tanks. Some use an agitating rod)
- **Thermometer,** accurate photographic type
- **Timer**
- **Graduated beaker,** at least 8 ounces (250 mL) for one 35mm roll on steel reel; 16 ounces (500 mL) for two
- (optional—recommended for color) Deep tray or dishpan for water bath, to keep solutions at the same temperature
- **Funnel**
- **Scissors**
- **Bottle opener** or cassette opener (for 35mm magazines)
- **Film clips** or spring-type clothes pins
- Drying cabinet or **clean place to hang film to dry**
- **Towels,** clean and dry
- Lab apron (otherwise, wear old clothes)
- **Developer** stock solution
- (optional) stop bath concentrate to conserve fixer
- **Fixer**
- (optional) washing agent to shorten washing time
- **Wetting agent** concentrate
- (optional) sponge or squeegee (must be clean)
- **Filing/proofing pages,** transparent archival type

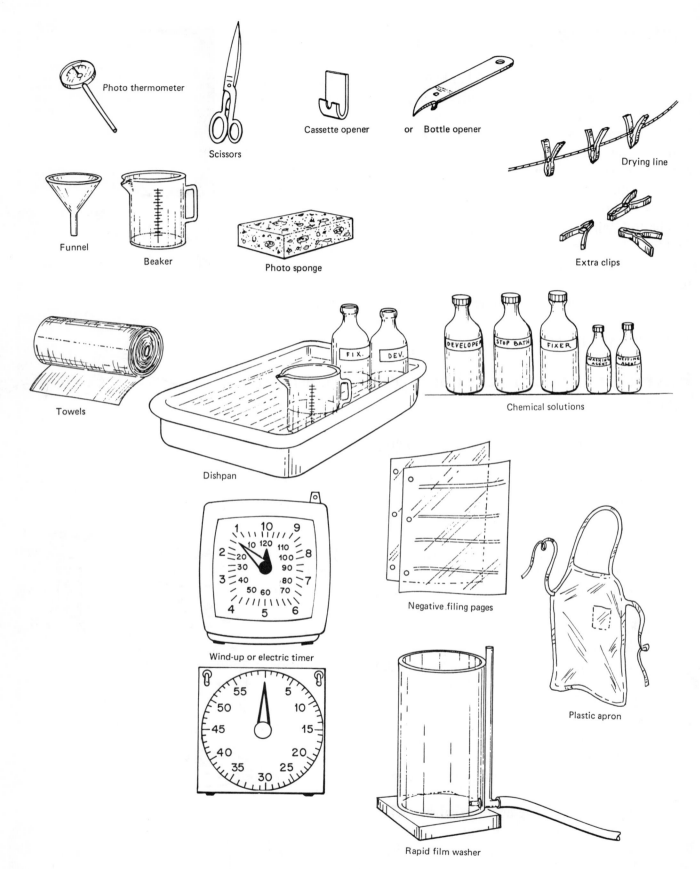

Photo thermometer

Scissors

Cassette opener   or   Bottle opener

Drying line

Funnel

Beaker

Photo sponge

Extra clips

Towels

Dishpan

FIX.   DEV.

DEVELOPER   STOP BATH   FIXER   WASHING AGENT   WETTING AGENT

Chemical solutions

Negative filing pages

Wind-up or electric timer

Plastic apron

Rapid film washer

Now that everything is together you're ready to start. Keep your wits about you, especially when working in the dark. That panicky feeling when you can't locate the developing tank cover in the dark is unlikely to occur if you practice ahead of time and lay everything out where you can find it by feel.

Control the water temperature

It is very important to maintain proper temperature. Turn on the tap water several minutes ahead of time and let it run into a beaker at a moderate rate until the temperature stabilizes. Adjust the hot and cold valves until the water is running at a steady 68°F (20°C). Keep the water running throughout the process if you can, but check it periodically because other demands on the water supply may cause the pressure and temperature to change. Be sure to use a thermometer that has been tested for accuracy; even one degree difference in the temperature of the developer can affect the quality of your negatives. Also, be sure to check the developer temperature inside the tank because it may not be the same as the running water.

In hot weather if your tap water won't cool to 68°F (20°C) you can work at up to 75°F (24°C) if you shorten the development time according to the film manufacturer's instructions (see table). Color reversal films may be processed at much higher temperatures, but all solutions should be kept within a degree or two of one another. The ideal temperature for developing most black-and-white film is 68°F (20°C) and even in hot weather you generally can maintain that temperature by circulating running water into a deep tray or plastic dishpan containing the tank and solution bottles. If your cold water isn't cold enough, you can immerse a plastic bag full of ice cubes into the water as needed. But don't put ice cubes directly into any of the solutions. If you can't keep solutions warm enough, try putting an electric immersion heater into the water that surrounds the chemical containers.

Preparing chemicals

For the same reason that you should stick with one type of film, I suggest that you start out with a standard developer and work with it unless you need to experiment with another formula. Although most developers are good for several rolls of film if used within a

Typical Time-Temperature Development Chart
Development Time in Minutes

Kodak T-Max 400 Film

Developer	65°F (18°C)	68°F (20°C)	70°F (21°C)	72°F (22°C)	75°F (24°C)
HC-110 (1:7)	6.5	6	5.5	5	4.5
D-76 (1:1)	14.5	12.5	11	10	9
D-76	9	8	7	6.5	5.5
T-MAX	NR	7	6.5	6.5	6

Kodak T-Max 100 Film

Developer	65°F (18°C)	68°F (20°C)	70°F (21°C)	72°F (22°C)	75°F (24°C)
HC-110 (1:7)	8	7	6.5	6	5
D-76 (1:1)	14.5	12	11	10	8.5
D-76	10.5	9	8	7	6
T-MAX	NR	8	7.5	7	6.5

few weeks after mixing, and replenisher solutions are available to prolong their life, many photographers prefer to use fresh developer for each roll, discarding the solution after use. Developer will lose its strength if kept for more than a few months or if it is reused without adding replenisher.

For convenience and economy, and especially to reduce the possibility of contamination, I recommend that you try a basic "one-shot" developer, such as Kodak HC-110 or D-76, that you can afford to dilute for use and then throw away. For either of these developers you mix a stock solution for storage from either concentrated liquid or powder. This stock solution usually is diluted still further with water immediately before use according to instructions on the film data sheet. For example, HC-110 stock solution usually is diluted 1:7—that is, 1 ounce (30 mL) of stock solution is added to 7 ounces of water to make 8 ounces (250 mL) of working solution. (8 ounces is just enough to cover one 35mm reel in a stainless steel tank.)

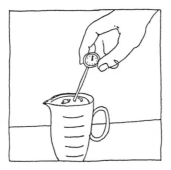

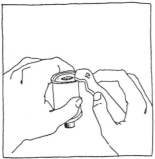

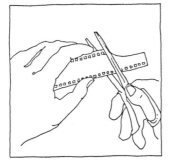

Mix the developer stock solution with 68°F (20°C) water and then put a thermometer into the beaker to verify the temperature.
Stop bath (if used) and fixer should be ready for use in beakers or bottles at about 68°F (20°C).

Developing Roll Film Step-by-Step

1. *(IN TOTAL DARKNESS) 35mm film:* Find the end of the spool that sticks out from the magazine and **pry off the metal cap** from the other end. Slide out the spool with the film wound around it. With scissors carefully **cut off the narrow part of the film leader.** Try not to touch the flat surfaces of the film with your fingers.

120 film: Break the paper seal with your thumbnail and separate the film from its backing paper. Let the paper hang down while the film rolls itself up in your hand. Handle the film by the edges only, except at the very end, when you have to tear off the tape. (If you tear the tape rapidly you may see a flash of light—a harmless effect caused by static electricity.

2. *(STILL IN TOTAL DARKNESS!)* **Load the film onto the reel.** Be sure the reel is completely dry and held correctly. The emulsion side (dullest appearing and lighter colored—although you won't be able to see this in the dark), should be facing the center of the reel. You can tell how it should go in the dark because roll film naturally curls toward the emulsion side. **Feel for the open ends of the wires. The film must start from that side. Center the end of the film in the clip or slot at the hub of the reel; then rotate the reel, keeping the film curved slightly downward with your thumb and forefinger as it feeds onto the reel.** You can feel it if the film buckles and misses a turn. When this happens, go back and rewind that section until it's going straight again. **The film must not touch itself anywhere or undeveloped spots will result.** If the film gets creased on the edges so it won't load, reverse it and start from the other end. Try not to touch the surface of the film or scratch it with your fingernails.

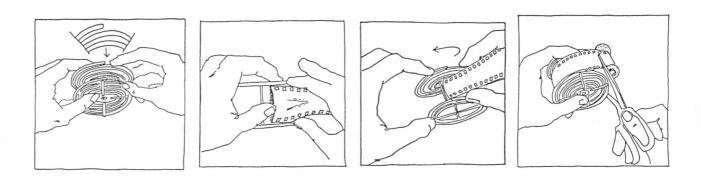

Plastic reels are loaded from the outside instead of from the hub. First, square off the end of the film with scissors between sprocket holes—it must be a smooth edge. Push the trimmed end under the outer flanges as far as it will go, then hold one half of the reel in each hand and rotate both sides back and forth until the film is drawn fully into the reel.

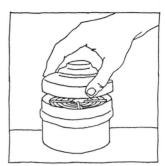

3. *(STILL IN TOTAL DARKNESS!)* **Put the loaded reel into the tank and put on the cover.** Although the cap can be removed to pour chemicals in and out, **the main part of the cover must stay on until after fixing.**

Alternative procedure: If your darkroom has running water, you can pour the developer into the tank first, then insert the loaded reel, put on the cover, and start the timer.

FROM NOW ON YOU CAN WORK WITH LIGHTS ON.

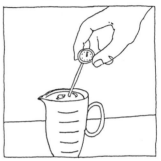

4. Recheck the developer temperature and set the timer according to the time-temperature chart.

5. Start the timer.

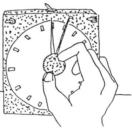

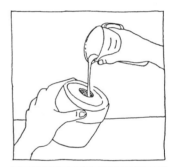

6. Pour the mixed developer into the pouring hole in the top of the tank. Hold the tank at an angle and fill it as quickly as you can.

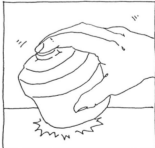

7. Rap the tank firmly three or four times on the bottom of the sink to dislodge any air bubbles, then **immediately begin agitation.**

8. Agitate. Holding the cap on with your thumb or forefinger, **turn the tank completely over with a gentle twisting motion five times in about five seconds.** Be gentle—don't shake the tank **Repeat this five-second agitation procedure every 30 seconds.** Rest the tank in the sink or in the water bath between agitation (if you hold it in your hand it will warm up). Some plastic tanks cannot be inverted, only rotated.

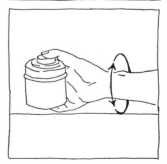

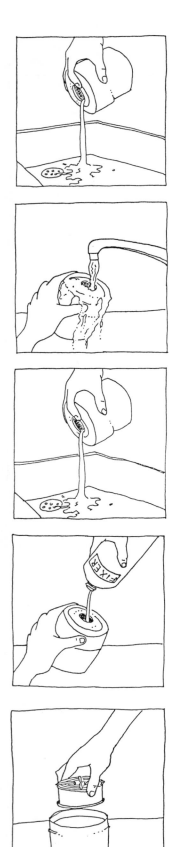

9. Remove the cap from the top of the tank about 15 seconds before the developing time is completed, *BUT DO NOT REMOVE THE WHOLE COVER!* Hold the tank so the cover can't come off and quickly **pour all the developer down the sink drain**.

10. Fill the tank either **with running water** at 68°F (20°C) or with prepared stop bath. Put the cap back on and agitate the tank. If water, empty it and refill it again as quickly as you can.

11. Empty the tank after about 30 seconds *KEEP THE CAP OFF, BUT DO NOT REMOVE THE COVER.*

12. Pour fixer into the tank until you can see that it's full. Set the timer for ten minutes (or less if recommended). Agitate the same way you did during development, except that the exact timing intervals are not as important.

13. Inspect the film. About halfway through the recommended fixing time you can remove the tank cover and check the end of the film to see whether it is still cloudy looking or magenta in color. Note how long it takes for all milkiness to disappear. Allow twice this time for total fixing. If T-Max film still is strongly magenta after fixing time is up, it should be put in fresh fixer until the color is gone or only a slight tint is left. Be careful not to drip or splash fixer around the darkroom— it dries to a messy white powder and contaminates everything. Rinse your hands and dry them before touching anything else.

14. Pour the fixer back into its container. You can leave the tank cover off because the film is no longer sensitive to light. Fixer can be reused until it begins to take longer than five or six minutes for the milkiness to disappear, or more than 10 minutes for most of the magenta to leave T-Max film.

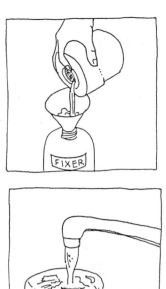

15. Wash the film. Leave the film on the reel and allow 68 °F (20°C) water to run rapidly into the tank for 10-20 minutes. Empty the tank and refill it several times during washing. One or two minutes in an optional washing aid such as Kodak Hypo Clearing Agent can shorten washing time, save water, and ensure removal of all fixer.

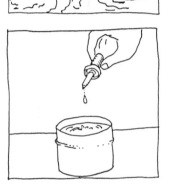

16. Add wetting agent. Turn off the water, leave the film in the tank, and add wetting agent such as Kodak Photo-Flo to the water. About 1 mL per roll will help prevent spots from forming on the film during drying. Too much wetting agent may cause oily streaks on the negatives. Agitate gently, but don't make bubbles. Leave the film in the solution for about 30 seconds.

16. Hang the film to dry. Attach a clip or clothespin to each end of the film and hang it in the most dust-free place available. Don't let anything touch the film while it is wet because it may get scratched or pick up and hold dust and dirt.

17. Wipe the film (optional). Hard water or other contaminants may cause spots on the negatives. These can be prevented by drawing a clean sponge (dampened with wetting agent then squeezed almost dry) once, *gently* down each side of the film.

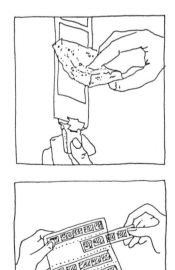

18. Protect the negatives. The film should be dry in one to two hours at average room temperature, or much less in a heated drying cabinet. As soon as they're thoroughly dry, cut the negatives into strips (35mm into five or six, 120 into three or four) and slip them into archival transparent filing pages. Keep negatives in their pages at all times to protect them from scratches, dust and fingerprints.

Handling and Processing Sheet Film

In the darkroom, sheet film must be loaded into special holders that take one sheet on each side. After exposure, each holder must be unloaded in the darkroom.

Processing sheet film is very much like roll film, except for the way the film itself is handled. If you have a special sheet film tank available, then the only difference is in loading the tank and agitating it. When only a few sheets are to be processed, the tray method is convenient and offers excellent control of agitation and individualized development time. Some people are able to shuffle as many as a dozen sheets of film simultaneously in a tray—but the risk is great of scratching and gouging the soft emulsion of one sheet with a corner of another.

Stainless steel developing hangers in large tanks frequently are used by professional photographers, but with this method you have to agitate very gently by lifting the bunch of hangers and draining from alternate corners. Too vigorous agitation forces developer through the holes in the hangers, leaving streaks visible in the negatives and, subsequently, in the prints.

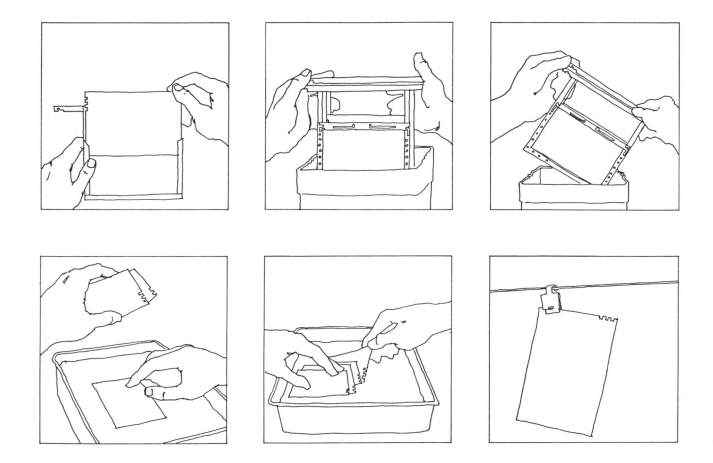

Sheet film can be processed either in tanks or in trays.
Great care must be taken to avoid damage to the emulsion while it is wet and soft.

Some Hints for Better Film Processing

1. Use clean water for mixing chemicals. City tap water usually is all right, but it should be filtered if it contains visible sediment. Well water often contains calcium, iron, and other impurities that cause spots and streaks on negatives. Wiping the film when it's hung to dry will help eliminate these problems, as will mixing your final wetting agent bath with distilled water. If water purity is a problem you also might mix developer solutions with distilled or bottled water.

2. Mix developer gently. Stir it according to directions and mix it at the proper temperature. Don't shake the bottle vigorously or stir the solution violently because oxygen in the air bubbles that are formed will partially reduce the strength of the solution.

3. Label all chemical storage containers clearly. If you pour developer or fixer back into a storage bottle, be sure it's the right one. Either solution should be thrown out if any of the other is mixed with it. Clean glass bottles and most plastic containers are safe for photographic solutions, but developer should be stored in a dark brown or opaque container to protect it from light. Never reuse a household bleach bottle for developer.

4. Don't touch the surface of the film with your fingers or allow it to rub across a table top or along the bottom of a sink. The emulsion side is very soft when wet, and it can easily be permanently scratched.

5. Wash everything every time, especially your hands. Make a habit of rinsing utensils whenever they are emptied, and rinse your hands every time you get any kind of solution on them. If you always rinse your hands in water before touching the towel, the towel will stay clean and prevent you from contaminating anything. Spilled chemicals may look like water when they're wet, but most of them leave a terrible mess when they dry. Sponge up any spills immediately and rinse out and clean up everything when you've finished working in the darkroom. Avoid getting chemical stains on good clothing. But if you

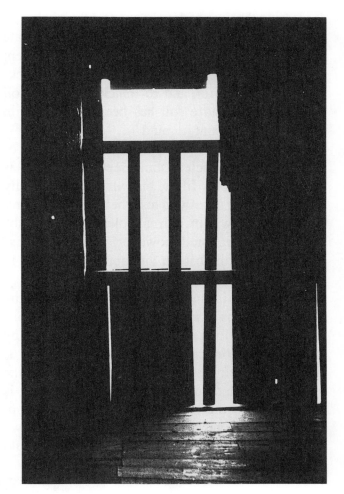

Rene Poch   *Abandoned Barn*
The visual impact of this photograph depends on high image contrast. High-contrast treatment emphasizes the forms themselves, without distraction from any background texture or additional detail.

do get a stain, a product called *Stainout!* may make it less visible.

Controlling Contrast Through Development

The old photographers' axiom that you should expose for the shadows and develop for the highlights was mentioned earlier. Half of the zone system is based on placing readings of the lower values in the scene in the appropriate zones (I through IV) by adjusting the exposure of the film.

Now, in developing the negatives, we have a chance to expand or compress the placement of the higher values (Zones VI through IX) by increasing or decreasing the time of development. Obviously you can't vary the high-value density of each separate negative on the same 35mm roll. The development control part of the zone system is ideal for black-and-white sheet film and for black-and-white roll film when the entire roll has been exposed with special development in mind.

This process does not apply to color negatives or to color transparencies; some speed "pushing" is possible with color films, but when you radically alter processing times you lose the ability to control color balance within normal tolerances. All the "rules" can be ignored, however, when you're experimenting with abstract and abnormal effects in color—a new frontier!

As exposure is placed on the proper low zone by adjusting f/stops—one stop adjustment equals one zone—so development time can be adjusted by increments of one zone in the higher values. If "normal" development, as recommended by the manufacturer and confirmed by your own tests, is represented by the letter N, then normal development plus one zone would be N+1; normal plus two zones would be N+2; normal minus one zone would be N-1, minus two zones would be N-2. Although further plus and minus extensions are possible with some films and special developing techniques, two zones each way seems to be the practical limit for standard films and developers. The table below gives suggested development factors as a basis for trial. They represent a starting point for your own experiments with any combination of black-and-white film and developer.

Development Factors for Trial With Various Combinations of Films and Developers		
	Result	Multiply
To expand gray scale (increase contrast)	N+1	N x 1.4
	N+2	N x 1.8
To compress gray scale (decrease contrast)	N-1	N x 0.6
	N-2	N x 0.4

It's OK to experiment. Try anything you want. See what comes out.

(David Posther, educator)

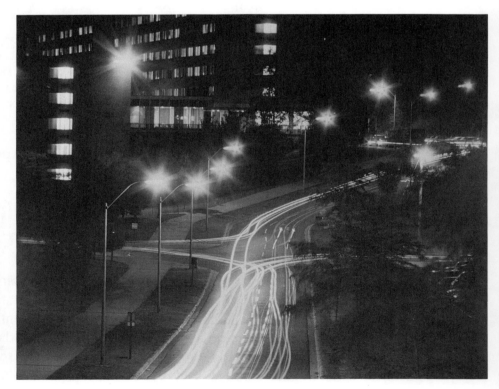

Dennis Griffin *Hadley Hall*
An exposure of five minutes at f/16 permitted the lights of moving cars to trace their patterns without being overexposed. Notice that the nonmoving street lights have built up so much density on the negative that star patterns (halation) have been formed. N-2 development reduced the overall contrast.

Suggested Exposure Indexes (EI) and Developing Times for Kodak T-Max Roll Films in a Small Tank				
Developer: HC-110 Stock Solutiion Diluted 1:7 (Dilution "B") at 68°F (20°C). Agitation five seconds every 30 seconds.				
*If these short times produce uneven development, pre-soak the film in water at 68°F (20°C) for one minute before development.				
T-Max 100	**EI**		**T-Max 400**	**EI**
N+2	13 min.	200	11 min.	800
N+1	10 min.	125	8.5 min.	600
Normal	**7 min.**	**100**	**6 min.**	**400**
N-1	*4.2 min.	50	*3.6 min.	200
N-2	*2.8 min.	25	*2.4 min.	100

Applying the zone system

One problem with the zone system is that when you manipulate the developing time of black-and-white film to expand or compress the contrast range of the negatives, you also change the effective speed of the film. If you don't compensate for this shift in speed when you intend to give N-minus development, your negatives may lack sufficient shadow density (you may not be able to separate Zones I, II, and III). On the other hand, giving N-plus development at the normal speed rating may result in unneeded density and excessive grain.

Exposing at a higher film speed and developing N-plus is not the same as "pushing" the film, which underexposes the shadows. See pages 168-169 for more about getting the maximum film speed possible under less-than-ideal lighting conditions.

The quality of your negatives can be affected by the accuracy of your camera shutter and exposure meter. If a densitometer is not available, you may not be able to make precise tests of effective film speed, but you can and should make practical tests.

To get started, you can use the effective film speeds and development times indicated in the table above. If your experiments agree, fine! Otherwise, don't hesitate to work up your own table.

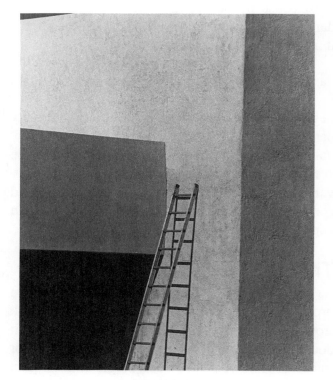

Beatrice Ray *Scottsdale Public Library*
The original print of this bold graphic image includes a range of gray tones from Zone I through IX. Although the inks used to print this book will not reproduce all of these values accurately, you should try to identify them in this picture and then previsualize them as you look at and photograph actual scenes.

Evaluating Your Negatives

If you look at a group of negatives against the light, you'll probably notice that they differ from one another in several ways. First, they will probably vary in overall density. Some may be nearly transparent all over because there was comparatively little silver deposited during exposure and development. Such a negative, low in density, transmitting a lot of light, is called a *thin* negative. Other negatives, appearing darker or denser because more silver was deposited, transmit less light and are called *dense*. A negative of very high density transmits very little light.

Besides differences in overall density, negatives vary from one to another in the relationship of dense and thin areas within each image. The brightest parts (high values), of each original scene appear most dense in the negative, and the shadows, or darkest areas (low values), of the subject appear thinner or more transparent.

The relative differences in density between the darkest and lightest important values within a single image is referred to as contrast. In a *contrasty* negative there is a great deal of difference in density between the high values (highlights) and the low values (shadows). In a *flat* negative there may be very little density difference between high and low values. You must learn to judge the density and contrast of all kinds of negatives before you can expect to make good prints from them.

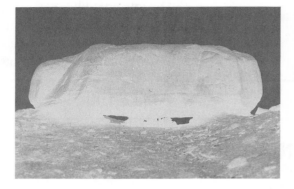

A *thin* negative appears to be relatively transparent overall. Especially if the result of underexposure, the negative may not have enough density and detail in the shadow (clear) areas to properly reproduce the darker values in the print.

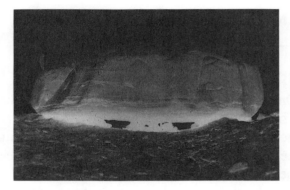

A *dense* negative is relatively opaque. Although plenty of detail probably will be visible in the shadow areas, there may not be enough separation of bright areas to ensure visible differences between high values in the print.

The ideal negative

You can't make fine prints unless you have properly exposed and developed negatives to work from. You can always make a print over again if it doesn't please you, but with negatives and color transparencies you have but a single chance. You have to do everything right the first time—or retake the photo.

The best prints will be made from negatives that are neither too thin nor too dense; neither too contrasty nor too flat; neither smudged, nor stained, nor scratched. Although you can burn and dodge and work minor miracles in the darkroom, the best prints will be made from "normal" negatives. You can be sure that most of your negatives will print well if you're always careful to give correct exposure in the camera, use fresh chemicals to process the film, and develop for the optimum time and at the proper temperature.

Dense negatives usually are the result of *overexposure*. If an overexposed film is also overdeveloped—that is, developed too long or at too high a temperature or with too much agitation—the resulting negative may be so dense in the highlight areas that it cannot be printed. What happens is that Zones VII, VIII, and IX tend to merge, making it impos-

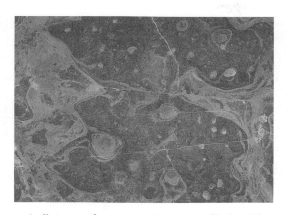

A *flat* negative may not necessarily be *thin,* but it lacks contrast. The density range of a flat negative is limited to relatively few adjacent values on a portion of the gray scale and may require expansion of the tonal range in printing.

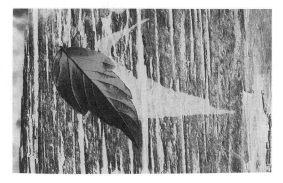

A *contrasty* negative shows a wide range of densities. Although adequate shadow and highlight detail may be visible in the negative, some dodging and burning-in may be required to retain separation within the highest and lowest values of the print.

sible to distinguish in the print subtle differences between such high values as white clothing, pale flesh tones, and blonde hair. Such a negative is said to be *blocked up.*

There is a direct relationship between density and grain. Overexposure and overdevelopment combined can give skies and skin tones the texture of a concrete sidewalk. Unless you want this effect, don't let excessive grain occur as a result of negligence.

Thin, or extremely transparent, negatives may be caused by underexposure, underdevelopment, or both. Underdevelopment is the result of not leaving the film in the developer for long enough time, not agitating sufficiently, or of using developer that is old and weak, contaminated with fixer or stop bath, or too cold. Thin negatives usually fail to record some of the lowest values (Zones I, II, and III), leaving clear film base where there should have been shadow detail. These areas without density print either totally black or lifelessly gray. Very thin negatives usually are *flat* or low in contrast, also.

Negative contrast depends mostly on the relative brightness values of important parts of the subject photographed. Contrast also is affected, and can be controlled to some degree, by development. If your negatives always have too much contrast, you can shorten the normal developing time or try a different developer or dilution. Correctly exposed, but consistently flat negatives usually result from underdevelopment. Be sure that your agitation procedure is the same every time (over and back gently for five seconds every thirty seconds). Over-agitation increases contrast unevenly; under-agitation decreases contrast, leaving a mottled, uneven appearance.

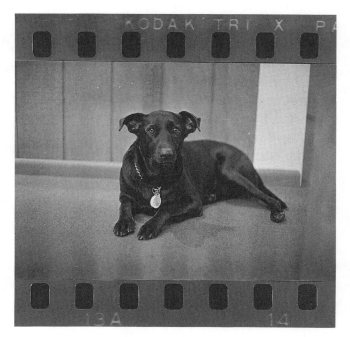

Careful and consistent agitation is very important. If agitation during film development is too vigorous or too frequent, streaks like these or mottled unevenness can result in the negatives and will show up in the print. Agitation problems will be most apparent in smooth areas of even middle tones such as skin tones and sky.

Determining Exposure Index

Are your negatives consistently too thin or too dense? If you've been controlling everything—previsualizing zones, making accurate exposure meter readings, compensating the film speed for minus or plus development, developing in the proper solution at the recommended time, temperature and agitation—yet your negatives seem always to lack shadow detail (suggesting underexposure) or always are excessively dense (implying overexposure), you may need to determine your own "personal ISO" exposure index.

Although the manufacturer's ratings are scientifically determined and they usually are quite accurate, all kinds of problems may affect the way you should expose film in your camera. The shutter may be consistently fast or slow; the meter may read consistently high or low; or your film processing procedure may produce differences from the norm established in the film manufacturer's tests. Such errors occasionally all fall in the same direction and the cumulative effect prevents optimum negative quality.

In black-and-white negatives, Zone I density should barely be distinguishable from the clear film (film-base density plus inherent fog) between frames and around the edges of the negative. By making the following test you can determine which exposure index yields the proper Zone I density. From this you can derive a modified exposure index for that particular film and processing combination with your own equipment and method of working.

The film speed test involves photographing a standard 18 percent gray card at various exposures:

1. Place the gray card in even, but not intense light, preferably outdoors in deep shade or on an overcast day. Adjust the angle of the card so there is no glare.

2. Mount your camera on a tripod and focus the lens at infinity (you want the gray card to be out of focus—you're testing for negative density, not for detail). Move the camera close enough to fill the negative completely with the image of the gray card.

Remember that your camera probably includes a little more than the viewfinder shows. Move in a little closer to allow for this. Be sure there are neither shadows nor glare on the gray card.

3. Read the gray card directly with your exposure meter. This reading will give you the exposure for Zone V. Be sure that the camera (or hand-held reflected-light meter) is close enough to the card so that you're not reading any background, but not so close that you read your own shadow.

4. Adjust your exposure reading from Zone V to Zone I. Do this simply by stopping down (closing) the lens four f/stops. Count zones to yourself as you stop down. For example:

> Meter reading (Zone V) 1/250 at f/4
> Minus one stop (Zone IV) 1/250 at f/5.6
> Minus two stops (Zone III) 1/250 at f/8
> Minus three stops (Zone II) 1/250 at f/11
> Minus four stops (Zone I) 1/250 at f/16

Of course you can use any combination of shutter speed and lens opening that gives equivalent exposure, but avoid the fastest shutter settings (1/1,000 and 1/500) because they tend not to be as accurate as the other speeds. If you can't stop down far enough, place the gray card in a darker location and make a new Zone V reading.

5. Make an exposure at the manufacturer's film speed rating for Zone I placement (1/250 at f/16 in the preceding example); then repeat the test at 25 percent, 50 percent, 75 percent, 100 percent (a duplicate of your first exposure), 150 percent, and finally 200 percent of the film manufacturer's exposure index. For example, in testing a film rated ISO 400, you would set your exposure meter at ISO 100, 200, 300, 400, 600 and 800. A test of ISO 100 film would include meter settings of ISO 25, 50, 80, 100, 160 and 200. For each different ISO setting, calculate the exposure for Zone I and keep very careful records of the sequence of exposures. If some frames are left over on the roll after finishing your tests, either repeat the tests or make pictures to finish up the roll. This is so the developer will have a normal amount of silver to work on and not skew the results of your tests.

6. After normal processing, read each of the test negatives with a densitometer. In most cases, the Zone I negative closest to a densitometer reading of 0.10 above film-base density will have been exposed at the correct exposure index for that type of film and your particular combination of camera, exposure meter, and processing procedure. For this test to have any meaning, however you must keep very careful records. You also have to standardize your developing procedure.

If a densitometer isn't available, you can make a very practical test that will indicate your working exposure index. Photograph a subject containing a large, very dark area with detail that would fall into Zone II. Dark, textured tree bark would be a good subject, or rough black soil or stone. Shoot at the various ISO settings suggested for the densitometer test, deliberately placing the dark, textured surface on Zone II (three stops less than the Zone V meter reading). Again, keep very careful records. After the negatives are processed, examine them through a magnifier, selecting the least-dense negative that seems to contain printable detail in the Zone II area. The ISO setting used to expose that frame is your working exposure index for that film.

> *Do not be afraid of the practical and mundane aspects of the medium; they will strengthen your technique and discipline and give you a broader perspective of the world we live in.*
>
> *(Ansel Adams, photographer)*

Negative Faults

If you see negatives that have noticeable overall gray "fog" density extending beyond the picture area into the margins of the film, you can suspect that the film was unintentionally exposed to some light before or after exposure or during processing. Or it could have been outdated film, or film that has been x-rayed or stored at high temperature. Dark streaks on negatives mean that some light probably got to the film either when it was in the camera—caused by a light leak or by opening up the camera back—or while the film was being loaded or unloaded in bright light. Color transparency films, of course, show fog and light leaks not as gray or black but as white or yellow.

Don't be alarmed if you notice a slight bluish or purplish cast to your negatives. This is an effect of antihalation dyes and is normal on many kinds of film. A slight overall magenta tint is typical of Kodak T-Max films, but if the color is intense or uneven the film should be refixed in fresh fixer and rewashed. An orange or brownish appearance is to be expected of color negatives, the coloration being caused by a contrast masking layer built into the film during manufacture.

Mysterious blotches or "fireworks" effects on negatives may be the static electricity fog that occurs in cold weather and low humidity when roll film is advanced or rewound too rapidly or the dark slide of a sheet-film holder is withdrawn or inserted too quickly.

Sometimes finger marks and scratches from careless handling of undeveloped film will show up as dark spots or lines on the finished negatives. Dark crescent-shaped marks result from pinching the film too tightly while loading the developing reel.

You can't make fine quality prints unless you have properly exposed and developed negatives to work from. You can always make a print over again if it doesn't please you, but with negatives and color transparencies you have but a single chance. Everything has to be done right the first time!

Processing problems usually are caused by carelessness. Most of the common negative problems that you are likely to encounter are described on pages 124-128. With care, most of these difficulties can be avoided.

> *The camera should be used for recording of life, for rendering the very substance and quintessence of the thing itself, whether it be polished steel or palpitating flesh.*
>
> *(Edward Weston, photographer)*

What's Wrong with My Negatives?

Images pale and light (negatives very thin and transparent), but frame numbers dark and legible. Shadow areas lack detail. (Color slides too dark).

Cause: Underexposure.

Prevention or Correction: Print with magenta filtration. Reshoot if possible.

Images and frame numbers thin and weak.

Cause: Underdevelopment.

Prevention or Correction: Print with magenta filtration. Reshoot if possible. Mix fresh developer. Verify dilution, time, temperature and agitation. Chemically intensify negatives.

Images very dark, dense and grainy, but frame numbers appear normal. (Color slides too light and "washed out").

Cause: Overexposure.

Prevention or Correction: Increase print exposure time, using filters if needed. Reshoot if possible.

Images very dense and contrasty, highlight areas opaque. Frame numbers extremely dense and fuzzy.

Cause: Overdevelopment.

Prevention or Correction: Increase print exposure time, using yellow filtration. Reshoot if possible. Verify developer dilution, time, temperature and agitation. Chemically reduce negatives.

Negatives evenly gray (fogged) all over, including area between frames and around sprocket holes. (Color slide film may appear yellowish or greenish over-all, even outside the image area).

Cause: Film exposed to light, extreme heat, or radiation.

Prevention or Correction: Check darkroom and bulk film loader for light leaks. Be sure not to remove tank cover during development. Store film away from heat. Protect from x-rays.

Image area gray fogged, but area outside and between frames is clear. (Color slides may appear washed out or yellowish, while area outside image is opaque).

Cause: Light leak in camera—probably shutter, lens mount, or bellows.

Prevention or Correction: Refer to camera repair technician.

Film fogged with dark streaks or blotches. (On color slide film the streaks are clear or yellow).

Cause: Light leak.

Prevention or correction: Load camera in shade. Keep film holders, magazines and rolls from bright light. Check reusable magazines and film holders for light leaks. If same fog pattern appears on more than one roll, consult a camera repair technician.

Strong overall magenta cast to entire roll or sheet of T-Max film.

Cause: Insufficient fixing.

Prevention or Correction: Return to fresh fixer until color clears. Rewash.

Milky translucency to all or portions of film.

Cause: Insufficient fixing.

Prevention or correction: Return to fresh fixer until milkiness clears, plus a few minutes more. Rewash.

Purplish-gray, opaque areas within image area of otherwise normal roll. (Or odd-shaped clear areas if film was taken off the reel before fixing).

Cause: Film stuck together during processing.

Prevention or Correction: Next time load reel more carefully.

Purplish-gray, opaque areas along edges of film, but outside image area.

Cause: Film stuck to flanges of reel during processing.

Prevention or Correction: This is normal. Ignore it.

Film overall fogged very densely over a few frames; rest of roll normal.

Cause: Camera back opened before rewinding film.

Prevention or Correction: THINK!

Clear, or less dense, round spots; may have dark edges.

Cause: Air bubbles clinging to emulsion during development.

Prevention or Correction: Pour developer quickly into tank. Immediately rap tank three or four times. When putting reels or hangers into filled tank, rap reel or hanger.

Tiny clear "pinholes" or irregular spots

Cause: Dust, lint, or film fragments on emulsion during exposure, or too-strong acid stop bath.

Prevention or Correction: Blow and brush inside camera and film holders before loading. Dilute stop bath or use water rinse.

Dense streaks in even areas of image such as sky, especially near sprocket holes in 35mm film.

Cause: Excessive or too-vigorous agitation.

Prevention or Correction: Agitate gently and consistently.

Mottled and uneven density or streaking from densest areas.

Cause: Insufficient agitation.

Prevention or Correction: Agitate gently and consistently.

Light (underdeveloped) strip across the length of all negatives on the roll.

Cause: Not enough developer in the tank.

Prevention or Correction: Measure carefully the amount of developer needed for each roll.

Slimy or crystalline scum on negatives.

Cause: Insufficient washing.

Prevention or Correction: Use washing agent; rewash; use fresh wetting agent.

Rounded spots or streaks dried on surface of film (usually on base side).

Cause: Deposits left by impurities in wash water or wetting agent.

Prevention or Correction: Remove spots gently with cotton swab moistened with photographic film cleaner or lens cleaner. Mix wetting agent with distilled water. Wipe wet film with sponge before drying.

"Dirt" particles embedded in emulsion.

Cause: Impurities in wash water or wetting agent. Wet film has touched a dirty surface.

Prevention or Correction: Soak film in washing agent and rewash. Bathe film in distilled water/wetting agent solution. Wipe film gently with clean, moist sponge or squeegee. Filter water supply if problem persists. NEVER LET ANYTHING TOUCH WET FILM!

Emulsion blistered, frilled, or reticulated.

Cause: Extreme temperature variation during processing.

Prevention: Monitor temperature, especially during rinse and wash, to avoid surges of hot water.

Dark, crescent-shaped marks.

Cause: Film bent or crimped during loading of reel.

Prevention: Handle film carefully.

Lightninglike lines or blotches.

Cause: Static electricity.

Prevention: In the camera, when the weather is very cold and dry, avoid rapid film advancing and rewinding. In the darkroom, separate roll film slowly from its backing paper; unload sheet film holders slowly. Avoid static.

Corners of image less dense than center (or corners rounded off).

Cause: Lens not covering film size; lens shade or filter cutting into field of view (especially with wide angle lens). This problem is referred to as vignetting (vin-yet-ting).

Prevention: Use proper lens and attachments

Thin dark lines parallel with edges of film May start and stop or go entire length of roll.

Cause: Scratching before development.

Prevention: Check camera back, film magazines, and bulk loader for burrs or embedded particles of sand or grit. Never *cinch* film (pull it tightly into a roll).

Light scratch lines.

Cause: Cinching roll, rubbing strips of negatives together, or other rough handling after processing.

Prevention: Cut roll film negatives into short strips. File all negatives in individual archival sleeves or pages. Keep them there.

Excessive curling or brittleness.

Cause: Too-rapid drying.

Prevention: Rewash and redry. Air dry with minimum heat.

Hazy, diffused, indistinct images.

Cause: Lens or filter may be severely smudged or very dirty.

Prevention: Inspect and clean with lens-cleaning fluid and lens tissue.

Entire image blurred equally.

Cause: Camera movement during exposure.

Prevention: Hold camera steadier. Use tripod whenever possible.

Moving subject blurred (when you don't want it that way).

Cause: Shutter speed too slow.

Prevention: Use faster shutter speed; pan camera to follow subject movement.

One plane of subject in sharp focus, remainder out of focus.

Cause: Too-large lens opening or lens focused incorrectly.

Prevention: Focus on principal plane of subject. Stop down lens for desired depth of field.

Corners of image unsharp, especially at wide apertures.

Cause: Poor-quality camera lens; or supplementary close-up lens or extender used at too-wide aperture.

Prevention: Use smallest lens opening possible (e.g., f/16)

One side of image or irregular area consistently unsharp.

Cause: Lens or film pressure plate out of alignment.

Prevention: Refer to camera repair technician.

Film completely blank (clear) except for frame numbers and edge printing. (Color slide film opaque with legible frame numbers).

Cause: Film not exposed. Camera probably not loaded correctly or dark slide not withdrawn from film holder.

Prevention: Load film carefully. Be sure sprocket holes are engaged in 35mm camera. Don't forget dark slide when using sheet film.

Film completely blank (clear) with no frame numbers or edge printing visible.

Cause: Film probably "developed" accidently in water or fixer.

Prevention: Check procedures. Label all solution containers.

Film completely opaque with no evidence of image. (Color slide film transparent).

Cause: Film totally exposed to light or strong radiation before development.

Prevention: Be careful!

Film heavily fogged, but with traces of image. (Color slide film may appear yellowish or greenish).

Cause: Film exposed to light or radiation before or during development.

Prevention: Be careful!

Multiple or overlapped images.

Cause: Accidental double-exposure; camera loaded incorrectly, or film transport malfunction.

Prevention: Check shooting and loading procedure. If problem persists, refer to camera repair technician.

Space varies between frames.

Cause: Film transport malfunction.

Prevention: Either live with it or have camera repaired or replaced.

Part of image normal; part totally unexposed or underexposed.

Cause: With flash: improper synchronization—shutter probably set at too high a speed (the edge between light and dark will be sharp and straight). Without flash: Something in front of lens, such as camera case or strap, coat collar, part of hand, etc.

Prevention: Most 35mm cameras synchronize flash at 1/60 or 1/125 second—see owner's manual. Be careful how you hold the camera.

Making Fine Black-and-White Prints 7

The Print as a Performance

The negative is comparable to the composer's score: the print to its performance. (Ansel Adams, photographer)

The print you make is the final revelation of what you saw, thought and felt when you were in the presence of the subject matter. Ansel Adams was a talented musician and a photographer whose awe-inspiring landscape prints are among the finest ever made. Adams' musical training influenced his photographic work and his performance analogy tells us that, in the darkroom, creative interpretation can improve your message.

It's at this final stage that you bring to bear everything you know about communication and about technique to make the print speak for you as eloquently as possible.

Esthetically, printing is alchemy: chemicals are converted magically into images. Technically, however, a print is made by exposing light-sensitive paper to light passing through a negative. A corresponding positive image is formed on the paper, the image appearing upon development. To make the image permanent, the print must be fixed, washed and dried.

I have been asked many times, "What is a great photograph?" I can answer best by showing a great photograph, not by talking or writing about one.

(Ansel Adams, photographer)

Photographers who work with view cameras as Ansel Adams frequently did, produce very large negatives that can be printed by contact. A contact print is the same size as the negative and is made by sandwiching the negative between a sheet of photographic paper and a sheet of glass. The great photographic artist Edward Weston worked in this way, most of his work being contact printed from 8 x 10-inch negatives. The contact printing technique is very convenient for proofing roll film negatives, but smaller format negatives usually must be enlarged for final viewing or reproduction.

Combine the optimum moment with the ambience of a fine print, and perhaps a successful photograph is achieved. (Ansel Adams, photographer)

When is bigger *better?*

Besides the spectacular effect of making big pictures from little negatives, the enlarging process allows many controls with which you can improve on a somewhat less-than-perfect negative. With these controls you can lighten or darken areas, alter the scale of values, modify perspective, soften or strengthen lines, combine images, or print only a selected portion of a single image.

Although color printing from both color negatives and transparencies is becoming much simpler and less costly—and more popular, the process of producing fine black-and-white prints for exhibition and reproduction will be emphasized here. In fact, there seems to be a renaissance in black-and-white photography for exhibition, publication and advertising. If you master the equipment and controls required to make quality black-and-white prints, you certainly will be able to follow the manufacturer's instructions for working with whichever color printing process you may choose.

The Enlarger

The two most common types of enlargers are referred to either as *condenser* or *diffusion,* depending on how light is passed through the negative. Some enlargers combine both types of illumination, having a relatively large diffused light source plus one or two condensing lenses above the negative to concentrate the light. A "cold light" fluorescent head is a diffusion source.

In comparing enlargers, we find that the condenser type will yield prints of comparatively higher contrast than those made with a diffusion light source, but the condensing lenses have an unfortunate tendency to emphasize all the defects in the negative, such as grain, scratches and dust. Some people claim that condenser enlargers yield sharper images, but the appearance of sharpness is only the effect of higher relative contrast. Assuming a sharp negative, the actual sharpness of the print depends on the quality of the enlarging lens, how flat the negative is held in the carrier, and how accurately it is focused. Sharpness has little to do with the type of illumination.

Filters control contrast

Most enlargers provide a place for variable contrast or color printing filters to be placed either in a holder beneath the lens or in a slot above the negative.

Separate filters aren't necessary with color enlargers that have built-in dichroic filters. These enlargers generally are of the diffusion type and are very convenient to use because you can dial in the exact amount of magenta or yellow filtration needed to print on variable contrast black-and-white papers.

Match lens to negative size

Most enlargers are designed to accept more than one negative size. You will require a negative carrier (film holder) of the right size, a lens of the appropriate focal length, and you may need to change either the condenser lenses or their position to match the negative size to be printed.

If either condensers or enlarging lens fail to "cover" the negative, the edges of the enlargement will receive less exposure than the center. The result can be light corners on the print and a "hot spot" in the middle. The normal focal length enlarging lens for 35mm negatives is 50mm; for 6 x 6cm, 75 to 80mm; and for 4 x 5-inch negatives it should be at least 135mm.

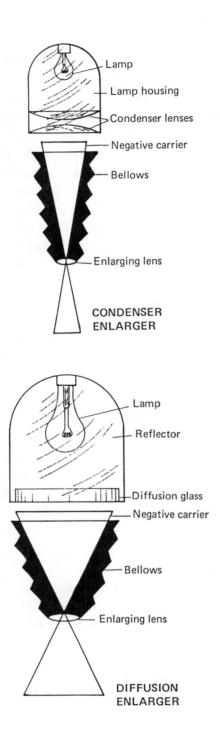

Lamp
Lamp housing
Condenser lenses
Negative carrier
Bellows
Enlarging lens
CONDENSER ENLARGER

Lamp
Reflector
Diffusion glass
Negative carrier
Bellows
Enlarging lens
DIFFUSION ENLARGER

The Darkroom

On the *dry* side of your darkroom you will need:

- **Enlarger**
- **Negative carrier**
- **Set of filters** and holder if required
- **Electronic timer**
- **Adjustable easel**
- **Contact proofing easel**
- **Focusing magnifier**
- **Anti-static brush**
- **Dodging and burning tools**
- **Negatives in file pages**
- **Enlarging paper** (8 x 10 variable-contrast RC recommended)
- **Paper trimmer** (rotary blade for safety)

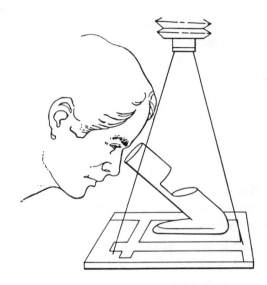

A focusing magnifier or "grain focuser" may make it easier to focus the image precisely on the enlarging easel. Be sure to re-check the focus before making your final print, however, because the negative may buckle slightly in the enlarger, throwing the image slightly out of focus.

The *wet* side of the darkroom should include:

- **Four 8 x 10 trays** (one may be larger, for washing)
- **Safelight(s)** type OC yellowish orange or sodium vapor
- **Timer or clock** with sweep second hand
- **Graduate** to hold one quart (one litre)
- **Thermometer** (dial type preferred)
- (optional) Print tongs
- **Towels** (clean and dry)
- (optional) Lab apron—or wear old clothes
- **Print developer** stock solution
- **Stop bath** concentrate
- **Fixer** concentrate
- (optional) Washing agent concentrate (needed only for fiber base paper)
- (optional) Print washer or tray siphon (needed for fiber base paper)
- **Squeegee board and squeegee**
- (optional) Print dryer or screen frames

Choosing paper

Because there are so many brands, types, and surfaces, your choice of enlarging paper will be influenced by availability and personal preference. A good beginning choice is 8 x 10 variable-contrast RC (resin coated) paper.

RC papers are available either with a smooth glossy surface or with a smooth or lightly textured matte (dull) or semi-matte finish. Be sure to examine the package carefully or ask advice before buying, because the coding can be confusing. For example, Kodak labels their Polycontrast RC glossy paper "F," their smooth matte "N," and a lightly textured semi-matte surface "E." Ilford Multigrade RC papers come either in *Deluxe* for tray processing or *Rapid* for processing either in trays or in a roller-transport machine. Ilford surfaces include *glossy,* similar to Kodak's "F," and *pearl,* which is a unique lustrous semi-matte.

Another reason to read the paper package label carefully is that Polycontrast and Multigrade papers are available with fiber base as well as resin-coated. Both RC and fiber papers also are available from several manufacturers with many names, contrast grades, weights and surfaces. Papers labeled with contrast grades one through five cannot be used with variable-contrast filters. The paper in a given package will yield prints only of that contrast level.

Although many fine art photographers prefer graded premium fiber-base paper for museum quality exhibition prints, RC paper has many advantages for everyday work.

Using RC paper

Prints made on RC paper require much shorter washing and drying time, and they usually dry with a smooth finish and lie perfectly flat for filing and mounting. The biggest disadvantage of RC paper is that if it is allowed to soak too long, water or chemicals may creep into the paper that is sealed between plastic layers, separating the edges and possibly affecting the permanence of the print. The most practical procedure is to batch process your prints. Fixing should require only two minutes. Shuffle the prints to keep them from sticking together. Prints can accumulate for a few minutes in a fresh water holding tray. Each batch then should be washed for about four minutes either in a rapid-flow archival washer or in a tray that is filled with running water from a hose and dumped and refilled frequently. If you are using the tray washing method, shuffle the stack of prints two or three times to keep them from sticking together. These prints should be placed immediately in a hot air drier or squeegeed and laid out on screen frames. Then you can return to the darkroom to expose and process the next batch.

Fighting dust in the darkroom

In the printing darkroom, dust is the biggest enemy. If your darkroom is air conditioned or ventilated so that filtered temperature- and humidity-controlled air is blown *into* the room at slightly higher pressure than outside, you'll have much less trouble with dust. In any event, good housekeeping is an absolute must. Vacuum away the dust regularly, but do this *after* a printing session rather than immediately before, to give the dust a chance to settle elsewhere than on your negatives. You'll probably notice the worst dust problems during dry weather when the air is heated and the humidity is low. Dried chemicals produce dust, so don't splash chemicals around. Mop up any spills immediately because chemical dust can leave horrible spots on sensitized materials. For this reason it's best either to purchase concentrated liquid chemicals or to mix solutions from powders *outside* the darkroom.

Making a Contact Proof Sheet

Contact proofs will simplify the filing of your negatives and make it easier to choose the best negatives from a series. You can make a contact sheet very easily using your enlarger as a light source. Here's how:

1. Set up chemicals exactly as for enlarging (see pages 134-141)

2. Place the proofer on the enlarger baseboard, directly below the lens. Put an empty negative carrier in the enlarger.

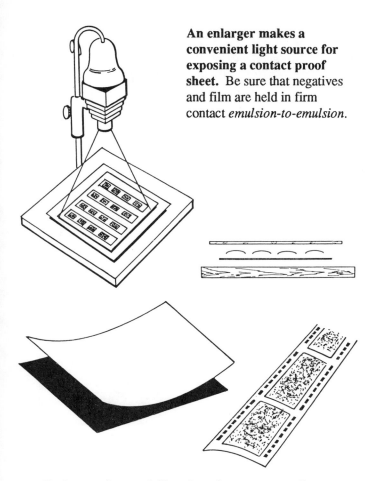

An enlarger makes a convenient light source for exposing a contact proof sheet. Be sure that negatives and film are held in firm contact *emulsion-to-emulsion.*

Both negatives and fiber-based paper normally tend to curl toward the emulsion side. RC papers, however, may sometimes fool you and curl backwards. Learn to tell the emulsion side of the brand of RC paper you use either by the gloss of the surface or by the printing on the back.

3. Set the enlarger timer for a test at 2 seconds.

4. Switch on the enlarger light, open the lens to its widest f/stop, and raise the enlarger head until the light beam covers the entire proofer and an inch or two around the edges. Turn off the enlarger light.

5. Under safelight, lay a sheet of 8 x 10 paper face (emulsion) up on the bottom of the proofer. Fiber-base paper usually curves toward the emulsion; RC paper lies flat. You can tell the emulsion side because usually it is shinier than the base. Sometimes the back has printing on it. If you can't tell the difference by looking, moisten a corner of the paper between your lips. (The slightly sticky

side is the emulsion). Place your transparent file page full of negatives *emulsion side down* over the paper. Lower the glass and hold it down firmly.

6. Holding down the glass, press the timer button and wait until the light goes out. Remove the paper, but leave the negatives in the proofer in case you have to make another exposure. Process the contact sheet according to the procedure below. If the entire sheet is too light, give the next one a few more seconds exposure time; if too dark, either give less time or close the lens opening one stop. When you get a good contact sheet, write down the number of seconds, the lens opening, the type of paper and the height of the enlarger so you can repeat what you did. If your negatives are consistently exposed and developed, the settings for future contact sheets will remain about the same.

Unless all your negatives are perfectly exposed some of the images on the contact sheet will be lighter, some darker. But you'll find that the proof sheet is very helpful in deciding which negatives to print. Examine each frame with a magnifying glass to check sharpness, facial expression, etc., and mark cropping directly onto the proof sheet with a marker or wax pencil.

Enlarging Procedure Step-by-Step

Processing prints is not very different from the procedure for developing film. The chemical solutions will be mixed from different formulas and in different dilutions, but they perform the same functions as they do with film.

The detailed instructions on pages 134-141 will show you how to make an enlargement.

> *I have never lost that initial thrill of watching an image surface in the developer.*
>
> (Jerry N. Uelsmann, photographer)

1

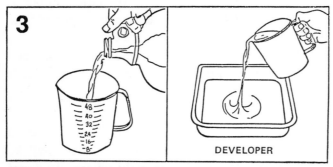

Arrange four clean trays in a row. Use trays that are slightly larger than the biggest print you plan to make.

2

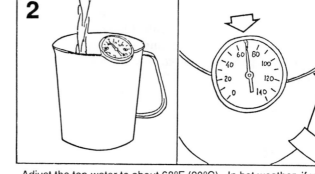

Adjust the tap water to about 68°F (20°C). In hot weather, if you cannot maintain 75°F (24°C) or below, you can use a plastic bag full of ice cubes to keep down the temperature of the developer.

3

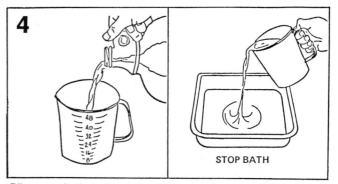

Mix print developer stock solution with approximately 68°F (20°) water according to the manufacturer's instructions to make 1 quart (1.1 litre). Pour developer into the FIRST tray. Rinse the beaker with water.

4

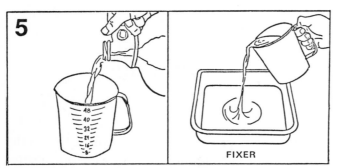

Dilute stop bath stock solution with water. The usual dilution is one ounce (30 mL) to make one quart (1.1 litre). Pour stop bath into the SECOND tray. Rinse the beaker.

5

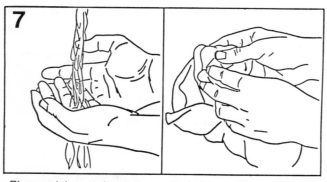

Dilute fixer stock solution according to manufacturer's instructions to make 1 quart (1.1 litre). Pour fixer into the THIRD tray. Rinse the beaker.

6

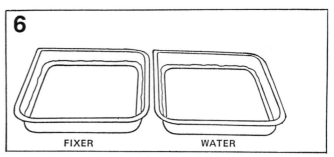

Fill the FOURTH tray with water as a holding bath.

7

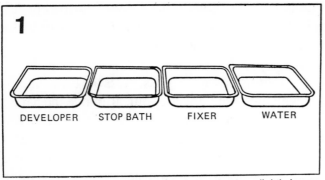

Rinse and dry your hands thoroughly before touching negatives, paper, or equipment.

8

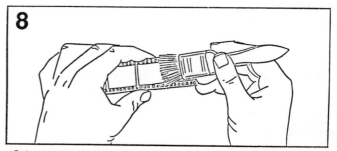

Select a negative to enlarge. Hold the film by the edges and gently remove dust from both sides of that frame with a soft brush.

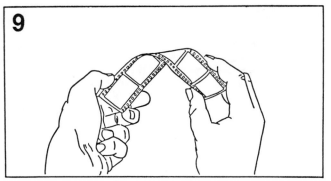

The emulsion side of the film is the *dull* side.

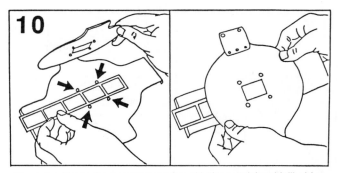

Place the film in the negative carrier with the emulsion (dull) side *down*. Center the negative between the pins. Close the carrier.

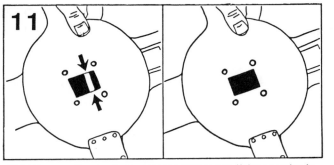

Hold the negative carrier toward the light to see if the negative is centered. Look for dust. Don't move the film without opening the carrier.

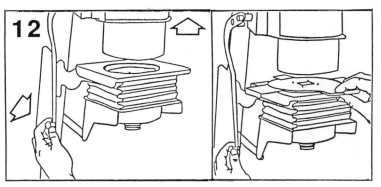

Raise the enlarger lamp housing and insert the negative carrier so the emulsion side of the film faces *down* toward the baseboard.

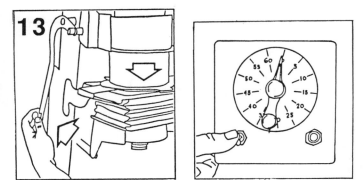

Lower the lamp housing. Turn on the enlarger lamp (switch to FOCUS on most timers).

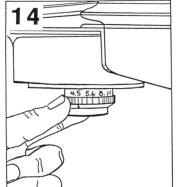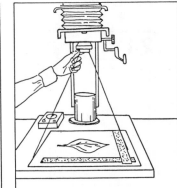

Rotate the aperture ring on the enlarger lens so the brightest image is projected onto the easel.

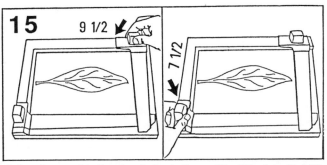

Adjust the easel to the size desired. For an 8" x 10" print with 1/4" borders, slide the side adjustment to 9 1/2" and the bottom adjustment to 7 1/2".

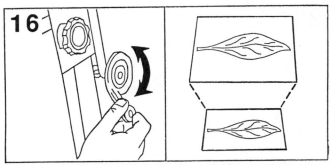

Make the image on the easel larger or smaller by raising or lowering the enlarger head.

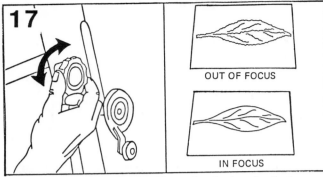

Focus the image on the easel by turning the focusing knob. Use a focusing magnifier if one is available.

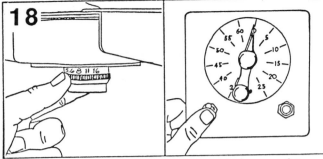

Rotate the aperture ring on the enlarger lens to decrease the brightness of the projected image by two click stops (f/8 or f/11). Turn off the enlarger lamp.

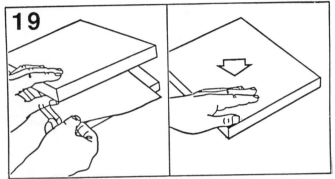

Remove a sheet of photographic paper from the box or envelope. Handle the paper only by the edges. REPLACE BOX COVER or CLOSE ENVELOPE!

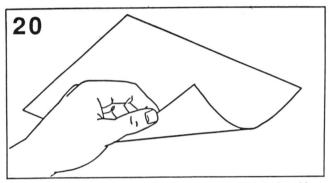

Determine the emulsion side of the paper. Usually it is the *shiny* side (the opposite of film). Handle the paper by the edges.

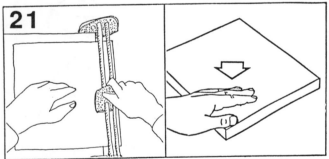

Cut the sheet of paper into test strips about one inch wide. Return the strips to the box or envelope and reclose it.

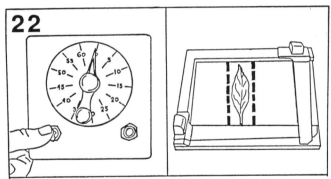

Turn on the enlarger lamp. Find an area of important detail with high values, such as skin tones or highlights in the image.

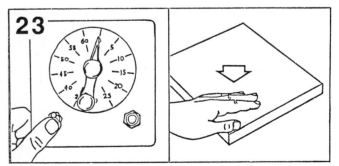

Turn off the enlarger lamp. Remove one of the strips of paper from the box or envelope and reclose it.

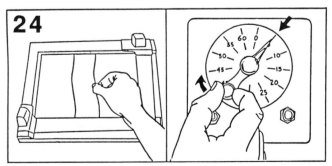

Place the strip of paper with the emulsion side (shiny side) up on the easel where the important detail will be projected. Set the timer for 2 seconds.

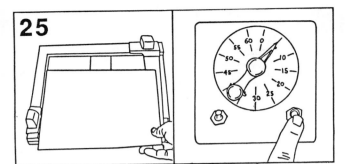

Cover 3/4 of the test strip by holding a piece of cardboard slightly above the easel but not touching the paper. Press the timer button to make a 2-second exposure.

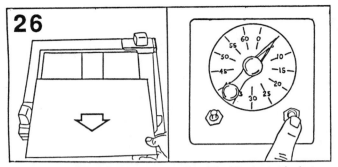

Move the cardboard to uncover another 1/4 of the test strip, but don't touch the paper and make it move. Press the timer button to make another 2-second exposure.

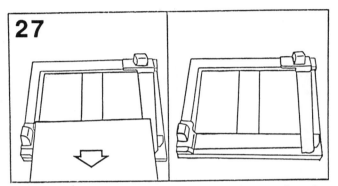

Continue until you have made four exposures of 2 seconds each. After developing, you will have a test strip with four exposures: 8, 6, 4, and 2 seconds.

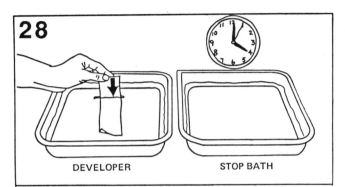

Without getting your hand wet, slide the test strip into the DEVELOPER so that the solution covers the entire strip. Note the time.

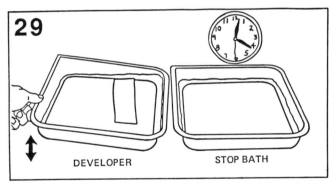

Constantly agitate the developer solution by gently rocking the tray. After 1 minute...

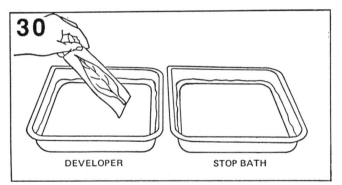

...lift the test strip by one corner and drain into the DEVELOPER tray for a few seconds...

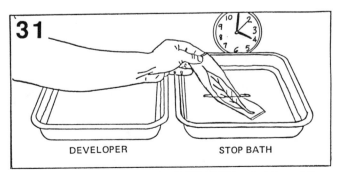

...then slide the test strip into the STOP BATH so that the solution covers the entire strip. Agitate. After about 10 seconds...

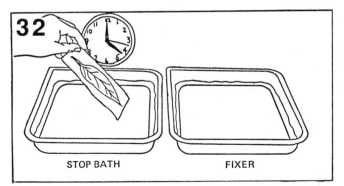

...lift the test strip by one corner and drain into the STOP BATH tray for a few seconds...

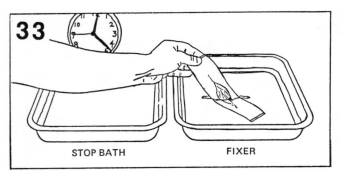

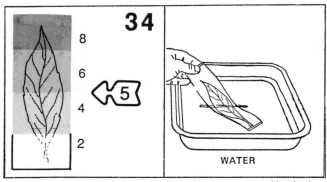

...then slide the test strip into the FIXER so that the solution covers the entire strip. Agitate. After about 30 seconds...

...examine the test strip by white light. If others are working in the darkroom, rinse the test strip in water, place it in a clean tray, and carry it outside the darkroom.

Determine the best exposure from the test strip and note the time. If the best time appears to be between two of the test sections, use an intermediate time.

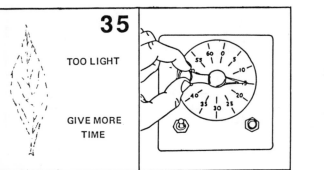

TOO LIGHT

GIVE MORE TIME

If the entire test strip is too *light,* make another test giving twice the time for each step.

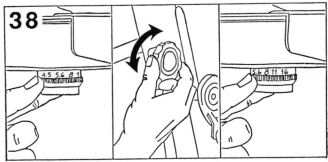

TOO DARK

GIVE LESS EXPOSURE

If the entire test strip is too *dark,* make another test at the same times as before, but *decrease* the brightness of the image by one more click stop on the lens (e.g. f/11 instead of f/8).

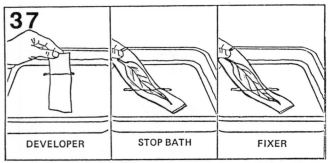

DEVELOPER   STOP BATH   FIXER

Process the test strip as before. Rinse it in water and examine it in white light. Afterward, rinse and dry your hands thoroughly.

When the test strip looks right, you're ready to make a full-sized print. Turn on the enlarger lamp.

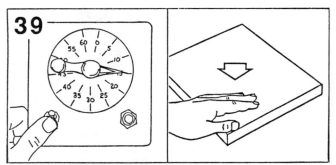

Rotate the lens aperture ring to project the brightest image. REFOCUS. Decrease the brightness of the image by stopping down the number of click stops determined by the test strips.

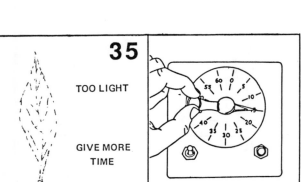

Turn off the enlarger lamp. Take a full sheet of paper from the box or envelope and reclose the package. Handle the paper only by the edges.

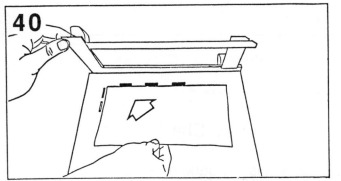

Raise the metal frame of the easel and place the paper—emulsion side up—against the corner guides. Lower the frame.

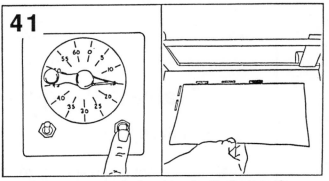

Expose the paper for the time determined by the test strip.

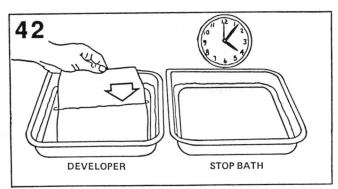

DEVELOPER   STOP BATH

Without wetting your hand, slide the paper into the DEVELOPER so that the solution covers the entire sheet. Note the time.

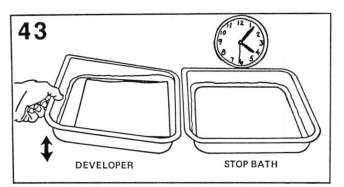

DEVELOPER   STOP BATH

Constantly agitate the developer solution by gently rocking the tray. After 1 minute...

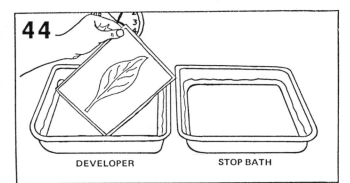

DEVELOPER   STOP BATH

...lift the print by one corner and drain into the DEVELOPER tray for a few seconds...

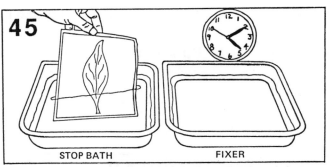

STOP BATH   FIXER

...then slide the print into the STOP BATH so that the solution covers the entire print. Agitate the tray. After about 10 seconds...

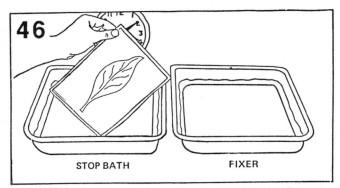

STOP BATH   FIXER

...lift the print by one corner and drain into the STOP BATH tray for a few seconds...

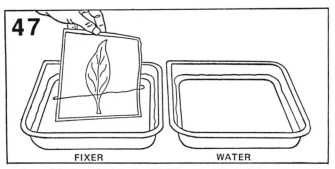

FIXER   WATER

...then slide the print into the FIXER so that the solution covers the entire print. Agitate the tray. After about one minute you can rinse the print in water and inspect it in white light.

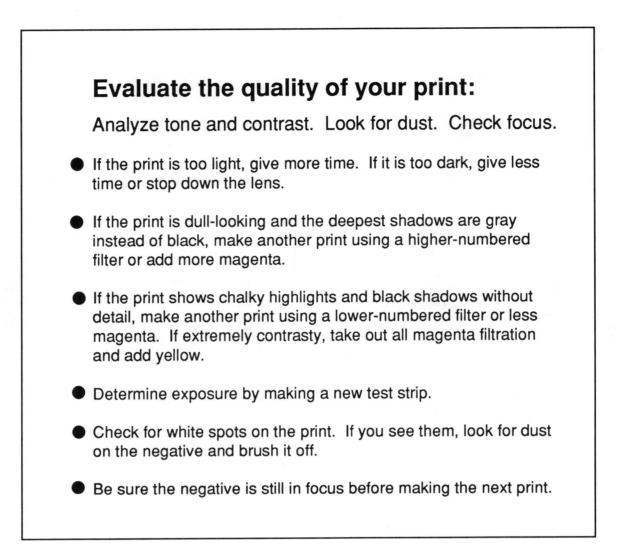

Evaluate the quality of your print:

Analyze tone and contrast. Look for dust. Check focus.

● If the print is too light, give more time. If it is too dark, give less time or stop down the lens.

● If the print is dull-looking and the deepest shadows are gray instead of black, make another print using a higher-numbered filter or add more magenta.

● If the print shows chalky highlights and black shadows without detail, make another print using a lower-numbered filter or less magenta. If extremely contrasty, take out all magenta filtration and add yellow.

● Determine exposure by making a new test strip.

● Check for white spots on the print. If you see them, look for dust on the negative and brush it off.

● Be sure the negative is still in focus before making the next print.

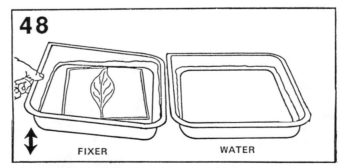

48

FIXER   WATER

When you finally are satisfied with your print, let it remain in the FIXER for about 2 minutes. Agitate the print every half minute or so by rocking the tray so the print always is covered by the solution. If several prints are in the tray, shuffle them so they don't stick together.

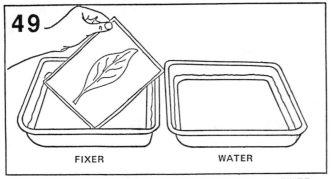

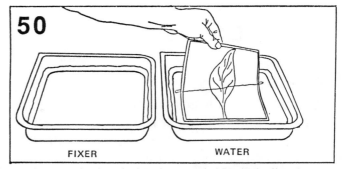

After fixing, lift the print by one corner and drain into the FIXER tray for a few seconds...

...then transfer the print into the water holding bath. If you're making several prints, they can accumulate in the water tray for as long as half an hour. Dump the tray occasionally and refill it with fresh water. Keep the prints separated so they don't stick together.

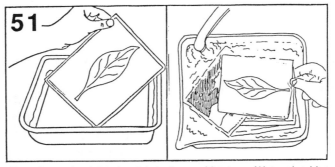

Transfer each print separately to the washing tray. Water should be flowing at about 68°F (20°C) if possible. Shuffle the prints gently to keep them separated. Dump and refill the tray a couple of times to accelerate washing.

While prints are washing, discard all solutions and rinse and drain all trays and accessories.

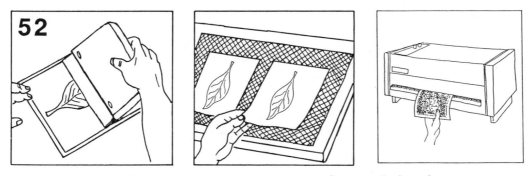

Transfer washed prints into a clean tray. Squeegee the face of each print and place it *face up* to dry on a screen frame or feed it into a hot-air dryer. (Fiber-base prints should be placed *face down* on a screen frame or dried in a blotter roll or canvas belt dryer.)

Printing Controls

Exposure

After you've made a good print from one negative, try working with other negatives of different density and contrast. You'll discover that although a normal negative may print well at 10 seconds, a very dense negative may require as much exposure as 30 or 40 seconds. On the other hand, a thin negative may need only one or two seconds to avoid coming up too dark in the developer.

Around 10 seconds is a practical exposure time—not too long to be boring, nor too short to allow some control. You may find that if you set your enlarger lens to about f/8 or f/11 the time will be about right. Otherwise, keep adjusting exposure time and lens opening as necessary. Make test strips. The rule about time vs. aperture is the same as adjusting a camera lens and shutter.

A group of so-called "normal" negatives all will print with about the same exposure. That's one of the advantages of using the zone system: your negatives will be much easier to print because they'll be more uniform in overall density and contrast.

Expose for light areas

Although "expose for the shadows" is the rule for negatives, you'll discover that exposing a print for the high values will give you better control. Once your tests show satisfactory tone and detail in the lightest important areas of the print (skin tones, snow, etc.), you can adjust relative values of the darker areas by filtration or choice of paper grade. By dodging, you can lighten shadow areas that print too dark. Incidentally, you'll have to increase the exposure if you raise the enlarger head to make a larger print or if you change filtration or use a different grade or type of paper. Each time you change something, make a new test strip.

Standardize development

With most papers, development time is not a control. A print developed for the recommended time (usually one to one and one-half minutes) will have the best quality. If the print comes up too dark

in the tray in less than a minute it's because it was overexposed. Leaving a light print more than a couple of minutes in the developer won't help much and the print may become fogged or stained. In either case, go back and make another test.

Allow for "dry down."

You'll soon discover that prints always look slightly darker under the safelight than they do when viewed under white light. So be sure to remember this when evaluating your prints: Let each print develop out for the full recommended time, then examine it under white light. If you're working in the darkroom with other people, I suggest that after fixing your print you rinse it in water, then place it in a clean tray and take it outside the darkroom where you can evaluate it properly.

But this isn't the end of the story. Your print will dry down somewhat darker and flatter than it looks while wet. Some very particular photographers actually sponge or blot off surface water from a print to get a preview of what it will look like when it's dry. RC paper requires such a short wash that you can go ahead and dry the print. Another useful alternative is to re-wet an extra print that has dried to your satisfaction and keep it in a tray of water as a sample to match similar values in the prints you're going to make later.

If you take a print out of the fixer to be viewed, rinse it off in water first to keep from contaminating the work area. But if you're going to keep that print, don't forget to put it back into the fixer for the required 2 minutes for RC papers or 10 minutes for fiber-base.

Control the contrast

Each print, with few exceptions, should have within it some tones of pure white and strong black. Sometimes these black and white areas will be very small, but usually they should be there. Also, with most subject matter there should be a full range of gray values in between the white and the black.

If you could use the zone system on every picture, controlling the entire process exactly, you could print every negative at a standard exposure setting without adjusting the contrast. In reality, each of us produces quite a few negatives that aren't quite

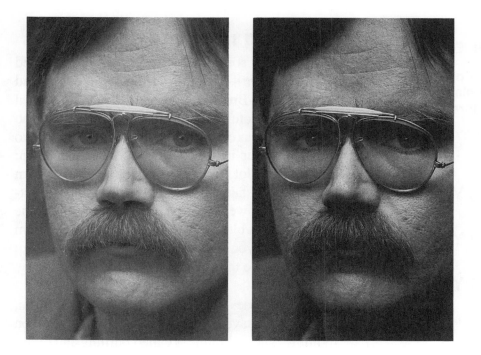

Filtration allows wide variations in print contrast. The same negative produced both versions on variable-contrast paper, the only variations being in exposure time and contrast filter (left: #1, right: #4).

perfect, and it's helpful to be able to do some compensating in the darkroom.

A flat, low-contrast negative may print very well when you add quite a lot of contrast, while a reduction in contrast may be needed for a negative that includes a range of brightness too great to record on the paper without help. Excellent prints never can be made from very *thin* negatives in which shadow detail has been lost due to underexposure. The same is true of extremely *dense* negatives that have opaque "blocked-up" highlights.

If you make your test strips of skin tones or other important values above zone V, and base your print exposure on those tests, then the dark values will indicate the contrast control you need.

If the areas that should be black in the print come out merely gray, then higher contrast is needed. To increase contrast with variable-contrast paper, use magenta filtration. If the shadows are so dark that important detail is lost and high values also lack texture, then you may want to reduce contrast by using either less magenta or yellow alone.

Color enlargers allow you to dial in magenta, yellow and cyan filtration. Only one color is used at a time because they will cancel each other out. Cyan is not used for printing black-and-white. White light (no filtration) is considered "normal" contrast, the same as grade 2 paper or *Polycontrast* or *Multigrade* filter number 2.

Contrast grades 1.5, 1, and 0 give progressively less contrast than "normal," while grades 2.5, 3, 3.5, 4, 4.5 and 5 give increasingly more.

Filters may change exposure

Make a new test strip whenever you change contrast. Exposure will be consistent between steps with some filter sets except for 4, 4.5 and 5. Others may vary over the entire range. Color enlargers require adjustment in time with every change of filtration. As magenta or yellow filtration is increased, less light is transmitted through the negative to the paper.

Black-and-white prints from color negatives

Kodak makes a special panchromatic paper called *Panalure,* that makes excellent black-and-white prints from color negatives. The trouble is, it has to be handled in the dark, like color paper. You can make pretty good prints, however, on regular paper if you add plenty of magenta filtration (equivalent to grade 3.5 or 4). Black-and-white *negative* prints can be made directly from color slides (page 203), but normal looking prints require that an internegative be made on film. This can be done most easily with a slide duplicator.

Approximate Contrast Filter Equivalents	
Paper Grade or Filter Number	Color Enlarger Filtration
0	80 Yellow
1/2	55 Y
1	30 Y
1 1/2	15 Y
2	0
2 1/2	25 Magenta
3	40 M
3 1/2	65 M
4	100 M
4 1/2	150 M
5	200 M

Each time you change filtration or paper grade there will be a change in exposure; so make a new test strip across the same high value as before. The greater the density of filtration, the more exposure increase will be required, but the increase will not always be predictable. Some electronic enlarging systems can meter for these changes, but most of us will have to use test strips.

Extraneous things get into photographs that you really have to weed out.

(Brian Lanker, *photojournalist*)

Cropping removes distractions

Although some of the most highly respected photographers—including Edward Weston and Henri Cartier-Bresson—apparently never trimmed any of their pictures, cropping is a way that we who do not yet see as clearly can have a second chance to recompose our images. Don't be afraid to crop; hindsight is a lot better than lack of sight. We learn by making mistakes, recognizing them, and correcting them. However, don't expect to get the same quality from a blow-up of a tiny portion of a 35mm negative that you could have achieved had you been able to enlarge the entire image.

As sometimes we second-guess on composition, we also can have a second chance to improve on lighting. The technique is called burning and dodging.

Dodging lightens areas

When part of the image prints darker than you want, you can shade that area during part of the exposure time. This process, called dodging, can be done with your hands or with a piece of opaque paper attached to the end of length of thin, stiff wire. The dodging device must be held well above the printing paper and kept moving to avoid a noticeable line between dodged and undodged areas. To find out how much dodging is needed, make a separate test strip of that area.

Burning-in darkens areas

The opposite of dodging, burning-in gives more exposure to selected parts of the print. This can be done by shaping your hands to cover all of the picture except the part to be darkened, but you probably can get better control by giving the extra exposure through a hole cut into a sheet of opaque paper or thin cardboard large enough to cover the entire print. Keep the paper with the hole in it well above the print and keep it moving so the effect isn't called attention to by a sharp edge or black spot. Pictures with light sky or a bright background often are improved by darkening the corners or edges by burning-in with a sheet of opaque paper or cardboard shaped to fit.

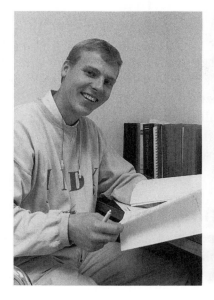 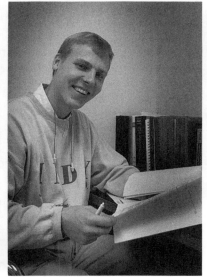

Ardyce Czuchna-Curl
Mill Engineer
Darkening the corners improves many pictures, especially portraits. Notice that in the print on the right, burning-in around the edges (dodging the center) helps concentrate attention on the subject's face, not the wall behind him, his white sweatshirt, or the papers in his hand.

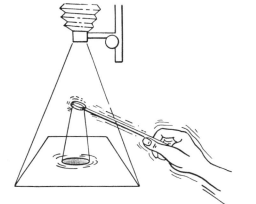

Ardyce Czuchna-Curl *Fire Chief*
Without dodging, the man in the cab printed much too dark. The same result could have been achieved by exposing for his face and burning-in everything else.

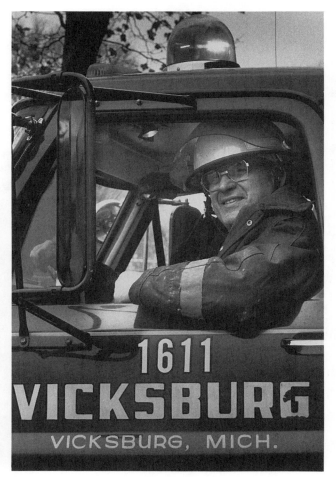

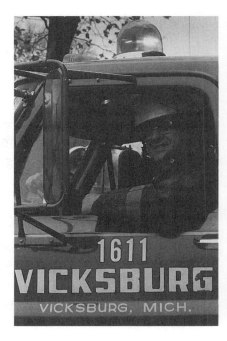

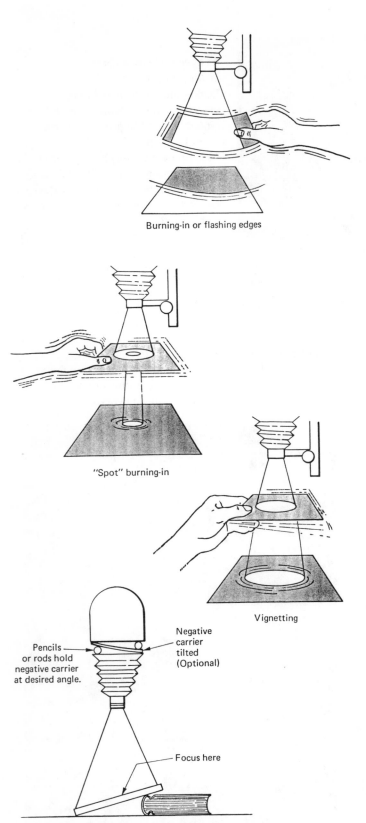

Burning-in or flashing edges

"Spot" burning-in

Vignetting

Pencils or rods hold negative carrier at desired angle.

Negative carrier tilted (Optional)

Focus here

Correcting perspective distortion: Focus carefully. Stop down the lens to achieve depth of field. Wrap opaque cloth around the bottom of the enlarger lamphouse to block stray light.

Flashing eliminates light areas

Flashing is burning-in with raw, white (or filtered) light to darken distracting highlights in a print. Either remove the negative and use the enlarger as a light source, or use a small flashlight with a paper or foil cone attached to selectively darken small light areas. Like dodging and burning-in, the flashed area must be blended smoothly into the rest of the image to avoid an artificial appearance.

Combining contrasts

Sometimes an image where part of the subject was in sunlight and part in the shade needs increased contrast in the shadows and decreased contrast in the highlights. This kind of control is possible with variable-contrast paper. The shadow areas are exposed with magenta filtration while the rest of the print is covered with opaque paper or cardboard, then the shadow areas are covered while the high values are exposed with yellow light (usually a much longer exposure). Making a separate test strip for each area will help you to determine the different exposure times.

Vignetting isolates a subject

Vignetting (pronounced vin-yet-ting) means burning-in the portion of the image that you want, while totally dodging out the rest (for example, taking one person's head out of a group picture). A commercially made adjustable plastic vignetter can be purchased, or you can make your own by tearing out an oval opening or whatever shape you want from a piece of black construction paper. Cut the edges of the opening sawtoothed or tear them raggedly. To avoid leaving a distinct edge, hold the vignetter well above the enlarging paper and keep it moving,

Tilting easel cures convergence

The most common example of convergence distortion occurs when the camera has been aimed upward to photograph a tall building. This makes the sides of the building seem to come together toward the top. A lot of convergence can be dramatic, but a little bit can be annoying when

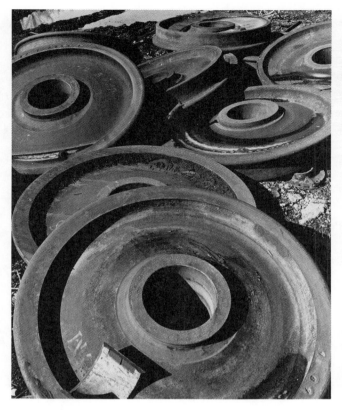

Straight print without flashing. Notice that light areas of contrasting shape and texture tend to compete for attention with the repeated oval forms of the wheels. Burning-in these areas would darken, but not eliminate them.

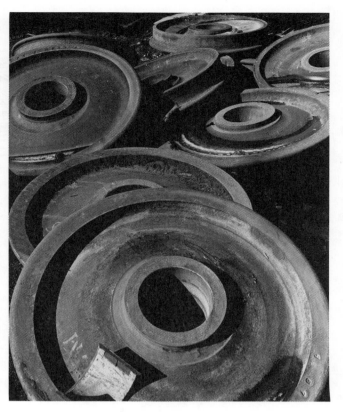

Flashing. **A small flashlight with a narrow "snoot" made from black tape was used to darken distracting light areas around the edges of this print.** A red filter under the enlarging lens allowed the image to be visible so that the exact places needing flashing could be located.

you're trying to keep the edges of a rectangular subject parallel with the margins of the print. You can correct this by tilting the easel, propping it up with a book or other support until the image looks right. You should focus about one third of the distance down from the highest point of the image and then stop down the lens far enough to bring the entire negative into sharp focus on the easel. If you can't get the image sharp enough by stopping down the lens, try tilting the negative carrier opposite the tilt of the easel by blocking it with a couple of pencils or strips or cardboard. Refocus carefully if you do this, and wrap a dark cloth around the negative carrier to block stray light from fogging your paper (or someone else's if others are in the darkroom).

Diffusion softens the image

Diffusion is the deliberate softening of an image. It is not the same as having the image out of focus. Diffusion makes dust, scratches, blemishes, retouching, and grain much less noticeable; and because it tends to hide skin wrinkles, diffusion is a favorite trick used by some portrait photographers to make aging subjects appear more youthful and glamorous. The process works best when a diffusion filter is attached to the camera lens, but it also can be done in the darkroom. You can make your own diffuser by holding beneath the enlarger lens a stretched-out piece of panty hose, fine metal window screening (black is best), or cellophane (crumpled, then smoothed out). The diffuser should be kept moving slightly during the print exposure and you should make a new test strip because the exposure probably will be longer than without diffusion. More contrast may be needed, also. The effect can be varied by holding the diffuser under the lens for only part of the exposure time.

Giant prints and posters

Most enlargers can be pivoted either at the base or at the head to enable a negative to be focused on the floor or on a wall. You may need to do this if you

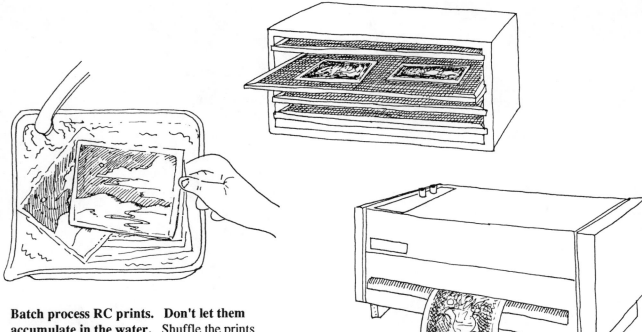

Batch process RC prints. Don't let them accumulate in the water. Shuffle the prints frequently in the washing tray so they don't stick together. Dry them either face up on screen frames or in a hot-air dryer.

want to make a print 16x20 or larger. Be careful to balance the enlarger so it doesn't fall. Enlarging paper comes in sheets up to 20x24 and in rolls 48 inches wide. If your easel isn't large enough, simply attach the corners of the paper to the wall or floor with loops of tape. Focus carefully!

Washing and drying prints

As you saw in the step-by-step instructions, prints on RC paper can be processed very quickly. Fiber base papers, however, should be washed in a rapid flow of water for at least one hour, or about 20 minutes if a washing agent is used to remove fixer and silver salts from the paper. In either case, prints should be agitated frequently and kept separated while washing.

Where water is scarce, an alternative method is to use a washing agent and then soak prints for a minute or two in each of six or more changes or water. Agitate the prints often and drain them well at each change.

Stains and fading are the result either of improper fixing or of not washing prints long enough. This effect may not be noticeable until several months, or even years, later. When permanence of the print is not very important, thorough washing is not necessary from the standpoint of the print itself. A serious side effect of insufficient washing is contamination of blotters, drying racks, or the canvas belt of a print dryer. Fixer left in prints by incomplete washing is transferred to other surfaces and soon even properly washed prints become contaminated by the drying equipment. Don't let this happen!

RC prints and matte prints on fiber-base paper may be dried in a number of ways. When a lot of prints need to be finished in a hurry, an electrically heated dryer can be very helpful. Special beltless dryers are available that remove the moisture from RC prints in seconds with a breeze of heated air. Some people dry fiber-base prints in a roll or stack of lint-free blotting paper, but the most popular drying technique for both RC and fiber-base prints is to squeegee the surface gently and spread the prints (RC prints face up, fiber usually face down) on fiberglass screening stretched over wooden or aluminum frames.

For that emergency rush job, an electric hair dryer will dry an RC print in a hurry!

A Dozen Paragraphs of Good Advice

1. Operate equipment gently. Learn where the adjusting and locking knobs are on the enlarger and please don't use brute force on them. Timer levers and switches will last years longer if operated with care.

2. Keep reference information. Read the printed data sheets that come with films, papers and developers. File a copy of each for future reference or tape them to your darkroom wall.

3. Handle film and paper only by the edges. Fingerprints can be forever, and they are almost certain to occur if you handle sensitized materials with damp hands.

4. Wear an apron or old clothes. Developer leaves a brown stain that's very hard to remove from clothing. According to Murphy's Law, the spots will occur on the front of your best white blouse or shirt!

5. Never reverse any processing steps. If you return a print or film to the developer after it has been in stop bath or fixer it will contaminate the developer. Always rinse your fingers or tongs before putting them back into the developer. Some photographers who use tongs reserve one pair for the developer and another for the stop bath and fixer.

6. Open paper carefully. Open each new package of photographic paper so that it can be resealed. Cut off a few strips of paper from one sheet for test exposures; then put the strips in the top of the package where they'll be handy when you need them.

7. Don't leave paper sitting out. Remove only one sheet of sensitized paper from the package at a time and then close the package. Even under safelights, photographic paper will fog if left out too long or kept too close to the light. Lifting the head of your enlarger with the lamp on to insert a negative or to check for dust will fog any paper that's on the counter top or in the developer tray. Accidentally turning on the room lights while the lid is off a full box of paper will be a memorable and expensive experience!

8. Ask before switching on lights. Don't turn on the white lights unless you check first to be sure that other people's paper is covered, as well as your own. Ask permission of anyone else working in the darkroom before turning on the lights or raising an enlarger lamphouse with the light on.

9. Reshoot poor negatives. Don't waste time trying to salvage a technically bad negative through the use of extreme paper-contrast grades, chemical reducers or intensifiers, and so on. If possible, correct your error by making another negative.

10. Refocus before reprinting. During the interval between the test strip and the final print, heat from the enlarger lamp may cause the negative to buckle or sag enough to throw your print annoyingly out of focus. Try using a focusing magnifier—this device makes it easier to focus sharply on the grain or fine detail of the negative. Don't forget to stop down the lens again after focusing!

11. Wash prints in batches. Washing time begins when the last print is put from the fixer or washing agent into the wash water. Another print will contaminate the batch if added to others already washing.

12. If in doubt, throw it out! Beware of chemical solutions in unmarked containers. The best practice is not to use any solution if its identity or age is in doubt. Developer and stop bath should be dumped after every printing session, even though only a few prints were made. Penny pinchers may want to reuse fixer and washing agent, although none of the solutions should be used for processing more than about 25 8x10 prints or the equivalent per quart (litre) of working solution. Developer turns brown with extreme exhaustion; some types of stop bath become purple. Worn out fixer may appear frothy, but by then it's too late. Keep track of the number of prints processed and make up fresh working solutions whenever they are needed.

What's Wrong with My Prints?

Image already too dark before one minute in the developer.

Cause: Overexposure.

Prevention or correction: Expose another print either for less time or at a smaller aperture. Make a test strip before exposing a large sheet of expensive paper.

Image still faint after one and one-half minutes in the developer.

Cause: Underexposure.

Prevention or correction: Expose another print either for more time or at a larger aperture. Make a test strip first.

Print exposed and developed properly, but the image looks gray and dull.

Cause: Not enough contrast.

Prevention or correction: Make another print with magenta filtration or grade 3 or 4 paper. First, make test strips to determine exposure and contrast.

Print dark enough overall, but lacks detail in high values.

Cause: Too much contrast.

Prevention or correction: Make another print using less magenta or all yellow filtration, or grade 1 paper. First, make test strips to determine exposure and contrast.

Corners of print very light; center appears normal.

Cause: Vignetting.

Prevention or correction: Use enlarger lens of correct focal length. If there are condenser lenses, be sure they are the right size and spaced properly. See if the filter holder is cutting off part of the light.

One side of print very light, rest of print normal.

Cause: Partial vignetting.

Prevention or correction: Straighten negative carrier and insert it all the way. Inspect alignment of enlarger and filter holder.

Highlights of print gray, but margins pure white.

Cause: Light fog.

Prevention or correction: Check for light leak in enlarger: around negative carrier, filter holder, or lens mount.

Print overall gray, including margins.

Cause: Light or chemical fog.

Prevention or correction: Keep unexposed paper in light-tight package at all times. Be sure paper is fresh and has been stored at cool or moderate temperature. Inspect darkroom for light leaks. Check safelights for proper filter and brightness. Be sure developer is fresh and properly diluted.

Black streaks on edges or corners of prints.

Cause: Paper partially exposed to light.

Prevention or correction: Be sure paper is covered before turning on white light.

Thin white line in same place on all prints from same negative.

Cause: Small scratch on negative.

Prevention or correction: Handle negatives carefully. Print with diffusion-type enlarger to hide the scratch.

Thin black line in same place on all prints from same negative.

Cause: Deep scratch on negative.

Prevention or correction: Handle negatives carefully.

Blurred double-image effect.

Cause: Vibration.

Prevention or correction: Don't bump the enlarger during exposure.

Small white spots and "snakes" in sharp focus.

Cause: Dust and lint on negative.

Prevention or correction: Blow and/or brush off dust before exposing print.

Fuzzy, unsharp light patches on print.

Cause: Dirt on enlarger lens, filter, or condensers, or obstruction in lamphouse.

Prevention or correction: Clean lens and filters; inspect inside of lamphouse.

Print fuzzy and diffused overall, but in focus.

Cause: Very dirty enlarger lens or filter. Poor quality lens or lens taken apart.

Prevention or correction: Clean lens and filters. Check lens. Don't unscrew anything!

Print partly out of focus.

Cause: Negative buckled, not held flat in carrier, or enlarger misaligned.

Prevention or correction: Reinsert negative. Check alignment. Refocus.

Short, dark random lines on faces of prints.

Cause: Abrasion.

Prevention or correction: Handle prints gently in developer.

Dark oval or teardrop-shaped stain in corner or along one edge of print.

Cause: Holding onto the print with thumb and forefinger while it is in the developer tray or draining.

Prevention or correction: Don't hold print more than a few seconds with your fingers. Use tongs.

Muddy-looking, mottled print.

Cause: Uneven development or underdevelopment.

Prevention or correction: Slide print under developer solution quickly and completely. Develop for full time, agitating tray constantly.

Irregular dark stains on face of print.

Cause: Excessive handling in the developer.

Prevention or correction: Keep your hands off the print while it's developing. Lift with tongs. Agitate by rocking the tray.

Overall yellow or purplish stain.

Cause: Insufficient fixing (overall yellow stain on RC prints may be from insufficient washing).

Prevention or correction: Fix and wash for proper time. Don't let prints stick together or float on the surface. If you inspect a print from the fixer tray, be sure to return it for complete fixing. Shuffle the prints gently two or three times in fixer and wash.

Brown or yellow stains on back of dried print.

Cause: Chemical contamination.

Prevention or correction: Wash prints fully. Clean squeegee board and clean or replace print drying surfaces.

Cracks in emulsion.

Cause: Wrinkling or folding.

Prevention or correction: Handle prints gently—don't let them get bent or tumbled roughly in washing. Watch prints as they go into dryer.

Scratches or gouges on emulsion.

Cause: Abrasion.

Prevention or correction: Be careful with tongs. Trim long fingernails. Don't let sharp corners of one RC print scrape the surface of another.

Emulsion frilled or separated on corners or edges of print.

Cause: Wash water too warm, or print soaked too long in water or washing agent.

Prevention or correction: Keep temperatures below 75°F (24°C). RC paper shouldn't stay wet more than about 30 minutes; fiber-base papers no more than a couple of hours.

Fiber-base prints curl excessively

Cause: Prints dried too fast or humidity too low.

Prevention or correction: Flatten in a mounting press or under weight. If necessary, moisten backs of prints and re-dry in a blotter roll.

Prints stuck together

Cause: Prints not completely dry when stacked.

Prevention or correction: Soaking stuck fiber-base prints in water may permit them to be gently peeled apart without damage. RC prints probably cannot be separated without tearing off the emulsion.

Print Finishing and Display *8*

The name of the game is to get your work seen.

(Ed Paschke, painter)

Making a quality print is only part of the process. You probably want to show your prints to people and you want your work to look its best—permanently. That means mounting, and/or matting and framing, and effective display. It may mean toning. And you may be one who is concerned with archival processing so that your photographs can be enjoyed by future generations.

Archival Processing

Most photographic materials including prints on RC papers will last for many years without apparent deterioration if they are processed carefully in fresh solutions, according to manufacturer's instructions, and stored with reasonable care. So unless you're producing prints for a museum collection, you might not have to worry about archival processing. If you are concerned, here are some major points to consider:

1. Overfixing RC prints can cause fixer to creep into the paper base that is sandwiched between plastic layers. Fix RC papers only two minutes in fresh fixer, wash immediately four minutes in rapidly changing water (don't let the prints stick together) and dry immediately.

2. Fiber-base prints should be treated four to five minutes (with agitation and separation) in each of two successive baths of fresh fixer. Don't allow prints to accumulate in the fixer. Use a water holding bath. Change the water in the tray every few minutes and wash batches of prints frequently.

3. The life of fiber-base prints can be extended by toning in gold-protective or selenium toner according to the manufacturer's instructions. An economi-

cal and satisfactory short cut procedure is to transfer prints directly from the final fixing bath into a solution of selenium toner and washing agent:

Kodak Hypo Clearing Agent working solution
1 gallon (4 litres)
Kodak Rapid Selenium Toner concentrate
3.5 ounces (100 mL)
Kodalk Balanced Alkali 2.5 ounces (75 grams)

Agitate prints constantly while they are in the toner solution, watching for any noticeable shift in image tone. Three minutes is enough time for protective toning. With some papers, a longer time in the toner solution will pleasantly intensify the blacks and may give a warm effect to the image. Discard the solution after about ten 8x10 prints or the equivalent have been treated per liter.

4. Wash treated fiber-base prints in an archival washer that completely separates the prints, or dump the wash water every five minutes and manually separate the prints, placing a different one on top each time. A total washing time of 30 minutes at 68-75° F (20-24° C) is probably adequate, although maximum permanence is attained by using a bath of Hypo Eliminator (Kodak HE-1 formula) followed by an additional 20-minute wash.

5. Squeegee or sponge excess moisture from both the front and back of each print. Use only a clean squeegee or sponge for this purpose, and lay the print on a smooth, nonabsorbent surface such as a stainless steel plate or a sheet of plexiglass. The bottom of a plastic photo tray should not be used as it may harbor chemical residue.

6. Air dry fiber prints face down on thoroughly clean fiberglass screening stretched onto frames.

7. Mount prints with dry-mounting tissue or corners on 100 percent rag or other sulfite-free board. If an overmat is to be used, it too should be cut from sulfite-free board.

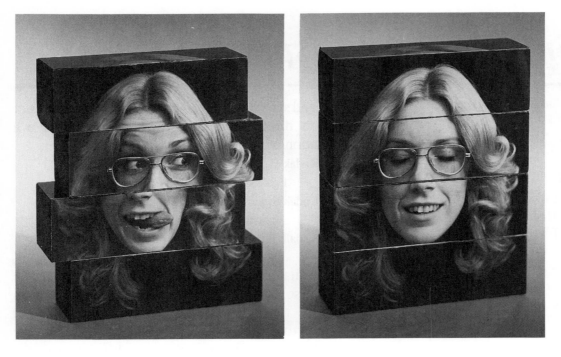

Betsy Hornbeck
Self-portrait
Only two of the many combinations of this entertaining, three-dimensional self-portrait are shown here. The photographer cut enlargements of four different poses into four equal-sized strips, mounting each strip on one side of a wooden block.

Permanent Mounting

Your portfolio will look more professional if the prints are consistent in format. For example, 8x10 prints look good on mounts cut to 11x14, 12x15, or 13x16. 11x14 prints often are mounted on 16x20. You probably will want to use 4-ply board, which is about 1/16" (1.5mm) thick. The size can depend on whether you buy ready-cut board or cut it down yourself from large sheets which come in various sizes. 22x28 cuts perfectly into four 11x14s, 30x40 cuts into six 12x15s, and 32x40 makes six pieces 13x16 with very little waste. Keep the mount dimensions to even inches because sectional frames come that way.

Acid-free conservation board is ideal, but expensive. Good illustration board usually costs less and will last for many years. It pays to shop around because the college bookstore or a local art supply store may have bargains in "slightly shopworn" smooth-surfaced illustration board that can be cut down perfectly for mounting photographs.

The kind of heavy-duty trimmer found in print shops is ideal for cutting mounting board, although you can do very well in your own studio with a razor-sharp, stout-bladed utility knife and a metal carpenter's square. When cutting with a knife and square, be sure to cover the work surface with a piece of scrap cardboard or building board and make several straight, decisive cuts until the knife cuts clear through. A few circular swipes on a pocket carborundum hone will keep your knife blade sharp and lessen the chance of leaving ragged edges. Be sure to cut away from the "good" part of the mounting board so you won't damage that part if the knife slips. The same cutting technique applies to foam core, which is a convenient backing material if you frame your prints. Be careful with the knife!

Overmats usually look better if all layers of the mat board are of the same color and texture, especially if the edges of the mat opening are to be beveled. Of course sulfite-free board should be used for both mat and backing if archival permanence is important.

What about colored mats and mounts? In photography, the general rule is to use white unless there is a very strong reason not to. Some prints look better with a gray or buff mat, and a few prints—very few—require black. Sometimes color prints can be matted effectively with a harmonizing color, but this is a matter of taste.

A photograph usually should be complete within its own borders and not need a mat to complete the graphic balance or enhance the tonal range of the print. A colored or textured mat seems more often to compete with, rather than to complement, most photographs. The support should be just that—a background to support the image; a mat is a window through which the image is viewed. Neither should distract or call attention away from the photograph.

When the tone of parts of the image tends to merge with the mounting board, you might want to choose a tone that separates well. When a white background doesn't show up against white, you could consider adding a thin black line around the photograph. A few photographers print all their negatives full-frame, using an oversize negative carrier that automatically leaves a slightly irregular border around each image. A more flexible approach that permits cropping is to add a black border by flashing the edges when the print is made. Other alternatives include offset mounting using two contrasting boards or careful use of black charting tape or a technical pen after the print has been mounted. Ink can smear and tape may peel off after a while, but either method will work.

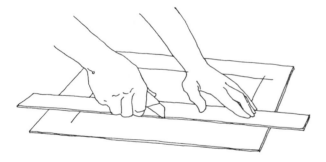

Work expands so as to fill the time available for its completion.

(Parkinson's Law)

Dry mounting is the most professional of all mounting methods because carefully dry-mounted prints are neat, flat, and permanent. Several types of adhesives are available including some "cold" processes using an adhesive with peel-off backing, but hot mounting with a press is preferred. The following procedure is for mounting RC prints using Seal *ColorMount* tissue. This same material can be used to mount fiber-base papers and the process is very similar. Other adhesives are available, some of which are intended for use at different temperatures. For best results, read the manufacturer's instructions.

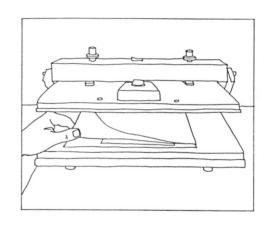

Creating a black border.
Some photographers use an oversized negative carrier to obtain thin black borders around their prints. But this means that the entire negative must be printed full-frame. A practical alternative method which permits cropping, is to flash the edges of the image with raw white light from the enlarger after the exposure has been made and the negative removed, masking the picture area with an opaque sheet of cardboard.

(photo by Brian Kuehn)

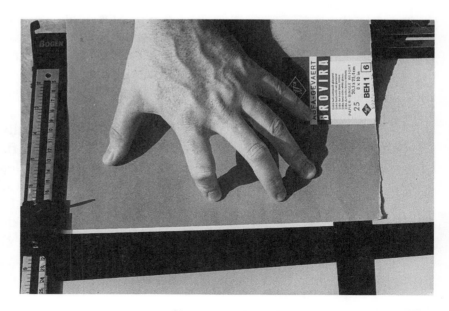

Dry Mounting RC Prints With a Press

1. Turn on the press and adjust the temperature control to 205°F (96° C). Allow about half an hour for the press to warm up.

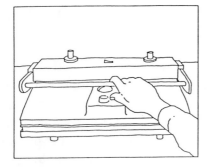

2. Plug in a tacking iron and set it for medium temperature. Allow it to warm up.

3. Predry the mounting board for 30 to 60 seconds between sheets of clean kraft paper or thin acid-free mounting board. close the press, but don't lock it. Open the press to allow moisture to escape, then repeat the process. Fiber-base prints should also be predried in the same way. It is not usually necessary to predry RC prints.

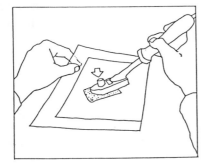

4. Attach a sheet of Seal *ColorMount* tissue to the center of the back of the print by holding the flat tip of the tacking iron against a small piece of release paper *(teflon side down, next to the adhesive)* for about 10 seconds. Be sure there are no particles of dirt or grit between the print and the tissue.

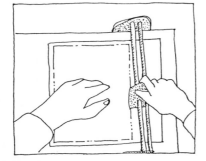

5. Trim the edges of the print with tissue attached. This is easiest and most precise with a rotary trimmer. With a guillotine paper cutter you should hold the materials firmly to keep them from slipping and being cut crooked.

6. Place the print face up on the mounting board. Center it the way you want. If you're going to use an overmat, it's easier to cut the mat first and use the mat as a guide for positioning the print.

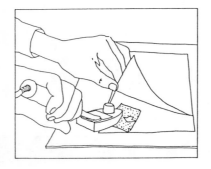

7. Attach two diagonally opposite corners of the tissue to the mounting board. Hold the flat tip of the tacking iron against a small piece of release paper *(teflon side down, next to the adhesive)* for about 10 seconds. Press out slightly with the tacking iron toward each corner so you don't gather a fold of tissue back under the print. Be sure there aren't any particles of dirt of grit between the tissue and the print and the mounting board.

8. Place the print, attached to the mounting board, face up inside the press on top of the foam rubber pad. Be sure no particles of dirt or grit are present, then cover the print and board with an oversize sheet of release paper *teflon side down,* next to the face of the print. Or place the print and board inside a folder made from release paper.

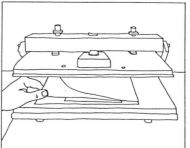

9. Lock press closed for about 30 seconds.

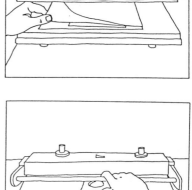

10. Open the press. Quickly transfer the print with its release paper cover to a clean flat surface. Cover immediately with a heavy metal plate (bonding occurs during cooling). After allowing a minute or so for cooling, inspect the bond. If the print has not adhered completely, return it to the press for a longer time and/or increase the heat slightly. If blisters or dull spots show on the surface of an RC print, the press temperature is too high. Remember Murphy? He always advises: *"Never mount your best print first!"*

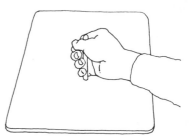

Cutting an Overmat

An overmat is a sign of professionalism that adds elegance to a print, especially if it is to be framed. A mat also serves to separate the print emulsion from the glazing, lessening the possibility of moisture condensation and fungus growth inside.

Mats are easy to make if you have access to a mat-cutting machine. They also can be cut by hand with a beveled knife holder and a metal square. The blade should be very sharp, so be careful with the knife! Practice first with scrap board. Be sure to cut against a smooth and expendable surface such as a discarded sheet of illustration board.

A mat may be cut from the same board used for mounting, unless the color of the inside laminations in unsuitable.

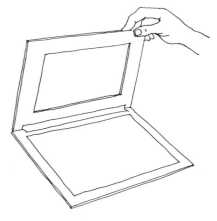

A hinged two-part mat.
Slip the print into mounting corners and you have a quick method for temporary display.

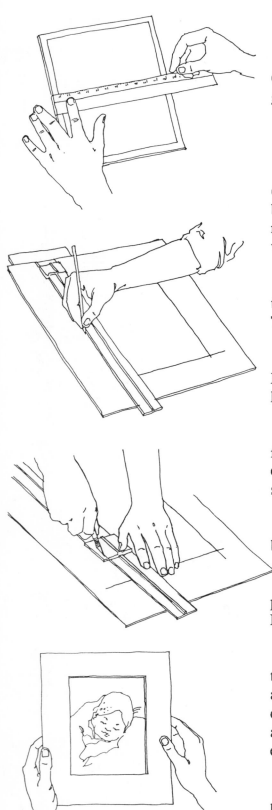

Here's how to cut a mat for an 8x10 print to be mounted on 11x14 board:

1. Decide how wide you want the mat opening (7")

2. Subtract the width of the opening from the width of the board (11 - 7 = 4), then divide by two to figure how wide the side margins should be (2")

3. Decide the height of the mat opening (9")

4. Subtract the height of the opening from the length of the board (14 - 9 = 5), then divide by two if you want equal spacing top and bottom. Artists often leave slightly more space below the print and make the top margin the same as the sides. If we do that, the top margin will be 2" and the bottom 3".

5. On the back of the mat board, pencil mark the margin widths for the top and sides of the opening. Use either a carpenter's scribe or a T-square.

6. Prepare the mat knife by inserting a new or sharpened blade. Place the knife into the slot for either a straight or beveled cut (X-Acto knife holder is shown. There are many types).

7. Hold your body against the base of the T-square and press down firmly on the end of it with one hand so it doesn't slip. Carefully cut each of the marked lines in turn, from the back of the board, cutting slightly beyond each of the corners.

8. Finish the corners, if necessary, with a new single-edge razor blade. Be careful to maintain the angle of the cut, and don't cut too far.

9. Line up the finished mat with the mounting board and insert the print so it is centered the way you want it within the opening in the mat. Lift the mat and mark the corners where the print should be mounted.

10. Dry mount the print as usual. If the mat opening is smaller than the photo, the edges won't show, so you won't have to be as careful about trimming them. Photographers who prefer full-frame images often cut the mat opening oversize and align the print within, leaving a wider space at the bottom for a signature. Assembling shows is much easier if all mats are cut to a standard size so they are interchangeable.

11. Hinge the mat to the backing board with a nonbleeding, nondrying tape made for library or office use. A hinge isn't needed if the print is to be framed.

Spotting

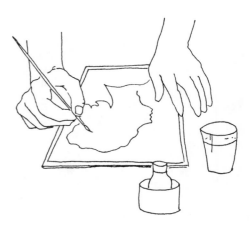

Along with dry mounting, spotting is another factor that sets apart professional quality prints. No matter how carefully you brush and blow before enlarging, a few specks of dust will cling to the negative. To camouflage those remaining dust spots you'll need a very fine (00), high-quality red sable watercolor brush and *SpoTone* dye, number 3.

Some people like to prepare a palette of various *SpoTone* dilutions, but you may find it easier to work directly from the bottle cap following this procedure:

1. Be sure the cap is on tight; invert the bottle and then right it again. Unscrew the cap and leave it on the worktable. Put the uncapped bottle someplace where it won't get knocked over (make a tip-proof bottle holder from the plastic cap of an aerosol spray can). Allow the dye in the bottle cap to dry for a few minutes.

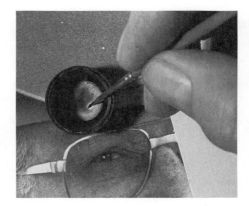

2. Moisten your brush enough to point it, then draw the tip of the brush over the dried dye in the bottle cap. Although it might not seem genteel, the tip of your finger moistened with saliva makes an excellent palette for moistening and pointing the brush. Or you can use a little water in a shot glass or small beaker and a paper towel or tissue for wiping the brush.

3. If you're spotting within a dark area, apply the dye full-strength directly to the spot with the very tip of the brush. Don't try to paint on the dye, but stipple with several tiny touches of the brush tip, working from the center of the white spot outward to blend the edges with the background.

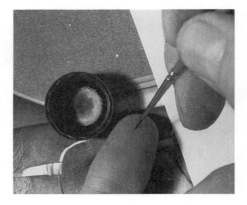

4. When the background of the spot is lighter, you'll have to dilute the dye. Use more water or saliva on the brush when you pick up the dye; then draw the tip of the brush across the end of your finger or the paper towel to get a lighter color and drier brush before touching the brush tip to the print. Keep the brush almost dry, and always dilute the dye more than you think necessary; then go back and add more. If you put on too much dye, it's permanent—you make another print!

Scratches and hair lines can be hidden with spotting dye, too. You do lines by drawing the tip of the brush very slowly and very lightly along the length of the white line to be covered, going back several times to make the blend undetectable. With patience, practice, and a strong light you can do it!

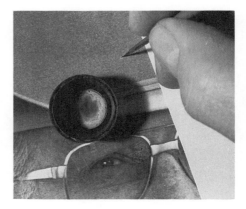

Etching and bleaching

SpoTone will take care of white spots on a print, but it won't do anything about black spots. These can be removed by etching or bleaching, but the cure may be worse than the problem. Etching nearly always mars the surface, although tiny spots on matte paper can be worked down with the tip of a very sharp razor knife. The idea is to shave away the emulsion a layer at a time, stopping before you remove everything down to the white paper base.

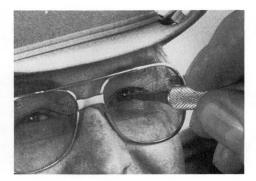

Etching catchlights. With a sharp razor knife you can etch tiny catchlights into eyes that otherwise would be dark and lifeless.

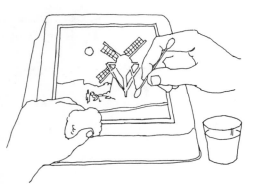

Another way to get rid of a dark spot is to bleach it with potassium ferricyanide solution (Farmer's reducer) or with a 10% solution of tincture of iodine. The same technique can be used to "dodge" very dark shadow areas. Here's what you do:

Lay the damp print over the back of a tray, then apply small amounts of the bleach solution with a small brush or a cotton swab, blotting away any excess bleach with a sponge or paper towel before it spreads. Bleach and blot several times until you get the desired result, then refix and wash the print. Fixer accelerates bleaching, so for major lightening of tone you can alternate between applications of bleach and fixer. The process may leave a yellowish stain that usually goes away when the print is refixed and rewashed.

Displaying Your Photographs

Framing adds a final touch of elegance to your work for public exhibition or permanent display. (How can it be *art* without a frame?) Ornate frames usually are inappropriate for photographs, but a tasteful silver or black narrow-edged frame can add to the appeal of a print, as well as keep it flat and protected.

Ordinary single-strength window glass commonly is used in frames, but acrylic sheet is popular because it is light, unbreakable (although it will scratch easily) and may help to protect the print from harmful ultraviolet radiation. You can buy either glass or acrylic and have it cut to size at a full-service hardware store. So-called non-glare glass seldom is used to frame photographs because its semi-matte surface tends to gray out the blacks in the print.

Better to avoid reflections in the glazing by hanging framed prints on walls that don't face windows, lights sources or light-colored walls.

Setting up gallery space

If you're preparing a gallery of your own, try lining one or more walls with either dark cork or soft building board (Celotex or Homosote) covered with rough, loosely woven material such as monk's cloth. Either of these surfaces will accept pushpins readily for temporary display of unframed prints. A convenient semi-permanent display for an office or hallway can be made by screwing two strips of wood molding to the wall. If the strips are positioned properly, the prints and their cover glass can be slipped in and out quite easily.

Assembling a Nielsen sectional aluminum frame

Very popular with photographers, this relatively inexpensive type of frame is available in art supply stores and photo shops everywhere and is quick and easy to assemble. Here's how:

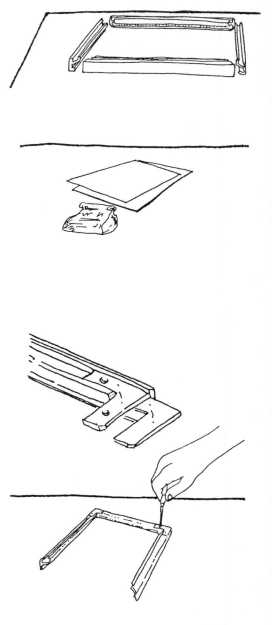

1. Lay out all the frame pieces on your work table. Open the bag of hardware and be sure you have four pairs of corner angles with screws, two hangers and two bumper pads. Also there probably will be several flat metal springs.

2. Clean the glass or slowly strip the covering from acrylic sheet. Gently brush off dust. If static electricity draws dust on plastic glazing, try grounding the sheet against a water pipe for a few minutes or simply let it stand until the charge goes away.

3. Assemble the glazing, mat, mounted print, and backing. Foam core makes a convenient backing. Because of the thickness of foam core, you probably won't need to use the metal springs to hold the materials in the frame. Be sure that no dust, lint or hair is trapped where it can be seen under the glazing.

4. Insert one pair of corner angles (with the name facing up on both pieces) into the track at each end of one short section of the frame. The thin angle goes inside and the thick one with the screws outside. Don't tighten the screws yet.

5. Slide the two long frame sections over the angles, making a "U". Holding the corners firmly together, tighten all four screws.

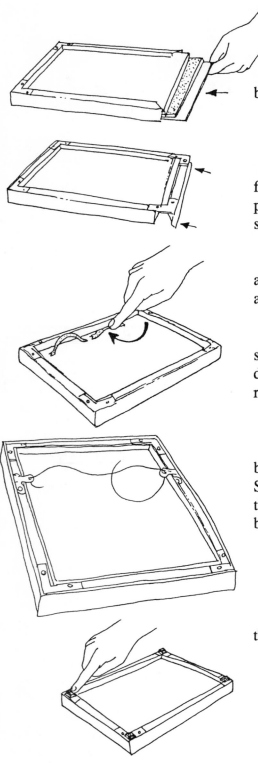

6. Slide the assembled package of glazing, mat, mounted print and backing into the channel in the frame.

7. Insert the remaining pairs of corner angles into each end of the final frame section. Slide the exposed ends of the angles into the side pieces of the frame, draw the corners together, and tighten all four screws.

8. Inspect the front of the frame to see that the corners are correctly aligned and that no dirt is trapped inside. Then check the tightness of all the screws.

9. If the backing isn't thick enough to fill the channel, space the flat springs around the inside of the frame and slide them into place. If you do use the springs, and you want to take the frame apart, be sure to remove them before unscrewing the corner angles.

10. Snap one hanger into each side of the back of the frame, just below the top corner angles. (There also are other types of hangers. See instructions). Picture wire may be strung between the hangers, but the best method is to hang the frame from two nails. If the nails have been leveled on the wall, the picture will never hang crooked!

11. Attach a rubber wall bumper to each bottom corner. Peel off the backing and stick them to the frame.

A...photograph need not be explained, nor can it be contained in words. My photographs are presented as ends in themselves, images of the endless moments of the world.
(Ansel Adams, photographer)

Photographing People and Things 9

Camera lens, film, developer and printing paper have but one purpose: to capture and present light...light is too often unknown, unstudied, and abused by photographers.

(Edward Weston, photographer)

In photography, light is everything! Light is the force that illuminates subjects so we can photograph them. Light reveals form and texture. If you're going to make successful photographs of people and objects, first you must learn to observe light as it falls naturally on shapes and surfaces; then you must control the quality, direction, and intensity of light so that your subjects are most significantly revealed

Notice the Light

Wherever you are, observe the effect of light on human faces. Notice how light can envelop a subject softly and gently, or harshly highlight irregularities. The way we see texture depends on whether light floods the surface with general illumination or skims the surface. Light coming from an angle creates shadows that emphasize and strengthen the natural feeling of roundness or roughness.

Become aware of distance, become aware of direction, become aware of bounce, become aware of the absence of light, become aware of reflectiveness...

(W. Eugene Smith, photographer)

There are certain cliches about light. Light that's bright and all-encompassing can imply a feeling of airy openness, space, and happiness. Lightness also may be associated with innocence or femininity. Absence of light creates mysterious shadows that may appear ominous and threatening—or deep tones that may imply drama, dignity, or strength.

Whether you're picturing people, pets or prod-

ucts; boats, buildings or boxes; rivers or rocks; snow or sand, the same general lighting principles apply.

When planning a picture, determine first the quality, direction and intensity of the *main* or *key* source of light. Study the desirable or unsatisfactory effects of the light as it falls on the subject. Note how the light will affect the exposure and development required to reproduce the subject naturally. Then decide how you will change the light or its effects to get the result you want. You may decide to return when the light is different.

Light is never stable and never the same a second time...Light makes each succeeding minute of every environment a new experience, and gives each situation the potential for aesthetic discovery.

(Charles Swedlund, educator)

Because we're accustomed to seeing the world bathed in various degrees of sunlight, "natural" photography of most subjects usually means reproducing the feeling of sunlight—or room light—coming from above. Any other illumination may seem contrived. Except when experimenting for unusual effects, the aim usually is not to call attention to the lighting, but to reproduce things the way they would naturally appear.

The natural look normally calls for a single *main* or *key* light source that appears to come from somewhere above and to one side, casting shadows that emphasize the form and texture of the subject. If additional lights produce more than one set of shadows, the picture may look weird, and facial features may seem distorted.

Every time you change position— every time there's a change in the light—there's a new world to see.

(Frank Gohlke, photographer)

William Beverly *Kris*
Soft "wraparound" lighting from large classroom windows gave a soft effect, yet retained directionality of the light and imparted roundness to the features. A chalkboard provided a conveniently contrasting background. Notice the vitality obtained by having the subject turn her head at an angle to her shoulders.

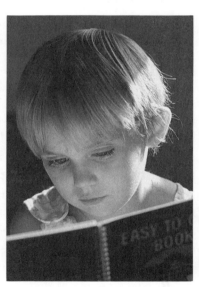

Robert Fleming *Window*
Natural window light is everywhere and can be excellent for photos, especially when the subject faces toward the light. Here, the mood suggested that no fill light or reflector be used. What exposure problems needed to be solved?

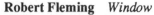

R. Vander Zwart
Easy Book
An open book makes an excellent reflector to counteract the extreme brightness range caused by strong backlighting by direct sunlight..

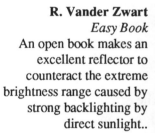

Larry Allen *Boo!*
Lighting from underneath seems mysterious, even sinister, as the head appears to be floating in space. Reserve this technique for special effects.

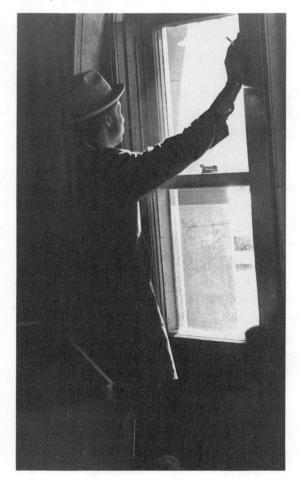

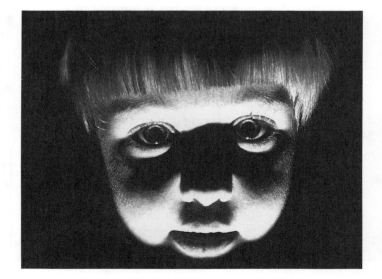

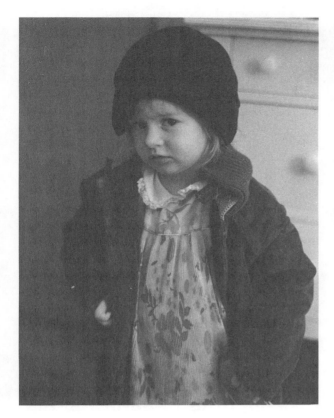

William T. O'Brien
Peggy
Soft, existing room light was sufficient for this appealing portrait of a little girl's relationship with the photographer—her father.

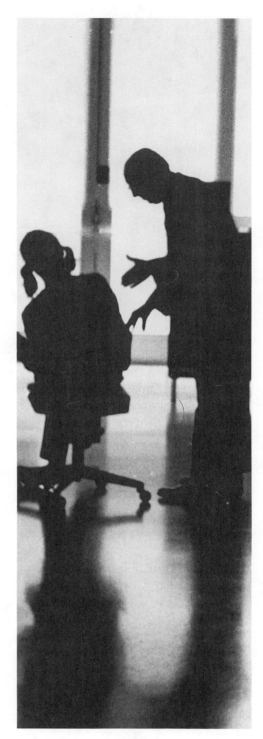

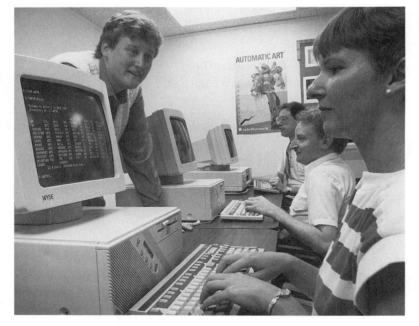

D. Curl   *Computer Class*
Existing overhead fluorescent lights were adequate for a "posed-unposed" exposure of 1/4 second at f/22 on 400-speed film. Visualize this same picture taken with direct flash on camera or with bounce flash. When would you *not* use the tripod and existing light?

Mary Cain   *Silhouettes*
Is this silhouette perhaps more provocative than the same photograph might be if it had a full tonal range? What serious problem of exposure determination exists when photographing directly into a light source such as this large window wall?

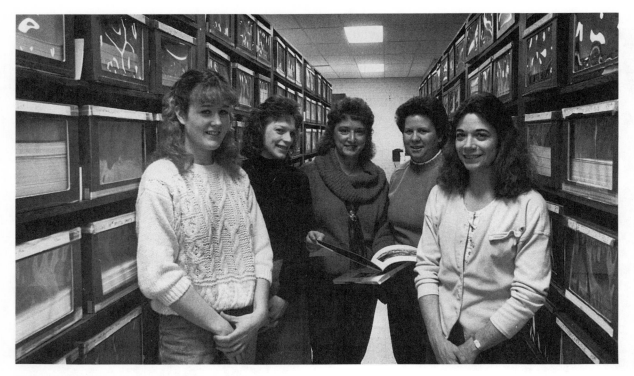

Ardyce Czuchna-Curl *Sample Room Staff*
Available light from fluorescents in the ceiling gave a
natural look to this obviously posed, but believable group
portrait for the company newsletter. 400-speed film was
used. Exposure, with the camera on a tripod, was 1/8
second at f/11.

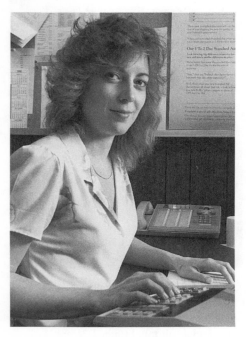

Ardyce Czuchna-Curl *Bookkeeper*
Existing light in the office was appropriate for this
employee portrait. Notice that a perfect 45-degree "short"
lighting effect was achieved by asking the subject to turn
her head until the existing light created the desired form
and shadows. 400-speed film. 1/8 second at f/11.

Look at pictures, observe people

You can learn a lot about lighting by studying
other people's pictures. Most of the examples in this
book were produced by students and these pictures
will be a good place to start, but get into the habit of
analyzing the lighting and composition of every
photo and painting you see. Also watch people as
they sit in class, in the office or plant, at home or
outdoors, and notice the way their faces and bodies
are illuminated.

Make the Most of Existing Light

Some people don't realize that good pictures can
be made with existing light, without using flash or
heavy studio lights. Actually, very excellent and
realistic photographs can be made indoors with
"fast" films if the existing room light is used properly. Instead of moving the light to the subject, as in
a portrait studio, you must move your subjects in
relation to the light. If you're shooting a group
activity, for example, arrange everyone so that each
person faces a light source, whether that source is a
window, a lamp, or a fireplace fire.

Try the "posed-unposed" technique

Arranging people doesn't necessarily mean posing them stiffly. You can group people informally and direct them to go ahead with some natural activity such as talking, working, playing a game, or examining an object. When you're ready to shoot, ask the people you're photographing to "hold it just like that" for an instant if your shutter speed is slow. Make several exposures and pretty soon your subjects will lose their self-consciousness. Before the people are in place, if possible, use your exposure meter to determine a basic overall exposure setting. Be extra careful not to let the meter pick up any stray light that might affect the reading. Move some people nearer to the light source, if necessary, so that all important parts of the picture are receiving about the same amount of light.

Evenly lighted rooms pose few problems for existing light photography, except perhaps that the light may be perfect for uniform exposure, yet uninteresting. If the light is strong and bright from windows along one wall and two or three stops darker on the other side of the room, you have three choices: First is to face the subjects toward the windows as a key light and allow the background to remain dark. The second approach would be to work for a dramatic effect by backlighting the subjects. With backlighting there is a risk of underexposing shadow detail, so either make incident-light readings or meter the shadow areas. As in other situations of extreme subject brightness range, the lowest important values should be placed in the proper zones. A third solution is to reduce the range of brightness.

Fill in the shadows

When the main subject is backlighted, a reflector may introduce enough light to supplement the shadows, or you can try bouncing light from the ceiling or walls. The bounce technique works well with either flash or flood, yet allows you to preserve the effect of natural illumination.

Don't forget to carry a tripod with you for shooting interiors. The extra trouble will pay off when

you need more depth of field and you're forced to shoot at a slow shutter speed such as 1/2 second. Some interiors are just too dark to allow shooting with a hand-held camera.

Some typical existing-light exposures with 400-speed films

Home interiors	1/30 @ f/2 or f/2.8
Candlelight close-ups	1/8 @ f/2.8
Classrooms, offices	1/30 @ f/4 or f/5.6
Floodlighted buildings	1/8 @ f/2
Outdoor sports at night	1/125 @ f/2.8
Indoor sports	1/125 @ f/2 or f/2.8
Auditorium stage	1/30 @ f/2 or f/2.8
Bright stage show, concert	1/125 @ f/4
Neon signs	1/125 @ f/4
Brightly lighted streets	1/60 @ f/2.8 or f/4
Fair midway and rides	1/30 @ f/2.8
Carnival rides patterns	B @ f/16
Traffic patterns	B @ f/22
Fireworks	B @ f/16
Lightning	B @ f/11

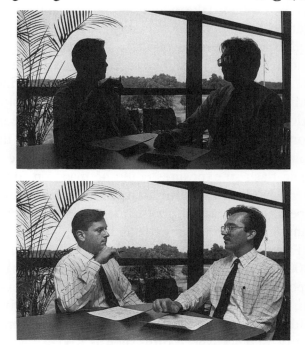

Bounce flash can fill in the shadows when a subject is facing away from existing light. When the subject is stationary and the camera is on a tripod, a reflector may be the best choice because you can see its effect.

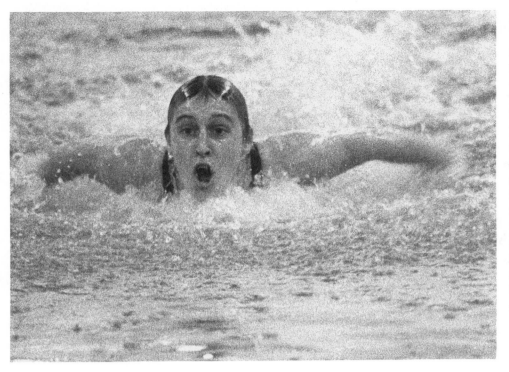

Pam Vogel *Swimmer*
"Pushing" your film may be the only answer when there isn't enough light for adequate exposure at the manufacturer's ISO rating and when flash may be unavailable or undesirable. Exposing the film at a higher exposure index and extending development time may result in a grainy but satisfactory negative when the subject matter is of relatively low contrast such as this indoor swimming meet. Pushing is less successful when the subject reflects an extended brightness range containing important shadow values.

Push Processing

If you want to take pictures of moving subjects in relatively dim light, such as stage action, indoor or night sporting events or industrial machinery in action, something has to be sacrificed to be able to use a fast shutter speed. What you give up is fine grain and shadow detail. The super-crisp color action shots of basketball or hockey that you see in sports magazines may have required setting up around the arena thousands of watt-seconds of electronic flash so exposures could be made on films rated EI 100 to 400. But for reproduction in newspapers, good enough photos are made every day using faster film under existing light.

Films such as Kodak T-Max P3200, Ektachrome P800/1600 and Ektapress 1600 all are intended to be exposed at EI 800 or higher, depending on processing. The instructions packed with these films give guidelines. Manufacturer's instructions for commonly used 400-speed films such as Kodak T-Max 400 and Ilford HP5 Plus also indicate processing for EI 800, 1600, or higher.

Film manufacturers build into their products a safety margin of about one stop, which means that if your equipment is correctly calibrated, you can expose most films at double their normal speed and still get an "acceptable" rendering of average subject matter. The penalty you pay for minimizing exposure is the risk of loss of shadow detail. By doubling the speed from 400 to 800 you're underexposing by one stop; in zone system terms, you're dropping the low values in the subject brightness range one full zone. For example, a dark, textured Zone III area photographed on T-Max 400 film would be rendered at EI 800 as Zone II. Doubling the speed again to EI 1600 will place that Zone III area in totally textureless Zone I, losing all shadow detail below Zone IV and resulting in an extremely thin negative.

The price of pushing

Pushing means *under*exposing the film and *over*developing it—sometimes in concentrated or high-energy developer. Developing underexposed negatives for extended time or in strong developer increases the density of the higher values (Zones VI through IX) without doing much for the shadows. This increase in highlight density makes the negative more contrasty, but it is also very likely to "block up" the high values so that the lighter zones cannot be separated in the print. High-energy devel-

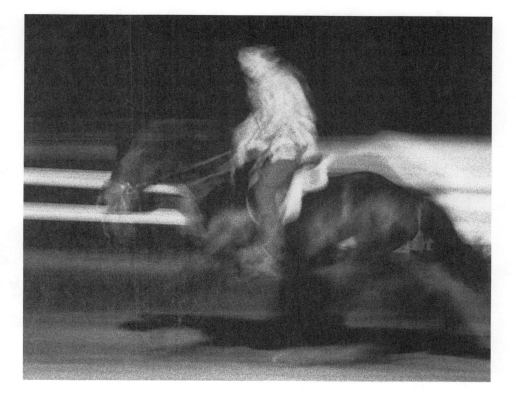

Blair Beitner
Night Rider
Kodak T-Max P3200 film was used to record an image outdoors at night where only dim light was available. At f/2, a 1-second shutter speed gave the negative printable density and the picture an exciting illusion of movement.

opers often build up a false shadow density through overall fog and increase the tendency for grain to clump together and become visible.

Because of the loss of shadow detail, pushing is poor practice when the subject has a wide brightness range, such as people doing things in an unevenly lighted room. Sometimes, as with night football, pushing is the only way to get pictures; but be ready for problems printing underexposed negatives showing dark-skinned players wearing dark-colored uniforms.

Pushing is useful, however, when you need to stop fast action in limited light and when the brightness range is so narrow that you would want to give N+ development anyway. Some examples could include football or soccer on an overcast day, or swimming or ice hockey in an evenly lighted arena. Under such conditions there are few significant low values to lose; hence, an underexposure of one or two stops (rating 400-speed film at 800 or 1600) and N+1 or N+2 development would be appropriate. Or try a film such as Kodak T-Max P3200. The negatives will be thin and somewhat grainy, but they should have a satisfactory tonal range and adequate contrast for printing and reproduction.

Pushing color films

The higher the exposure index, the greater the grain; and "push" processing increases contrast. These rules apply to color films as well as to black-and-white. But you have to decide whether a sacrifice of shadow detail and a gain in contrast are acceptable prices to pay for results. Aerial photography is one field in which it is routine to push color transparency film. An extra stop or two of speed is desirable, and the extra contrast from push processing helps reduce the effects of haze in the air.

Since magazines and newspapers are printing many more color photos, staff photographers and correspondents have to come back from assignments with color negatives or transparencies that will stand reproduction. Fortunately, grain doesn't show as much in the halftone reproduction on a printed page, so many photojournalists routinely shoot 400- or 1600-speed color negative film on daily assignments.

This is the most important rule to remember about pushing: Do it when you have to, but don't expect the same quality as when you give correct (zone system) exposure and processing

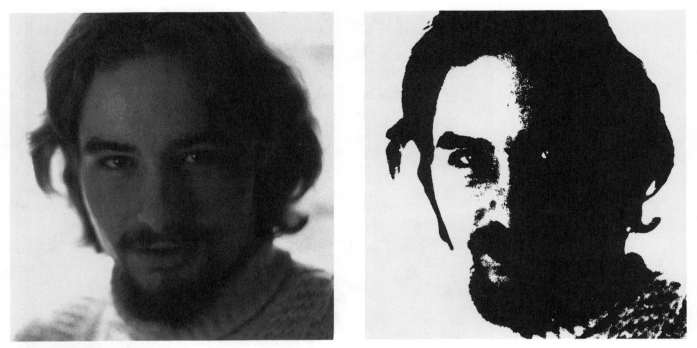

John Willerton *Two Faces*
Although the angle of the key light is slightly different, these two photographs of the same subject illustrate a difference in mood created by extremes of contrast. Do you react differently to the personality, as you imagine it, of the young man as he is represented in each photograph?

Portraiture

If you wait long enough and someone is looking at you—sooner or later you will see their soul, providing you don't talk too much. (Bruce Davidson, photographer)

A portrait should emphasize the subject as a person. A good environmental portrait can reveal much more about the subject than merely what he or she looks like; surroundings or background may contribute by indicating something about the person's home life, work, or interests. A fleeting expression on the subject's face may reveal deep truth.

A portrait...if it's handled right...is the closest thing to climbing inside somebody's mind and experiencing what they are about. (Brian Lanker, photojournalist)

Careful selection of pose and lighting by the photographer can bring out grace, poise, dignity, and character, as well as emphasize or de-emphasize certain features. The subject's eyes, facial expres-

sion and body language often will reveal a great deal about your own relationship with the individual you are photographing—tense and formal, casual and relaxed, amiable and intimate. You might be surprised to realize that your instinctive choice of camera angle, subject distance, and lighting will reveal something of your attitude toward the person.

The good photographic portrait is a collaboration, a transaction between photographer and sitter...and it reveals the personalities of both...Photographer and...subject are connected by a thread that is delicate and tenuous. If the two establish rapport, the photograph will be a success. The subject will feel that the photographer has had the insight to see his best qualities, and the photographer will feel that he has perceived the essential human being. Thus, it is the photographer's responsibility to choose the particular fraction of a second by which the person would wish to be remembered. (Margery Mann, photographer)

The attitudes of people are so different in front of a camera. Some are embarrassed. Some are ashamed. Some hate to be photographed and others are showing off. You feel people very quickly. You see people naked through the viewfinder...and it's sometimes very embarrassing.

(Henri Cartier-Bresson, photojournalist)

At one time, a 4x5-inch or even larger negative was thought to be necessary, for portraits always were believed to require retouching. But many excellent portraits now are being made with 35mm and 120-size roll film cameras. Small negatives are difficult or impossible to retouch with pencil and an etching knife, but much of the demand for retouching has disappeared. Many portraits are made for publication, and reproduction processes suppress enough detail to effectively diminish many facial faults. Soft lighting and simple diffusion techniques either at the camera or in the darkroom can soften the effects of wrinkles and blemishes when it's important to satisfy the subject.

The difference between a portrait and a snapshot is that the portrait is [when] the person agreed to be photographed. It's not at all like somebody you see and catch on the street.

(Henri Cartier-Bresson, photojournalist)

Although excellent informal portraits can be made in existing light with a small hand-held camera, a tripod and controlled artificial lighting are still important equipment for making "formal" portraits. You also will need a plain, neutral background.

It's hard to converse with your subject and observe spontaneous expressions while looking through a viewfinder (it makes your subject uneasy); however, with a tripod and a cable release, you can concentrate on the subject and forget about the camera, except to trip the shutter. If you have a choice of lenses, a lens about twice the normal focal length is ideal for portraiture.

A shorter focal length lens at close range tends to make the subject uncomfortable and to distort facial

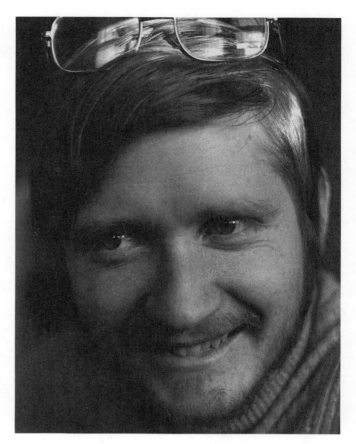

Lin Childs *Jim*
Awareness, spontaneity, intimacy. An image of a relaxed moment that seems to reveal something about the personality of the subject and about his relationship with the photographer.

features, making whatever part of the anatomy is closest to the camera appear abnormally large.

One reason photographs don't look natural is that photographers always tell their subjects to look pleasant.

(Author unknown)

Placing the key light

"Studio" portraits usually require a minimum of two lights: the *main* or *key* light and a fill-in light, or one light source plus a reflector for fill. Nowadays most studio work is done with electronic flash systems that have built-in "modeling" lights for positioning. Maximum control is possible with flash (sometimes referred to as strobe) lighting— large tent-like soft-boxes, reflectors, grid and focusing spot attachments all make it easier to get exactly the quality, intensity and direction of light desired.

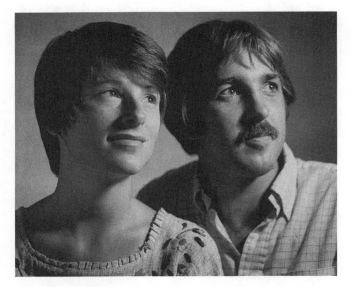

Mike Deines *Couple*
This informal portrait illustrates use of a single light source to provide uniform short key lighting on both faces. A window can give this effect, or any kind of direct light source. Enough light was scattered around the room from light-colored walls to fill the shadows with some reflected light.

Professional Studio Lighting

Each of the four lights shown in the diagram below has a specific function. For a portrait of a person, a product layout or a machine part, the function would be the same, but the placement might be different.

1. KEY or MAIN light—All shadows should appear to come from this light, which largely determines the exposure. Start with this light placed about 45° above and 45° to one side of the subject.

2. FILL light—Less than half as bright as KEY. Close to lens axis or bounced. Softens shadows without casting visible shadows of its own. A reflector sometimes is used instead of a lamp.

3. ACCENT or BACKLIGHT—Adds highlights on hair and shoulders. Should not strike camera lens or front of subject's face.

4. BACKGROUND light—Separates subject from background. Eliminates any shadows cast on background by FILL. Should not light subject.

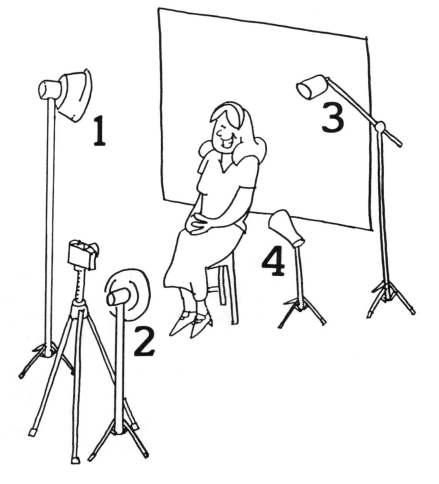

The very quick, bright discharge of electronic flash eliminates the problem of motion and its brightness permits great depth of field.

Incandescent "hot" lights will do almost as well; they're just not as convenient for the photographer nor as comfortable for the sitter.

Whatever the light source, the *key* or *main* light should be the brightest and it should cast the only *noticeable* set of shadows, comparable to the sun's light outdoors.

The 45° formula

Usually the best place for the key light is high enough so that the light falls on the subject's face from about 45° above eye level, and 45° from the subject's face *on the side away from the camera.* In other words: 45° high and 45° from the side. And place the camera on the *dark* side of the face. This 45° formula produces a result that, among pros, is referred to as *short* lighting because, assuming the subject isn't facing squarely toward the camera, it illuminates the *short* (narrow) side of the face. Short lighting is appropriate for most faces. Notice the examples in this chapter and look for other examples of short key light placement everywhere: still photos, movies, television, and on the stage.

An alternative 45° key light placement is *broad* lighting; so-called because the camera is looking at the lighted (broad) side of the face instead of the

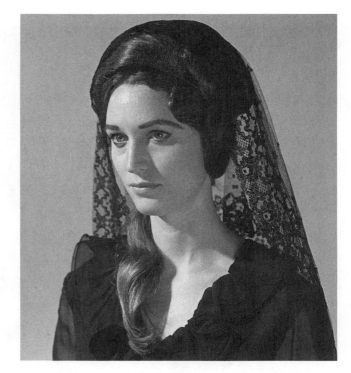

W. A. Moss *Satin and Lace*
This portrait illustrates placement of the 45° key light and diffused fill. Notice how the key light forms a triangle of light on the model's left cheek. This is what is referred to as *short* lighting, because the key is placed to illuminate the *short* or *far* side of the subject's face. Notice that the camera is on the *shadow* side.

shadow side. *Butterfly* lighting places the key light 45° high, directly above the subject's face, producing a "butterfly" shadow directly below the nose.

Placement of the key light emphasizes facial form. Compare short lighting (left); broad lighting (center) and butterfly lighting (right). The key light was the same in each example—a single quartz lamp bounced off a silvered umbrella. The only change was moving the light. No other lights were used.

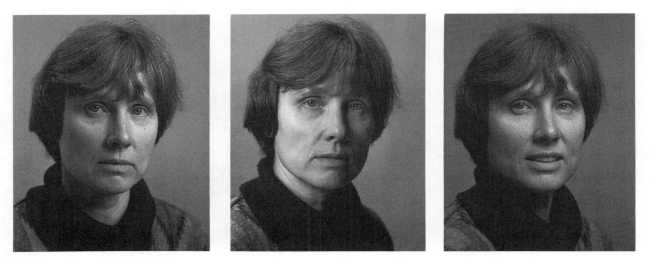

Short   Broad   Butterfly

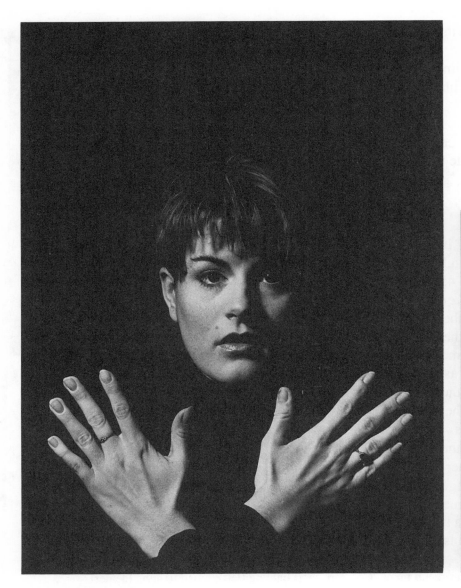

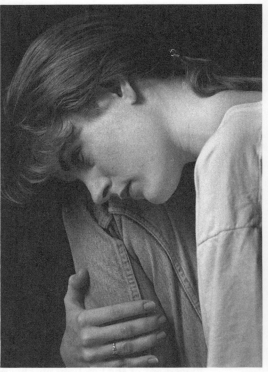

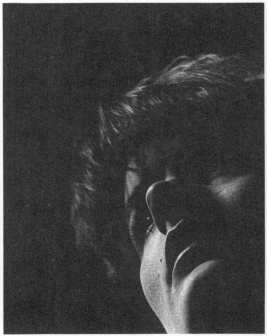

Jorg Jasper *Mary*
Did you recognize that the same person is the model in all three portraits? How is your impression of the "personality" of the subject affected by variations in pose, lighting, camera viewpoint and image contrast? How far can (or should) photographer and film directors go toward creating a persona for a subject in front of their cameras?

Light the eyes

If your subject has deep-set eyes, or is wearing a hat that shades the eyes, either tilt back the hat or lower the key light until the eyes no longer are in shadow. Try to get a "catch-light" in each eye from the key light. These tiny bright sparkles add life to the portrait.

Fill in the shadows

The shadows cast by the key light alone usually will be too dark for anything but a dramatic theatrical effect; so you probably will want to add a fill light or use a reflector to reduce the subject contrast. Using too much fill is a common mistake. If the fill is too bright, it will wash out the effect of the key light and cast shadows of its own. The fill light should be only one-half to one-fourth as bright as the key, and it should be placed as near as possible to the camera (or bounced) to prevent extra shadows.

Experiment with the lighting ratio, remembering that for a one zone difference in brightness the fill should be half as bright as the key. If the fill is one fourth as bright, the difference will be two zones.

Caucasian skin in full light should ordinarily be Zone VI and the shadow side of the face no darker than Zone IV. Dark faces often reproduce well at Zones V and III. You can control the relative brightness of the fill by moving it toward or away from the subject or by "feathering" the lamp by turning it toward one side to control its brilliance. Other good techniques are to attach a white fiberglass diffuser over the fill light or to "bounce" the light from a convenient white wall or reflecting surface. Remember that a two zone difference in brightness represents a lighting ratio of 4:1 between key and fill. You can verify this with your exposure meter, reading first the highlight side of the face and then the shadow side.

Separate the subject
from the background

When dark-haired people are being photographed with only one or two lights, their hair sometimes lacks detail and sparkle and it blends into the background. Dark hair can be brought up to Zone III,

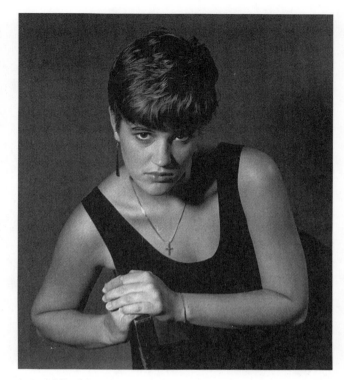

Ashaki Smith *Corinna*
A sophisticated theatrical appearance has been achieved with *broad* lighting, no fill, and a subtle accent light behind the subject's left shoulder. Notice how the hands and arms are carefully posed to unify the composition.

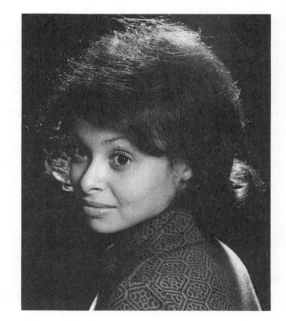

Johnny Yee *Maria*
Another example of *broad* lighting, in which the key light illuminates the broad, or near, side of the face and is somewhat nearer to the camera than usual, so no fill has been used. Notice that a strong accent or backlight adds sparkle and dimension to the hair and separates the shoulders from the background.

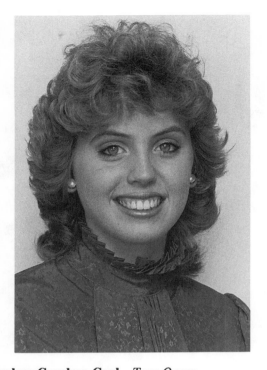

Ardyce Czuchna-Curl *Teen Queen*
Bounce lighting gives a very soft, nearly shadowless
effect without casting an annoying shadow on the
nearby background. The bounce technique can be
used anywhere there is a low, white ceiling or other
reflective surface.

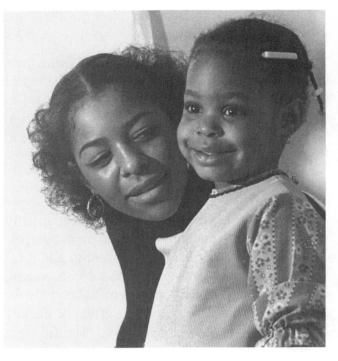

Wallace Kirk *Mother and Daughter*
A single key light plus fill provided sparkling short
lighting to both faces in this informal home portrait.
Notice that the fill is just bright enough to show detail
in the shadows without eliminating them.

improving its texture and adding some sparkling
highlights, by using a third light, called an *accent*
light, high above and behind or to one side of the
subject. Carefully aim the accent light at the area
you want to lighten, being careful not to let any of the
light spill over onto the subject's face or into the
camera lens. When you add an accent light, it's
generally a good idea to put a lens shade on your
camera and use "barn doors" or a "snoot" on the
accent light to keep glare out of the lens. Don't
forget to turn off this light when making a meter
reading of the face.

If the background seems too dark, a fourth light
can be placed behind the subject and directed onto
the background. Move the subject farther from the
background if an objectionable shadow of the subject falls on the background from the key or fill. If
the shadow is weak, the background light can eliminate it; if not, move the subject still farther from the
background. A painted wall or plain drapes can
serve as a portrait background if you don't have a
roll of seamless paper or a painted canvas flat. A

makeshift background rigged from a blanket or
sheet usually shows wrinkles and looks fake. For
environmental portraits a natural background is best
of all. Try to avoid strong patterns and lines unless
you can include them as part of the composition.
Strong background elements often distract by competing with the subject for the viewer's attention.

Camera angle

Most portraits of a seated subject look best if the
camera height is near to the subject's eye level.
Looking down on a person can make them appear
submissive (children often are photographed from
an adult's eye-view). Looking up at a person either
adds stature or a feeling of aloofness. If your camera
is on a tripod, as it should be, direct the subject's
eyes to the lens or to wherever you want them to
look. Otherwise, in trying to get an animated expression, the subject's eyes might follow you; if
you're not standing directly behind the camera you
might get a lot of "white of the eye" which looks
unnatural.

Often, a head-on front view of a person (passport style) is unflattering and gives an unpleasant feeling of confrontation. For most subjects, a three-quarter view is better, showing only one ear. Turning the head in relation to the body gives a feeling of poised action. You'll learn a lot by trying to emulate portraits that you like. Invite your favorite model to help you experiment with variations in posing and lighting.

> *Promote visual health...photograph a friend.*
> *(Walt Burton, photographer)*

Solving Portrait Problems

> *So many people dislike themselves so thoroughly that they never see any reproduction of themselves that suits. None of us is born with the right face. It's a tough job being a portrait photographer.*
> *(Imogen Cunningham, photographer)*

Professional portrait photographers have to lie a little—and sometimes a lot—to make a living. Very few people really are willing to be photographed the way they actually look, especially when they're paying for the pictures!

> *After a certain age you've got the face you deserve, I think.*
> *(Henri Cartier-Bresson, photographer)*

But you can be a portrait photographer and not resort to diffusion or retouching to make your subject appear at his or her best. If you study your subject carefully, you'll see that camera angle, lighting, and choice of lens all can affect a person's appearance for good or ill. Let's look at some examples of how to solve the most commonly encountered portrait problems:

> *As people grow older, there is written on their faces not only what life has brought to them but what they have brought to life.*
> *(John Mason Brown, essayist)*

Texture: Wrinkles, crow's feet, and laugh lines are signs of life, and everyone past the age of twenty has a few. A middle-aged or older person pictured without wrinkles would seem ridiculous (look at a portrait studio window display). But nevertheless, when you photograph your mother, maiden aunt, or a favorite friend, the facial lines may seem a bit severe. But take heart; soft lighting will soften the lines. Diffusion can do the rest. Try using a filter made for the purpose, or produce your own diffuser from a snippet of mesh window screen, a piece of pantyhose, or a sheet of cellophane that has been

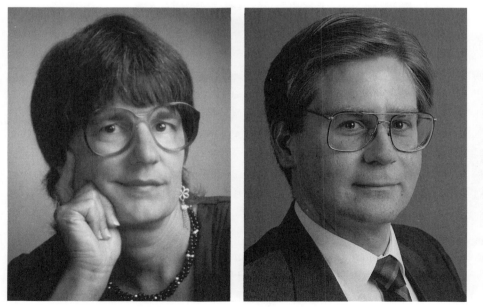

Notice that *short* lighting was used on both of these portraits. The lighting ratio was about 3:1 (key light three times as bright as the fill). No reflections are visible in the glasses, because the key light was high enough and the fill carefully adjusted. Also the bows (ear pieces) of the glasses were raised slightly to direct reflections downward. Shadows from the key light would conceal texture and any blemishes on the near cheek and neck. The portrait on left was softened by placing a diffusion filter over the camera lens.

wrinkled up and then flattened again. Either put the diffuser over the camera lens, or diffuse during enlargement. While enlarging you can control the effect by holding the diffuser under the enlarging lens for only part of the exposure time. Keep it moving. You can hide wrinkles on a person's neck or conceal a double chin by "short" lighting the face and throwing the neck into shadow.

Distorted Facial Features: On close-ups of people, a normal focal length or wide-angle lens tends to enlarge the nose or chin or whatever part of the anatomy is closest to the camera. An extra-long telephoto lens tends to flatten out the features, giving a paper doll effect. The favorite focal length of most portrait photographers is about twice "normal," that is about 105mm for 35mm cameras, 150-180mm for 6cm cameras, and 300-360mm on 4x5.

But suppose you want deliberately to emphasize or suppress a certain facial feature—a weak chin, for example. Choosing a relatively short focal length lens and a low camera angle will strengthen the chin in proportion to the rest of the face. Shooting slightly down on a person with a large forehead will emphasize the brainy or "egghead" feeling. A long nose can be shortened by approaching the subject from a slightly low camera angle, and a crooked nose sometimes looks better from the side toward which it bends. When eyes aren't at the same height, shoot from the side where the eye is lower and the face may appear normal.

A burly person tends to look even heavier when photographed full-face. Heavy-set people appear slimmer with a three-quarter pose and short lighting. Or you can add a few pounds to a thin-faced subject by use of broad or butterfly lighting.

Facial Blemishes: Look carefully at your subject to see whether you can conceal acne scars and other marks by choosing your subject's "best" side; then use short lighting to throw the offending areas into shadow. In severe cases, makeup may be needed; but diffused short lighting usually will do the trick. For extreme cases, the obvious solution is to throw the offending side of the face into total shadow—a dramatic effect, but flattering to certain people.

Baldness: The rule here is simply to keep the light away from the top of a bald man's head and not to emphasize his baldness with a high camera angle. To save burning-in time in the darkroom, pre-dodge a bald head by using barn doors on the lights or block some of the light with a head screen made from a piece of cardboard clamped or taped to a light stand. The same trick can be used to keep an ear or shoulder from being too light and distracting attention from the face.

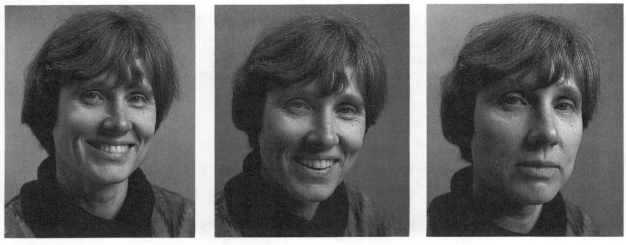

105mm   55mm   35mm

The lens makes a difference. Compare the rendition of facial features, especially the nose and chin, in the photograph on the left which was made with the equivalent of a 105mm lens on a 35mm camera, with the version in the center made with the equivalent of a 55mm lens, and the result on the right equivalent to a 35mm wide angle lens on a 35mm camera. (The camera was moved for each exposure to keep the same image size).

Prominent Nose: A good look at your subject will tell you whether the nose requires special attention. Tilting the chin up will minimize a long nose, while carefully controlled short lighting will straighten a crooked or an arched nose. A person whose nose points to one side should be photographed from that side.

Deep-set Eyes: The problem is to get enough light into the eye sockets. Either place the key light lower than usual, or reduce the lighting ratio by moving the fill closer or using a reflector to bounce light into the eyes.

Glasses: A person who wears glasses only occasionally can be shown holding them in their hands, perched on top of their head, tucked into their shirt collar or pocket, or hung by a chain around the neck. But if the person wears glasses all the time, he or she often looks and feels strange without them.

Leave the glasses on, but be extra careful about shadows and reflections, adjusting the lights or positioning the subject's face so that shadows from the frames don't cut across the eyes. Tilting the face slightly downward usually will get rid of reflections from the key and fill lights. With existing lamp or window light, the key often is reflected in the glasses; in the studio, reflections usually are caused by the fill. Raising the bows (ear pieces) of the glasses or tipping the face down slightly will usually get rid of the most severe reflections. If reflections remain, try bouncing the fill from a surface above the camera.

Heavy eyeglass frames require careful placement of the key light to avoid shadows across the eyes. Watch out for secondary shadows from frames if the fill light is too bright or too far from the camera position. When very thick lenses are worn, sometimes the only way to eliminate reflections in the glass and distortion of the face through the lenses is to ask the sitter to borrow a pair of empty frames from an optician.

Clothing: Plain dark clothes usually are best, because the face, being lighter, tends to stand out. Loud designs and bright, complex patterns draw attention to themselves. Unless the lighting is carefully balanced, bare arms and shoulders may compete for attention with the face and require burning-in in the darkroom. So, unless it's a glamour session, it's best for the model to cover up.

Get to know your subject

Take time to talk with people you're photographing. They'll feel less uncomfortable in front of the camera. You don't have to entertain your subject. It's usually better not to try to dominate, but ask sincere questions to assure them you are really interested in them as a person.

If you study each person intelligently and perceptively, you can capture his or her likeness, as well as some of their essence and spirit. Fortunately the heavily retouched ("mortician's ideal") portraits of the past no longer are very popular. Good posing, lighting and camera techniques will keep you from having to resort to much retouching.

Perhaps you will become one of those happy photographers who genuinely enjoys working with people. If so, you may be able to make a career of portraiture or photojournalism, because the public is beginning to appreciate informal and more natural-looking pictures of themselves and their families and associates.

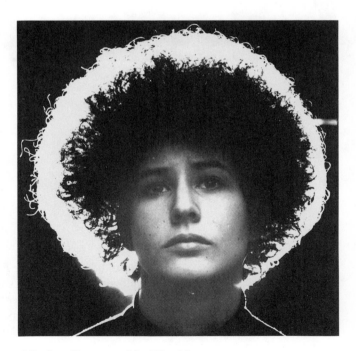

Marion Grzanowski *The Afro*
Extremely strong backlight provided the halo effect, with diffused *butterfly* lighting on the face.

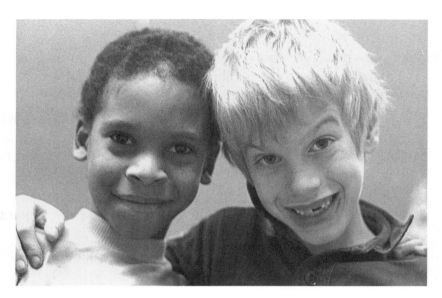

Nancy Bly *Friends*
Children seldom are shy about having their picture taken. Like adults, they will simply stand and "mug" for the camera unless given direction. Unlike adults, children soon become absorbed in whatever activity they are involved in and forget that a photographer is present.

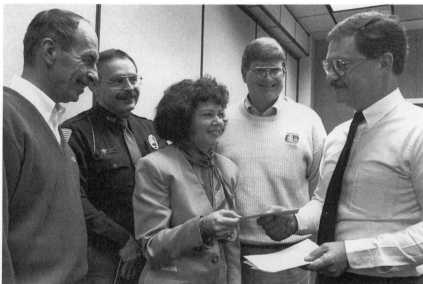

Ardyce Czuchna-Curl
Check Presentation
Unless directed by the photographer, people will simply stand in a row with their arms hanging down at their sides. Notice here that the three key people (on the right) are arranged in an informal triangle and they have been given something to do with their hands.

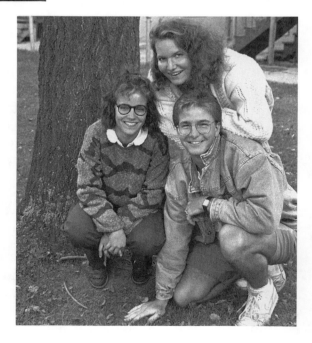

Fumiko Yarita *Three Friends*
Instead of allowing them to stand stiffly in a row, the photographer directed her friends into an informal triangular pose that appears to be spontaneous and natural.

Full-length and group portraiture

A good group portrait consists of several individual portraits taken at the same time. Be sure each face and figure is properly lighted to bring out the form and best features of each person. But in group photography, the whole actually is greater than the sum of its parts because the total effect must be compositionally interesting, as well as technically well-lighted and photographed.

Avoid deadly, static, row-on-row groupings. Use enough imagination to arrange everyone in a unified and varied way. When people agree to be photographed, they look to you, the photographer, for guidance and direction. Tell them what to do, whether you merely want them to look toward the camera and "Smile, please," or pretend to be doing something.

This is your big chance to act like a Hollywood director. And the most successful method of preparing your "actors" often will be the posed-unposed technique. First you decide how to arrange people, props, and background the way you want them in relation to the lighting, and then you determine exposure and focus. After all the technical problems are solved, you direct the people either to continue what they would normally be doing (working on machines, examining an object, or talking informally with one another) or you give directions: "Joe, please hold up the trophy like this—with both hands—and be telling about how you won it; Mary and Jim, you'll be looking right at Joe." Or "Pick up the phone, Sally, and pretend that you're having a pleasant conversation with your boyfriend." Or "Be adjusting the horse's bridle with both hands, Jennifer, then turn and look directly at me...now smile!"

Full-length portraits require much greater attention to background detail and to the pose, especially if you're photographing outdoors. Obvious things to watch out for include wires, poles and branches growing out of people's heads, and excessively bright or "busy" areas especially in corners or along edges, that might distract from the main subject(s). Avoid awkward placement or amputation of arms, hands, legs, and feet.

Hands should be holding something, tucked into belt or pockets, or posed together in a natural way. Arms should not be just hanging down. When included, legs and feet ought to placed naturally and comfortably, but usually not "at attention." Fashion models learn to stand with most of their weight gracefully on one foot, with the other foot slightly forward and at an angle. A seated figure looks more active if the weight is shifted slightly to one side instead of distributed equally onto both buttocks.

Body grace is especially important in fashion and figure photography because an awkward pose and crude lighting can make even a beautiful person appear grotesque. For a full-length figure, the camera angle generally should be lower. Eye level

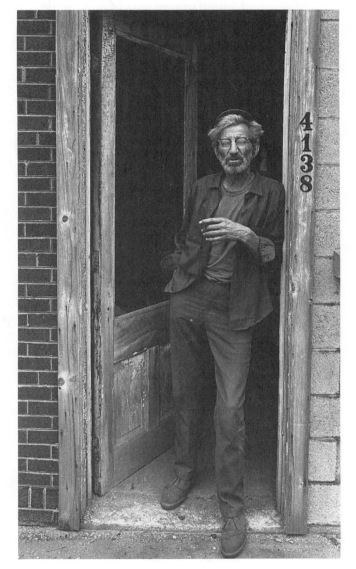

Jim Nixon *Man in Doorway*
A full-length portrait—straightforward and eye to eye. Notice the relaxed, natural positions of hands and feet.

usually is right for a head-and-shoulders portrait, but a chest- or even waist-high camera position often lends dignity and grace to a standing figure.

> *Beauty is its own excuse.*
>
> *(Ralph Waldo Emerson, poet)*

The nude figure is the most challenging of all to photograph. Because art is never absolute, but relies on the sensibilities of the beholder, a clear distinction has not always been made between conscientious representation and crass pornography. A beautiful nude photograph should not be thought of as a portrait of a specific person unclothed, but should be viewed as an informed impression of an esthetically satisfying natural form. Perhaps, in such a fine photograph, some will discover metaphoric meaning.

> *To make a photograph of the human body express something more than mere physical nakedness or suggestive sex, one has to look for qualities that make the human body a...beautiful part of nature. The nakedness of a body is as natural as the nakedness of a tree.*
>
> *(Wynn Bullock, photographer)*

Self-portraiture

Self-portraits and fun and challenging. Knowing how it feels to be in front of the camera helps us to empathize with people who pose for us. The biggest challenge is judging lighting, focus and depth of field from the other side of the lens.

Of course the simplest solution is to have a stand-in pose for you until everything is ready, then you take his or her place as model, letting the stand-in release the shutter. Another way is to work with a large mirror propped up near the camera. Or you can use a video camera and monitor, although seeing exactly how one looks before the exposure tends to take away some of the sponteneity and surprise. If you're working alone, the shutter can be operated with the camera's delayed action self-timer, with a long cable release, or with a remote-controlled electrical release.

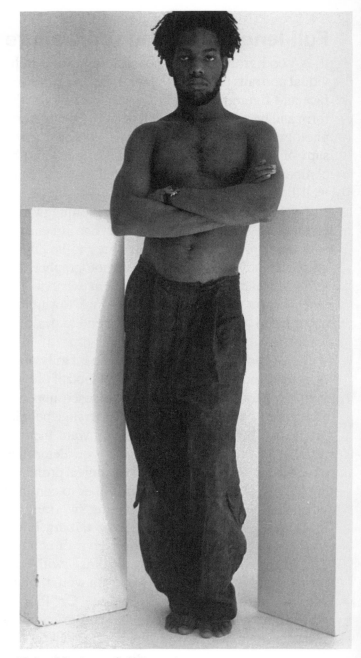

Kolen Mackey *Self-Portrait*
Do we try to photograph our ideal self? To realize a fantasy? Think of self-portraiture as a way of releasing inhibitions and developing empathy for those we photograph. Posing for pictures, one learns quickly the awkwardness and discomfort felt in front of a camera by most inexperienced models.

> *When the subject is in any way uneasy, the personality goes away where the camera can't reach it.*
>
> *(Henri Cartier-Bresson, photographer)*

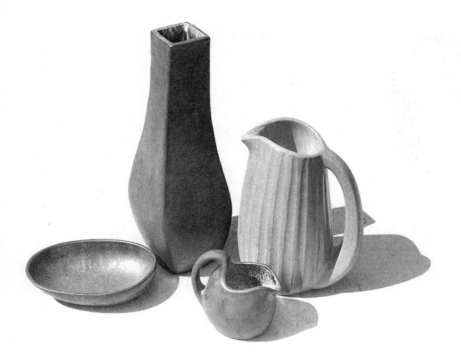

Richard Strader *Ceramics*
Photographing objects requires the same care and attention to arrangement and lighting as making portraits of people. A single source of shadows (key light) is usually mandatory, plus sufficient fill light to retain adequate texture in the shadows. Still-life subjects often are most effectively lighted with the key light coming from behind or strongly from one side. Remember the 45° rule for a portrait key light. Imagine that the subject is a face, determine which direction the "face" is facing, then place the key light accordingly.

Product Illustration

Most of the same principles that apply to creating portraits of people apply also to photographing a structure, a sculpture, or a cereal box. The lighting principles are similar (key, fill, accent, background), and so are the elements of perspective and composition. Always think first in terms of reproducing the shape or form and texture of any subject. Then you'll be able to work out the details of lighting, lens choice, camera position, and so on—one problem at a time.

Find the "face"

As each person has a face, so too has each building. Because of this, the most successful architectural photographs will be made at a time of day and season when light creates the strongest feeling of form and texture. It is the same with large outdoor sculptures, fountains, storage tanks and silos, and certainly with natural forms such as mountains, rocks, and trees.

Photographing small objects in the studio offers a fine opportunity to find the "faces" of products and to study the effects of light placement. Working with a miniature model, you can simulate the sun with a lamp. As you shift lights about in your studio, you should notice the way the shadows fall and the way in which lighting angle can reveal and emphasize texture. Strong shadows may add to the effectiveness of studio illustrations, even to the point where the shadow may be more interesting than the object itself. Dramatic lighting can produce a three-dimensional effect, the highlights tending to come forward while the shadow areas recede.

Start with simple lighting

So you can see what you're doing, it's always a good idea to begin with only one light, but there are two basic approaches: (1) Start out with a key light, as in portraiture, to reveal basic shape and texture through shadows; then add a fill light or reflector and finally accent or background lights if required. (2) Begin with a broad, diffused "base" light, either bounced or from a large translucent softbox. Then add direct key and accent lights to create highlights and shadows as needed within the composition. Instead of using many lights, commercial photographers often employ large and small reflectors made from cardboard, foam board or foil to brighten small areas and to bring substance to reflective surfaces.

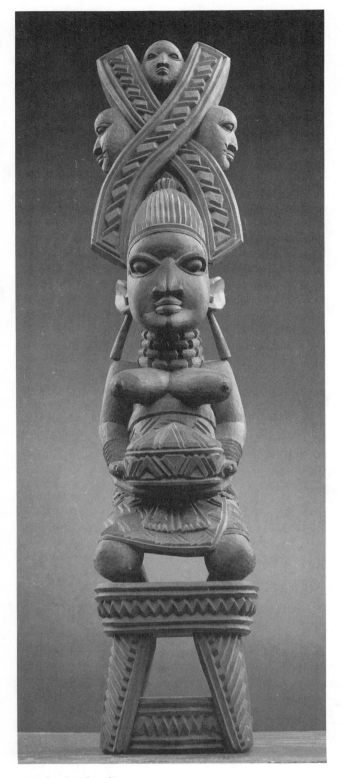

D. Curl *Ose Sango*
A softbox in the *butterfly* position provided basic light for this wood sculpture by noted Yoruba carver Lamidi Fakeye, while large foil reflectors behind and on both sides emphasized its three-dimensional form.

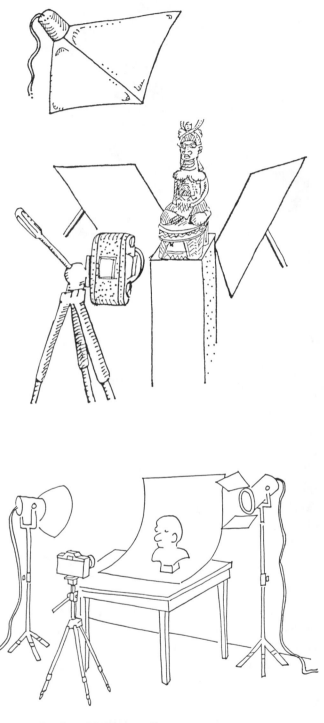

A simple table-top studio.
Improvise yours with seamless paper or poster board.

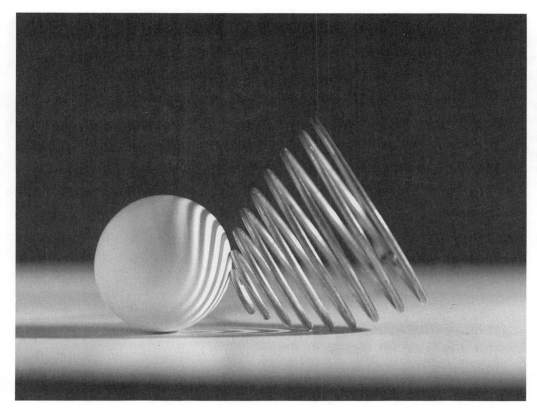

Doug Hauk
Ball and Spring
A commercial subject in which imaginative use of lighting has emphasized and repeated the basic forms.

Your choice of background will depend on the tone and texture of the subject. If the background is white or very light in color, you can vary the contrast between it and the subject simply by directing more or less light onto the background. Unless background texture or pattern contributes to the picture, as it does frequently when illustrating food, the background should be unbroken by seams, edges, or wrinkles.

Some small objects can best be photographed on a pedestal several feet from the background. For others, a miniature stage can be improvised by curving and taping a large sheet of lightweight poster board or seamless paper along the top of a small table and part way up a wall. If the background is large enough to allow the subject to be placed well forward, the table can be pulled away from the wall far enough to allow lights to be placed behind it. Instead of a plain paper background you might choose a material that can give added information about the subject if you're careful not to introduce too much additional texture or pattern. Native backgrounds such as stone, sand, cloth, woven matting, or tree bark can establish location and add character and realism to certain illustrations.

D. Curl *Transmission*
This large truck component was lighted as if it were a sculptural form. The general shape was noted, then five lights and three reflectors were placed to emphasize form and texture and to separate light and dark values.

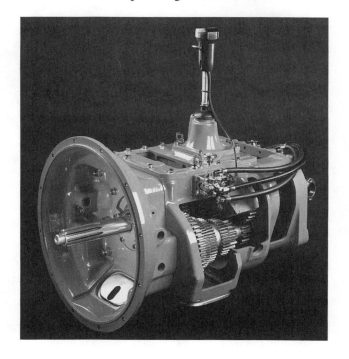

Ardyce Czuchna-Curl *Library*
Bounce flash has given the effect of natural overhead light, but the picture was made with the camera hand-held instead of on a tripod. Although the room was large, the ceiling was white and low enough for adequate exposure. The sensors on most modern flash units will compensate automatically for bounce lighting.

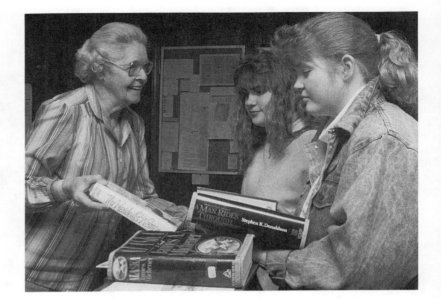

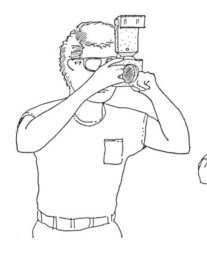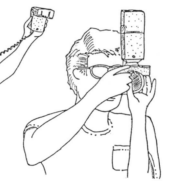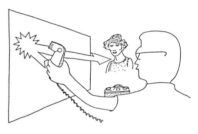

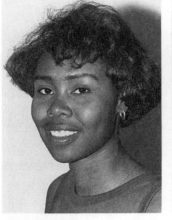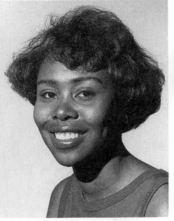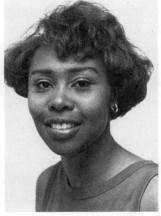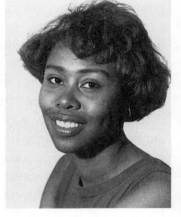

Direct flash on-camera. This is the "point and shoot" method—convenient and quick, but the lighting is so flat it gives a "paper doll" effect with little form and texture. Note the typical dark shadow on the background.

Direct flash off-camera. Hurried photojournalists use this technique to get some feeling of roundness when there isn't time to set up lights. Aim carefully because lighting can be uneven. The shadow on the background is hidden behind the subject.

Bounce flash on-camera. This soft lighting is convenient, flattering to most subjects, and works well in smaller rooms with average-height white ceilings and light-colored walls. The flash was aimed straight up at the ceiling.

Bounce flash from a large reflector. Softer than direct flash off camera, but shadows are more noticeable than flash bounced from the ceiling because the white reflecting surface was closer. A reflective umbrella is often used.

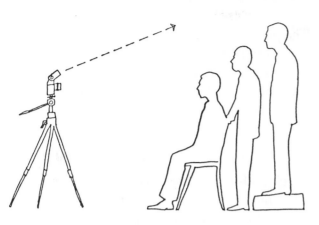

If your flash unit swivels, you can "feather" the light to make it more even. When you have to photograph people at various distances from the camera, aiming the flash at or slightly beyond the farthest subject will reduce the tendency for the nearest subjects to be overexposed. Use this technique outdoors or in a large gym or banquet hall when bounce lighting is not practical.

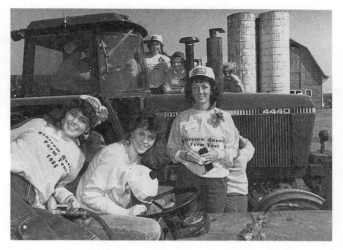

Ardyce Czuchna-Curl *Blossom Queens*
Fill-in flash erased dark shadows on the girls' faces. Use this technique outdoors when you can't control the light in other ways. Be sure to use the maximum synchronized shutter speed on your camera. Determine the sunlight exposure first, then adjust the flash for the lens opening required.

Using Flash

Flash is a handy way to get a picture when there isn't enough existing light for satisfactory exposure. Most professional portrait and commercial studio photographers use flash almost exclusively for their work because of its uniform quality, consistent high intensity, incredible motion-stopping ability, and lack of uncomfortable heat and glare—whether the subject is a person, an animal, or an ice cream sundae. But these professionals seldom shoot anything with only a small flash unit on the camera. They work with expensive, heavy-duty multiple lighting units.

Effective lighting with flash, like good lighting with any other source, is the result of previsualizing the effect you want to achieve. Do you want shadows to be harsh, soft, or nonexistent? Do you want to emphasize texture, or accent a certain part of the subject? Do you want to use light to separate the subject from the background? All of these questions should be answered before photographing any subject with flash or with any kind of light.

The common method of using flash—with the flash unit clipped into a metal shoe mounted on top of the camera or held by a bracket at one side of the camera and aimed directly at the subject—violates all of the principles of good lighting. Use direct-flash-on-camera only as a fill-in to illuminate harsh shadows cast by the sun, for personal "snapshooting," and as the sole light source only when there's no other way to get the picture.

A flash on the camera aimed directly at the subject gives flat, uninteresting lighting. It may cause an ugly black shadow on the background, overexpose foreground objects and underexpose subjects farther away. Another problem with flash-on-camera is red-eye. The eyes of subjects looking toward the camera may reflect spots of light the way the eyes of animals on the road reflect a car's headlights. The solution to this problem is to move the light source away from the camera.

By placing the flash unit to the side or above the camera, shadows are cast on the subject more from the ideal 45° key-light position, giving a feeling of form, texture, and depth. Off-camera flash requires a cord sufficiently long to hold the flash at arm's length, or farther if you want to mount the flash on a stand. Take care to aim the flash so that the reflector is aimed where you want it. It's easy to tilt the flash unknowingly up or sideways. This can cause uneven lighting.

The simplest way to get decent lighting with a flash mounted on the camera is to tilt the flash straight up at the ceiling or sideways to a nearby wall. Called "bounce" flash because the light is bounced off a reflective surface and back down to your subject, the bounce technique gives soft, low-contrast lighting that looks very natural. But bounce flash works only in relatively small rooms with white ceilings or light-colored walls. It won't be effective outdoors, of course, or in a large gymnasium or auditorium. With color film, unless the bounce surface is white, the picture may take on the color of the ceiling or wall.

Aim the flash straight up at the ceiling or directly at a reflecting surface. Be careful not to partially tilt the flash so the subject is too bright on the top or one side from direct light and too dark at the bottom.

Flash exposure

Most small flash units automatically give the right amount of light if their controls are set to the proper f/stop and distance range. Exceptions may be with bounce and when shooting direct flash outdoors at night or in a very large room. Since some light is lost under these conditions, you may need to open the lens one or two stops more than indicated. Be sure to run tests with new equipment, and attach a label to your flash so you won't forget the settings.

Dedicated flash units make it easier to fill in shadows outdoors on a sunny day. If your equipment doesn't have automatic fill flash, begin your tests by setting the maximum shutter speed that your camera will synchronize (see owner's manual or set at 1/60 if the shutter speed dial is not clearly marked). Then, either by meter or "Sunny 16" rule, set the lens opening. For example: 100-speed film on a sunny day should be 1/60 at f/22. Check the charts on your flash to find out the distance range within which you can work at f/22. If your tests show that the flash is too intense, either use the next lower brightness setting or tape translucent diffusion material over the flash.

Copying and Close-ups

The photographic reproduction of flat objects is known as copying, whether you're making a new negative from an old photographic print, or reproducing a map, an illustration from a publication, or a painting or drawing.

Line copy is just black & white

Black-and-white material to be copied usually is divided into two categories: *line* and *continuous tone*. Line copy materials consists only of black-and-white without gray tones. Examples of line copy are the kinds of things we would think first to reproduce on an office copy machine: a printed or typewritten page, an ink drawing, or a screened halftone reproduction (the image being broken up into a pattern of black-and-white dots). Such materials are best photographed on special film such as Kodalith Ortho or Kodak High Contrast Copy film. If high contrast film is not available, you can use ordinary film, but you should reduce the Zone V exposure by one or two stops and give N+2 development to increase the contrast. (NOTE: get a Zone V exposure either by using an incident meter or by reading a standard 18 percent gray card).

Continuous tone includes grays

Continuous-tone originals contain many shades of gray between the lightest and darkest tones. A good photographic print fits into this category, as does a painting or drawing containing various shades of tone or different values and intensities of color. Slow, fine-grained films are suitable for most continuous-tone copying. The highlights may tend to print with a grayish cast, however, so special copying films are available in sheet film sizes that are designed to make reproductions that more exactly match the tonal values of the original.

Special techniques for color

Copying in color requires using a film balanced for the light source. While natural light can be used, the most consistent results will come from using a

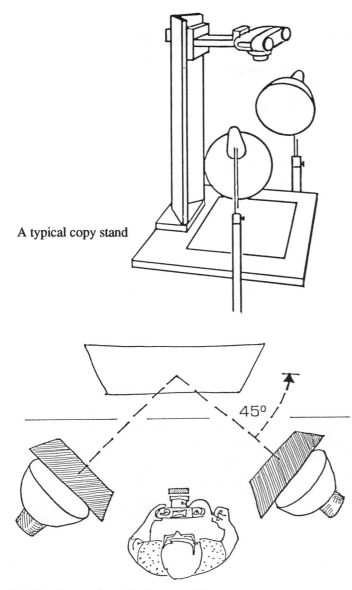

A typical copy stand

Copies of artwork can be improved by placing polarizers over lens and lights.

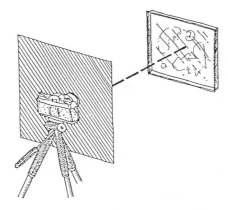

Reflections of the camera in the glass of a picture frame or display case can be minimized by shooting through a hole cut in a black card or cloth.

sturdy copy stand with two studio lights to ensure even illumination. Either quartz lamps or 3,200 K incandescent bulbs are commonly used because they match tungsten balanced color films such as Ektachrome 64 and 160. An 80A blue filter will balance tungsten light with daylight color films or you can use blue filter gels over the lights or blue-tinted bulbs. Color negative films can be corrected in printing. The color of the light isn't important with black-and-white.

Place lights at 45°

The lights should be placed at equal distances from the material to be copied, set at an angle of 45°, and aimed so they slightly overlap the center of the copy. Check the evenness of the light with a hand-held incident exposure meter. Move the meter across the area where the artwork will be, adjusting the lights as needed. Determine exposure with the incident meter or, if you must use the meter in the camera, read from a standard 18 percent gray card held directly in front of the material to be copied.

Polarizing filters properly placed over each light and on the camera lens will eliminate nearly all traces of surface reflections from glossy inks or paints and improve the color saturation of the copy. The axis of the polarizer on the camera must be set 90° from the axes of the lamp polarizers. This combination usually will require about one and one-half stops more exposure (a factor of three).

Increase exposure up close

Additional exposure will be needed when photographing things that are very small. This is in addition to any increase required at one second or longer because of reciprocity. A general rule is to give four times normal exposure (two stops) if the subject is about the same size as the negative—for example, a postage stamp or an insect photographed life-size on 35mm film. If the subject is reproduced approximately half natural size, such as copying a small snapshot photo with a 35mm camera, the exposure should be increased by one stop or double the exposure time. Remember that you should always base the exposure for close-up and copy work on a Zone V reading from a gray card or an incident meter.

If you have neither an incident meter nor a gray card, read a non-glossy white card and divide the ISO setting on the camera by five. This will give you Zone V because a white card reflects about 80 percent of the light, five times as much as an 18 percent gray card.

While copying flat material doesn't require much depth of field, photographing small three-dimensional objects requires all the depth of field you can get— f/16 or the smallest opening on your lens. Even with flat materials, however, the lens probably will be sharpest overall around f/5.6 or f/8. Better to use a sturdy copy stand or tripod and give whatever exposure time is necessary including increases for both reciprocity and close-up factors.

I respond initially to the texture, form and the effect of light on my subject. The visual challenge and delight for me is bringing all of these elements together into a cohesive composition.

(Susan Carr, photographer)

Jorg Jasper *Swimmers*
Simple 45° lighting emphasizes the repetition of forms and textures

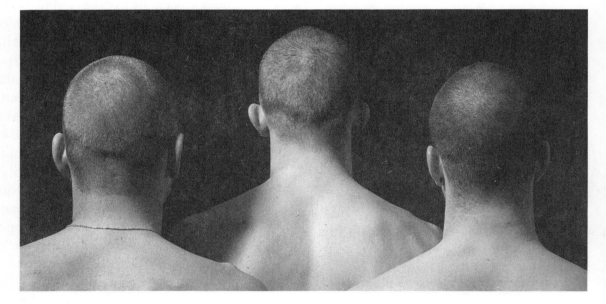

Darren Hathaway *Jeff*
Notice the perfect 45° short lighting in this available-light portrait. Because of the wide lens opening, the depth of field is very shallow.

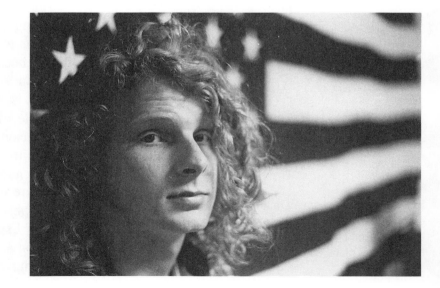

Special Camera Techniques   *10*

Unexpected Experiences

Events that never happened—photographs of strange things and strange visions in strange places.
      (Peter Gold, photographer)

People believe in photographs. Because most of us subconsciously accept the old adage that "the camera never lies," photographs can shock us by twisting what we have quietly expected to be a faithful reproduction of reality into an unexpected experience.

The universe is full of magical things patiently waiting for our wits to grow sharper.
      (E. Phillpots, philosopher)

Frequently there is conflict between interesting subject matter and interesting photographs. Great photographs exist that are superb renditions of interesting subject matter, yet in other great photographs the subject matter is scarcely recognizable. Artists use the term surrealism to describe work that transcends reality; but unique to photography is the ability to produce an image that exists in a world of its own, halfway between the real and the imaginary.

Surrealism is freedom. It is the power of imagination. What you dream...what comes out of you when you don't know it.
      (Henri Cartier-Bresson, photojournalist)

Sometimes, because of subtly revealed textures and forms or bizarre juxtaposition of subject matter, a "straight" photograph may offer us a surrealistic surprise. But more often, such interesting images are the result of inspired manipulation.

I frequently attempt to show in my work...the unreality of the "real" and the reality of the "unreal." This may result, at times, in some disturbing effects. But art should be disturbing; it should make us both think and feel; it should infect the subconscious as well as the conscious mind.   *(Clarence John Laughlin, photographer)*

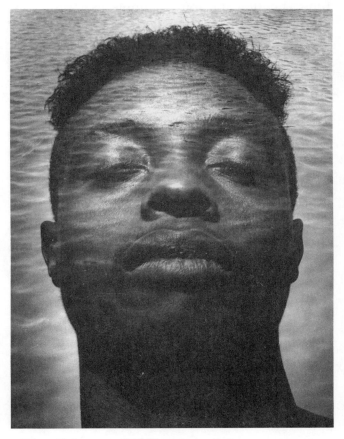

Diane Osborne   *Still Water Runs Deep*
Two negatives were sandwiched in the enlarger to create this provocative image that served as the lead picture in an exhibition.

Great photographs exist...in the electric tension between real and unreal.

    (Charles Harbutt, photographer)

When examining the work of certain contemporary imagemakers, sometimes it's hard to tell for sure where photography has ended and handwork or optical/electronic manipulation begun. Widespread overlapping of technologies is creating an ethical dilemma, as well as an artistic "gray area" within which it is sometimes difficult to distinguish concept from craft, and message from technique.

Some photographic special effects are good, clean fun. Some of the more obvious "tricks" that can make a strong artistic statement, produce a visual joke, or sometimes sell a product include special films, lighting illusions, multiple exposures, and optical manipulation with lenses and filters.

Darkroom and computer effects range from the obvious to the amazing, with many steps in between. Photographic effects are created in one of three ways: by accident, by trial and error, or by deliberate design.

In this chapter we will describe several special effects that you can achieve with your camera and accessories. Chapter 11 will continue this concept into the darkroom where many more techniques await your experimentation. Finally, although electronic manipulation is becoming more and more common, we will wait until the next edition to catch up with computer imaging software!

Reflections and Distortion

The mark of an educated person is to see something in a mud puddle besides the mud. (anonymous)

One rainy day as I was stepping off the curb to cross a street, a little girl splashing around nearby shouted, "Mommy, Mommy, look at the pretty rainbow in the gutter!"

"Silly girl," replied Mom, "Can't you see that's just dirty oil floating on the water. It's nasty. Don't get it on your boots!"

So much for imagination. When that little girl goes to school, will her teacher show her how to draw a turkey by tracing around her hand? Will she

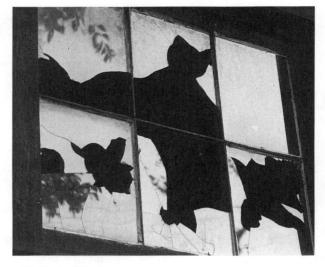

D. Curl *Window*
Which form is surface, which form is behind the glass, and which is the reflection? Reflective surfaces can yield endless relationships between positive and negative space.

be told that the country landscape she has crayoned isn't right because the sky is not blue and the grass is not green?

It's OK to trust your instincts
(Ed Paschke, painter)

So I hope you will learn to see puddles, polished metal and stone surfaces, windows and glass doors as mirrors, too. Notice what you see in reflective surfaces, what's on the surface, and what is revealed beyond.

Special Filters

In Chapter 4 we discussed how filters work and when you might want to use them. But there are special ways to use ordinary filters, and special filters that can be used, with imagination, to create stunning effects.

Any colored filter will create an overall tint of that color on color film, and sometimes that's what you want. One interesting technique is to make a triple exposure (on a tripod) through each of three colored filters (#25 red, #61 green, and #38A blue). Ignore the filter factors, exposing each time for the basic exposure without a filter. Bracket, of course.

The effect is most dramatic when part of the subject remains stationary during all three exposures, while other parts such as flowing water, blowing leaves, or other moving objects appear in the scene. For this project your camera must permit multiple exposures without moving the film.

Diffusion filters give a soft-focus "romantic" effect to landscapes and, when used on portraits, tend to obscure wrinkles and facial blemishes. Experiment, because the strength of the effect often depends upon the lens opening (larger openings show more diffusion).

A piece of black metal screening or nylon mesh will diffuse the image, but glass filters seem to give more sparkle to the highlights.

Some filters are available with a clear center and a diffusing effect around the edges, or with color surrounding the center. You can make your own diffusion filter by smearing a circle of petroleum jelly around the outer portion of a clear UV filter (don't do this on the lens!)

Some split-field filters increase apparent depth of field by giving near and far sharpness. Others are half clear and half graded neutral density (useful for darkening a light sky or the top of a snow-capped mountain); others consist of bands of color.

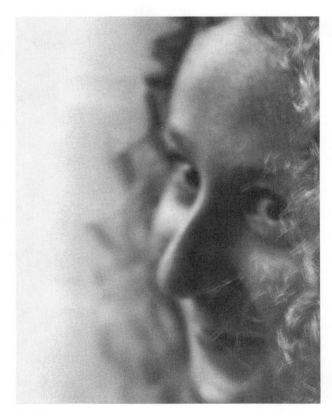

D. Morenz *Imp*
Is this not a case where unsharpness of the image actually contributes to a sense of motion and fun—a feeling of impish intimacy? **Q:** When is fuzziness *not* a flaw? **A:** Only when technical imperfection improves the effect of the photograph.

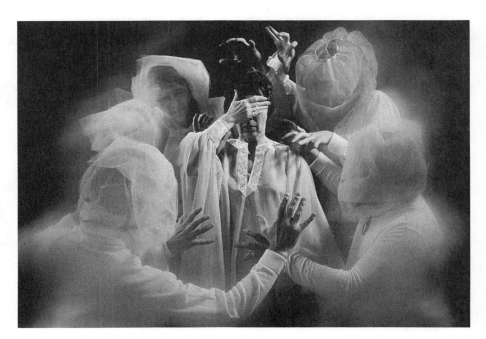

David Harrison *Ellie's Dream*
Diffusion is a technique rarely employed today, except by some professional portrait photographers. The desired dreamlike quality was given to this photograph, however, by placing a ring of petroleum jelly around the outside surface of a UV filter, leaving only the center clear. A *center sharp* filter could have been used for a similar effect.

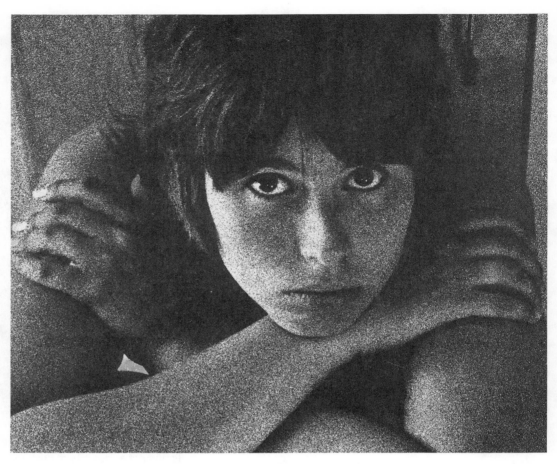

Mickey Howell *Ann*
Although grain usually is something we try to minimize, course grain occasionally strenghens the statement. The portrait (above) is a small portion of a 35mm negative made on very high-speed film that was push processed.

Jane Horton *Harrow*
Snow can simplify complex subjects by concealing distracting elements and outlining forms. High-contrast treatment made this image into a composition of repeating lines.

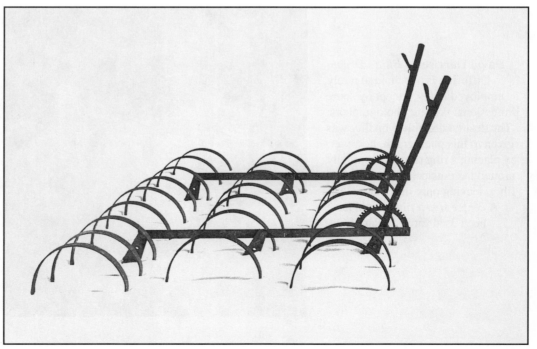

A star filter can add a dramatic cross-line flare effect to light sources and slightly diffuse the image. A piece of silver aluminum screening also will give this effect. Other filters use a diffraction pattern to create various starburst rainbow illusions. All are most effective when light sources or bright highlights appear in the picture.

Multi-image filters repeat the image of a person or object three or more times. Some designs give an illusion of linear motion. All perform best when a distinct subject is separated from a relatively dark, plain background. The multiple images appear closer together with a wide angle lens and farther apart with longer focal lengths.

Special Films

For special effects, sometimes the "wrong" film can be right! For example, if you want grainy texture in a portrait, instead of 100-speed film choose a very fast emulsion such as Kodak T-Max P3200, then push process the film and make a big, high-contrast enlargement from the negative. You'll be sure to get grain!

Extreme contrast effects such as silhouettes and outlines are easier to achieve when special film is used for the original camera negative or used to make an intermediate negative or positive for printing. Kodalith Ortho film, when processed in Kodalith developer, yields black-and-white negatives with no grays. Ektagraphic HC Slide Film can be processed either for ultra high contrast or moderately high contrast such as when copying faded old photos or low-contrast drawings. Kodak Technical Pan film also depends upon processing to determine its contrast. This slow, ultra fine-grain film is intended for scientific photography, but has many other uses as well.

Infrared film is another scientific tool that has been adopted by experimenters for bizarre pictorial effects. Unusual because its speed varies widely due to subject and lighting conditions, infrared must be exposed through a red (#25) or visually opaque (#87) filter. Turn back to page 92 to examine two examples of the special appearance of photographs made with infrared.

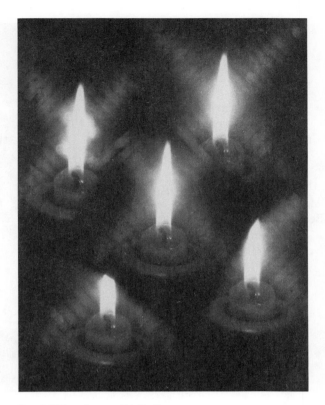

David Harrison *Light Patterns*
Novel and sometimes spectacular effects can be achieved with special filters. Here, multi-image and star filters were combined to glorify a single candle flame.

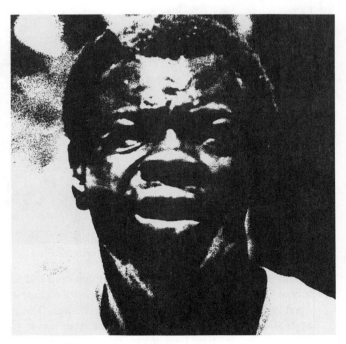

Debi Reda *Contrasts*
High contrast film transformed an ordinary continuous-tone image into an abstraction.

Fumiko Yarita *Suzy*
This double-exposure was made in the studio against a black background that kept "ghosting" to a minimum. (Note the very slight overlap that shows only in the center). Because each exposure was at a different distance, the camera had to be refocused.

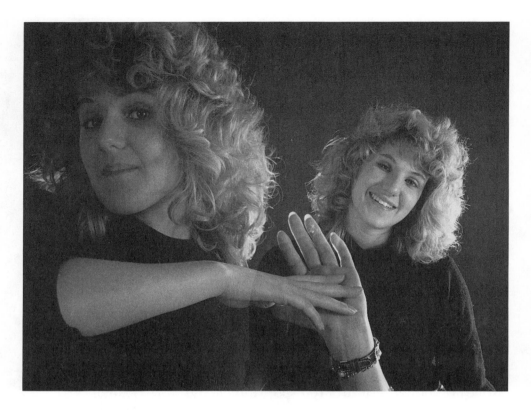

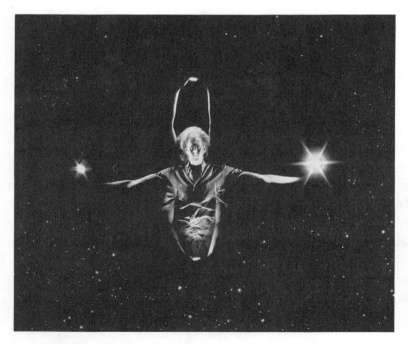

Todd Wickersham *Angel*
In this unusual self-portrait, a flash unit was held and fired manually at each of four positions while the camera shutter was held open on "B" setting with a locking cable release. The lens was set at its smallest opening (f/16) because the flash was so close to the subject. The star field background was achieved by sprinkling baby powder on the enlarging paper before exposure, and then blowing it off before putting the print into the developer.

Todd Wickersham *Myself and I*
As with *Angel* (left), the flash was fired manually in a dark room with the shutter locked open.

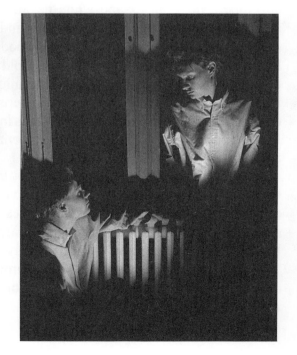

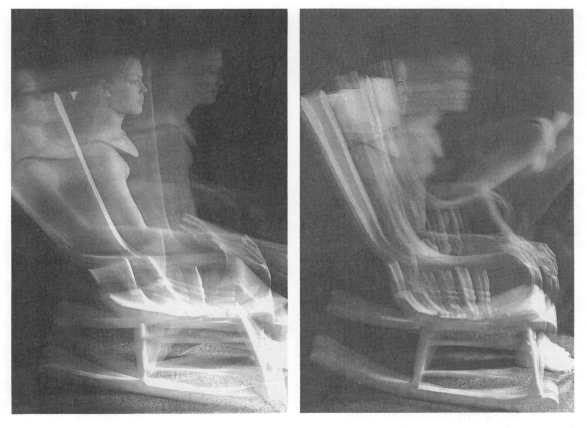

Steve McNut *Rocking*
Sharp images were recorded as the model paused briefly, blurred images as she moved during the brief time exposure (shutter set on B, cable release depressed for about five seconds).

Multiple Exposures

Repeated images of an animated subject can be created with a multi-image filter, but more control is possible with in-camera multiple exposure or with flash fired in sequence during a time exposure.

You can make multiple exposures easily if your camera provides a means for cocking the shutter without moving the film. Many 35mm cameras do, but not all. Check the owners manual to see whether yours has this feature. If not, you could consider acquiring an inexpensive older camera that does, such as a venerable Argus C-3

When using a dark background for a multiple exposure, normal exposure should give good results. But if the background is light or if the subject overlaps much of itself, you may need to divide the total exposure by the number of images (for two exposures, stop down one stop; for four exposures,

two stops). Experiment!

With the camera on a tripod and the shutter locked open at "B" setting, a flash can be fired repeatedly as the subject slowly moves across the picture area. Combining sharp with blurred motion images is another interesting technique. If you're using only hot lights, direct the subject to move, then hold; move, then hold; leaving sharp images connected by blurs to give the appearance of motion. A variation is to direct your subject, side lighted with tungsten lights, to move slowly and then end the blurred sequence with a single pop of the flash. Of course all of this must take place either in a darkened room or outdoors at night, otherwise light reflecting from the background will build up too much density and obscure the subject.

A final variation, useful to photograph a large unlighted interior or an outdoor space at night, is "walk-around" flash. You lock open the shutter and walk around within the picture area firing the flash.

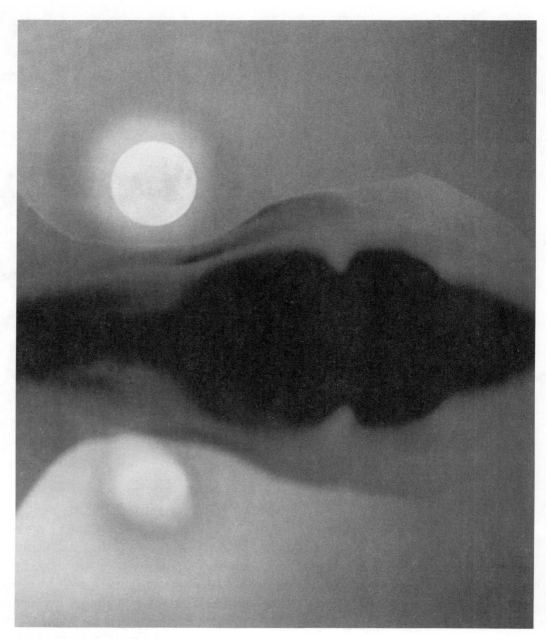

Darren Hathaway *Landscape Reflections*
Carefully masked images from four slide projectors
were superimposed to blend the "landscape," the moon,
and both reflections. Rephotographed off the screen
with 35mm color negative film, the final result was a
spectacular 16x20 color print.

*The problem with fantasy is that it's not
real. And the problem with reality is
that it is!*

(Marilyn Rowens, photographer)

Be sure to direct the light away from the camera, hiding yourself if possible behind pillars, doorways, furniture, etc. The lens opening will depend on the power of the flash unit at the chosen flash-to-subject distance.

It is the relationships between things that gives meaning to them.

(Hans Hofmann, philosopher)

Projected Images

If you're working with color slides, ingenious combinations are possible. Slides with objects against light backgrounds can be removed from their mounts, sandwiched together, and remounted for projection or printing. If two, three, or more projectors are available, try projecting together slides of subjects against dark backgrounds. The pictures can be overlapped and blended by moving the projectors around. Brightness can be adjusted simply by stretching strips of black masking tape across the front edges of projector lenses. (Don't stick the tape to the glass). Projected images can be overlapped and blended together seamlessly by using soft-edge slide masks available from audiovisual suppliers.

When you get an arrangement on the screen that you want to keep, take a picture of it from the screen with your 35mm camera. Distortion can be minimized by setting up the camera on a tripod slightly above and behind the projectors, framing the projected image tightly with a zoom or telephoto lens. The closer the projectors are to the screen, the brighter the image will be.

Either slide or color negative film can be used, but with 100-speed film, you may have to expose for several seconds with the shutter on "B." Make tests based on meter readings made directly from the screen. Bracket toward longer times, because reciprocity will lengthen the exposure needed.

Art is the only way to run away from home without leaving home.

(Twyla Tharp, choreographer)

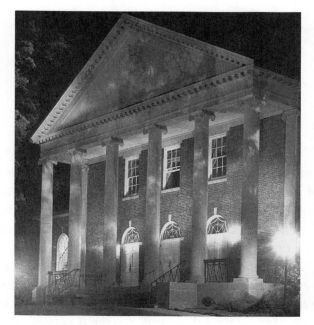

David Harrison *Chapel*
This night-time image was created by firing a hand-held flash unit 15 times as the photographer walked around the building and hid behind columns.

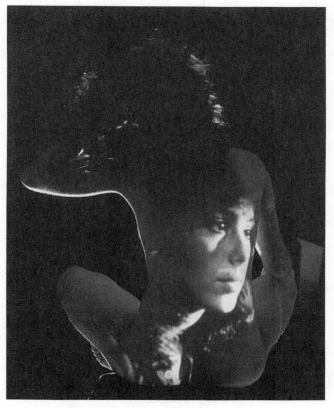

Darren Hathaway *Corina*
A color slide was projected onto the model's back in a darkened room and then rephotographed. Notice how backlighting prevents the outline of the model's body from blending into the background.

Color Temperature

Color should be convincing, appealing and enjoyable; but not necessarily accurate.
(Eliot Porter, photographer)

Accurate color sometimes is very important, as in commercial work; but at other times the *impression* of color may enhance a picture's mood and meaning. Once you know how to get correct color you can then use this knowledge to create any kind of variation or fantasy you like.

Each type of color film is designed to be exposed by light within a particular part of the spectrum, which is known as the Kelvin temperature scale. (See page 94 for a diagram). To put it very simply, candlelight and firelight are on the very "warm" or reddish end of the Kelvin scale; tungsten lights such as household bulbs and studio "hot" lights are still on the warm side (most studio tungsten and quartz lights are 3,200 K). Electronic flash is on the bluer side, similar to mid-day sunlight (5,500 K), while the extreme blue end of the spectrum consists of light reflected from a blue sky, which can measure 12,000 K or more.

What happens when you use the "wrong" film?

Because the color of light varies so much, color films have to be selected and/or filtered to match the light when accurate color values are wanted. But what about dramatic effects? Well, one common Hollywood technique is to shoot "day for night." Scenes that appear to take place under the blueness of moonlight really have been shot in sunny daylight, but on film balanced for tungsten—and underexposed to drop out shadow detail. You can do the opposite to enhance the colors of neon signs, fireworks, etc. or if you're using gelled (filtered) lights in the studio. Daylight-balanced film may cause these colors to appear more intensely saturated.

Unintentional use of the wrong color film for the light is a common beginners' mistake. So when the skin tones come out orange, what happened? That's right, you probably exposed daylight film under tungsten light. If an outdoor color picture is very blue? Well, if it's in sunlight it probably was shot on tungsten film; but if the picture was taken in heavy shade it may simply have required a warming filter. With color slides these mismatches can be catastrophic; but color negative film usually can be corrected when it is printed.

I found that I could say things with color and shapes that I couldn't say in any other way—things that I had no words for.
(Georgia O'Keeffe, painter)

Time Exposures

Night can be an exciting time to photograph city skylines, buildings, fountains, etc. A tripod is necessary, and so is exposure bracketing. You can start with an exposure table such as the one on page 167, but since every subject is so different you'll still want to bracket to be sure (don't forget about reciprocity). Motion effects such as panning and zooming can be done at shutter speeds from about 1/30 down to 1 second. But holding the camera shutter open (set on "B" and operated with a locking cable release) for several seconds or even several minutes can give a dramatic illusion of time and motion as lights from moving objects trace themselves onto the film (turn back to example on page 118). A small lens opening usually works best to keep the lighted subjects from losing shape and color due to overexposure. Also you may need to use a slow film.

Perhaps the biggest surprises will be found not in the far reaches of outer space, but rather in the near reaches of inner space—that special space where wonders are wondered, new worlds are imagined, and happenings are understood.

(Bill Stonebarger, educator)

Special Darkroom Techniques *11*

Darkroom effects range from the obvious to the amazing, with many steps in between. Photographic effects are created in one of three ways: by accident, by trial and error, or by deliberate design (Uelsmann's *postvisualization*). In this chapter are examples of several of the special effects techniques that my students have been most interested in trying.

Photograms

A cameraless shadow picture or photogram is the first assignment given by many teachers of photography. Because a photogram project requires no negative, it can be done on the first day of class; the experience with chemicals and an enlarger or other light source provides an excellent initiation for beginners into the mysterious rites of the darkroom. But making photograms can be more than an exercise. Exploring this simple process may challenge your imagination to find forms that will reproduce themselves in varied tones and to place them in graphically interesting patterns.

Any photographic paper will do for photograms—in fact, this is a good way to use up old surplus paper of any size, surface, weight, or contrast grade. Simply make a trial exposure to determine the deepest black you can get without producing flare around the images of the objects you've placed on the paper.

Also, instead of placing objects on the paper, thin, flat cutouts and patterns that will fit into a glass negative carrier can be inserted into an enlarger and projected as large as the paper available.

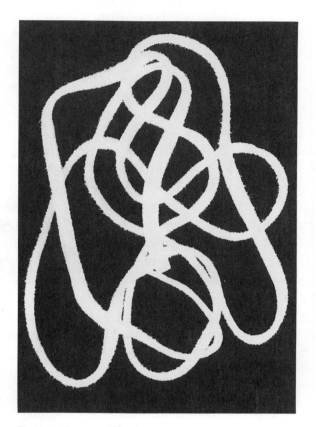

James Alvaro *Photogram*

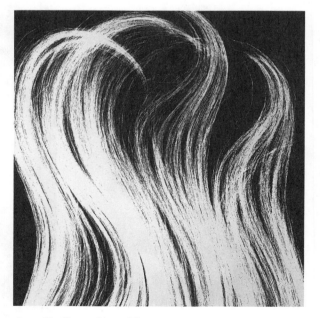

Aurelia Spengler *Photogram*

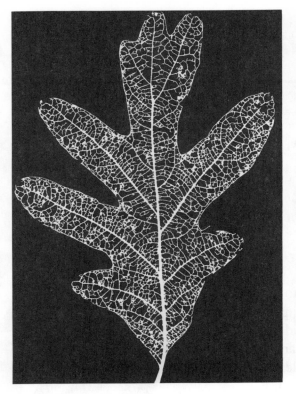

D. Curl *White Oak*
A leaf skeleton found on the ground was placed between glass in a 4x5 enlarger and projected with maximum contrast.

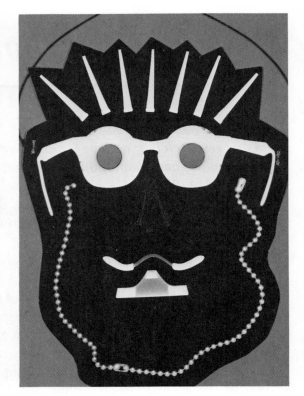

D. Curl *Mask*
A class Halloween party provided the occasion for everyone to make and wear their own photogram mask.

Lois Henry *Leaves*
The various tones of gray in this photogram were achieved by giving a series of short exposures, removing one leaf each time until only the part of the paper beneath the maple leaf in the center received no light and remained white.

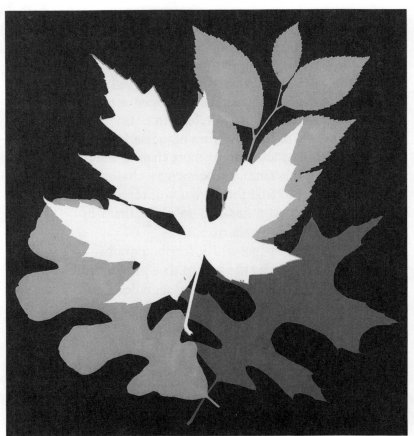

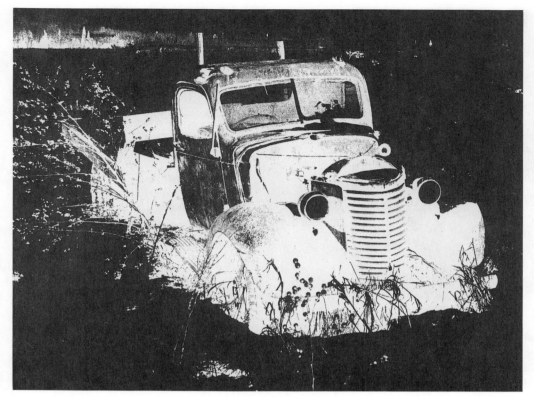

Steven Hunt
Junked Truck
An image like this can be enlarged directly from a color slide or made by contact from a positive print.

Negative Prints

A negative print? Why not! If you put a positive image such as a color slide into the negative carrier of an enlarger and make an enlargement, the result is a print that is reversed in tonal values and usually higher in contrast.

Starting with an ordinary negative, you make first a normal print, then produce the negative print by contact—paper to paper. For maximum sharpness, contact imaging of dry prints should be done emulsion-to-emulsion, either in a vacuum frame or a spring-backed glass printing frame. Lacking either, you can use a contact proofer if you firmly hold down the glass. If the positive print has just been processed and is still wet, try soaking the unexposed paper in a tray of water and laminating it against the paper positive, emulsion-to-emulsion, with a print roller or squeegee. After exposure, peel apart the two sheets and develop the final print normally. During exposure you can adjust contrast with filtration and make parts of the image lighter or darker by dodging and burning, as with a conventional print.

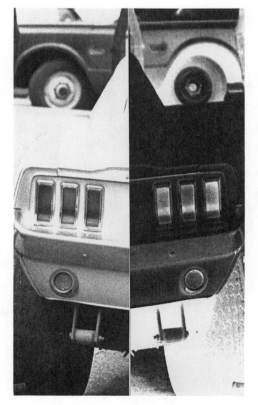

Linda Chick   *Motor Monster*
Positive and negative prints were mounted side by side to create this mask-like image.

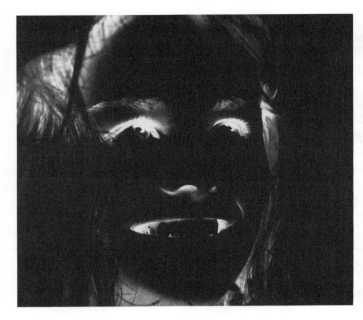

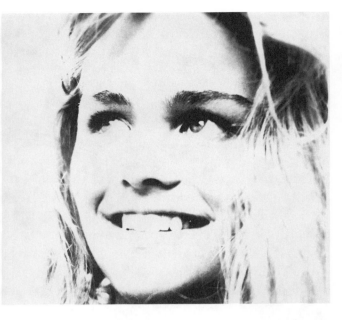

Jorg Jasper *Nina*
The negative print (left) was made directly from a color slide. The high-key positive print (right) is a contact print from it. Does the process sound complicated? It's not, really, but choose a subject that will be improved by increased contrast.

Constant creativity and innovation are essential to combat visual mediocrity.

(Jerry N. Uelsmann, photographer)

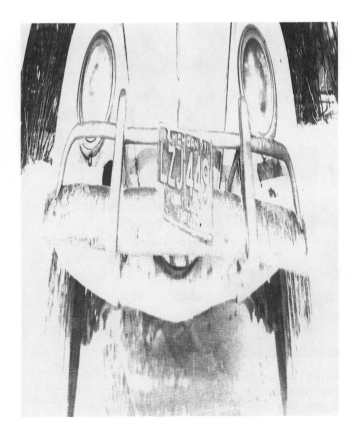

Image Distortion

The same technique that corrects for converging verticals and similar errors in perspective can be reversed to produce distortion in a normal image. Try going even further than tilting the easel: actually curving the paper, for example, can make a "stopper" from an ordinary photograph. Another idea you might want to try is to aim your camera into a highly polished distorted surface and then add to the effect by holding the paper out of square when printing. Further distortion can be achieved by copying (re-photographing) the distorted print. This is one way graphic artists make lettering appear to conform to an angled or irregular surface.

Jim Scherrer *Volksface*
A curiously distorted, facelike image has been produced by holding the enlarging paper in a sharply curved position during exposure.

Combination Printing

Sometimes it's effective, and often amusing, to print from more than one negative onto the same sheet of enlarging paper. There are several ways of doing this so the images combine to form one, the choice of method depending on the relationships of the images and on the size of the negatives and whether their backgrounds are black (transparent on the negative) or light (dense on the negative). If you have a pair of negatives with transparent backgrounds, and if the subjects are in scale with each other, a simple negative sandwich in the enlarger will work. To see whether two negatives will sandwich effectively, simply hold them up to the light together and move them around to see whether they will register satisfactorily. Beware of dust on the negatives and trapped between them, or you may have a lot of spotting to do.

Negatives with dense backgrounds must be printed separately. The background of the second negative, if it is dense enough, will mask out all but the image you want to print, so it doesn't affect the image from the first negative already printed. Careful dodging or vignetting will be necessary if the backgrounds of the negatives are not dense enough. A carefully cut mask can be useful when you want to print in a background, such as sky, around a clearly defined subject.

Most difficult of all is the blending of portions of two or more separate negatives to create what appears to be a single, unmanipulated image. It is easier to do this when each negative is in a separate enlarger and focused, masked, and with exposure determined in advance and timer set. Then you can produce several prints nearly alike, and perfect the process with a minimum of mistakes. Although a great deal of setup time and testing is required to make a blend line that doesn't show, the results can be strikingly surreal.

The true magician can explain his trick, but the magic is still there.

(*Jerry N. Uelsmann, photographer*)

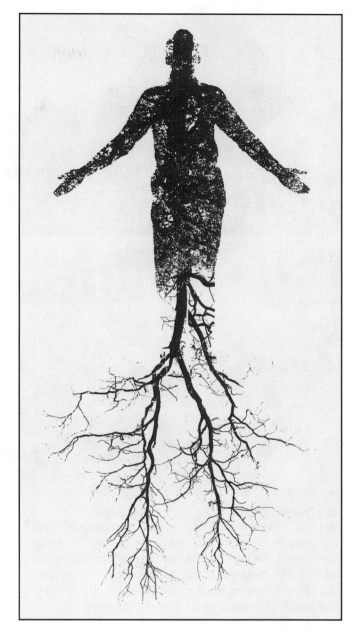

D. Curl *Roots*
Two negatives were sandwiched, one of them upside down, to produce a "roots" effect from bare branches. The completely white background resulted because the backgrounds of both the tree and the silhouette figure negatives were very dense and overlapped when the two negatives were sandwiched for printing.

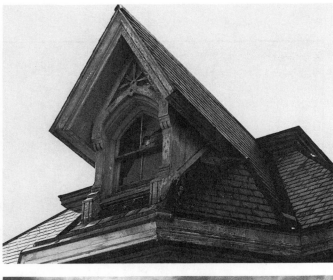

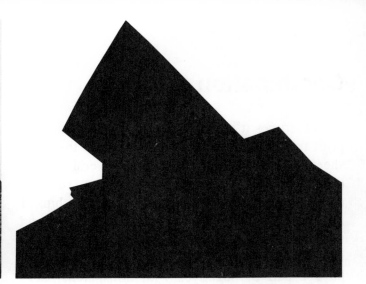

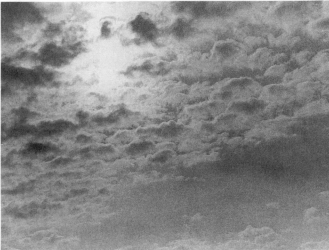

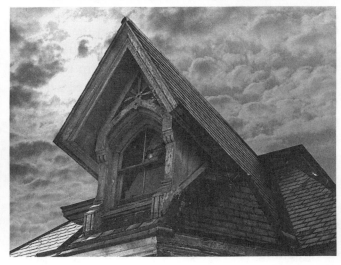

Jim Nixon *Gable*

Dramatic clouds were needed to add dimensions of depth and mystery to the gable of this old house, but the sky was blank white that day. Double printing did the trick. First, the negative image of the gable was projected to the desired size on the enlarging easel and an outline of the gable traced with pencil onto black paper. Cut out precisely with scissors, the black paper mask then was used to cover the area where the gable was exposed, while printing in the clouds from another negative. A red filter under the enlarger lens was very helpful in aligning the mask and the second image. Careful spotting of the print usually will correct minor imperfections in registration.

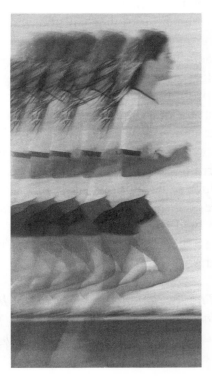

Rene Poch *Runner*

The illusion of motion in this photograph was achieved by making five separate exposures on the same sheet of enlarging paper, moving the easel an inch each time. The white background enabled the runner's face and form to stand out because the paper remained unexposed in those areas.

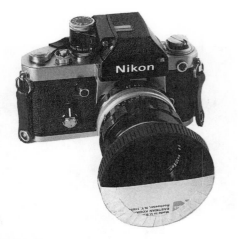

Blends can be made either in the camera or under the enlarger. A piece of matte black paper taped over half of the lens shade will do. (In the illustration, we have used a piece cut from an enlarging-paper envelope). If the blend line is too apparent, place the black paper mask inside the lens shade, closer to the lens, but be careful that it cuts the circle of light exactly in half. Try putting black paper in the enlarger filter holder beneath the lens and experimenting with placement of the blend line and lens opening until you get the effect you want.

(photo by Brian Kuehn)

D. Curl *Daymare*

This blend was achieved in the darkroom, using two separate negatives. First the top half was printed while the bottom half of the paper was covered with a black paper mask in the filter holder under the enlarger lens. Then the negative was changed and the bottom portion of the print was exposed while the top was covered. A red filter under the enlarger lens allowed positioning of the blend line without removing the sensitized paper from the easel. If two or more enlargers are available in the same darkroom, it is much easier to make this kind of blend because you can set up each negative in a separate enlarger. Then, after all tests are made, move the paper from easel to easel.

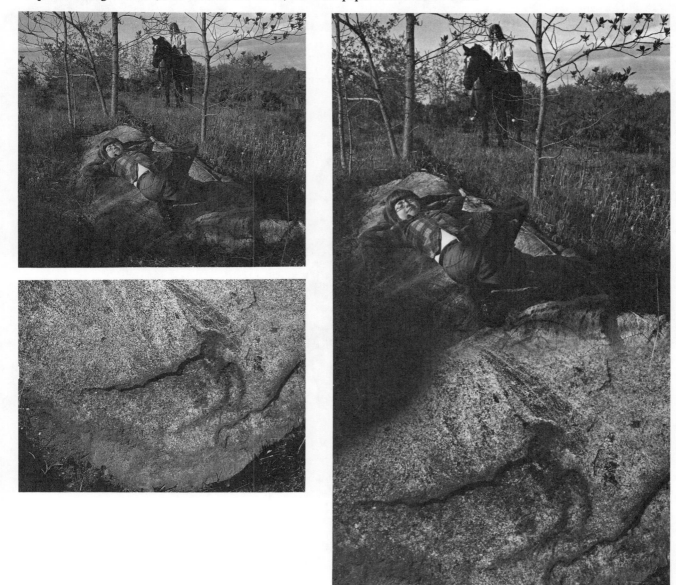

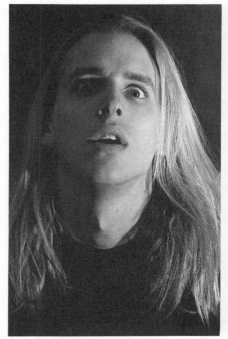 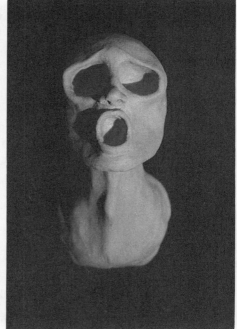 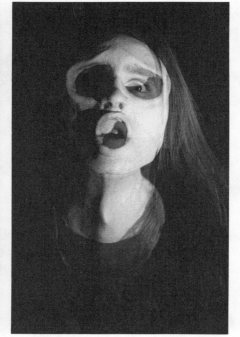

Darren Hathaway   *Ophelia*
This negative sandwich was preplanned.
The face and sculpture were photographed to the right size and against a
black background so the negatives would
superimpose easily without blending the
images with a mask.

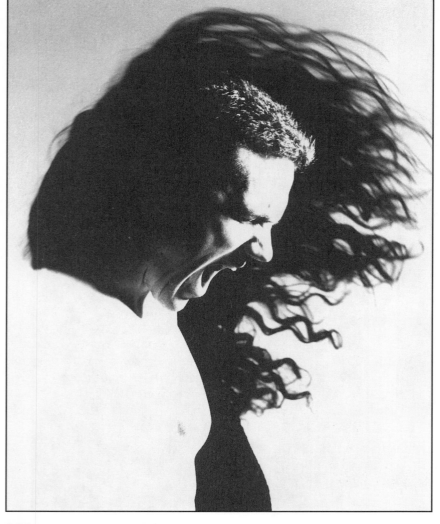

Jeff Keyes   *The Scream*
The man was photographed against a
black background so that his head would
fit inside the silhouette of the larger head.

Lowell McCoy *Sunflowers*
A negative sandwich resulted in this dramatic effect. Because the sky portion of the sunflower negative was virtually opaque and the foreground nearly transparent, the bubble negative printed through only the foreground.

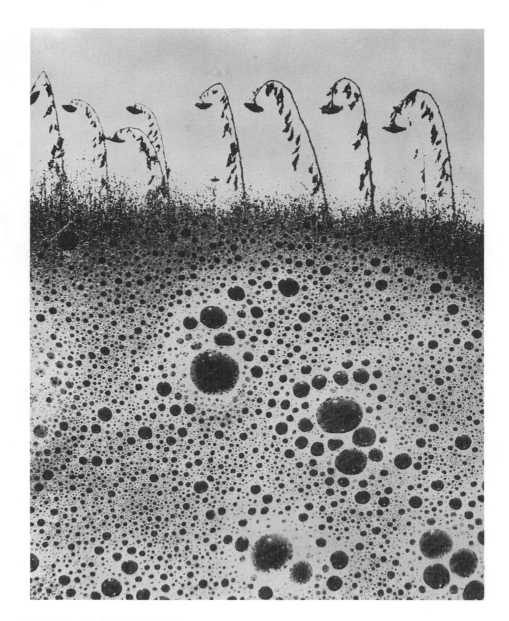

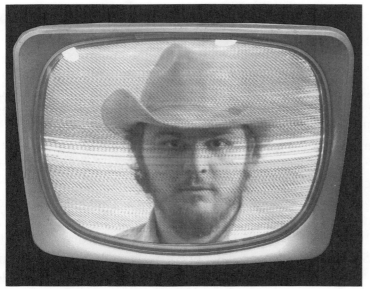

Dan Fetters *Self-portrait*
This photographer put himself on TV by the simple method of exposing the same sheet of enlarging paper separately to two different negatives. The cutout mask used to separate the shoulders from the frame of the TV set would have been unnecessary if the entire portrait negative, except for the face, had been white (opaque on the negative). This process is easiest when you use two enlargers.

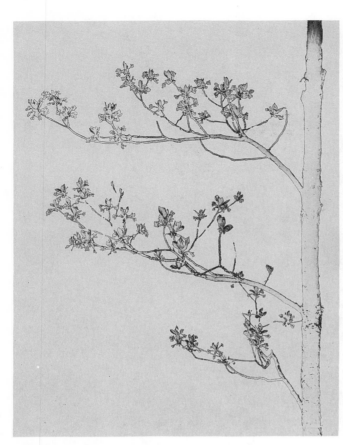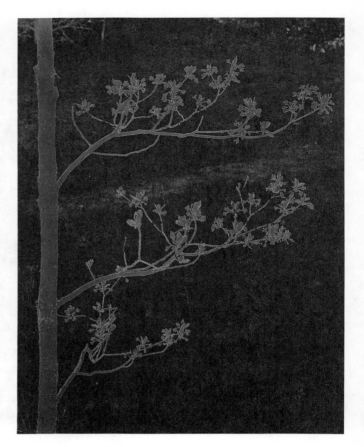

D. Curl *Young Sassafras*

Solarization (the Sabattier effect) in the conventional manner. The very dark image on the right was exposed with maximum contrast from the original negative. After one minute of development, a 100-watt bulb in the darkroom ceiling was turned on and then immediately turned off. The print was allowed to develop, without agitation, for 30 additional seconds before being stopped, fixed and rinsed in water. This dark print was then squeegeed face to face with an unexposed sheet of wet enlarging paper and the sandwich exposed to maximum contrast enlarger light, through the back of the paper "negative," for about 10 seconds. The two sheets of paper were then peeled apart and the second sheet was processed normally, resulting in the print on the left.

Solarization (the Sabattier effect)

Intriguing, partly negative, partly positive images are the result of exposing either film or paper to light after development has been partially completed. The part of the image already developed acts as a mask, while the previously unexposed emulsion is being exposed. If the image has strong contrasts between light and dark areas, delicate white or black outlines, called Mackie lines, may be formed.

Don't give up in despair if the first results aren't what you expected—part of the joy of the Sabattier effect is its unpredictability. You'll find that you can vary the effect if you experiment with the length of the white light "flash" exposure and also if the exposure occurs when the print or negative is only partially or almost fully developed. When you try the Sabattier effect on film, of course, you have only one chance. If the effect isn't right you have to make another negative. For this reason, I suggest you expose several duplicate negatives on sheet film or space your frames on roll film so you can cut the roll into perhaps three sections for separate development and solarization. Kodalith Ortho film is recommended when you want to make duplicate sheet film positives or negatives for solarization, as this film gives the added contrast usually needed and it can be developed by inspection under a safelight either in Kodalith developer or in print developer if you don't want maximum contrast.

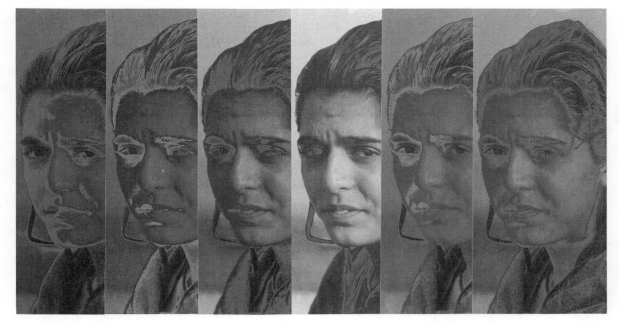

Rebecca Allen *Solarizations*
Each of the six prints above was produced on variable-contrast paper using maximum magenta filtration (200M). The process used was the double-exposure method described below. Differences were created by varying the first and second exposure times, but the 1:3 ratio between the exposures remained the same. Dull-looking prints usually result from using paper or filtration that is not maximum contrast, or from trying to work with a negative that lacks tone separation.

How to "solarize" a print by the double-exposure method

1. On the enlarger baseboard, lay a piece of glass or plexiglass at least a couple of inches larger all around than the size print you're going to make. Focus a negative with good separation between black and white onto a sheet of plain white paper the same size as your printing paper that is laid on top of the glass. Mark with tape on the baseboard where the corners of the image will be.

2. Set the enlarger lens at f/5.6 for your first trial.

3. Insert a red filter into the enlarger's filter holder.

4. If you are using variable contrast paper, set the enlarger color head for maximum magenta, or insert a #5 filter.

5. Soak a sheet of enlarging paper in fresh print developer at normal dilution for about one minute. (This should be grade 5 paper if not variable contrast).

6. Move the glass to the sink. Lay the wet paper, emulsion side up, on the glass and gently remove all of the developer from the surface. Wipe with a rubber squeegee blade or blot with a paper towel. The way this step is done may affect the texture of the image.

7. *Without dripping developer,* move the glass back to the enlarging easel, turn on the enlarger lamp with the red filter in place, and position the glass so that the paper is where you want it.

8. Turn off the enlarger lamp, remove the red filter, and make the first exposure. Try four seconds at f/5.6 for your first test. *After making the exposure, don't move the glass or the paper!*

9. Watch the print develop under the enlarger for about 30 seconds. The print should appear rather light and very contrasty.

10. Make a second exposure three times the length of the first exposure (12 seconds for your first test).

11. Peel the print off the glass and slide it back into the developer tray for at least 30 seconds to deepen the blacks.

12. Stop, fix, wash and dry the print as usual.

13. Clean up everything especially well. Be sure to wash the glass!

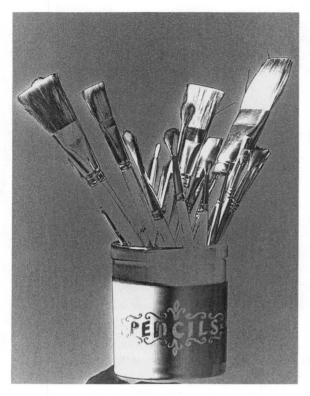

Shirley Bale *Brushes*
The Sabattier effect can be
especially pleasing when the
negative is solarized instead of
the print. Be prepared to experiment with *duplicate* negatives!

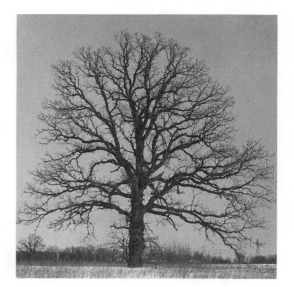

John Stites *The Oak*
Conventional print from original continuous-tone
negative (see Kodalith derivations on right).

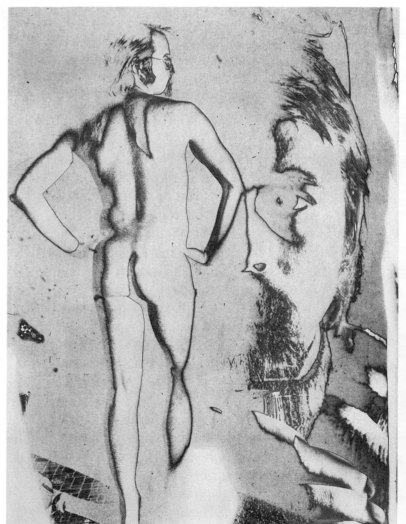

Lowell McCoy *Self-Portrait*
Double-exposure, paper-negative,
and solarization (Sabattier effect)
techniques were combined to
create this unusual image.

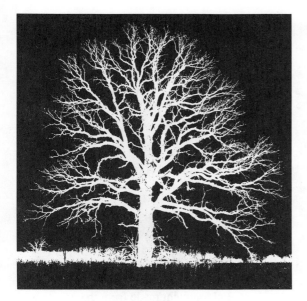

Negative print made from Kodalith positive produced from the original continuous-tone negative (third generation)

High-contrast "solarizations"

Because high-contrast litho film can drop out all middle tones, it can be used to produce very dramatic images using the Sabattier effect. In these examples John Stites made positive and negative images by contact on Kodalith ortho type 3 film from the original continuous-tone negative. Some of these negative and positive film images were exposed (solarized) for one second to the light of a 25-watt bulb four feet above the developing tray. The entire process can take place under illumination from a red series 1A safelight.

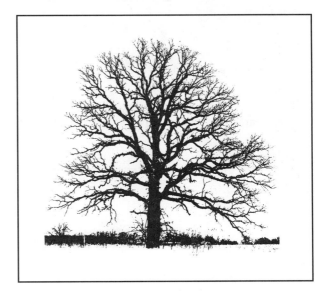

Positive print made from Kodalith negative produced from Kodalith positive (fourth generation).

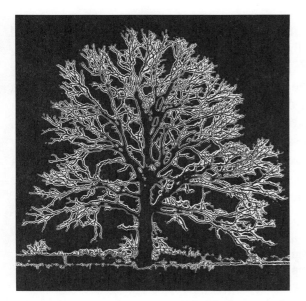

Negative print made from *solarized* Kodalith positive produced as follows:

1. Normal contact printing exposure as determined by test.
2. 45-second development in Kodalith developer, in a tray with constant agitation.
3. 15-second still development (no agitation)
4. Additional exposure (one second, 25-watt bulb, four feet above tray).
5. 1.5-minute still development (no agitation).
6. Normal stop, fix and wash.

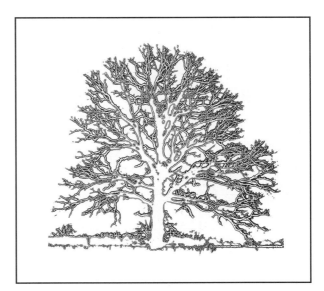

Positive print made from Kodalith negative produced by contact from *solarized* Kodalith positive (fifth generation).

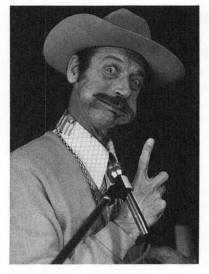

John Stites *The Entertainer*
Conventional enlargement from the
original continuous-tone negative.

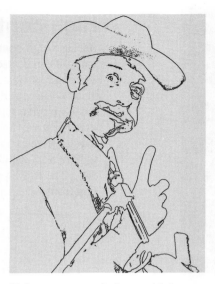

Enlargement made from a high-
contrast positive made by contact
from the negative produced in step 5.

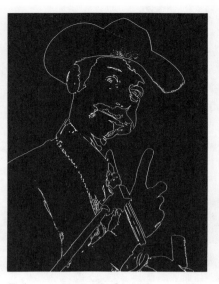

Enlargement made from the negative
produced in step 5 (below).

> ## *If you don't try, you'll never know if you can do it!*
>
> *(poster caption)*

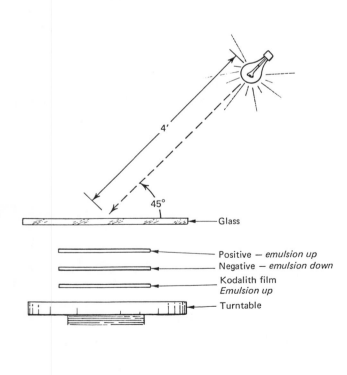

Positive — *emulsion up*
Negative — *emulsion down*
Kodalith film
Emulsion up
Turntable
Glass

Spin Drop-Out (Tone-Line)

A line-drawing treatment sometimes confused with the Sabattier effect is achieved by registering positive and negative images and then printing this pair onto Kodalith film, exposing the film sandwich to an oblique light source while whirling it on a turntable! Although this seems to be a very weird process, the resulting detail and strength of line may well be worth the effort. As with all special-effect processes, you'll have to experiment a bit to get the optimum exposure.

The spin drop-out process (sometimes referred to as tone-line) can convert a continuous-tone photograph into an image resembling a pen and ink drawing. The examples at the top of this page were produced by the following procedure:

1. Conventional 35mm negative enlarged onto Kodalith film to make a high-contrast film positive.
2. Kodalith positive contact printed onto Kodalith film to make a high-contrast negative.
3. Kodalith negative opaqued to conceal dust-spots.
4. High-contrast negative and positive taped together in register and placed into a pressure-back printing frame with a sheet of unexposed Kodalith film. Printing frame placed on turntable (see diagram).
5. Exposure with turntable rotating at 45 rpm was five seconds with a 60-watt bulb three feet from the turntable and at a 45° angle. Rotation does not have to be rapid, but it should be even. (A kitchen "lazy Susan" will serve as a turntable if you don't have an old phonograph).

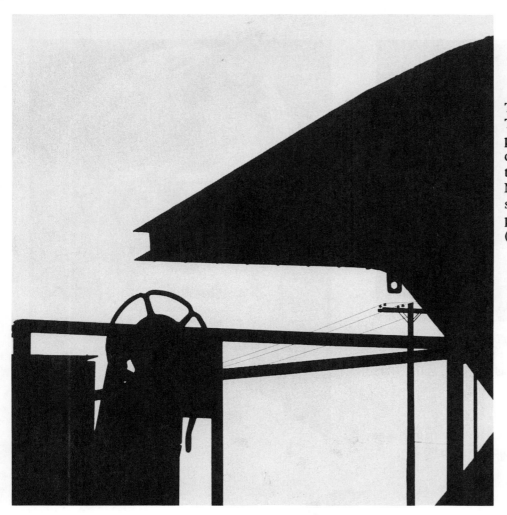

Therese Douville *Vectors*
The high-contrast drop-out process eliminates extraneous detail, focusing attention on the underlying graphic design. Notice in this example the strong interplay between positive and negative space (foreground and background).

High-Contrast Drop-Out

Some photographs have more impact if the middle tones are "dropped out"; that is, if the image is reduced from a full scale of tones to pure black and white. Obviously this isn't an effect that you would use too often, because it would lose its novelty and defeat the purpose of striving for a rich tonal scale. A straight enlargement with maximum magenta filtration (contrast grade 5) often will yield a very satisfactory high-contrast print from a negative that already is a strong near-silhouette or that includes prominent light and dark elements. Additional tones can be dropped out by making a high-contrast intermediate positive or negative by projecting the continuous-tone original either on paper or on Kodalith Ortho film.

Kodalith is a graphic arts film that is intended to yield completely clear lines against an opaque black background if exposed properly (ISO 3-6) and developed in Kodalith developer. Kodalith solarizes

beautifully, and it can be developed to somewhat lower contrast in ordinary print developer. A red (1A) safelight lets you develop by inspection until you see the result you want. Kodalith Ortho film is available in 35mm bulk rolls and in 35mm magazines as Ektagraphic HC film so it can be exposed directly in a 35mm camera. The exposure is extremely critical, however, and it's much easier to control the results when you convert a normal negative or color slide to high contrast in the darkroom.

Unless you make a print really *"bad," it won't be any* good! *(Anonymous)*

One must learn by doing the thing; for though you think you know it, you have no certainty until you try.
(Sophocles, philosopher)

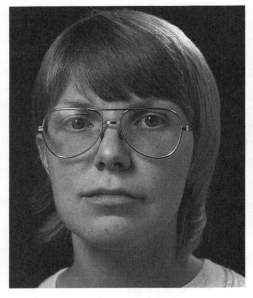

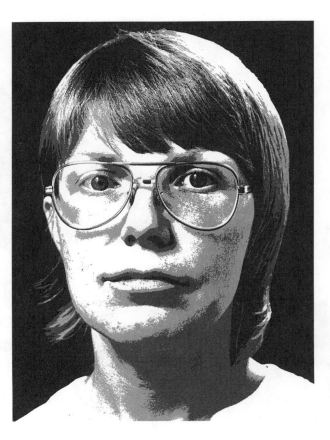

John Stites *Virginia*
Conventional print from original negative (left) and final result of posterization (right).

Tone Separation

(Below) Appearance of shadow negative (left), midrange negative (middle) and highlight negative (right).

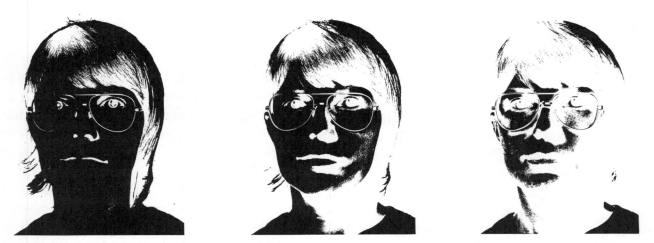

Posterization converts a conventional photographic image into something resembling a screen print. Instead of a full range of gray tones, the scale is limited to three or four values. This example was produced by the following procedure:

1. Three Kodalith positives were made from the original continuous-tone negative Exposures were 2.5, 5, and 10 seconds, as determined by test.
2. Three Kodalith negatives were made by contact from the Kodalith positives made in step 1 (same exposure for all three).

3. The final enlargement was made with three different exposures, from the three different Kodalith negatives, all on the same sheet of paper:
     a. Shadow negative (most dense): 35 sec.
     b. Midrange negative (middle density): 7 sec.
     c. Highlight negative (least dense): 4 sec.

Exposures were determined first by making separate test strips. Each negative was registered visually with a print made previously, then the enlarging paper was returned to the exact same position in the easel. This process is much simpler if you can use a separate enlarger and easel for each negative.

Tone Separation (Posterization)

Another way to produce a strong graphic image from an "ordinary" photograph is to make a posterized print from three or four high-contrast separation negatives on Kodalith film. Start with a fairly contrasty film positive and expose the duplicate negatives either by contact or by projection. You should deliberately underexpose one negative so that only the highlight areas are recorded. The intermediate negative(s) should receive somewhat more exposure, therefore the opaque areas will be larger. Finally, the negative receiving the most exposure will record the largest area of density and cover the deepest shadows that you'll be able to reproduce. The separation negatives must be printed in sequence of the most dense through the least dense, and they must be registered exactly with one another, similar to the way in which screen-process stencils are registered when printing with inks.

Reticulation

One of my students "discovered" reticulation quite by accident. She came to me in tears, having "ruined" an entire roll of negatives. Luckily, however, the subject matter was enhanced by the neat pattern embossed onto the film by her "mistake." Deliberate reticulation can yield extremely interesting texture effects, but I suggest that you try the process on a roll of film that contains *copy* negatives made from prints of simple subjects with large areas of even tone. Here's how to do it:

Immediately after normal development, place the film in a rinse of hot stop bath at least 140°F (60° C). Leave the film in the hot stop bath for one minute, and then plunge it immediately into a bath of ice water for another minute before fixing and washing. Dry the film quickly with hot air.

Mary Kay Payne *Reticulation*
The abstracted shapes of positive and negative space are strengthened by eliminating detail and superimposing texture.

> *A painting can be abstract from the beginning; a photograph, to be nonobjective, must either be selected with infinite care from a corner of nature or tortured out of all recognition in processing.*
>
> *(Thomas W. Leavitt, photographer)*

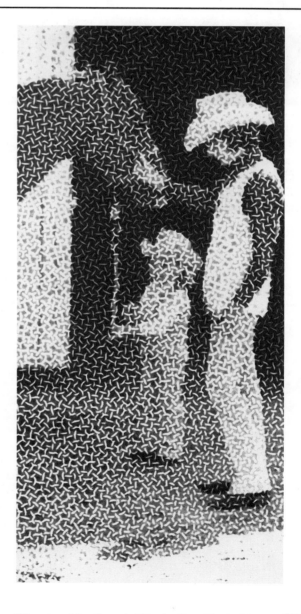

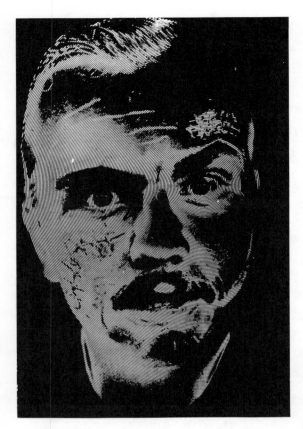

Dan Klaasen *Scarface*
The concentric circle pattern on this negative portrait resulted from a commercial texture screen being placed over the Kodalith film positive when the enlargement was made.

J. Savage *Old House*
Texture effects can be simulated by placing a transparent pattern in contact with either the negative or the paper and printing through the combination. This cobweb effect was obtained by sandwiching a sheet of lens cleaning tissue with the negative.

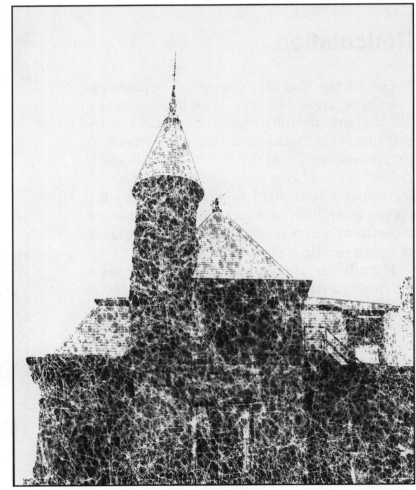

Texture Screens

Besides grain or reticulation in the negative, another way to superimpose an overall pattern onto a photograph is to print through a transparent material with the desired design.

Texture screens can be purchased, or you can make your own by photographing a textured surface on high-contrast film. A color slide of a textured surface can be mounted and projected or printed together with another slide or with a negative. Graphic arts textures and patterns can be reproduced with Kodalith film, and some materials such as lace, netting, or rice paper can be used directly as texture screens. The screen either can be sandwiched with the negative or placed over the enlarging paper when the print is made. Ordinarily, you should use a sheet of glass or a negative proofer to hold the texture screen and the paper in firm contact. A glass negative carrier may be needed in the enlarger, too, but usually stopping down the lens will keep both negative and screen in good focus.

Halftones are texture screens

Continuous-tone photographs must be printed through a kind of texture screen if they're to be reproduced in ink on a printed page, such as in a book or magazine. The special screens used for this purpose break up the image into a regular pattern of black dots of various sizes that, if the screen pattern is small enough, give the illusion of various tones of gray. You can get a sort of "pop-art" effect by superimposing a photolithographer's halftone screen on your negative and then enlarging it until the dot pattern becomes visible. A transparent contact screen can be placed tightly against the enlarging paper in a proofer, or sandwiched with the negative and then enlarged, or a duplicate negative can be made on Kodalith Autoscreen Ortho film. Autoscreen film has a built-in 133 lines-per-inch dot pattern that can be enlarged to the degree desired. Such a screened negative can be used to produce a screened positive on regular Kodalith, the first step in making photographic screen process prints.

Diffusion

As discussed in Chapter 10, a diffusion filter can be placed under the enlarger lens as well as in front of the camera lens. Usually the results are better on the camera, but the effect is permanent. Diffusion in the darkroom lets you experiment to get just the amount of softness you want. Commercial diffusion filters work well on the enlarger, but black window screen, nylon pantyhose and crumpled cellophane are commonly used.

If you're using a makeshift diffuser, hold it just beneath the lens and keep it moving during the exposure; or move it out of the way so that part of the exposure is with the diffuser, part without. You may need to increase the exposure slightly. Also increase the contrast because diffusion tends to flatten the image.

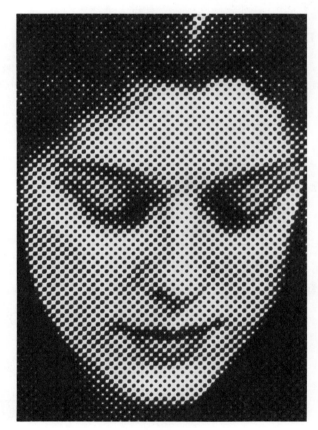

Bob Lane *Laura*
The dot pattern was achieved by enlarging a duplicate negative that had been exposed through a 133-line halftone screen of the type used by printers.

Photo Sketching

A final derivation eliminates the photographic image altogether, converting it into a line drawing by hand instead of optically. Photo sketching is a controversial technique—purists insist that it's cheating, although many technical illustrators and commercial artists use similar methods regularly, apparently without pangs of conscience. The most obvious and expedient method simply is to place a negative or a slide into the enlarger and trace the outline of the projected image with pencil or marker the size you want it onto paper on the baseboard. Shading effects and other details can be added later.

Another process involves making an enlargement and bleaching away the photographic image after tracing over it. Here's how it's done:

1. Make an enlargement of the desired size. This print should be light and flat—just dark enough to see the wanted detail (underexposure and underdevelopment will produce this kind of print).

2. Process and air dry the print. A long wash is not required.

3. Ink-in the detail you want, using a draftsman's technical pen and waterproof black India ink. (If the print is made on matte surfaced paper, the drawing can be done with a pencil). Detail you don't want should not be traced. Shading can be done by stippling. Allow the ink to dry thoroughly.

4. Bleach away the silver image in a solution of Farmer's Reducer. You can buy packets of prepared powder or you can mix up a longer lasting two-solution bleach consisting of 25 grams of potassium ferricyanide crystals dissolved in 1 liter of water in the first tray and regular fixer in the second. Alternate the print between the two trays until the bleaching is complete.

5. Agitate the print in ordinary fixer until the yellowish stain is gone. Wash, then air dry.

Enlargement for photo sketching

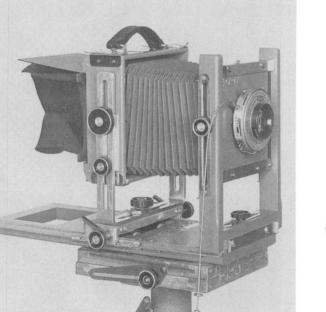

Completed photo sketch

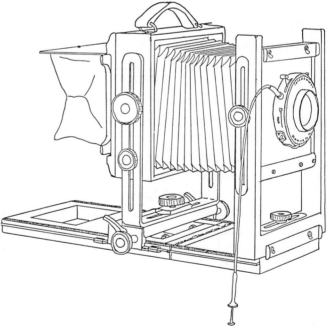

Electronic Imaging

Still-video cameras and printers. Computer graphics software. These are the new "darkroom" tools of the '90s. No, optical/chemical photography is not dead, nor even dying. But our old concepts are expanding to include technologies undreamed of only a few years ago.

> *What is happening now is that electronics is more important after image capture— for publishing, storing, organizing, transmitting, editing, retouching, and creating montage images or images combined with type or other graphics. Such procedures can be easier and better via electronics.* (Ken Lassiter, educator)

Everything described in this chapter can be done with electronics faster, easier, and in color. But not necessarily as well—yet, nor as cheaply. And the image has to be created before it can be modified.

Processes such as tone drop-outs, line separations and photo sketching can be done like this: First you scan a conventional photographic print or "grab" a video frame; then with digital "darkroom" software in a personal computer, you crop, eliminate, add, retouch, modify, distort, reverse, adjust contrast, add color, change color—anything imaginable. You see what you're doing on a video monitor and experiment until you get just the effect you want. Then print it out with a couple of keystrokes or transfer it directly into a page-layout program.

> *If you want to go somewhere, you gotta get on the bus.*
>
> (Tom Bodett, writer)

What should each of us be doing about these changes? Well, I'm rewriting this book entirely on a Macintosh computer and laying out the pages with Aldus *PagerMaker* desktop publishing software. (Would you believe that personal computers didn't even exist in 1978 when the first edition of this book was published!)

Now the line drawings can be scanned in and placed onto the pages electronically. Everything except the halftone photographs can be done "modern." At today's state-of-the art, the halftones will be sharper and print with a better tonal range if they are reproduced by traditional optical-mechanical processes. Storing halftones also requires an enormous amount of hard disk space. For the next edition, that may not be true!

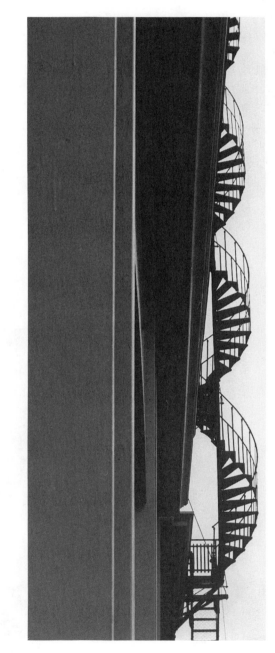

Lou VanderHave *Staircase*

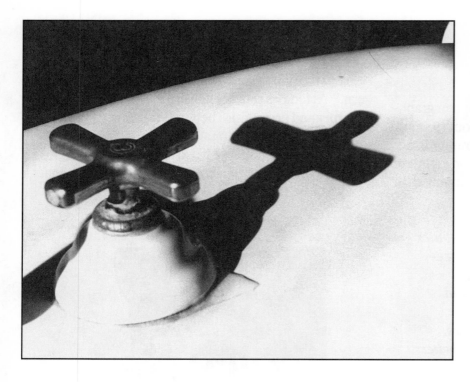

Todd Wickersham
Baptismal Cross
This dramatic image presented itself one morning as the sun shone brightly into the bathroom window. Marvelous visual experiences await us every day. Will you be tuned in?

Jennifer Harris *Collage*
This clever graphic design was created by mounting together a series of test strips.

Photography as a Profession **12**

Q. As an ethical professional, I'm compelled to do things as well as I know how, but I'm frustrated by the corporate liaison who insists that I do everything her way. I have a difficult choice to make. Do I compromise my artistic judgment to please her, or do I stand firm and risk offending her? So far I haven't made a decision and I'm a nervous wreck.

N.H., Los Angeles, CA

A. We all must choose, but we cannot choose not to choose. Fortunately for you and your client, the choice is very simple. You were hired to produce exactly what the client wants and it must be done exactly as the client, through its corporate liaison, wants it done. That nonsense about artistic integrity must come to a screeching halt. Use your ability to produce great work to your client's specifications, not to second guess the world.

(Adapted from a column by Leo Lukowsky,
***Industrial Photography** magazine's Answer Man)*

Creativity vs. Craft

If you truly love photography, perhaps you should not become a professional. On the other hand, the idea of being paid to do that which you most enjoy is enormously appealing. Despite having squarely faced this dilemma throughout forty years of earning a living from imagemaking, I haven't fully resolved the conflict between creative freedom and financial security; but then few photographers have resolved it, and in other media even fewer artists have. Nevertheless, students constantly are asking for advice on how to make a living by making pictures.

It's not easy being in love with photography and trying to make a living from it.
(Ralph Gibson, photographer)

The source of the dilemma remains the ancient paradox of creativity versus craft. Craft sells regularly and predictably; creativity sells sporadically. The best compromise is to approach your craft creatively, but not *too* creatively, because in the changing marketplace the value of "art" lies less with the artist than with the beholder.

"Whoever pays the piper calls the tune" is not just a folk saying. It is equally true that whoever pays the photographer usually sets the rules for the assignment. If eventually you become one of the celebrities in our industry, some clients may give you blanket assignments and be delighted with whatever images result. Then you will be able to measure success by the size of your bank balance. To reach this exalted status, however, requires much more than mere talent, it requires an extraordinary knack for both salesmanship and showmanship.

Another paradox is of more recent vintage—the incredibly rapid advance of technology from the traditional optical/chemical to the electronic. Foreword looking visual communicators today refer to their field as "imaging." Think of that when you're deciding whether to sign up for video and computer courses. Remember it when writing your resume.

> *Work consists of the things you have to do that you dislike doing—everything else is either play or a labor of love.*
> *(Roger E. Greeley, humanitarian)*

To earn a living as a professional imagemaker I see three choices open: (1) seek a salaried staff position, (2) be a self-employed freelancer, or (3) set yourself up in business as an entrepreneur. A fourth option may lie in one of the allied fields related to imaging, or in a profession or trade that employs visual communications technology. Obviously, the prerequisites for success vary greatly depending on which road you decide to travel.

The Corporate Imaging Technician

Industrial firms, government agencies, newspapers, and large photographic studios need to hire competent technicians. These big organizations already know the kinds of work they want done and they will buy the services of skilled craftspeople who will come to work in the morning, do the assigned job promptly and acceptably, and then go home in the evening (although overtime is all too frequent in photo departments).

What about creativity? Yes, definitely. You might eventually get praises—and raises—if you can make images of an automobile, a milling machine, a stylish dress, a bottle of beer, or a group of people so that the composition is subtly balanced and the lighting adds sparkle to the subject. But too often the corporate imagemaker is expected only to carry out the ideas of the "Creative People" in the advertising or public relations department. I remember how disillusioned I felt when I realized that the benevolent midwest Fortune 500 corporation I was working for actually sent out to a New York advertising agency all the jobs that called for imagination and originality. The agency then farmed out the work to a commercial studio and added the agency's sizable commission to the cost. Often it doesn't occur to an executive that creative visual work of all kinds can be produced by people within the organization.

Working for someone else

Perhaps the greatest challenge facing you as an employee will not be how to solve technical and creative problems, but how to sell yourself, to raise your own stature—subtly—in the eyes of your employers. Being active in professional organizations will provide some opportunities for recognition through seminars, awards, publications, and continuing education.

Corporate imaging offers important trade-offs that help to compensate for the frustrations. When you sell your services to a large employer, you do so in exchange for relief from such problems as hustling to find clients, filling out endless small-business paperwork, and considering such anxiety-pro-

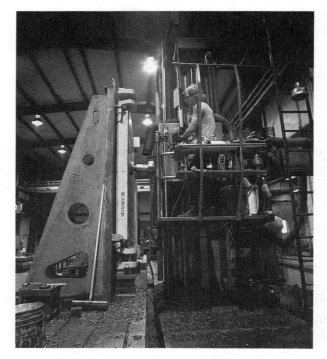

D. Curl *Industrial subjects*
These two photographs are typical of daily assignments facing an industrial photographer. The challenge is to record all the detail wanted by the client, but still to produce an image that is both excellent and interesting.

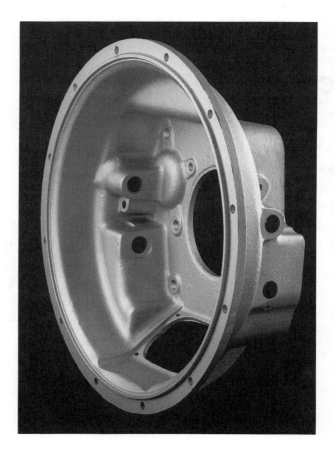

voking issues as hospitalization and disability insurance for yourself and for your dependents. Most big corporations also will relieve you from part of the responsibility of putting aside money for your eventual retirement. That biweekly paycheck and employee benefit package can look pretty good when you consider the alternatives.

Luck is when preparation meets opportunity. (Harvey Frye, educator)

You have to *work* to get a job

Landing a staff job doesn't always require a college degree, but getting—and holding—a job with advancement potential does demand mastery of the fundamental skills of photography, video/electronics, and computer graphics. Graduates of recognized technical schools and colleges and universities with respected degree programs generally have an advantage not only because of the degree, but because they can show a portfolio of good work.

Successful job seekers master certain prerequisites such as how to write up an application and resume. But some employers avoid hiring advanced degree holders to fill technical positions. A master's degree could even be a handicap. Employers often are unwilling to pay the higher salary that an MFA would seem to demand, and a few "School of Hard Knocks" managers have been known to feel intimidated by an applicant's degree. But such academic jealousy seems to be largely a problem of the past.

In many industries and organizations today, the best preparation, grounded on a sound basis of liberal arts, would seem to include photo, video, graphic arts and computer experience plus a bachelor's degree in business administration or communication. "Here's a young person," goes the logic," who can do a good technical job for us now, yet who may be potential management material."

Corporate imaging can be a very interesting way to make a living. Skilled visual communicators contribute significantly to the productivity of the organizations that employ them, but few of my colleagues who are "staff" photographers take pictures for a hobby—most of them prefer to spend weekends sailing or playing golf.

Photojournalism

When [things] go on in my town, I've got to photograph them. There aren't any big events here. The rest of the world really doesn't care...But they're very important...to everybody who lives here.
(Brian Lanker, photojournalist)

Daily and weekly newspapers occasionally hire an ambitious young photographer, but usually the jobs go to the best graduates of journalism schools and the openings are not created by expansion, but by retirement. Many newspaper photographers at first find their jobs fulfilling because they feel involved in community happenings; but it soon becomes quite a challenge to keep coming up with fresh, new ways of handling routine assignments and still meet daily deadlines.

When advertisers shifted much of their money from print to television, different kinds of opportunities were created for photojournalists.

Many magazines that once retained large staffs of adventuresome and imaginative photojournalists now either are defunct, or they buy much of their photography from freelancers who work independently, through agencies or cooperatives, or on contract to the publisher.

Television has changed forever the public's media habits. The *Evening News* and various talk shows and specials have replaced, for most people, the daily newspaper and weekly magazines as major sources of current information and entertainment. When advertisers shifted much of their money from print to television, different kinds of opportunities were created for photojournalists.

The demise or reformatting of many magazines, however, has created more demand for specialized

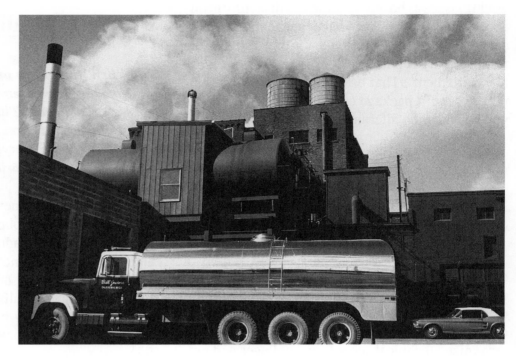

Berta Stauffenberg
Kalamazoo Creamery Co.
Can a commercial subject be "art?" Here, repetition of forms with variation in size, texture and value presents an interesting image of an industrial subject.

publications. There seems to be at least one magazine or newsletter for every hobby, interest, and profession in the world; and most of them use photographs!

Production of documentaries and news for television is almost a totally different field from still photography. Although the "good eye" and human sensitivity of the photojournalist are needed by the filmmaker/videographer, the still photographer making the switch to professional motion pictures or video finds it very difficult to finance and complete a production independently. Because of the enormous costs involved and the tremendous amount of work, producers nearly always need to draw a salary or to have a commercial sponsor. One person rarely completes a production alone—a crew consisting of director, camera operator, and sound, lighting, and editing technicians usually is required. Electronic photography certainly is where much of the action is, but to get to the top one needs specialized training, intensive experience, and often labor union affiliation.

Talent doesn't come in a box. It comes from within us. It can't be bought, but it can be rented. (Joe Farace, photographer)

How to Sell Yourself

There's psychology in applying for a job in imaging, as in any career field. First you have to do a good job of writing yourself up. Your resume, or vita, must provide prospective employers with the basic facts about your personal status and educational background, plus a chronological listing of your previous work experience. Make this section of your vita brief, but emphasize those aspects of previous jobs and internships that relate to the position you seek. For example, if you're applying for work as an imaging technician with an aerospace firm, and you shot video and stills of aircraft activities and tests while you were a photographer in the Navy, say so. Remember that your resume represents you to someone you haven't met. Try to impress the human resources office with your effectiveness and your neatness, if not with the depth of your experience.

The portfolio is important

Your portfolio shows what you have actually accomplished and suggests the kind of work you can be expected to do without additional training. Your pictures and sample videos should look good and so should you. Just as you wouldn't show up for an employment interview wearing tattered jeans and messy hair, you shouldn't expect an employer to be impressed by dog-eared, unmounted, unspotted prints or sloppily edited video clips, no matter how good the content and technique. Don't try to show more than 20 to 30 prints unless you're asked for more, and select examples that show you have an idea of the kind of work the company does. You wouldn't include abstractions, nudes, or fashion illustrations in a portfolio intended to show how well you might handle a nuts-and-bolts industrial job. Your prospective employer probably will be looking for well-corrected view camera illustrations, competently lighted product photos, and perhaps an example of your best "company magazine" picture story feature. A prospective employer wants to hire someone who can produce the kind of images he or she expects.

What employers are looking for

The expectations of advertising and publishing executives can be a bit different. An art director or picture editor will want to see your most imaginative work to determine whether to take the risk of offering you a challenging assignment. The editor or art director sees competent professional work every day. What he or she probably is looking for is not only someone who can do routine assignments in an unusual way, but someone who can be counted on to deliver promptly and according to client specifications. Competition is so keen that ad executives seldom are willing to take a chance that might cost them a client. Editors have pages to fill and deadlines to meet. Your portfolio and your personality have to inspire confidence that you can do what you say.

> *Say what you mean. Mean what you say.*
> *Do what you say you're going to do.*
> (*Morris Massey, motivator*)

The pictures in your portfolio should show exactly what you can do. Begin with several attention-getting images, include a sequence showing your skill and versatility in the prospect's field of interest,

then close with a few more blockbusters. And don't talk too much. Let the pictures speak for themselves. A good mount size is 16 x 20; 11 x 14 is adequate and more portable, but the mounts should all be the same size. Carry your prints in a neat nylon or vinyl case and you will have an attractive presentation that will help you to sell yourself.

The Freelance Business

If you begin to feel restless in the security of corporate employment, you may soon begin to look longingly at the glamorous life of the freelancer who, it would seem, flits care free from client to client like a butterfly, sampling the nectar from only the choicest opportunities. Don't you believe it! Freelancing can be a killing grind. It is a fierce competition in which only the very fittest survive.

Nevertheless, the flame of freelancing attracts, like moths, thousands of aspiring young photographers every year. As a successful freelancer you can be an artist, but you also have to be a canny business person. Many among the self-employed choose to work through a "rep" (agent), who can relieve them from making sales calls and free them from some routine business matters in exchange for a percentage of each assignment contract.

Freelancing, demanding and uncertain, is nevertheless a good way to make some pocket money, especially if you're good at a speciality and if you research your specialized market carefully. Nearly every young professional starts out by freelancing or moonlighting (moonlighting is part-time freelancing). There will be more on how to break into the business a little later in this chapter. Meanwhile let's look at some other career possibilities.

Opening Your Own Studio

There's always money to be made from portrait, wedding, and general commercial photography. Although the field is somewhat crowded, there seems to be room in almost every community for a *quality* studio. Usually there is an untapped market for photographic sales that cries for an enterprising person to develop the market by advertising and to maintain sales by offering excellent service at a fair price.

To be successful at establishing and operating a studio you must have an insatiable drive for achievement. You and your spouse or partner should expect to work 16-hour days routinely, at least for the first few years, to earn a modest financial return. You have to enjoy running the business fully as much as you enjoy photography, perhaps more.

Because human contact is such an important aspect of operating a studio, it's essential to develop a friendly, open, somewhat extroverted attitude. Contacts made through service clubs and community activities will pay off for you at the cash register just as they do for other business people. Like the florist, the real estate broker, and the neighborhood merchant, the successful photo studio owner becomes an integral part of the community as he or she goes about earning a living.

> *One of the best things about being on my own is that when a client calls, I know that they're calling for ME. I try to treat each client like they're the only one I have. The bottom line is...*
> *If they're happy, they'll come back.*
>
> *(Bill First, photographer)*

Other Career Opportunities

Many careers related to photography are open to men and women who are interested in the field in some capacity other than as a practicing photographer. Video is an attractive field of its own, and the graphic arts encompass the wide world of printing, color separation, and computer imaging. Scientific and biomedical imaging includes photomicrography, photogrammetry, spectroscopy, metallography, ballistics, and many other finely differentiated specialities in industry, medicine, and law enforcement.

Photographic and electronic manufacturing and retailing is a multibillion-dollar industry in itself, employing scientists, engineers, managers, techni-

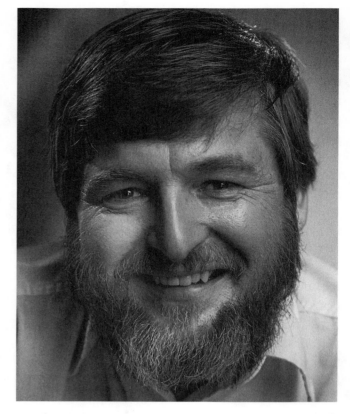

D. Curl *Werner*
Portraiture is perennially profitable. Many owners of small studios have begun a growing business by doing model and performer portfolios for friends and acquaintences.

cians and salespeople, most of whom require considerable knowledge of at least certain aspects of photography. Although much of the imaging equipment sold in the United States and Canada is imported, the distributors of equipment and manufacturers and distributors of materials and supplies employ experienced photographers as technical representatives and salespeople.

Photofinishing, video postproduction, and computer imaging provide options for those with technical skills and management ability. Custom laboratories and service bureaus provide high-quality support services for professionals, while huge automated finishing plants and shopping mall mini-labs process and print the billions of images exposed each year by weekend snapshooters.

> *Photography is a magic thing.*
> *Nothing will ever be as much fun!*
>
> *(Jacques-Henri Lartigue, photographer)*

How important is a degree?

A two-year degree from a community college or technical institute often is the entry-level qualification for many jobs in the career fields mentioned here or for a position as a corporate imagemaker or assistant or a studio intern/assistant. A bachelor's degree is required by some employers, and is often a prerequisite for advancement to a management role or, if photography is combined with science or engineering, to a specialized technical or supervisory position.

> *After graduating from college, I got my education from two years working in a studio.* (David Kamm, photographer)

The MFA (Master of Fine Arts) is considered by most colleges and universities as a terminal degree for the individual who will teach in a department of art, with the Ph.D. being a credential for the academic administrator, researcher, or art historian. Teachers in secondary and elementary schools require a bachelor's degree plus a teaching certificate. For permanent certification, most states require teachers to obtain further credits in education, leading eventually to a master's degree.

Full-time teaching openings in photography are rare, there being many more aspiring teachers than vacant positions. Part-time teaching, however, is pleasant and relaxing for some working imagemakers; more of these opportunities are becoming available as public interest increases in photography, video and computers as leisure-time activities. For teaching evening or weekend courses, community colleges, art centers, and adult education programs often employ experienced professionals who have demonstrated a talent for teaching.

How to Begin

Back, as promised, to freelancing. Many successful professionals started out this way, often gaining experience and making pocket-money-plus while in high school or college. Here's advice on how to begin:

1. *Specialize!* Become especially skillful at photographing certain types of subject matter that you particularly enjoy and know something about. One of my former students is a model airplane buff; he submits regular how-to-do-it illustrated articles to the model-building magazines. He has become so well known in this field that editors send him assignments and he has sold a number of color covers.

What is your hobby: horses, dogs or cats, wildlife, hunting and fishing, gardening, weaving, woodworking, custom cars, antique aircraft, spelunking, stamp collecting? You name it—there are special interest publications, organizations, and individuals who will buy photographs. One girl was taking pictures of some of the animals she admired at a pet show. Some of the animals' owners asked her for prints and now she has become official photographer for all of the cat and dog shows in her corner of the state—and she has all the reprint business she can handle.

Another former student follows his passion to all of the regional motor speedways and auto shows. He makes good money every summer and sells stock photos during the off-season. But the work wouldn't continue coming along if each of these individuals wasn't interested enough to keep going after it. That brings us to point number two:

2. *Hustle!* Another student enjoys architectural photography. While he was in high school he made a series of construction progress pictures of a public building being erected in his home town. Putting 8x10s of those photos neatly into a ring binder, this enterprising young photographer went to see the contractor on the job. The contractor, very impressed, bought the book on the spot and commissioned the young man to shoot aerial and ground progress pictures at regular intervals of every subsequent project that his firm did in the area. Out of this contact grew sales to subcontractors, architects and occupants of the buildings. But the photographer had to go around to contact and sell to these people. They would never have come to him.

If you study collections of old photographs made in the 1880s and 1890s, you find that itinerant photographers traveled about photographing families posing out in front of their houses or farm buildings. Many of these century-old photos not only are historically valuable, they are technically

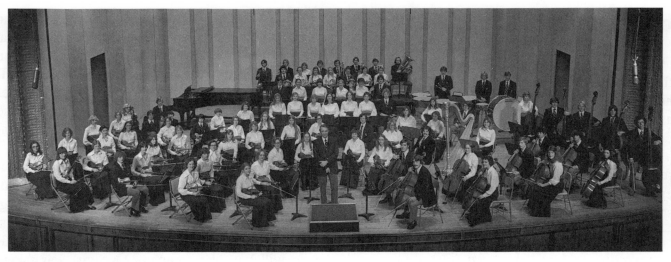

Brian Kuehn *Orchestra*
Rather ordinary group photographs and athletic team pictures can be a ready source of income for anyone with a medium- or large-format camera, some patience, and lots of hustle. Every face must be recognizable so everyone (or their parents) will want to buy a print. A wide-angle lens is very useful, along with one or two large flash units to supplement uneven existing light.

excellent—sharply focused, well exposed, and obviously made with a properly adjusted view camera. But George Eastman's snapshot Kodak killed much of this business, convincing most people that they could take their own snapshots of their homes and families. Today, people still will buy photographs of themselves and their property, but not many will call up a photographer and order the work done. Maybe you don't feel comfortable doing door-to-door sales, but one neighbor does tell another, and if you can wangle a few jobs—even for free or for barter—other people will want photographs made if you're on the scene at the right time.

"Kidnapping" is another way to collect some cash (this term means *photographing* children, of course, not abducting them). In formal child and baby photography, you're competing with the established studios as well as with cut-rate shopping mall operators. It doesn't occur to many parents, however, to have their kids photographed around the home, or in a park, in natural childhood settings and typical activities. Even if the parents own an expensive camera, chances are their snapshots of the kids are stilted, too far away, and poorly exposed.

Another of my former students, who now makes his living as an elementary school teacher, started out making informal portraits of the kids in his classes. When parents saw the photos, they loved them. Parents told other parents. Now this teacher enjoys a lucrative home portrait business that keeps him busy every summer and on weekends and adds a nice supplement to his salary.

Other photo and video opportunities in every community include kids' athletic teams, adult sports leagues and corporate olympics groups, scouts, 4H, and local pageants and festivals of all kinds.

The quality freelancer cuts into the established professional's business less than you might imagine. The smart freelancer will use imagination and hustle to profit from a largely untapped segment of the community's portrait and commercial photo market. Most studio operators depend on the formal and conventional walk-in and telephone trade, so they often make little effort to go out to the public. The part of the potential market that the pros overlook is *your* fair share! Then, after you gain enough experience, you, too, can become part of the established profession—if you choose.

3. *Be professional!* You *become* a professional as soon as you begin earning a substantial amount of your income from photography. If you're operating as a professional, the public will expect you to be dependable, to produce quality work, and to price your work fairly and competitively. If photography is a moonlighting business for you, don't try to take work away from established studios, but try to mine the gold that they may be overlooking. Above all, don't compete unfairly on price. If your work is as good as the studio operator's, your price should be very nearly competitive.

The established pro has overhead expenses that you don't have, so you can charge less—right? Wrong! People often tend to value services according to what they have to pay. Not only does a competitive price make your work appear to be of higher quality, but if your costs actually are less than the studio's you can pocket the profit without feeling that you're taking away someone else's livelihood by undercutting prices.

Weddings are a case in point. With so many automated color processing and printing laboratories providing a complete wedding package at a very low price, the wedding photographer can spend all of his or her time shooting and selling, and no time at all in the darkroom. If you're a moonlighter and you like to shoot weddings, leave the upscale formal bridal portraits to those who do the job best and concentrate on providing a uniquely personal type of candid wedding coverage tailored to the desires (and the financial resources) of the bride and groom and their parents. Through friends and satisfied customers you could create a demand for quality custom wedding coverage, including video, that might actually increase business for some of the better studios, as well as give you a comfortable extra income.

But weddings are very important occasions, so you have to deliver like a professional or your budding business will evaporate overnight! Plan ahead with the bridal couple, be punctual and polite, be neat and courteous, yet boldly competent; and whatever happens, don't goof up technically. These rules apply not only to weddings, but to any assignment. The professional is competent and confident, dresses like a business person, and behaves maturely.

4. *Keep trying!* If you're determined to make money at photography, you've got to keep at it until you develop a reputation for quality and dependability. It may take a while before the work begins to come to you, instead of your having to go out after it all the time. This is especially true of sales to publications, as all freelance writers know. In publications work you'll be dealing with many of the same markets as writers, and you can expect to collect rejection slips and polite letters at about the same rate. There are excellent references available at your public or college library that can give you up-to-date information about publishers and agencies and how they should be approached.

If you sell directly to publications or to commercial and advertising markets, it's very important to price your work fairly and competitively because you're competing directly against full-time professionals. Find out what the going rates are. Many publications specify the rates they will pay; this and other valuable information can be found in some of the guides, such as *Writer's Market* and *Photographer's Market*. Assignment work should be priced at current rates, as listed in the *ASMP Guide to Business Practice* and other references available through the Professional Photographers of America, Inc., and state and local professional photographers' associations. You should consider joining one or more of these organizations. The membership benefits usually far outweigh the cost. One of the major benefits is continuing education.

> *If you're determined to make money at photography, you've got to keep at it until you develop a reputation for quality and dependability.*

5. *Keep learning!* Most of the best professional imagemakers are happy to share their secrets with young people entering the field, because they have not forgotten that they learned from others much of what they know. Every year there are hundreds of workshops in all aspects of professional imaging and fine art photography that are attended by working pros from all specialties. Many of these programs occur in pleasant resort areas so participants can simultaneously relax and recharge. Professional organizations, manufacturers, and vendors often sponsor clinics and short courses in hotels and on college campuses. The industry's most comprehensive schedule of intensive, hands-on courses is offered year-round in the Chicago suburb of Mt. Prospect, Illinois by the Winona School of Professional Photography.

For a Winona catalog call **1-800-742-7468**.

Selling Stock Photos Through an Agent

Editors looking for specific kinds of pictures often make their first call to an image library. These research and sales agencies are referred to in the trade as stock houses. When you first start out as a freelancer you should try to sell some pictures directly to publishers, especially if you have a strong specialty. You might be lucky with sales, and if you can establish a name for yourself, your chances of having work accepted by a stock house are greater than if you've never had anything published. Agencies work on a 40 to 50 percent commission, but an active agent will show your pictures to markets that you might never have imagined, nor had the time to approach. Barbara Van Cleve, formerly an agent specializing in travel and textbook markets, offered my students some pretty sound advice:

"Young photographers," she said, "usually have an inflated sense of their ability and a naive knowledge of the market, which makes them very impatient should sales not be forthcoming immediately. They need to know that their work is competing with the work of famous professionals who market on their own to all kinds of clients, with whom we also deal. To be really involved in this business they ought to be sending us at least 50 new slides per month, until they build up a file of around 1,000 shots with us. These should cover a wide range of subjects in order to be most saleable."

The advice offered by Ms. Van Cleve to aspiring young photographers is to "look at a lot of pictures as they appear in ads, textbooks, and magazines, make assignments to themselves to shoot these assignments, do a lot of highly selective shooting, edit their work carefully, send it to us...and be patient. All sales through an agent should be considered 'gravy' or 'icing on the cake,'" she said. "No one can live on stock sales alone, and no professional does. Some work from very good photographers will sit in our files for a year before we can market it, because textbook publishers follow cycles in their revisions.

"If young photographers want to bypass a service such as ours," suggests Ms. Van Cleve, "they can use the *Writer's Market* or *Photographer's Market* as a guide and send out letters of inquiry accompanied by some sort of inexpensively printed brochure as a sample of their work. When a buyer contacts them they can send out their slides for review and take their chances. But they will soon learn the economics of postage!" When you send out work to a publication you're trying to get the attention of an appropriate editor.

Dealing With Editors

Every day major publications receive so many unsolicited manuscripts, photos and story ideas that sometimes the best they can do is to return them unopened. Editors like to receive material they can use, but they don't have time to handle photos and articles that are wildly inappropriate or of unsatisfactory quality. If you want to hit a particular market, first study recent issues of the publication you aim for, then query the editor briefly by letter, enclosing a few representative samples of your work. Always enclose a self-addressed stamped envelope (SASE) with enough postage for return of anything you want to get back. Editors expect a SASE and most won't return your material unless you enclose one.

Publications pay for accepted work either upon receipt (desirable but uncommon) or upon publication. When you do sell photographs or an article, be sure there's written agreement whether the editor is buying full, exclusive rights to your material, or only reproduction rights for one-time publication. Naturally, you're entitled to much more money when exclusive rights are involved. Rates vary widely for single photographs, from a pitiful low of only a few dollars for a single black-and-white print, $100 or more for a color cover, up to more than $2,000 for an illustrated article bought by a major magazine.

Some editors, if they like an article idea that you've queried them about, will give you some suggestions for making it more saleable and then "assign" you to do the story. Unless you're a well-known pro, however, this kind of assignment is still

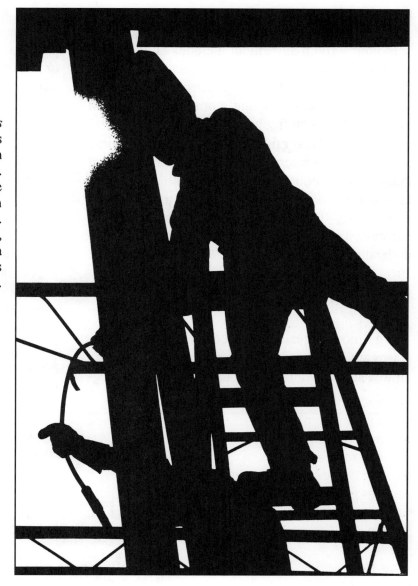

Raimonds Ziemelis *Welders*
Try to visualize subject matter in its most abstract or graphic form, even when working on a routine assignment. The high-contrast drop-out technique simplified this construction photograph to forms in positive and negative space. If you can produce enough dramatic, generic images, they can produce extra income for you as stock photos placed with an agency.

on speculation—the editor is not obligated to publish your material or to pay you for it if the results don't measure up to expectations. But on the other hand, the editor is ethically bound not to "steal" your idea and assign it to another photographer or writer until you've had a good crack at it. You're bound ethically, too, not to submit the same story or photographs to competing publications at the same time. You could, for instance, submit similar fishing photos to an outdoor magazine and to a calendar publisher, but not to another hunting and fishing magazine until your material has been rejected by the editor of the first magazine. Simultaneous submission of queries is OK, though, because it often takes so long to receive replies.

Some picture editors, especially those who pub-

lish industrial stockholder and employee magazines and annual reports, may be willing to contract for your services by the day, rather than by the picture or by the story. Day rates are individually negotiable, of course, but rates reported by the ASMP (see the Selected References) for small publications begin at a *minimum* of $350 per day plus expenses. The photographer usually retains rights to the photographs, selling one-time reproduction rights unless it is agreed in advance that all negatives and transparencies made while on that assignment belong to the client. In such cases, referred to as "work for hire," you should negotiate a job rate that includes a specified number of prints or transparencies as well as a definite fee.

Advertising photos usually bring higher prices

than those used editorially. Find out what other photographers are charging for similar work, and be sure your written agreement includes all the terms and prices, so that your invoice comes as no surprise. Being specific also protects you from the shock of being told: "Sorry, but that's not what we had in mind." Successful freelancer Fred Tonne suggests avoiding the "Never time to do it right; always time to do it over" problem by being certain at the outset that everyone concerned with a photo assignment knows what to expect from the other parties. "Get it in writing," Tonne advises, "unless you've worked before with the same client and you're sure you understand each other."

Model Releases

The model release is a necessary bother. Releases are such a nuisance to get signed that they're almost never obtained for routine editorial photography. Legally, a photographer or publisher is in little danger of a lawsuit, unless the subject of the photo is being held up for ridicule by miscaptioning or a clear invasion of privacy is evident. You wouldn't, for example, publish a telephoto picture of someone sunbathing by their backyard pool, but almost anything occurring in a public place is fair game if the facts and circumstances are not misrepresented. It's almost impossible to get a release for travel pictures, and one is seldom expected for editorial use.

Advertising use of pictures of recognizable people is another story. Most clients won't even consider buying a picture for use in an ad unless you can provide a signed release from any person appearing in the picture and from the owner of private property such as a home or business. Exhibition of a photograph in a gallery or display, however, is not usually held to be advertising, unless a product is being promoted. You're usually quite safe if you exhibit nonderogatory photos of people in a public park, at

---

Release No. _____

Date _____

Subject _____

Consideration _____

Check No. _____

Photographs taken on this

release _____

_____

_____

PERMISSION TO USE PHOTOGRAPH

Release No. _____

Date _____

I am (am not) of legal age. For good and valuable consideration, the receipt of which is hereby acknowledged, I hereby authorize _____

to take photographs of me and/or my property and authorize him and his assigns and transferees to use and publish the same (including use and publication with my name, no name, or a fictitious name, use in the form taken or with intentional or unintentional alterations, and use for the purpose of publicity, illustration, commercial art, and in the advertising of any product or services).

Signed _____

Address _____

Witness _____

_____
Parent or guardian (if not legal age)

Assignment: Date _____

For value received I assign full rights in this release to _____

_____ for purposes covered in Order No. _____

or as follows _____

_____
Photographer

Model release forms, although a nuisance, are good business if you plan to use your photographs for purposes other than non-commercial exhibition or editorial publication. (Form courtesy of Professional Photographers of America, Inc.)

a school, gallery, art fair, or camera club. If prints are sold, however, and the subject finds out about it, you might be expected to share the proceeds with your subject or remove the prints from display. But if prints are going to be exhibited to promote the sale of a certain brand of film or camera, for example, you should always obtain a release.

If you're on assignment for an advertiser, or if you're planning to sell stock pictures later, you'd be wise to get a signed release from anyone portrayed prominently in the pictures. Always get a routine release from anyone modeling for you, especially nudes. Without releases, picture agents' hands are tied. Many clients simply won't buy pictures without releases. Professional models who are being paid for posing expect to sign a release form as a matter of course. A few free prints often are compensation enough for most amateur models.

Copyright

Placing a copyright notice on each of your photographs announces that you intend to challenge unauthorized publication of your work, but few photographers actually file the forms. Many freelancers routinely stamp on the back of each print or the face of each slide mount a statement in this form: "© 1992 John Lensman," thus giving notice of intent to copyright and securing what is, in effect, a common-law copyright that takes effect when the work is "published." According to the law, however, public exhibition of your photographs or showing them to editors without the copyright notice does not relinquish any rights you have to your work. Current law defines "publication" as actual *sale* to the public.

You may not actually be able to recover damages from an infringer, however, unless you have followed the registration and deposit requirements which include filling out Form VA, paying a $10 fee, and depositing two copies of the work Several photographs made in the same year and "published" together can be copyrighted as a group on the same form for a single fee. Pages of duplicate slides or contact sheets will meet the requirement.

For details and forms, write to: Copyright Office, Library of Congress, Washington, DC 20559 or phone (202) 707-9100.

Starting a Filing System

If you continue as a photographer, soon you'll be overwhelmed with negatives, contact sheets, prints and slides. Unless you begin *now* with a simple filing system, you won't be able to find things when you need them. Everyone has their own way of coding and cross-referencing, but here's what I do:

1. Place all negatives in clear polypropylene or polyethylene archival filing pages. Label each page with the date and subject.

2. Punch contact sheets for a 3-ring binder.

3. File each contact sheet chronologically, next to the appropriate negatives, in a 3-ring binder.

4. Store slides also in archival pages. Label by date and subject.

5. Keep slide pages by date either in a 3-ring binder or in a hanging file.

6. Maintain a simple card or computer file by subject matter and/or by client. Whenever you add something to an existing category, put on the card the date (everything is filed by date). If several subjects are on the same roll and filed together, just add frame numbers or slide numbers. If several rolls are shot on the same day, number them consecutively. For example: Flowers, daffodils: 4-15-91 (3) 1-10; Birds, robins: 4-15-91 (3) 11-24. If you add a new category, start another card.

7. Slip finished, mounted prints into individual polyethylene archival bags and store them in acid-free boxes. Label the boxes by subject and/or by date.

8. Keep all photo files in the driest place available, away from bright light and heat.

9. I keep some irreplaceable negatives and transparencies in my basement food freezer. Not only does freezing retard deterioration of the dyes in color films, but firemen have told me that they've seen the contents of the freezer intact after a house has burned to the ground. Zip-lock bags can be used, or special heat-sealed negative storage bags.

A final word of advice: don't allow unfiled work to accumulate or it can become a useless mess.

Anything worth doing
is worth doing now!

(D. Curl, photographer)

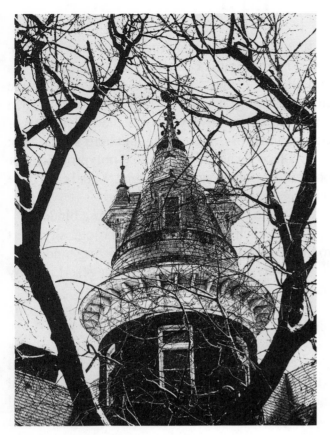

Larry Daly *Henderson Castle*
A good filing system will help you retrieve saleable negatives like this unusual view of an architectural landmark.

The Picture Story

> *One picture is worth a thousand words.*
> *(Confucius, ancient philosopher)*

> *If a single picture is worth a thousand words, imagine the possibilities of two, three, or more photographs working together to convey more complex layers of meaning.* *(Judy Dater, photographer)*

During the 1940s and '50s *Life* and *Look* and other popular weekly magazines perfected the still photo and text sequences that we call picture stories or photo essays to a high form of communicative art. Then television took the public's attention, along with special-interest publications. But those great word/picture formats are not dead; a few magazines continue the tradition and photographic books offer the imaginative photographer opportunities to communicate personal ideas while commenting on society.

> *A sequence of several images can be thought of as a single statement.*
> *(Minor White, photographer)*

Fine art photographers including Minor White have long realized that the emotional impact of a series of related images viewed together can be greater than if each image is considered alone. Another storytelling method is to create a chronology in which actions occur. Perhaps the best known contemporary exponent of this approach is Duane Michals, whose hand captioned, comic-strip-like sequences are full of whimsy, mystery, and surprise endings.

> *I...prefer those photographs that had no life until the photographer's imagination called them into being...Photographs should ask questions, suggest dramas, reveal, rather than merely describe.*
> *(Duane Michals, photographer)*

Journalistic picture stories usually follow some form of chronology or other continuity, employing words as captions or supplementary text, either to provide background for the pictures or to explain their meaning. Strong photographs, ideally, require a minimum of words to explain them, if any at all; the words and pictures should complement one another. The photo essay, a highly refined form of picture story, deals, in the literary sense, with a selected topic from an interpretive, highly personal point of view.

> *After all, isn't that what life is all about, the ability to go around back and come up inside other people's heads...and say: oh, so that's how you see it!?*
> *(Ray Bradbury, author)*

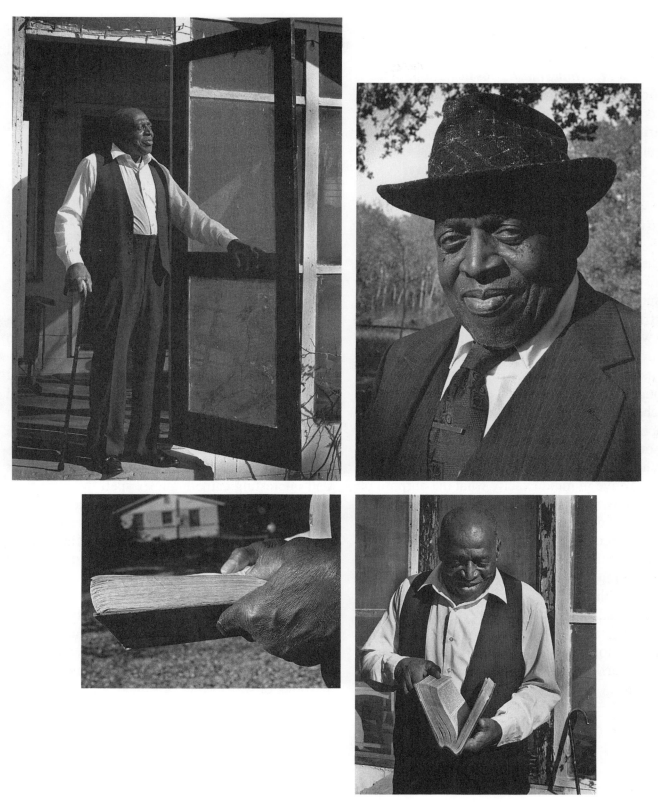

Reverend Gadsen   *Diane Osborne*
A serial portrait has been created with this photo essay.
Multiple images often can reveal much more than could be
glimpsed from a single photograph that records only
one moment in time.

There's a strong temptation to overshoot on a picture story assignment. Beginners often take pictures of everything that moves in the hope of later discovering great image sequences on the contact sheets. This "shotgun" approach can work if you're covering a fast-breaking news or sporting event, but it's much better to plan ahead of time the kinds of shots you think you'll need to tell the story.

Journalism is the first rough draft of history. (David Broder, historian)

The script for a picture story or photo essay may consist merely of an outline that lists each aspect of the subject to be covered. A simple checklist often is sufficient when you do your own planning.

If you prepare a detailed shooting script, each picture idea should be described in enough detail that its part in the sequence is clear and any special techniques, equipment, props, etc. are noted. Simple sketches will help you to previsualize the format and composition you'll be looking for during shooting sessions.

Whether or not you prepare a detailed script, you ought to have in mind exactly what the purpose of your story is, who the intended audience will be, and just what kind of reaction you expect from them: Do you want people to become amused, enlightened, saddened, angered, aroused? Do you want them to *buy* something or to *do* something? Or would it be sufficient if those who view your efforts shared your very personal feelings of concern, elation, appreciation, or nostalgia? If, as a communicator, your purpose is not clearly in mind, how can you expect your viewers/readers to respond to the message as you intend?

Every story should have a beginning, middle and end—but not necessarily in that order.

(Jean-Luc Godard, filmmaker)

But don't be a slave to the script. If what you thought you would find, or what you thought would happen, doesn't turn out as expected, be flexible. Even while shooting, if you feel the need for a different approach, or if you encounter interesting aspects of the subject that you hadn't anticipated, don't hesitate to change. If you've thought out all aspects of the story, you can always change the script as you see fit. Without enough advance planning, however, you may discover, too late, that you have to go back and reshoot some key parts that you missed. Reshooting is seldom convenient and not always possible.

Story ideas

One of the simplest types of picture story is the how-to-do-it series. These sequences are simple to produce because the continuity is already determined by the actual steps in the process. All you have to do is to write down the order of events and decide how each step can best be presented. An example of a how-to-do-it might be a story on the manufacture of a hand-tooled leather belt or the erection of a log cabin home. Imaginative treatment and interesting camera angles spell the difference between a mundane record of a process and an interesting and motivating experience for the viewer/reader. You can see what kinds of stories are selling, by studying current issues of magazines that interest you.

"A day in the life of..." has become a common picture story theme. You've probably seen the cooperatively-produced photo books with variations on this title. Another approach is "What it's like to be a..." in which you present an occupation, pastime, or way of life.

Another popular theme is to photograph similar subject matter, but in different locations. For example, a story on how people have restored historic houses may be told effectively by photographs made in several different towns. Or you might do an essay in depth on a singularly interesting and inviting old home in your community and about the people who are restoring it. A deeply personal essay on *being alone*, or *daybreak*, or *flight* or *the sea* could contain several related visual poems interwoven with free verse or prose. Such essays can be enormously rewarding, both for the sake of doing them and for the possibility of publication.

How extraordinary the commonplace world can be. (Robert Adams, photographer)

We see things not as they are, but as we are. (High Museum of Art, Atlanta)

The starting point for any picture story or photo essay is the idea. Ideas may come easily to you if you've become an expert in a specialized field; or you may need to do quite a bit of research. After the initial story idea, you need to learn as much about the subject as possible, taking notes for later copy and caption writing. You should ask—and answer—the journalist's traditional questions: Who? What?

Art is a means of communicating with people; not an aim in itself.

(Modest Musorgski, composer)

Why? When? Where? and How? You'll need to get to know the people involved and to become accepted by them. Virtually everyone will be friendly and cooperative if they believe you care about them and that you're genuinely interested in what interests them. Get to know your subjects: observe how they talk and act. Listen to what they say and pay attention to their advice.

I think photographers sometimes forget how difficult is is to stand on the other side of the camera. We forget how intrusive a camera can be.
(Lynn Johnson, photojournalist)

I try to be sensitive to people, to treat them with kindness and dignity.
(Robert Maxwell, photojournalist)

I do not believe in photography just to invade people's lives. I go into people's lives constantly, but only to make their motives, their ideas, understood.
(Cornell Capa, photojournalist)

I find no photographs superior to the decency of a man's feelings and his right to those feelings. When there is such a conflict, I...put the camera down and take no pictures.
(W. Eugene Smith, photojournalist)

An experienced photojournalist, comfortable in a situation, can imagine what an image is going to look like as a finished photograph. You can train yourself to do this and to sense the exact instant when subject arrangement and action feel "right." Henri Cartier-Bresson calls this *the decisive moment.* Preplanning can help you to recognize these important instants when they occur. Self-confidence and a good relationship with your subjects can help you set up significant situations in an unobtrusive "posed-unposed" manner. Unless you plan ahead, it's easy to lose purpose and direction and end up merely with a hodgepodge of routine pictures. Successful stories have unity and continuity.

Every picture story needs a strong "lead" picture to engage the viewer's curiosity and interest and give incentive to examine the rest of the story. Most stories, even photo essays that do not have rigid continuity, require a beginning, a climax, and a conclusion. The lead picture often is an overview or an introduction, or it may be the one most dramatic photograph, which sets the mood, introduces the main character, or establishes the environment. The lead is the picture that the editor often will run largest in the layout to catch the attention of the reader.

As you study effective published picture-story page layouts, notice that seldom are the pictures the same size and shape, nor are they usually arranged in static rows. Editors and art directors want to avoid monotony in their layouts, so you'll be wise to include verticals as well as horizontals and shoot plenty of close-ups, as well as medium and long shots. Don't forget that magazine covers and book jackets usually are vertical in format. If you want to crack the lucrative cover market, your compositions have to be oriented correctly and there must be enough space allowed for the name of the magazine or title of the book, as well as other copy.

Picture captions should be complete, containing all names (spelled correctly), plus all the other important data (who, what, why, when, where, and how). Captions should be neatly typewritten or laser printed and attached to the prints in such a way that they can be read while the editor is looking at the print. This is done by fastening the caption to the bottom of the reverse side with nonbleeding "magic mending" or library tape and then folding the paper up over the face of the print to save space in handling and mailing. Slides should be submitted in file pages and keyed by number to captions on a separate sheet.

Conclusion

It doesn't occur to [clients] that photography is work. (Andrea Krause, photographer)

Here in this final chapter you've read a few suggestions about how to turn your interest in photography into income. Broader than photography, the field of imaging, even more than most professions, requires energy, talent and persistence because of the very popularity of the medium. People who never would consider trying to be their own doctor, lawyer, accountant, plumber or farmer will believe that they can be their own photographer—until in a gentle way you educate them to see how your pictures are better then theirs. And millions of people consider themselves "experts" with a camcorder or a computer. That's one of the problems faced by imagemakers everywhere. And sadly, not all clients will appreciate the quality difference. But if you're good at what you do, you can find a market for your work. Being successful means doing your best at all times. You *will* succeed if you

believe in your ability to learn and to produce. Most of all, happiness can be the reward of a life spent seeking vision and humanity.

As you learn and grow as a human being, that becomes what you bring to your art.
(Victoria Littna, painter)

*It is not half so important to **know** as to **feel**.* (Rachel Carson, author-naturalist)

You can tell that you're doing the right kind of work, if: (1) you keep on doing it; (2) you love the details; (3) the process is even more important to you than the finished product.

(Lisa Palchick, painter)

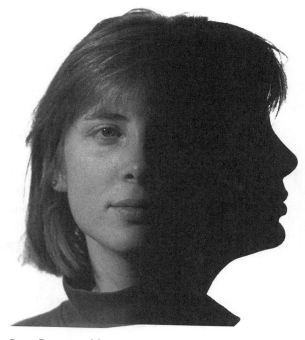

Jorg Jasper *Mary*
This provocative multiple portrait was created by exposing both negatives the same size and with a white background. The two images registered perfectly and print as a negative sandwich.

Self-Assignments

1. Feelings About Photographs

Choose several photographs that communicate something to you. Discuss them with friends and classmates. Observe what each picture *shows* you, then consider how it makes you *feel*. Try to imagine the thoughts and feelings of the photographer at the moment of exposure. Do you think that your reactions to viewing each image are similar to those experienced by the photographer who actually was there? Identify any techniques that you think the photographers might have used, either deliberately or subconsciously, to influence the reactions of those who would later see the pictures.

2. Emulation

Study the work of several photographers whose work you admire. Make at least one photograph of typical subject matter as you imagine it might have been done by each of these admired artists or photojournalists. Try, for example, an "Edward Weston" vegetable or tree root; an "Ansel Adams" landscape; an "Aaron Siskind" wall; an "Arnold Newman" portrait; a "Bruce Davidson" portrait; a "Mary Ellen Mark" portrait; and a "Cartier-Bresson" street photograph. Note: This work should be *emulation,* not imitation. Don't simply copy something that you've seen published, but try to react to the subject matter as you imagine that particular photographer would have reacted. Try to identify yourself with your chosen photographer, interpreting the subject matter, as well as you can, through his or her "eyes."

3. Types of Cameras

Arrange with your instructor, your friends, or a cooperative professional photographer or photo dealer to examine several different types of cameras. Examine, if possible, each of the following: 35mm single-lens reflex, 35mm rangefinder, 6cm single-lens reflex, 6cm twin-lens reflex, 4x5 or larger view camera.

With help from someone familiar with each camera, practice handling them and adjusting the controls. Pretend to take pictures. Sight through the viewfinder, focus, operate the shutter at various speeds. Learn how to load each camera with film.

Find out the following information about each of the cameras you have available: (1) name of camera, (2) size of negative, (3) types of film used, (4) focal length of standard lens, (5) other lenses available, (6) largest f/stop, (7) smallest f/stop, (8) fastest shutter speed, (9) slowest shutter speed, (10) provision for Bulb and Time exposures, (11) how flash is attached and synchronized, (12) how the camera is focused, (13) does it have a self-timer (delayed release), (14) provision for preventing accidental double exposures, (15) provision for intentional double exposures, (16) the kind of photography for which the camera is best suited, (17) any special precautions that must be exercised when using the camera, and (18) its greatest limitations.

4. Photograms

Exposing with light from an enlarger or overhead lamp, arrange opaque or translucent objects on a sheet of photographic paper to create an interesting design without the use of a camera. Experiment with many variations of pattern and illusion. Try combining hand-drawn or photographic images with the shadows of real objects.

5. The Lens

This project has two parts:

(A) Using lenses of different focal lengths, make a series of photographs comparing image size and perspective rendering of similar subjects photographed at the same distance from the camera.

(B) With different lenses, fill the frame by varying the distance between camera and subject. Use both a wide angle and a telephoto. For example, if you are using a 35mm camera, you should try using, in addition to the normal 50mm or 55mm lens, a 28mm or 35mm wide angle and a 105mm to 135mm lens, or longer. If you have access to a zoom lens, try it out over its entire range.

6. The Aperture

This project has two parts:

(A) *Using slow film or in weak light,* photograph a subject such as a person, small sculpture, flower, etc. using selective focus. Set your lens at its widest aperture (about f/2 with most 35mm cameras) and adjust the shutter speed for correct exposure. Focus carefully on the main subject, allowing the background to remain completely out of focus.

(B) Mount the camera on a tripod and set it on manual mode. Make a series of photographs with your normal lens, comparing depth of field and overall sharpness at apertures (f/stops) ranging from the widest (about f/2) to the smallest (about f/16). Include an object approximately two feet (0.5 m) from the camera, something else at three or four feet (1 m), then five to six feet (2 m), 10 to 12 feet (3 m), 20 to 30 feet (7 m), and farther (infinity). Focus at about five feet (1.5 m), then notice what happens to the sharpness of objects at other distances.

Do this experiment with slow film such as Kodak Ektar 25 color negative, *or in relatively weak light,* because your exposure settings should be something like this: 1/1000 at f/2, 1/500 at f/2.8, 1/250 at f/4, 1/125 at f/5.6, 1/60 at f/8, 1/30 at f/11, and 1/15 at f/16. In bright sunlight with 100-speed film, these settings will give three stops (eight times) overexposure unless you use a filter such as red (#25) that will absorb the extra light.

7. The Shutter

This project has four parts:

(A) Using 400-speed film, try some shots of fast action using the fastest shutter speeds on your camera. (1/1,000 etc.) As you change from one speed to another, be sure to compensate for exposure by adjusting the lens opening.

(B) Load your camera with *slow film,* place it firmly on a tripod, and make a series of exposures from 1 second to 1/15 second of a subject moving past the camera. (Be sure to adjust the lens opening each time you change the shutter speed).

(C) Try a series with the same shutter speeds, only hand-hold the camera and use the panning technique: Follow the action with the camera, releasing the shutter while the camera is moving, and keep it moving until the shutter closes. (The image will disappear while the mirror is up, but keep following the action anyway).

(D) At night, put your camera on the tripod again, set the aperture at f/16 and the shutter at "B". Find a place where moving lights create a pattern in time (traffic at an intersection, carnival rides, fireworks) and make some exposures lasting several seconds. Try to fill the frame with a design traced by the lights. Also focus on bright neon signs or other patterns of light and then create interesting streaks and shapes by moving the camera.

8. Contrast Filters

Photograph subjects that contrast strongly in color hue with the background. Choose filters that will exaggerate or diminish the separation of each subject from its background: a red apple against green leaves, or a light colored stone or concrete building against blue sky. Another possibility is to eliminate contrast between colors, such as in copying a stained document or old photograph, using a filter to remove or lessen the effect of a stain. Calculate exposure using the filter factor. Compare these settings with the reading you get through the lens with the filter attached. If they differ, expose both ways and keep a record so you'll know what to do next time.

9. Flash Techniques

Produce a series of photographs illustrating various uses of flash illumination. Compare:

(A) direct flash on camera,

(B) off-camera flash aimed directly at the subject, but at least at arm's length from the camera;

(C) flash bounced from ceiling or wall; and

(D) fill-in flash outdoors in bright sun. If your flash unit does not automatically adjust intensity according to the distance you will need to make practical tests to determine a guide number. To do this, place a subject 10 feet from the camera and shoot a series at different lens openings. Choose the best negative. Multiply the lens opening used for that shot by 10 to get your guide number (for example: f/8 x 10 feet = 80). Divide the guide number by any subject distance to get the appropriate f/stop.

10. Architectural Forms

Photograph both the exterior and the interior of a building that interests you. Your photographs should show something of the function of the building as well as its appearance. Experiment with a wide angle lens and with the perspective correction of a view camera if one is available. If you are using a 35mm or roll-film camera try to keep it as level as possible so the walls don't converge. Also try some dramatic angle shots and close-ups of details.

11. Close-ups and Copying

(A) Photograph a small sculpture, household object, or natural form so that its shape and texture are clearly shown. Use either natural or artificial light, but determine exposure and development with care, compensating if necessary for light loss due to lens extension.

(B) Make a copy negative from a photographic print. Then make a duplicate print the same size as the original, trying to reproduce as accurately as possible its tonal values.

(C) Make color slides from a painting using 45° lighting and polarizers. Adjust the lights for evenness and bracket exposures to get the best possible quality in the reproductions.

12. Product Illustration

Illustrate a familiar household product so that it becomes tempting to buy or to consume. A view camera, if available, may be desirable for this project because of its controls, but any format will do if you conceive an interesting idea and compose and light the subject imaginatively. It's OK to *emulate* good illustrations that you've seen.

13. Portraiture

(A) Make several significant portraits of someone who is important to you. Photograph this person in various settings, under different conditions, and with both natural and studio lighting. Try to capture the "essence" of your subject—beyond a mere likeness—and attempt to visualize the relationship between your subject and yourself.

(B) Attempt a *non*portrait of an individual, indicating as much as you can about him or her without showing the subject's face.

(C) Photograph a person in their surroundings. Include as much of the background and other objects as you feel explains the subject's work, interests, or personality without cluttering the image. It's OK if this part of the project overlaps with (A) and (B).

(D) Create a revealing portrait of yourself.

14. The Nude

Find a suitable model who is willing to pose for you, either indoors or out. Try to portray the sensuous grace, the line, form, texture and symmetry that have made the human form a favorite subject of artists throughout history. Attempt to capture an illusion of flowing movement as well as static beauty.

15. Evidence of Mankind

Without including any people in the photographs, show how humans have changed their environment. Examples could range from an unmade bed or a half-eaten apple to a strip mine, a polluted stream, or a monument; but you should try to give viewers evidence enough to make inferences about the nature of the person or people who had been there.

16. Visual Equivalents

Search for visual parallels or analogies:

(A) *Simile*—something that reminds you of something else (for example, a vegetable that looks like an animal).

(B) *Metaphor*—an object that symbolically represents another (for example, a lone tree symbolizing an individualistic person).

(C) *Equivalent*—a natural arrangement of forms that evokes an esthetic sensation (for example, a pattern of leaves or clouds that elicits the feeling of having heard a musical chord).

17. The Real and the Surreal

Photograph the same subject or theme in at least two different ways:

(A) as literally and realistically as possible.

(B) in a highly unreal or surreal fashion.

18. Visual Paradox

Produce a photograph in which familiar subjects are juxtaposed or joined to create a new significance. In other words, make a "double-take" image, the meaning of which appears at first glance to be obvious, but which, on second examination, becomes something else: i.e., a visual paradox or pun.

19. The Junkyard

Visit a junkyard, with permission from its owner, and photograph as many abstract compositions as you can discover among the jumbled, twisted and corroded remnants of man's industry. Work close-up with a single-lens reflex or view camera on a tripod, observing and recording line, form, texture, and color.

20. Your Own Back Yard

Spend one or several days photographing only the subject matter you discover within the bounds of your own yard, farm, city block, or campus. Look up, down, and around. Notice how many objects, shapes, surfaces and relationships you may have passed by hundreds of times, yet may never have "seen" before.

21. A Sense of Place

Find a landmark or location that intrigues you, and explore it thoroughly with your camera. An abandoned barn, a historic home, a school building, a church. Try to convey the "feel" of the place. See whether you can evoke in your photographs the "presence" of the occupants without showing them.

22. A Common Theme

Decide on a motif such as rocking chairs, vans, windows, doors, satellite dishes, the number *3*, the color *yellow*, or (more difficult!) an emotional state such as love, joy, solitude, despair, or death. Produce a group of photographs (a photo essay) that, viewed together, illustrate your choice of theme.

23. A Picture Sequence

Produce a series of photographs that depend upon continuity for their meaning. Each image should be a strong one, but the sequence should have a beginning and an end: a linear relationship leading to a definite conclusion.

24. Documenting an Event

Document an actual or imagined event or happening, so that essentials of the participants and the occurrence can be understood and shared by viewers of the photographs.

25. Image Magic

Experiment in depth with one or more special effects techniques in black-and-white or color. Subject matter can be from another assignment, but emphasize the technique.

26. Interviewing the Pros

Identify several successful imagemakers and interview them. Study their work. Find out how they feel about the field of visual communications as a profession and as an avocation. Find out whether they received formal education or were self-taught. See whether you can learn some "tricks of the trade" from these experts.

Tell me, magic moth—
from a groping, sleeping thing
what could I become?

(Robert F. Mainone, poet)

A Photographer's Vocabulary

aberrations Inherent defects in a lens that cause the image to be unsharp, particularly around the edges.

accent light A light directed at a subject from the side or back to add highlights and to separate the subject from the background. Sometimes referred to as a backlight or kicker.

acetic acid Used in diluted form to make stop bath and fixer. Commonly available in 28 percent dilution. Concentrated (glacial) acetic acid is corrosive and must be handled very carefully.

achromatic Color corrected. A lens designed to eliminate most chromatic aberrations.

activator Alkaline processing solution that energizes emulsion-incorporated developer; generally used in a stabilization processor.

acutance Sharpness. The inherent capability of a photographic emulsion to reproduce fine detail.

additive colors The red, green and blue wavelengths that theoretically add up to make white light.

AE Automatic Exposure.

AF Automatic Focus

agitation Movement of the film or paper as it is processed, or movement of the processing solutions, to ensure uniformity.

air bells Bubbles of air causing transparent spots on negatives, resulting from insufficient agitation of film when first immersed in the developer.

airbrush A small compressor-powered paint sprayer used to drop-out backgrounds and retouch areas of prints that require an even tone and to add highlights or outlines.

aliasing The jagged, stair-step effect along the edges of computer graphics; also called "jaggies."

amateur One who engages in photography or other activity primarily for pleasure rather than for profit.

ambient light Light existing naturally at a location (available light).

analyzer An electronic device used to determine filtration and exposure for color printing.

anastigmat A lens corrected for astigmatism.

aperture Lens opening, controlled by an iris diaphragm and expressed as an f/number or f/stop.

aperture priority On automatic cameras, the mode in which the user selects the aperture and the camera automatically adjusts the shutter speed.

apochromat A highly corrected lens with an extremely flat field.

archival An image processed to remove chemicals that may cause fading, staining, or disintegration; storage methods and containers that prevent chemical deterioration.

artificial light Light brought to the scene by the photographer.

ASA (now *ISO*) A system for comparing light sensitivity of photographic emulsions. Acronym for American Standards Association.

ASMP The American Society of Magazine Photographers. A professional organization for the benefit of photographers working primarily for periodicals and mass media.

astigmatism A lens aberration that prevents points of light in the image from being brought to a sharp focus.

automatic exposure A mode in which aperture, shutter speed, or both are adjusted by the camera instead of by the photographer.

automatic flash A flash unit containing a light-sensitive cell that shuts itself off when exposure is correct.

automatic focus A system by which a camera adjusts its lens to the distance of whatever is in the center of the viewfinder.

available light Normal illumination found by the photographer in a place where photographs are to be made (ambient, or existing light).

B "Bulb" setting on a shutter. A shutter set on B will remain open as long as the release is held down.

backdrop A piece of cloth or other material used as background for a subject to be photographed.

background The part of a scene visible beyond the principal subject; also backdrop or wall covering behind the subject; also *negative space*—the area surrounding the subject.

background light Light aimed at the background to silhouette the subject or to prevent the subject from visually merging with the background.

backlighting When the main source of illumination comes from behind the subject, toward the camera.

back projection (see *rear projection*)

barn doors Adjustable flaps on a studio light, used to shade parts of the subject or background or to prevent the light from shining into the camera lens.

base Material on which light-sensitive emulsions are coated. Modern films usually are on transparent acetate or polyester base, although paper, glass, metal and cloth can be used.

baseboard The work surface beneath an enlarger, to which the enlarger column is attached and on which the easel is placed; also the base of a copy stand.

base-plus-fog The density of an unexposed area of a developed film.

bas-relief A low-relief effect created by printing positive and negative images slightly out of register.

beefcake Slang for sexy photos of attractive men.

bellows A flexible, light-tight connection between a camera lens and the body of the camera.

bellows factor Increase in exposure required when a lens is focused on a very close subject.

between-the-lens shutter A type of camera shutter in which the leaves that open and close are located in the space between lens elements.

bit A single binary digit; the smallest unit of computer information.

bit map Grid of pixels forming an image on a video display terminal. The intensity and color of each pixel is controlled by bits.

bleach *(reducer)* A chemical treatment that lightens or removes the visible silver image.

bleed An image printed or trimmed without a border; also, when a image flares out and loses sharpness, usually from overexposure.

block out To paint over parts of an image, such as background, to eliminate unwanted detail.

blocked-up Describes a very dense area in a negative that should have detail, but prints white without texture; usually the result of overexposure and/or overdevelopment.

blotter roll A strip of lintless blotter paper and cloth in which fiber-base prints may be rolled up to be dried.

blowup An enlargement.

boom A stand with adjustable arm, generally used to hold a light, a gobo, or a microphone.

bounce light Light reaching the subject indirectly because it was aimed at a ceiling, wall, or some other reflecting surface.

box-camera A simple, inexpensive camera with few or no adjustments.

bracketing Making exposures both over and under what "normal" exposure has been determined to be.

brightness Lightness or intensity of a color.

brightness range The extent of the scale of values present in a subject, ranging from the deepest shadows to the most reflective highlights.

broad lighting In portraiture, when the main or key light fully illuminates the side of the subject's face closest to the camera. The effect tends to broaden a thin or narrow face.

bulb The B setting that allows the shutter to remain open as long as the release lever is depressed. (Photographers used to release their shutters by squeezing a rubber bulb on the end of an air hose).

bulk film 35mm film purchased in long rolls that must be cut into shorter lengths and loaded into cassettes for exposure in a camera.

burned out The result, in the print, of blocked-up highlights in the negative.

burning-in Giving additional exposure to darken relatively small areas, while shielding the rest of the print from light.

butterfly lighting A portrait lighting technique sometimes employed for glamour portraits of young women. The main or key light is placed above and directly in front of the face, casting a symmetrical shadow directly beneath the nose.

byte A number of bits, usually eight, composing each character or pixel displayed on a video screen.

C Abbreviation for Celsius temperature scale.

cable release A flexible attachment that allows the shutter release to be depressed smoothly from a short distance from the camera and without moving the camera.

camel's-hair brush A high-quality soft brush used for spotting prints and removing dust from negatives and lenses.

camera A light-tight box fitted with an image-forming lens or pinhole that focuses onto a light-sensitive surface.

candid photography Making unposed pictures with or without the subjects' knowledge.

carrier The negative holder in an enlarger.

cartridge *(cassette, magazine)* The light-tight metal or plastic container that 35mm films are packaged in.

cassette (see *cartridge*)

catchlights Tiny reflections of light in a subject's eyes.

CC filters Color Compensating filters that are used to balance the color of the light used to expose color films and papers. CC filters are available in six colors: additive primaries of red, green, and blue; subtractive primaries of cyan, magenta, and yellow; and in various densities.

CD ROM Compact Disk storage medium for reference files of digitized images.

center of interest The part of a scene or image that has greatest attraction to the eye of a viewer.

center weighted A through-the-lens metering system that, in calculating exposure settings, automatically bases the exposure more on light reaching the center of the viewfinder area than light at the edges of the frame.

changing bag A light-tight cloth bag with elastic openings for the photographer's arms, that can be used for loading or processing film when a darkroom is not available.

characteristic curve A graph depicting the response of a particular emulsion to exposure and development. Also referred to as the D-Log E curve because silver density is plotted against the logarithm of the exposure.

cheesecake Slang for sexy photos of attractive women.

chiaroscuro Compositional arrangement of light against dark, and dark against light.

chroma Color saturation or intensity.

chromatic aberration Inability of a lens to focus all colors of light in a common plane. The result is a blurred image in black-and-white, or color fringing with color materials.

chrome A color transparency.

chromogenic Emulsion in which the image is composed of dyes instead of silver.

cinch marks Scratches on roll film, caused by pulling on the free end of the roll.

circle of confusion A tiny cluster of light rays that are slightly out of focus at the image plane. The size of acceptable circles of confusion determines the limits of depth of field.

circular polarizer A special polarizing filter for use on automatic and autofocus cameras.

clearing agent (Hypo clearing agent). A chemical solution used after fixer to shorten washing time.

clearing time The length of time required by the fixer to remove all visible traces of undeveloped silver halides from film emulsion.

click stops Slight indentations that give positive indication of f/stop or shutter-speed settings. Some lenses have click stops between the marked f/stops; these half-stops should not be confused with whole f/stops when calculating exposure.

close-up A photograph made nearer to the subject than the normal focusing range of the camera; may require use of a close-up lens, supplementary bellows, or other attachments.

coating A chemical layer applied to lens surfaces to reduce flare caused by reflections within the lens.

cocking Tensioning the shutter mechanism before making an exposure.

cold-light Fluorescent light source for a diffusion-type enlarger.

cold mounting Attaching prints to a backing with peel-off adhesive sheets, spray adhesive or cement. None of these methods is archival. Dry mounting in a heated press is recommended.

cold tones Bluish or blue-black overall tinting in a monochrome photograph; in color, the green-blue-violet portion of the spectrum.

collage A composite "paste-up" image assembled from photographs combined with other media.

color analyzer A device for determining filtration and exposure when making color prints.

color balance Apparent accuracy or naturalness of colors as reproduced in a color photograph.

color cast An overall tint of one color in a color photograph.

color head An enlarger lamphouse equipped with a system of adjustable dichroic filters for changing the color of the light source.

color sensitivity The effective response of an emulsion to different wavelengths of light. Panchromatic emulsions are sensitive to all visible colors; Orthochromatic materials are not sensitive to red; some special copy films are sensitive only to blue.

color separation The process of photographing or electronically scanning an image through three primary color filters (red, green and blue) to produce black-and-white separation negatives used for color reproduction.

color temperature A system for measuring the color of light sources in terms of relative warmth in degrees Kelvin (K). Daylight and flash are relatively cool, or bluish white, whereas incandescent lamps are warm, or yellowish by comparison.

coma A lens aberration that causes unsharpness around the edges of the image.

compensating developer A self-limiting formula that tends to develop shadow areas (low zones) fully, without overdeveloping or blocking-up the higher values.

complementary colors Any two hues of light that combine, in the additive system, to reflect white; or, in the subtractive system, to absorb all wave lengths, resulting in black or gray.

composition Consciously assembling and arranging the visual elements within a photograph.

condenser enlarger An enlarger in which a system of large lenses collects light from the lamp and directs it uniformly through the negative.

contact print A same-size print made by placing the emulsion sides of the negative and the printing paper together under pressure and exposing the paper to light passing through the negative.

contact screen A film screen containing halftone dots. When placed into contact with photosensitive material during exposure, the resulting screened image may be reproduced by offset or screen-process printing.

contact sheet (Proof sheet) A contact print made from several negatives at the same time on one sheet of paper.

continuous tone An image consisting of continuous gradations of gray values.

contraction Shortened development, resulting in a negative with reduced contrast.

contrast The range of difference in density between dark and light areas of the same image.

contrast filter (1) A filter used on the camera lens in black-and-white photography to lighten or darken one color to separate it from another. (2) A filter used on the enlarger to adjust print contrast on variable-contrast paper.

contrast grade The contrast produced by a particular printing paper that is not variable-contrast.

contrasty An image with a wide range of difference in brightness between dark and light areas.

convergence Parallel lines that do not appear parallel in a photograph.

conversion filters Colored filters enabling color film balanced either for daylight or for tungsten light to be exposed satisfactorily in the other kind of light.

converter A supplementary lens attachment that changes the effective focal length.

convertible lens A lens that can be taken apart and the two major components used either together or separately at longer focal lengths.

cool colors The green-blue end of the color spectrum.

copyright Exclusive legal right to the marketing and distribution of published copies of photographs, films, videos and other works of art and literature.

copy stand A camera support with baseboard used for copying documents and photographing small objects.

correction filters Warm or cool colored filters used to improve color rendition when illumination differs from the color temperature for which the film was balanced.

covering power The ability of a lens to produce a sharp image large enough to fill the format for which it was designed.

CP filters Color Printing filters usually placed inside an enlarger lamphouse.

critique Authoritative evaluation and constructive criticism.

cropping Trimming or masking the borders of an image to improve the composition.

cross lighting More than one main light source appearing to come from opposite sides of the subject.

curvature of field An aberration causing the center of a lens to focus on a different plane than the edges.

cut film Sheet film.

cutter (see *gobo*)

darkroom A light-tight room for carrying out photographic processing.

dark slide The light-tight cover of a film holder that must be removed before making an exposure.

daylight film Color film balanced for use with light of about 5500 K, such as midday sunlight or electronic flash.

day rate A pricing arrangement whereby a photographer agrees to make as many photographs during a working day as the client requests, for a fixed price plus expenses.

dedicated flash A flash unit that sets the camera shutter speed automatically and shows in the viewfinder when the flash is ready to fire.

definition Sharpness; clarity of detail.

density The opacity, or light-stopping power, of a negative. A *dense* negative appears quite dark, or opaque, compared to a *thin* negative.

densitometer An instrument for measuring the darkness or density of a negative or print.

depth of field The distance between the nearest and farthest objects that appear to be in acceptable focus in a photograph.

depth of focus the shallow zone inside the camera within which the plane of focus (the film) can be moved toward or away from a focused lens without a significant change in the sharpness of the image.

derivation An abstract special effect created from a photographic image.

design Intentional arrangement of visual elements such as line, form, texture, color, etc. within an image.

developer A chemical solution that make visible an exposed latent image.

developing tank A container, usually light-tight, into which film is placed for processing.

diaphragm An adjustable device, ordinarily located between lens elements, that controls the size of the aperture that allows light into the camera.

dichroic filters Specially coated adjustable glass filters in the head of an enlarger designed for color printing.

diffraction The tendency for light waves to bend and scatter as they pass around the edge of an obstruction.

diffusion The scattering of light waves in random directions as they are reflected from a rough surface or transmitted through a translucent filter.

diffusion enlarger An enlarger that uses translucent glass or plastic instead of condenser lenses to even out the light that passes through the negative.

digitizing Converting an analog (visual) image to electronic data that can be enhanced, manipulated and stored by a computer.

DIN Deutsch Industrie Norm. A film-speed comparison system used in Europe.

diopter A measure of the relative magnification of a supplementary close-up lens. Such lenses are commonly provided in +1, +2, +3 and +4 diopters. The higher the number, the "stronger" the effect.

dissolve A smooth visual transition in which one projected or video image fades out on the screen while another fades in; a cross fade.

Dmax Refers to the maximum density possible in high-contrast film or in a transparency.

dodging Shading part of the image from light during printing to make it appear lighter.

double exposure Two or more exposures made on the same frame of film, either intentionally or accidentally.

double-weight Photographic paper thicker than single-weight.

dropout A high-contrast image from which the intermediate gray tones have been eliminated, leaving only black and white; also describes eliminating the background from around an object in a photograph by masking with opaque material.

drum A cylindrical plastic container generally used for processing color prints.

dry down To become darker when dry. Most prints appear slightly darker and less contrasty when dry then during processing.

dry mounting A permanent bonding process in which a sheet of thermoplastic material is placed between a print and a sheet of mounting board and then subjected to heat and pressure.

dulling spray A removable aerosol compound that reduces glare in highly reflective surfaces.

DX coding Checkered markings on 35mm film magazines that automatically set the film speed in automatic cameras.

dye transfer A high-quality color printing process in which full-sized black-and-white separation matrices are dyed yellow, magenta and cyan; the dye images are transferred in register onto a single sheet of prepared paper.

easel The paper holder, usually with adjustable masking strips, for use on an enlarger baseboard.

EI (or E.I.) Exposure Index (film speed).

electronic flash A repeatable light source, producing a brilliant flash of light usually less than 1/500 second in duration. Sometimes referred to as strobe.

element One of the glass components of a lens.

emulsion The gelatin coating on photographic films and papers in which are suspended light-sensitive image-forming chemicals.

enlargement A photographic image, made by projection, that is larger than the original negative or transparency.

enlarger A projection printer for making enlarged (or reduced) reproductions of negatives or transparencies.

esthetics (aesthetics) Study of the perception of beauty.

etching Removing small areas of unwanted density from a photographic image by shaving away the emulsion with a very sharp blade.

existing light Ambient or available light naturally occurring in a scene to be photographed.

expansion Extended development, resulting in an effective increase of negative contrast.

exposure The total amount of light allowed to reach photosensitive material. Exposure is the product of light intensity, as controlled by the aperture, and the length of time the shutter is permitted to remain open.

exposure factor The amount exposure must be increased when extending the lens for extreme close-up photography.

exposure index Film speed. Usually the same as ISO rating.

exposure latitude (see *latitude*)

exposure meter An instrument for measuring the intensity of light either falling on or reflected from a subject for the purpose of determining exposure settings.

extension tubes Light-tight rings or tubes placed between the lens and the camera body to enable focusing on very close objects.

f The symbol engraved on some lenses to indicate focal length—for example, f=13.5cm.

F Fahrenheit temperature scale.

fade-in Gradual appearance of a projected or video image from black.

fade-out Gradual disappearance of a projected or video image to black.

Farmer's reducer A bleaching solution of potassium ferricyanide and sodium thiosulfate (fixer).

fast Film or paper that is very sensitive to light (high ISO number); also a lens with a relatively large maximum aperture, e.g. f/1.2 or f/1.4.

feathering Evening out intensity of illumination by tilting a light source so that the brightest part of the beam is directed toward the more distant parts of the subject.

fiber-base paper "Conventional" paper that requires longer processing time than resin-coated (RC) papers.

fill light A light source or reflector directed into the shadow areas of the subject to reduce the brightness range or lower the lighting ratio (contrast) of the subject.

film Material on which the image is recorded in a camera. Usually consists of a light-sensitive emulsion coated on a flexible acetate or plastic base.

film back Removable device for holding roll film used on a medium- or large-format camera.

film clip A toothed, spring clamp or a spring-type clothespin used to suspend processed film during drying.

film holder Removable device for holding two sheets of film, one on each side, for exposure in a view or press camera.

film magazine *(cassette)* The metal or plastic container that 35mm films are packaged in.

film pack A metal or plastic container holding several individual sheets of film. Each sheet is moved into place for exposure by pulling a paper tab.

film plane The place inside a camera where the lens focuses the image.

film speed (Exposure Index or ISO) The relative sensitivity of film to light.

filter A piece of transparent gelatin, glass, or plastic, usually colored, that will absorb selected wave lengths of light while transmitting others.

filter factor The number of times basic exposure must be multiplied (for example, 4x=four times, or two stops) to compensate for light absorbed by a filter.

fisheye lens An extremely wide-angle lens (as much as 180°) that usually gives noticeable curved distortion around the edges of the picture.

fixer The processing solution that dissolves unexposed and undeveloped silver halides from the emulsion, making the film or paper no longer sensitive to light; also called *hypo* or *fixing bath.*

flag (see *gobo*)

flare Non image-forming light reflected from within the lens and/or camera and resulting in overall fog density, halo effects, or repeated patterns of density that often take the shape of the lens diaphragm. Flare is most noticeable when photographing subjects that are strongly backlighted or when light sources appear in the picture.

flash A brief, intense discharge of light from a flash unit.

flashing Selective darkening of part of an enlargement by exposure to raw light from the enlarger lamp with the negative removed or by local use of a small flashlight; also brief, uniform exposure of film to light for the purpose of reducing contrast.

flash meter An exposure meter that determines exposure for photography by flash lighting.

flash synchronization Adjustment of camera timing so that the flash unit fires when the shutter is fully open.

flat A photographic negative or print that is low in contrast; also a large panel or screen used as a studio background, space divider, or reflector.

flood A light source designed to illuminate a relatively large area uniformly.

floppy disk Magnetic storage medium for digitized images.

f/number A number obtained by dividing the focal length of a lens by the effective aperture. When marked on a lens it is referred to as an f/stop.

focal length The distance from the center of the lens to the film when the lens is focused at infinity.

focal plane. The surface inside the camera where light from the lens forms a focused image.

focal plane shutter A curtain shutter located in the camera just ahead of the film, which exposes the film through a slit of adjustable width.

focus To adjust the relationship between lens, film plane, and subject, so that a sharply defined image is formed on the film.

focusing cloth An opaque drape used to shield the ground glass of a view camera from extraneous light while composing and focusing.

fog Overall density in a negative or print, not part of the normal image, resulting from extraneous light or chemical action.

format The size and proportions of the image area produced by a particular camera. 35mm cameras are considered to be of small format; 6x6cm and 6x7cm cameras of medium format; and 4x5 and larger cameras as large format.

four-color The process generally used to print color photographs in books, magazines, posters, etc. Black-and-white separation negatives are scanned through color filters from the original image, then four separate plates are made for printing on a press with cyan, magenta, yellow and black inks.

frame To compose; also a single negative or slide from a roll, or the useful picture area on the film.

frame grabbing Converting a still video image (frame) to digital data for storage and manipulation with a computer.

freelancer A self-employed person who produces photographs for sale, either on assignment or on speculation.

fresnel A shallow, concentric lens used to focus the illumination from a studio spotlight.

frilling Loosening and detachment of emulsion from along the edges of film or paper during processing; usually caused by high temperatures and prolonged soaking.

f/stop An aperture setting on a lens.

front projection Rephotographing a projected image or projecting a background behind a subject, using a projector on the same side of the screen as the camera.

full-frame An image as framed in the camera; not cropped.

full-scale A photographic image with a wide range of tonal values from deep black to brilliant white, with many gray values (zones) in between.

fuzzy Not sharp; blurred or out of focus.

gel A colored gelatin or acetate filter placed in front of a lens or light source.

gelatin A jellied animal protein substance used as the basic medium in which the light-sensitive silver salts in photographic emulsions are suspended.

ghost image A blurred, secondary image of a moving subject recorded on the film by ambient light when flash is used in daylight or in a brightly lighted interior; also a second image recorded out of register, caused by slight movement of the camera or enlarger during exposure.

glossy Photographic paper with a highly-reflective surface sheen.

gobo A small opaque or translucent panel, usually mounted on a boom stand, used to shade part of the subject or to protect the camera from light that could cause flare; also called a *flag* or *cutter*.

gradation A scale of tonal values ranging from white, through gray, to black.

graduate A calibrated cylindrical container used to mix and measure liquids.

graduated background A screen-printed plastic or paper sheet that begins in one color or value and gradually changes to another.

graduated filter A filter that is partly clear with increasing density across the other part.

grain Particles or clumps of metallic silver or dyes that form a photographic image. Grain is not usually noticeable unless the image is enlarged.

grain magnifier An optical device resembling a miniature microscope that is used to aid in focusing the image from an enlarger.

graphic arts The science and technology of reproducing images, usually in the fields of art and printing.

graphics card (or board) Circuit board installed in a computer that enables it to capture and process digital images.

graphics tablet An interface surface upon which an artist draws with a stylus to create images in a computer.

gray card A standard, neutral test card of 18 percent reflectance. Representing Zone V of the zone system, a gray card is the basis for determining average exposure and a neutral reference for determining color balance.

gray scale A standardized rendition of tonal values, usually in 10 steps (Zones 0 through IX) arranged one stop apart in a sequence of increasing density. Computer imaging programs break up continuous-tone images into up to 256 levels of gray.

ground glass The focusing surface in view and reflex cameras.

guide number Number used with non-automatic flash units to determine f/stop setting at any given distance. Divide the guide number by the distance to get the f/stop.

halation Blurred density surrounding extremely overexposed areas of a negative, such as light sources in the picture.

halftone Printer's term for a continuous-tone image that has been broken up into a dot pattern for reproduction.

halides Silver compounds that provide the light-sensitive component of photographic emulsions.

halogen lamp A compact and highly efficient tungsten light source with a quartz envelope instead of glass.

hanger A frame, usually stainless steel, for tank processing of sheet films.

hard High contrast

hard copy A paper or film printout from a computer printer or microfilm reader.

hard disk Magnetic storage medium for storing and accessing large amounts of digital data.

hardener A chemical solution, usually incorporated in the fixing bath, that toughens the emulsion and increases its resistance to scratching, frilling and reticulation.

haze filter (see *UV filter*) A colorless glass filter often used as a protective lens cover.

high contrast Predominantly black-and-white with few, if any, intermediate values of gray; a scene or image with an extended brightness range.

high key An image predominantly light or white in overall tone, dark areas or bright color accents being very small, if present.

highlights The brightest areas, or highest values, in a scene or image; the corresponding dense areas of a negative.

holder A film holder.

hot shoe A clip on top of the camera for mounting a flash unit that has an electrical connection in its base.

hot spot An unwanted concentration of light, usually toward the center of the beam of a studio light, enlarger, or projector.

hue Color identification such as red, green or blue.

hydroquinone A vigorous developing agent; a chemical component of many developer formulas.

hyperfocal distance The distance from the lens to the near limit of depth of field when the lens is focused on infinity.

hypo Fixer.

hypo clearing agent Washing aid. A bath used between fixing and washing to shorten washing time and increase permanence of the image.

image Photographic representation of the subject; the visible picture.

image capture Recording of a visual (analog) image later to be digitized and enhanced.

image enhancement Improving or modifying an image; usually refers to computer-manipulated digitized images.

imaging The broad field of visual communications technology and allied arts. Including, but not limited to photography, film making, videography, graphic arts and computer graphics.

incandescent light Light from a tungsten filament bulb as distinguished in color temperature from fluorescent tubes, vapor arcs, electronic flash, and daylight.

incident light Light reaching, or falling on, the subject, as distinguished from light reflected from the subject.

incident meter An exposure meter designed or adapted for measuring the intensity of light falling on the subject.

infinity The distance, usually 50 to 100 feet from the camera, beyond which distant subjects will be in focus without further adjustment of the lens. Indicated by the symbol ∞.

infrared Invisible, long wave lengths of electromagnetic radiation that may be used to record images on specially sensitized film exposed through a deep red filter that blocks all or most visible light.

intensifier A chemical solution for increasing image density and/or contrast; usually for making printable an underdeveloped negative.

intensity Brightness or value of a color.

interchangeable lens A lens that can be completely removed from the camera body and replaced by another.

internegative A copy negative made from a positive transparency for the purpose of making prints.

inverse square law A principle of physics that intensity of illumination varies inversely with the square of the distance from the light source. This means that if you double the distance between the light source and the subject, only one fourth as much light reaches the subject; so you have to open up the lens two stops to compensate.

iris The adjustable part of the diaphragm, controlling the size of the aperture admitting light through the lens.

ISO (formerly ASA) A system for comparing light sensitivity of emulsions. Acronym for International Standards Organization.

K Abbreviation for Kelvin temperature scale.

Kelvin temperature A system for comparing visual warmth or coolness of light sources. Daylight and electronic flash average about 5500 K (bluish) and most professional incandescent studio lamps operate at 3200 K (yellowish).

key light (*Main light*); the principal source of directional illumination and shadows.

kicker (see *accent light*)

Kodalith™ (see *litho film*)

lamp A light bulb or light source.

lamphouse The part of an enlarger or projector that contains the light source.

latent image The invisible image produced by exposure of photosensitive material to light. The latent image must be developed to become visible.

latitude The amount of over- or underexposure possible without the result being an unprintable negative or unacceptable transparency.

leader A strip of film or paper provided at the beginning of a roll to aid in threading the material into a camera, processing machine, or projector.

leaf shutter An irislike series of overlapping metal leaves, usually placed between elements of the lens, that opens and closes to allow a predetermined amount of light to enter the camera.

lens The image-forming part of a camera, usually glass, the varying thickness of which causes light rays to be bent predictably as they pass through the denser medium, forming an image in a single plane.

lens barrel A metal tube in which lens elements are mounted, usually containing an iris diaphragm, but often without a shutter.

lens board A metal or wooden panel on which an interchangeable lens is mounted for use on enlargers and large-format cameras.

lens cap An opaque protective cover placed over either the front or rear element of a lens. Many photographers keep UV filters on each of their lenses for this purpose.

lens cleaner A special solvent that is effective in removing fingerprints, smudges, salt water, hard water, and wetting agent smears from lens and film surfaces.

lens hood (*lens shade*) A tubular or rectangular attachment for shielding the front of a lens from extraneous light that might cause flare in the image.

lens mount Both the part of the camera body that supports the lens, and especially in 35mm cameras, the metal barrel that contains the lens elements, diaphragm, and focusing mechanism.

lens shade (see *lens hood*).

lens tissue A special nonabrasive, lintless paper recommended for cleaning optical glass surfaces.

light Visible electromagnetic radiation; illumination.

lighting ratio A measure of the relative brightness of highlights and shadows; for example, a ratio of 4:1 means two stops difference.

light meter An exposure meter.

light-tight Capable of excluding all light, such as a camera, darkroom, or changing bag.

light trap A maze-like arrangement that excludes light, yet permits people to enter or leave a darkroom; or allows processing solutions to be poured into and out of a tank.

limbo A scene or image in which the subject is brightly lighted against a very dark background.

limn effect A scene or image in which the subject is very flatly lighted against a light background; a dark line (limn) appears around the subject.

line copy A high-contrast image consisting only of black and white, without middle tones.

litho film An extremely high-contrast film intended primarily for line and halftone reproduction in graphic arts processes; referred to by manufacturer's trade names, such as Kodalith.

long lens A lens of greater than normal focal length for a particular format camera.

loupe A magnifying glass of high quality used to examine fine image details.

low key An image predominantly dark or black in overall tone, usually with only relatively small white or brightly colored accents.

M Flash synchronization mark on some older camera shutters to indicate the setting for flashbulbs.

Mackie lines Thin outlines that appear around areas within a solarized image (see *Sabattier effect*).

macro lens A lens especially corrected for close-up work An extended focusing range allows very close camera-to-subject distances without accessory devices. Sometimes the term *micro* appears in the name of a macro lens.

main light (see *key light*).

magazine Light-tight film container that fits into or attaches to a camera.

masking Blocking out portions of the image area, such as the background or edge, with an opaque medium such as paint, tape, paper or film; also, the use of a low-contrast film positive in register with a negative, or a low-contrast black-and-white negative in register with a color transparency to reduce contrast in printing or duplicating.

master An original reserved for printing or duplicating.

manual mode When the photographer adjusts the aperture, shutter speed and focus.

mat A cut-out cardboard frame placed around a print or transparency for presentation and display.

matrix A positive gelatin relief image used in dye-transfer color printing.

matrix metering A system whereby an exposure meter samples portions of the entire scene, using a microprocessor to calculate which portions represent the subject and which are background.

matte Dull, nonreflective surface.

matte box A large lens hood, into which are inserted gelatin filters or cutouts for making multiple-exposure photographs.

megabyte One million bytes.

menu A list of user options presented on a computer screen.

metol A relatively soft-working developing agent that is a chemical component of many developer formulas.

microprism The structure of the focusing circle in the center of the viewing area in some single-lens reflex cameras.

middle gray Zone V; the standard 18 percent reflectance to which exposure meters are calibrated.

middle tones Gray values falling between black and white.

model A person posing for photographs.

model release A document signed by the subject of a photograph, or parent if the model is underage, or owner of a pet or property, giving permission for editorial or commercial publication.

modeling light A small incandescent lamp placed within a studio flash unit to allow visual placement of the light.

monochrome An image or process employing a range of tones of a single hue, or grays if black-and-white.

montage (see *photomontage*)

mottling Uneven or splotchy tones cause by underdevelopment with insufficient agitation.

muddy An image that appears flat, gray or mottled.

multi-image A slide presentation that uses two or more projectors programmed together.

multi-media An audiovisual event that incorporates various presentation modes, e.g: slides, film, video, lasers, musicians, live performers.

narrow lighting (see *short lighting*)

ND filter Neutral-density filter.

negative A photographic image in which the tones are reversed from the original subject— that is, shadows appear light or transparent while light areas in the subject appear dark or dense; opposite of a *positive* image.

negative carrier A frame for holding negatives in position for printing in an enlarger.

negative space The background of an image that surrounds the main subject.

neutral-density filter A gray filter intended to reduce the intensity of light without changing its color. Available in increments of .30 density which equals one stop.

NFS Not For Sale.

nonsilver processes Techniques used by printmakers to reproduce photographic images with dyes and other chemicals instead of silver compounds.

normal lens A lens with a focal length approximately equal to the diagonal of the film format the lens is designed to cover; the standard lens normally supplied with a camera.

notching code A system of notches cut into one edge of most sheet films to identify the type of film and to indicate the emulsion side when loading film holders in the dark.

NPPA National Press Photographers Association; a professional group for photojournalists.

one-shot developer A developer that is stored in concentrated stock solution, diluted for one-time use and then discarded.

opaque Incapable of transmitting light; also, a red or black paint used for blocking out or masking areas of a negative that are not to be printed.

opaqueing Painting out small imperfections in a high-contrast negative or positive.

open flash Method for taking flash pictures in which the camera is placed on a tripod, the shutter is set to B or T and opened, the flash is fired manually, and the shutter is closed.

opening up Increasing the size of the aperture of a lens. Using a smaller f/stop number—for example, opening up from f/8 to f/5.6.

ortho film (orthochromatic) An emulsion sensitive to blue and green wave lengths of light, but not sensitive to red.

overdevelop To give more than the normal amount of development. With film, overdevelopment increases contrast.

overexpose To give more than normal exposure to light, resulting in an excessively dense negative, an unacceptably dark print, or a color transparency or slide that is lacking in density and color saturation.

oxidation Deterioration of chemicals from contact with oxygen in the air.

page rate A pricing arrangement by which a publication agrees to pay a fixed rate for photographs and copy based on the amount of space they occupy in the publication.

painting with light A technique for moving a single light source around a darkened interior or back and forth across a stationary subject while the camera shutter is kept open. The effect is soft, diffuse lighting.

palette The selection of colors available in a computer graphics system.

panchromatic An emulsion sensitive to all colors of visible light.

panning Following a moving subject with the camera during exposure.

panoramic camera A special instrument that uses either a very wide-angle lens or a pivoting lens to record a wide horizontal view.

paper The sensitized paper used in making photographic prints.

paper grade Numbers that refer to relative contrast from 0 (very soft), 1 (soft), through 2 (normal), to 3, 4, and 5 (hard and very hard). Photographic papers are available graded in this way or as *variable-contrast* papers.

paper negative A negative image on photographic paper, either exposed directly in the camera or printed from a positive transparency; usually the paper negative is printed again, resulting in a positive print. If the paper negative is a final product, it properly would be referred to as a negative print.

parallax The difference in framing between what is seen through a camera viewfinder and what is actually recorded by the lens.

PC Abbreviation for Personal Computer.

PC cord An electrical cord that connects the flash contact stud on a camera with a flash unit.

perspective Two-dimensional representation of three-dimensional space; refers to relative size of objects, convergence of parallel lines, variations of tone with distance, and camera viewpoint.

pH Measure of acidity or alkalinity of a chemical solution.

photo CD Laser-optical storage medium for digitized images.

photocomposition Setting printer's type photographically.

Photo-Flo™ Kodak trade name for a wetting agent commonly used as a final bath to aid in rapid and even drying of film.

photo essay A group of pictures that collectively describe subject matter or create a mood or feeling.

photoflood An incandescent lamp bulb of high intensity but limited life, and a color temperature of 3400 K.

photogenic Someone or something that looks good in pictures.

photogram A shadow picture made by placing objects on the sensitized surface of a sheet of photographic paper or film and exposing to light.

photogrammetry The technology of creating maps from aerial photographs; also uses of photography in scientific measurement.

photojournalism Editorial use of imaging as distinguished from commercial use and advertising.

photolithography Offset printing process.

photomacrography The making of extreme close-up photographs of small objects without using a microscope.

photomicrography The making of photographs through a microscope.

photomontage A composite image consisting of several photographs assembled together.

photomosaic A single image assembled from smaller photographs of portions of a subject or scene.

photomural A *very* big enlargement, usually for wall decoration.

photosensitive Capable of chemical change from the effects of exposure to light.

pictorialism "Romantic" or "pleasing" pictures, as contrasted with realistic representation.

picture story A series of photographs with an intended sequence.

pinhole A tiny, clear spot in a negative or reversal positive resulting either from a speck of dust on the film during exposure or from an air bell during development; also, the image-forming aperture in a pinhole camera.

pinhole camera A simple camera that focuses light through a tiny pinhole aperture instead of a lens.

pinup Slang for a sexy glamor photo.

pix Abbreviation for "pictures."

pixel A basic unit of digital information used to form an image that can be stored and manipulated in a computer.

plate Photosensitive emulsion coated onto a glass support.

polarizing filter A neutral gray filter that, because of its optical structure, can reduce or eliminate glare reflected from some surfaces.

Polaroid® Trade mark of Polaroid Corporation; often used generically to mean "instant" photograph.

POR Price On Request.

portfolio A group of photographs assembled to show when applying for a job or soliciting work from a client; also a limited edition selection of prints offered for sale.

portrait Image of a person or animal.

positive A photographic image in which the tones or colors are similar to those in the original subject; opposite of a negative.

positive space Area occupied by subject matter in a picture; background is referred to as *negative space*.

posterization A high-contrast process in which some detail is eliminated and the tonal scale usually is limited to three or four values or colors.

postvisualization Creating images, especially composites, in the darkroom or at a computer terminal, that were not fully conceived when the original photographs were taken.

power pack Case containing capacitors and batteries or AC connection for powering an electronic flash unit.

PP of A Professional Photographers of America, Inc.—a major trade association principally for studio owners and corporate imagemakers.

presoak To soak film briefly in water before development.

preset diaphragm An adjustment on some lenses to allow focusing at maximum aperture and then manual stopping down to a predetermined f/stop for exposure; accomplished automatically on most modern single-lens reflex cameras.

press camera An obsolete type of large-format camera with many features of a view camera but designed for hand use.

press-focus A button or lever on some shutters that allows the image to be seen on the ground glass without setting the shutter to B or T.

previsualization Anticipation of the forms, relationships, and tonal values of a scene or subject as they will appear in a finished print.

primary colors The basic hues, or colors, of light or pigment from which other colors may be blended.

print A final photographic image, usually a positive representation on paper.

printing frame A frame with glass and a removable pressure back used for holding negative and paper together when making contact prints.

printing out A process of printing in which a visible image is produced by direct exposure to light, without development.

prism A solid, transparent optical form that bends light. Most single-lens reflex cameras use a prism to provide a large, bright viewfinder image that is right side up and laterally correct.

process camera A large-format sheet-film camera, usually fitted with a highly corrected apochromatic lens, designed for line and halftone copying.

processing Subjecting photographic materials to chemical treatment in sequence, such as develop, stop, fix, and wash.

processor A machine that automatic processes film or prints.

professional One who earns a significant portion of income from a trade or profession; also work meeting a high standard of quality.

programmed An exposure mode that can be set into the camera so that both aperture and shutter will be set automatically.

projection printing Enlarging.

projector A camera in reverse; a machine with a lens and light source that projects an image, usually greatly enlarged, from a small transparency, negative, print, or video recording.

proof A test print or sample.

proof sheet A contact print made from several negatives simultaneously on one sheet of paper; a *contact sheet*.

props (*properties*) Accessories used in setting up a studio photograph.

push To increase film development in an attempt to compensate for known underexposure.

quartz lights Compact, highly efficient incandescent light sources characterized by relatively long life, consistent light intensity, and uniform 3200 K color temperature (see *halogen lamps*).

rangefinder A system of prisms and lenses that aids focusing by presenting two images simultaneously. When the two images are brought together, the camera is in focus.

RC paper (*Resin-Coated* paper). Printing paper with a water-resistant base that allows for rapid processing, short washing time and quick drying.

ready light An indicator that an electronic flash unit has charged sufficiently to make an exposure.

rear projection Projecting from the back of a translucent screen (the side away from the audience or a camera using the projected image as a background).

reciprocity law The principle that the amount of exposure varies directly in proportion to changes in light intensity or time. Reciprocity *departure* occurs at very long exposure times or with extremely short exposures with high-intensity flash.

recycling time The time required for a flash unit to recharge sufficiently for another exposure.

red eye The effect of light near the camera reflecting back from the retinas of the subject's eyes.

reducer A chemical solution that reduces the density of a negative or print by dissolving some of the silver that forms the image.

reducing agent Chemical term for a developing agent such as metol or hydroquinone.

reel A metal or plastic spiral-flanged spool on which roll film is wound for processing.

reflected-light meter. The type of exposure meter that reads light reflected or emitted by the subject.

reflection The rebounding or redirection of light from a surface; also, an image that appears to be beyond or within a shiny surface such as water, a window, or a mirror.

reflector A surface such as cardboard, fabric, or foil, used to redirect light onto a subject.

reflex camera A camera in which the image formed by the lens is reflected by a mirror to a ground-glass surface for focusing.

refraction The bending of light rays as they pass from one transparent medium into another of different density, as through a lens.

register To superimpose one image over another so that their outlines coincide.

Rembrandt lighting Portrait lighting in which the shadow side of the face is toward the camera (*short lighting*).

replenisher A concentrated additive placed into a used developer or other processing solution to maintain constant strength and to prolong its useful life.

resolution Sharpness of the image. Resolution depends primarily on the resolving power of the lens and the acutance of the sensitized material used.

resolving power The ability of a lens to reproduce fine detail.

restoration Repairing or improving the appearance of faded, stained or damaged images.

reticulation A wrinkled emulsion surface usually caused by subjecting film to extreme temperature changes during processing.

retouching Hand or computer alteration or enhancement of an image.

reversal Transformation of a negative image into a positive, or vice versa.

reversal film Transparency film intended to produce a positive image from first processing (direct positive). Actually, reversal film is first developed to a negative, which is bleached away during processing; a positive image is then formed from the silver not previously used to form the negative.

revolving back Camera back that permits changing between horizontal and vertical formats without tilting the camera or removing the film back.

rim light Light coming from behind the subject that produces a bright outline, such as on a portrait profile.

rise and shift View-camera adjustments that allow some control over framing and perspective; generally used in conjunction with swings and tilts.

roll film Usually refers to rolls of film (for example, 120 or 220 size) that are supplied on a spool with paper backing and/or leader instead of in a metal or plastic magazine such as 35mm.

rule of thirds The principle of placing the horizon or main subject away from the center of the image.

Sabattier effect Partial reversal of image tones caused by exposure of an emulsion to light during development; commonly referred to as *solarization.*

safelight Darkroom illumination of a color that will not fog or expose certain sensitized materials during normal handling and processing.

saturation The intensity or relative brilliance of a color.

scale Range of values that make up an image.

scanner Electronic device for converting a print or drawing into digital data so that it can be enhanced, manipulated and stored by a computer.

screen A surface on which images are projected for viewing or rephotography; also, a sheet of glass or film containing a closely spaced pattern of dots or lines for producing a half-tone image for reproduction or for an overall texture effect in a print.

scrim Translucent material placed between a light source and the subject to partially shade the subject or lessen the intensity of the light.

seamless A long roll of background paper; also describes "perfect" blending of composite images.

secondary colors Complementary colors; for example, cyan, magenta, and yellow each contain equal amounts of two of the primary colors of light.

selective focus Shallow depth of field, concentrating attention on one plane of the scene and throwing other objects out of focus.

selenium toner A chemical solution used between fixing and washing to give a slightly brownish tint and deeper blacks to a black-and-white print and/or to increase archival permanence.

self-timer A device on some cameras that can be set to delay release of the shutter for several seconds, usually so the photographer can get into the picture.

semi-matte Printing paper surface between glossy and matte.

sensitometry Measurement of the light sensitivity of photographic materials.

separations Color separations or tone separations for reproduction processes.

sepia A yellowish-brown color associated with antique photos. Can be achieved by bathing a black-and-white print in sepia toner or exposing color film through a sepia filter.

set An arrangement of background, furniture, etc. constructed for photography.

shadows Dark parts of a scene; corresponding light parts of a negative.

sharpness Apparent clarity and crispness of definition in a photographic image.

shelf life Length of time chemicals and sensitive materials may be stored without noticeable deterioration.

sheet film Film supplied in individual sheets instead of rolls; also referred to as cut film.

shoot Slang for taking a picture; a photo session.

short lens A lens of shorter than normal focal length; usually a wide-angle lens.

short lighting In portraiture, when the main or key light fully illuminates the side of the subject's face that is turned *away* from the camera. The effect is to narrow a broad face, emphasize facial contours, and conceal blemishes on the face and neck.

shortstop (see *stop bath*)

shutter A mechanical device, sometimes electronically controlled, that determines the length of time light is allowed to enter the camera.

shutter priority A mode of automatic camera operation in which the photographer selects the shutter speed and the aperture is adjusted automatically.

shutter speed The duration of exposure; usually indicated on the camera as the denominator of a fraction of a second—for example, 250=1/250 second.

side light Light shining on the subject from one side.

silhouette A scene or image in which the subject is dark against a brightly lighted background.

silica gel A moisture-absorbing material used in packing and storing photographic equipment and materials.

silver halides Light-sensitive chemical compounds in photographic emulsions.

silver recovery Chemical processes for reclaiming silver from processing solutions and scrap emulsions.

single-lens reflex A camera in which the image formed by the lens is reflected by a mirror, usually through a prism, onto the ground glass of the viewfinder. The mirror swings out of the way during exposure.

single-weight Relatively thin photographic paper.

skin tone Usually the most important value in pictures of people. Zone VI for Caucasians, Zone V for darker complexions.

skylight filter A pale pinkish filter intended to absorb ultraviolet and some visible blue light, giving a warmer hued color image under hazy or overcast conditions.

slave A flash unit that is not wired to the master unit, but is triggered by its flash or by a radio signal.

slide A transparency mounted in cardboard, plastic, metal or glass frame and viewed by projection on a screen; also the opaque cover of a film holder.

slow An emulsion that has relatively low sensitivity to light; also, a lens with a small maximum aperture; also, a long shutter speed.

SLR Abbreviation for Single-Lens Reflex camera.

snappy Slang for contrasty.

snapshot A casual photograph made with a hand held camera; a personal picture that may not appeal to other people.

snoot An opaque tube placed over the front of a studio light to narrow its beam.

sodium thiosulfate The main ingredient in most fixers.

soft Low in contrast; also, lacking in sharpness.

soft box A large, tent-like diffuser placed around a light source.

soft focus Blurred, diffused, or slightly out of focus.

software Programs stored on magnetic or optical disks or other media that enable a computer to process digital information.

solarization Partial reversal of tones caused by extreme overexposure; often used somewhat inaccurately to describe the *Sabattier effect*.

solutions Processing chemicals dissolved in water for use.

soup Slang for developer.

SPE Society for Photographic Education. An association primarily for educators and students interested in fine-art photography.

spectrum The systematic arrangement of electromagnetic energy according to wave length. Visible light makes up a portion of the electromagnetic spectrum, which can be observed in the rainbow effect of a prism.

specular highlights Very bright, mirrorlike reflections without detail.

speed (see *fast* and *slow*)

spherical aberration A lens defect that permits light rays to form the image in a curved, rather than in a flat plane.

spill Stray, unwanted light from a source improperly aimed or masked..

spin drop-out The *tone-line* process.

split-image Type of rangefinder in which two halves of an image must be brought together to focus the camera.

split toning Partially toning an image to vary the color effect.

spotlight A studio light using a lens or reflector to concentrate the light to a narrow beam.

spot meter An exposure meter especially suited for use with the zone system because it can measure the reflected brightnesses of very small areas.

SpoTone® Trade name of a spotting dye used for retouching prints.

spotting Dyeing, penciling, painting out, or bleaching small defects in a photographic print.

squeegee A sponge or rubber blade for removing excess surface water from films and prints.

stabilization A rapid processing technique that yields prints of good quality but limited permanence.

stain A unwanted darkened or colored area within a photographic image, usually caused either by incomplete processing or by oxidation or chemical contamination.

static eliminator A device or substance for reducing the accumulation of dust on films.

step wedge A transparent gray scale used either for calculating print exposure or for calibrating a densitometer.

stereo camera A camera for making 3D pictures. Usually equipped with two lenses separated by the distance between human eyes.

still video camera A single-lens reflex that records images electronically onto miniature magnetic disks instead of film.

stippling In spotting a print, making small adjacent dots that blend together when viewed from a distance.

stock solution A chemical solution stored in concentrated form but intended to be diluted into a working solution for use.

stop An f/stop or aperture setting; also any change in exposure that doubles or halves the previous setting; also *stop bath* or *shortstop,* the acid rinse bath between developer and fixer.

stop bath A dilute solution of acetic acid used between developer and fixer to neutralize the alkalinity of the developer and prolong the life of the fixer; also called *shortstop* or simply *stop*.

stopping down Decreasing the size of the lens aperture; using a larger f/number—for example, *stopping down* from f/8 to f/11.

straight print Unmanipulated; with no dodging or burning-in.

stringer Slang for a freelancer employed occasionally by a publication or agency.

strobe An electronic flash unit capable of flashing several times per second; generic term referring to electronic flash.

studio A room for making photographs; also, a photographic business.

study A carefully composed still photograph.

stylus A pen-like device for creating computer images on a graphics tablet.

subject A person, object, or view photographed. The term *object* generally refers to an inanimate subject, although the terms are considered interchangeable.

subminiature A still camera that uses film smaller than 35mm.

subtractive colors The secondary hues (cyan, magenta and yellow) that are complementary to the red, green and blue primaries of light. Cyan, magenta and yellow are the basic colors used in color emulsions and graphic reproduction because each of the three colors subtracts from white light all wave lengths except that of the desired primary.

superimpose To place one image over another.

supplementary lens A simple lens or lens system attached to a camera lens to effectively shorten or lengthen its focal length.

swing and tilt View-camera adjustments that allow control over framing and perspective and maximum use of depth of field; generally used in conjunction with *rise* and *shift* adjustments.

sync cord An electrical wire connecting a flash unit to a shutter.

synchronization (see *flash synchronization*)

T (*Time*); a marked speed on some shutters; similar to B (*Bulb*), except that a shutter set on T will remain open until the shutter release is depressed again or the shutter is recocked.

tabletop photography Still-life photography of small objects or miniature models.

tacking iron A small electrically heated tool used to attach dry-mounting tissue to the back of a print and to the mounting board before insertion into a dry-mounting press.

take-up spool The spool or core upon which film is wound in a camera or processor.

taking lens The lower lens of a twin-lens reflex camera; the lens that forms the image reaching the film.

tank (see *developing tank*)

tear sheet A page (or copy of a page) showing published work to be filed or included in a display or portfolio.

telephoto A compact lens of long focal length. A telephoto lens is designed to form a large image of a distant subject on smaller format film than a lens of similar focal length would ordinarily be expected to cover.

tenting Surrounding a reflective object with white or translucent material that, reflected in the object, will produce the effect of a smooth surface.

test strip A small test print made from a representative area of the negative. Usually exposed in segments at progressively increasing times, the developed test strip provides a range of print densities from which to estimate the exposure time and contrast required for the final print.

texture screen A pattern of lines, dots or designs printed on film; the pattern is superimposed on a print from any negative printed through it.

thin A transparent image, usually a negative, of very low overall density.

three-quarter view A viewpoint intermediate between front and side, or between full face and profile; a portrait that includes head and torso.

through-the-lens meter An exposure meter with sensors placed inside the camera, often on the mirror of an SLR or on the ground glass of a view camera, so that reflected light readings are made of the light transmitted through the lens. A TTL meter usually eliminates the need for compensating for lens extension and filter factors.

thumb spot A mark placed on the lower left front corner of a slide mount to show how the slide should be held for viewing and projection.

tight framing Filling the viewfinder with the subject so that later cropping will not be required.

time and temperature The method for controlling film development by strict adherence to a predetermined development time at a carefully maintained temperature.

time exposure An exposure usually ranging from more than one second to as long as several minutes, the shutter generally being set either to T or B.

TLR Abbreviation for Twin-Lens Reflex camera.

tonality The range of gray values in a black-and-white photograph or the quality of color.

tone A value of gray or color intensity (see *tonality* and *values*); also to impart an overall color to an image by soaking in a chemical toner solution).

tone-line process A method for producing a high-contrast photographic image from a negative combined with a positive transparency. Also referred to as a *spin drop-out*.

toner A chemical solution used for overall coloring of an image or for improving archival permanence.

toning Changing the color of a photographic image, usually a print, by immersing it in a chemical solution following the fixing bath. Special toners are used also to increase archival permanence.

translucent Describes material that diffuses light passing through it, but does not allow objects to be seen clearly.

transparency A photographic image, usually a positive, that is intended to be viewed either directly by transmitted light or by projection.

transparent Clear; capable of transmitting light without diffusing it.

tray A shallow, open, rectangular dish in which prints, and sometimes films, are processed.

tripod An adjustable three-legged camera support.

TTL Abbreviation for Through-The-Lens exposure meter.

tungsten film Color film intended to be exposed by tungsten or incandescent light, usually of 3200 K.

tungsten light Incandescent illumination at the warm (yellowish) end of the Kelvin color temperature scale.

twin-lens reflex A type of camera that employs two similar but separate lenses: one for viewing and focusing and the other for taking the picture.

ultraviolet A band of short, invisible electromagnetic wave lengths adjacent to the visible blue-violet, to which most photographic materials are highly sensitive.

umbrella A reflective umbrella-shaped reflector attached to a light source; a black non-reflective umbrella-shaped shading device.

underdevelop To give less development than normal because of shorter time, cooler temperature, insufficient agitation, or diluted, exhausted, or contaminated developer; the effect is less density and lower contrast.

underexposure Too little light reaching photo-sensitive material, resulting either in a thin negative, an unacceptably light print, or a reversal transparency with excessive density.

unipod A camera support with only one leg.

UV filter A clear glass or very pale yellowish filter intended to absorb some of the invisible ultraviolet wave lengths that may cause hazy effects and overall bluishness in photographs of distant scenes. Often referred to as a haze filter, a UV filter is used by many photographers as a protective lens cover.

values The relative intensities or brightnesses of gray or color comprising a photographic image.

vapor lamps Common ambient light sources such as sodium and mercury lamps that give light of a color temperature that must be corrected with filters to balance with color films.

variable-contrast paper Printing paper that permits varying the contrast of the image with filters or by adjusting the amounts of yellow or magenta light transmitted through the negative.

videographer Operator of video camera and recording equipment.

videography Electronic photography.

view camera A large-format, tripod-mounted sheet-film camera used mostly for photography of the natural landscape and for architectural and commercial illustration. The inverted image must be focused on a ground-glass screen at the back of the camera. In addition to a long bellows for copying and close-up work, most view cameras provide extensive adjustments, called *swing, tilt, rise* and *shift* that allow considerable control over image perspective and depth of field.

viewfinder A device for aiming a camera and framing the image.

vignetting Isolating part of an image from the background or blending the image into the background by dodging around the desired area with a mask called a vignetter. May be done at the camera or during enlargement of the negative (pronounced vin-nyet-ting); also unintentional cutting off of the corners of a picture by a lens shade, filters, etc.

warm tones Brownish or reddish overall tinting in a black-and-white image, particularly in the darker areas; in color, the red-orange-yellow portion of the spectrum as well as the brown or "earth" hues.

washed-out A weak, pale, unsaturated image such as results from underexposure of a print from a negative or overexposure of a reversal transparency.

washing aid A chemical bath used to remove fixer from film or prints, shorten washing time, and increase permanence.

water-bath development A technique of soaking film alternately in water and developer. The purpose is to obtain maximum shadow detail in the negative without overdeveloping the highest values.

watt-seconds A relative measure of the power output of electronic flash units.

wavelength The distinguishing characteristic of each portion of the visible electromagnetic spectrum that causes it to be perceived as a distinct color.

weight Thickness of photographic paper base or mounting board.

wet mounting Attaching a print to a surface with a liquid adhesive.

wetting agent A final rinse for film that reduces surface tension so the film dries faster and with fewer water spots.

white light Illumination, usually consisting of a mixture of all wavelengths, to which photographic materials are normally exposed. The proportion of each wavelength present determines the color temperature of the light.

wide-angle A short focal-length lens with an angular coverage greater than that of a normal lens of the same focal length.

wipe A transition in which one projected or video image replaces another along a border that moves across the screen.

working solution Photographic chemicals properly mixed, diluted, and ready for use in processing.

X Flash-synchronization marking on some shutters and cameras to indicate the setting or contact point for electronic flash.

zone A value or tone of gray corresponding to one step in the 10-step gray scale that is the basis for the Zone System of exposure and development control.

zone focus To preset the focus of a lens in anticipation of action to take place within the expected depth of field.

Zone System A systematic exposure and development method for controlling the relationship between subject brightness range, negative density and contrast, and print values.

zoom lens A lens adjustable within a specified range of focal lengths.

> *There are a lot of pictures that have what I call "magic" in them where you can look at the photograph and have some delight that is beyond just a reproduction of the real thing.*
>
> *(Barbara Crane, educator)*

Selected References

Books

The following titles represent a cross section of references that have been found to be most useful to me and to my students. They have been selected from the more than one thousand photographic publications currently in print.

Adams, Ansel. *The Camera.* New York Graphic Society, Boston, 1980, 203 pp. A survey of equipment in all formats, with Adams' own point of view of the effects of cameras and lenses on visualization. Excellent brief summary of view camera adjustments.

Adams, Ansel. *The Negative,* New York Graphic Society, Boston, 1981, 272 pp. Explains the Zone System and reveals technical procedures recommended and followed by this master of large-format photography.

Adams, Ansel. *The Print,* New York Graphic Society, Boston, 1983, 210 pp. Describes Adams' procedures for making and finishing his own extraordinarily fine prints.

Adams, Ansel. *Examples—The Making of 40 Photographs.* New York Graphic Society, Boston, 1983, 177 pp. Adams describes here some of the circumstances and technical considerations involved in the making of several of his favorite photographs.

ASMP Professional Business Practices in Photography. ASMP—The American Society of Magazine Photographers, Inc., 419 Park Ave. South, New York, NY 10016, revised periodically. Describes pricing guidelines and contract procedures used by many freelance professional photographers.

Kodak Index to Photographic Information, Publication No. L-1, CAT 843 8319, Eastman Kodak Company, Dept. 412L, 343 State St., Rochester, NY 14650, revised periodically. This inexpensive publication is an annotated index to hundreds of books and pamphlets sold or distributed by Kodak on nearly every photographic topic.

Newhall, Beaumont, *The History of Photography,* 5th ed.. The Museum of Modern Art, 11 West 53rd St., New York, NY 10019, 1982, 216 pp A classic survey of practitioners and masters from the very beginnings of photography.

Photographer's Market. Writer's Digest Books, 1507 Dana Ave., Cincinnati, OH 45207, revised annually. A directory of buyers of photographs, including agencies and galleries. Advice to the freelancer on exhibiting and selling.

Szarkowski, John. *Looking at Photographs.* The Museum of Modern Art, 11 West 53rd St., New York, NY 10019, 1973, 215 pp. Penetrating essays commenting on one hundred significant photographs selected from the collection of the Museum of Modern Art.

Weston, Edward. *The Daybooks of Edward Weston: Volume I—Mexico; Volume II—California.* Horizon Press, New York, 1966, 504 pp. Through his personal journals, Weston gives us extraordinary insight into the creative process.

Uelsmann, Jerry N. *Process and Perception.*
University of Florida Press, 15 NW 15th
Street, Gainsesville, FL 32603, 1985, n.p.
A collection of several of Uelsmann's most
provocative composite images, with step-by-
step explanations of how some of them were
created in the darkroom.

Sources of Books About Photography

Hundreds of fine books of photographs and books about photography are available for every level of interest and taste. Some are monographs featuring the work of one photographer; others reproduce collections of photographs on a theme or catalog an exhibition representing the work of several photographers. Many books are how-to-do-its on every aspect of the craft. Some of these publications can be found in local libraries, bookstores, museum stores, and photographic dealers. Among firms publishing catalogs of books for sale by mail are the following, which specialize in photography:

Aperture, 20 East 23rd St., New York, NY 10010.
(212) 505-5555.

Light Impressions Corp., 439 Monroe Avenue,
Rochester, NY 14607-3717. 1-800-828-6216.

The Maine Photographic Resource, 2 Central
Street, Rockport, ME 04856.
1-800-227-1541.

photo-eye, PO Box 1504, Austin, TX 78767.
(512) 480-8409.

Periodicals

No one has time to read all of the photographic magazines. But if you examine an issue or two of each of the following major periodicals at a library or newsstand, you should quickly form an impression of those that appeal most to you at your present level of interest:

American Photo
PO Box 51033
Boulder, CO 80321-1033

Darkroom and Creative Camera Techniques
7800 Merimac Ave
Niles, IL 60648

Modern Photography and Video
825 7th Ave
New York, NY 10019

Outdoor Photographer
Box 50174
Boulder, CO 80321-0174

Outdoor & Travel Photography
1115 Broadway
New York, NY 10160-0261

PHOTOGraphic Magazine
PO Box 56498
Boulder, CO 80322-6498

Photographer's Forum
511 Olive St.
Santa Barbara, CA 93101

PhotoPro
5211 S. Washington
Titusville, FL 32780

Popular Photography
PO Box 51805
Boulder, CO 80321-1805

The Professional Photographer
Professional Photographers of America, Inc.
1090 Executive Way
Des Plaines, IL 60018

Workshops

When everyone works together a work-
shop can be a truly inspirational event,
one that can start you on a career or open
your eyes to a new way of thinking,
seeing and photographing.

(George Schaub, photographer)

Workshops are everywhere. Most of them are expensive, many are held in scenic resort areas, but workshops are the best way to meet and learn from men and women who are tops in their field. Whatever your interest, there's a workshop. Most attendees find the change of scene important and the experience worthwhile, but to help find the right workshop for you there's an annual guide:

Photography & Travel Workshop Directory,
   Serbin Communications, Inc., 511 Olive St.,
   Santa Barbara, CA 93101.

Special mention should be made of professionally-oriented workshops offered by:

Brooks Institute of Photography
801 Alston Road
Santa Barbara, CA 93108
(805) 966-3888

Rochester Institute of Technology
One Lomb Memorial Drive
Rochester, NY 14623
(716) 475-2200

The Maine Photographic Workshops
2 Central St.
Rockport, ME 04856
(207) 236-8581

Winona International School of Professional
   Photography
350 N. Wolf Rd.
Mt. Prospect, IL 60056-2724
1-800-742-7468

Professional Associations

Most people belong to associations so they can interact with others, have job placement opportunities, and qualify for group insurance. There are many specialized and local organizations, but these three form the foundation of professional photo groups in the U.S.A.

ASMP (American Society of Magazine
   Photographers)
419 Park Avenue South
New York, NY 10016
(212) 889-9144

PP of A (Professional Photographers of America)
1090 Executive Way
Des Plaines, IL 60018
(312) 299-8161

NPPA (National Press Photographers
   Association)
3200 Croasdaile Drive, Suite 306
Durham, NC 27705
(800) 289-6772

Index

(Page numbers in *italics* refer to photographs or quotations by the person named.)